In My Petticoat:
A Touch of Insanity

By:

LINDA L HUTCHISON

ISBN: 1466487771
ISBN 13: 9781466487772

Library of Congress Control Number: 2011960030
CreateSpace, North Charleston, SC

Dedicated To The Ones
I Love Most, My Children
James, Joey, Eric and Leeann

To All The Other Mom's Who Have Traveled This Road

We Can Make The Needed Changes. Together We Can Do It.

Thank you to everyone who encouraged me to write this book. Those who kept telling me that this is a story that must be told and I kept saying " Who will really care." To my sister Nancy Ann Reif, who acted as my sounding board and my personal dictionary, not only for this book, but for my entire life. A special thank you goes out to the women of the Thurber House Writing Group, your inspiration and immeasurable input from some very talented and creative writers. Holly Bardoe, Marty Ross Dolen, VivianWitkind Davis, Margaret Feike, Patricia Liddle and especially Becki Stamm, whom without your help in my attempts to edit the manuscript, I may not have gone forward. Therefore, I am giving you credit for all the right things and I will take credit for all the wrong things.

Prologue

A Knock on The Door

The knock on the door I knew would someday come was here. It was a bitter cold January night, about 11:15 pm. Two very kind but somber police officers brought news I already had felt in my heart—that my son was never coming home again. My son Joey had been killed earlier that evening. He was the victim I saw wrapped in a white sheet, laying on the pavement on the evening news.

I tried to prepare for this day, for most of my life. Now that it was here I wanted to scream, "No! Not yet! Not now! I'm not ready. It's too soon. I just talked with him this afternoon and he seemed fine." But the truth was, he was a little manic; writing a new essay on his computer, making lists for items he would need to begin a new career path—refurbishing properties—preparing to paint his room, and going out to buy a new wristband for his watch.

Since the mental health professionals wanted him to be emancipated from his family I had looked at a property that a friend had that was for sale, that needed to be refurbished, and one in which Joey might live. Although Joey had some experience refurbishing properties, I honestly didn't understand how the "professionals" thought this plan was supposed to work. He was 45 years old and had never lived on his own. Nevertheless, Joey said, "Yes," he would be home when I got there around dinnertime. "Yes," he said, we would then go look at the property.

This would have been the first property that he could live in while he worked on renovating it. He could become independent, which is what his mental health providers had been pushing him to do. During his efforts to pursue a second degree, he had dropped out of Columbus State College, because he had been told, by his mental health providers, that he was hiding from the "real" world. They thought he needed a job, more than he needed a second degree.

He had been scheduled to see one of his mental health providers but she had called and canceled his appointment. The only other thing I can remember him saying, that last day of his life, was: "Mom, I am so sorry for all the worry I have given you. It will get better soon. I love you." I have searched my memory many times trying to remember anything else we might have said to each other during that last exchange. But I always came back to those last words: "I love you" because ultimately, what else matters?

What happened between the time I received his telephone call that afternoon and 6:23 pm. that evening, when he ran into interstate traffic is open to speculation. It is my opinion that he just gave up the fight. Do I believe he committed suicide? No, not consciously. Whatever went on in Joey's mind was not preplanned. It just happened, on the spur of the moment, like so many other things that had happened in his life. It happened without reasoning of the consequences. You see my son was mentally ill.

I can say that now as casually and as a matter of fact as a parent might say, "My child is diabetic," or "My child has asthma," or "My child is class president." Saying someone is mentally ill is usually said—in jest—when your child, or someone does something incredibly stupid. However, I can tell you there is nothing funny about mental illness. When did I stop thinking that discussing the fact that you have a child with mental illness was not something you talked about in polite conversation? Sadly, not until the day he died.

The reasons most people don't talk about mental illness are varied and multiple. With me it was because of how my son dealt with his illness. It seemed he often felt ashamed; ostracized, as if no one would accept him as a person worthy of love. Most of the time he thought that if he tried hard enough to be "normal" the mental illness would go away. There were times I know he just didn't believe he was ever mentally ill; times he would pretend that he wasn't. I suspect that could be said of someone who had leprosy, or who was presumed possessed by "demons" (think of epilepsy and how it was diagnosed 2000 years ago). Most likely signs and symptoms of these afflictions were ignored for as long as possible.

Today it might be someone with HIV, Herpes, STD's, or those who are thought to live outside traditional acceptable behavior. Now with few exceptions, most everything is accepted in society, with fewer stigmas for those with serious mental illness. But this is the 21st century; surely we can do better.

We brought mental retardation, Down's syndrome, epilepsy and other such illnesses, and disorders into mainstream acceptance. In the past, these children were kept in attics or basements, and families felt the "shame" of having a child who was less than perfect. The optimum word here being "perfect."

On May 13, 1962, Mother's Day, a perfectly beautiful 10-pound baby boy was born. Perfect in every way at the moment of his birth...or so I thought. This child had all ten toes, ten fingers, a beautiful little body and an angelic little face. For all accounts he was a perfectly normal newborn. We, as his parents, were ecstatic, and we thanked God for the safe delivery of our much-wanted son. At that moment there was no reason to believe that our child would not have a happy and healthy life.

It is still not clear when and where mental illness begins and the argument over "nature vs. nurture" rages on. For all the advances we have made in diagnoses and the treatment of mental illnesses we still have yet to break the social barrier. How is it we can talk about erectile dysfunction on TV from a man running for President of the United States (Bob Dole) and yet we can't talk about someone's mental condition?

A small breakthrough seems to have emerged as we have recently begun to air commercials on television for drugs aimed at depression. However, we are still not talking about the "Big Three:" schizophrenia, bipolar disorder and paranoia. The reasons mental illness is so scary is that you can't vaccinate for it, you can't cut it out with surgery and as of today there is no permanent cure.

I hope my story will help remove the stigma from those with mental illness, and bring those who suffer from this condition an opportunity to come out of "the closet" and be allowed the dignity to live a productive life; one that does not include jail or prison, as that is how society seems to control a large percentage of our mentally ill population. To effect changes to the system that is currently in place, we must start by talking to our loved ones. We must be unafraid to share with the world what it's like to live with those afflicted with mental illness. Mental illness is not the fault of the person. Mental illness is a biological fault sometimes made worse by environment.

We seem to have a need to blame someone for the condition; especially the afflicted one. Hopefully my story will put the "blame" where it belongs; with man's inhumanity to mankind. When the answers and solutions are not at our fingertips, experts shrug their shoulders and walk away. Excuses should no longer be tolerated. I believe this is one of the last "closet doors" we need to open. Mental illness affects almost everyone; most simply do not even realize.

With all the many knocks on the door; telling me of the dangers my son faced, I was not prepared for the final one. I can however, honestly say it was my privilege to be Joseph David Hutchison's mother. I would not have wanted anyone else to have that title. God gave him to me, and as much as I prayed for this challenge to be lessened, and to take this cup from him, no one could have loved him more than I.

Even with my belief in God's will, the hole in my heart had become unbearable and the pieces so broken, I thought I might not survive. I eventually suffered from what doctors called "Broken Heart Syndrome" or "Takotsubo Cardiomypathy." Yes, you can die from a broken heart. This condition can have fatal consequences or a full recovery. Thankfully, I have recovered. Apparently, God has other plans for me.

As I prayed, "Lord, you have taken one of my most precious reasons for living. What am I supposed to do to fill that void? What more do you want from me? What more must I do?"

My answers came in a dream....

"Linda, I want you to tell your story. There will be those who will only see this as a piece of fiction. They will be critical and judgmental; but do not be discouraged... for I am with you always, and for as many as who will not see the truth, there will be those who will see the big picture... I promise. There will be those who will find a lesson or two, and those are the ones whom I want to reach. Let Me help you get started....

In The Beginning....go on, I'm Listening"

CHAPTER 1

In The Beginning:

The Happiest of all Childhoods

Who would have guessed that this journey into madness would begin with an incredibly precocious child, (me) growing up oblivious to anything more painful in life than a scraped elbow or banged up knee? How could my life have had so much drama and turmoil when I had had such a wonderful childhood? Could my life have been preordained? Did I have the power to change the big picture? I can envision my life's story eventually titled, "While on Your Way to Eternity, You May Have to Step Into Hell." Even with the happiest of all childhoods there are no guarantees.

My earliest memory is of visiting what would be our new home in a well-lived in neighborhood in North Dayton, Ohio. It was the spring of 1947. I was about four years old, and everything loomed large. So big were all the houses and trees. Most of the houses on our street had huge porches with stoops out front. The house that Gramma would turn into our home was on a main street, but it had a quiet little backyard with an alley that separated us from the neighbors who lived on the street behind us.

In front of this house, streetcars ran up and down the middle of the road. We could hear the click, click, clicking and the clanging of their bells and whistles as they passed. There was a trolley stop right in front of our stoop. When I saw people waiting to board the streetcar, I wanted to go, too. Gramma said, "Not today, little girl. Some day I will take you uptown; just not today." That was the day I learned that you have to wait for things you want in life.

My Childhood Home

Soon the streetcar was to be replaced by a new transportation vehicle called a bus; it too would run on electricity that came from the wires and cables, and just as changes came for the streetcar, changes were coming for me too.

According to well-known writer/psychic, Sylvia Brown we choose the life we want to live here on earth. During the times we are content with all of the wonderful things the spirit world has to offer, in the grand splendor of heaven, we plan how we would like to be challenged as a mortal. It's possible we may chose to do this more than once, by being reincarnated; then take those lofty plans and bring them to life here on earth.

If Sylvia Brown's premise it true, then I wrote all my challenges and chose my life. What in God's name was I thinking?

As I entered the foyer on that first day in our new house, I knew I would soon claim this space as my own personal play area. This is where I would pretend to be waiting in the wings for my entrance on "stage." Every actress needs a stage entrance and at the age of four, an actress is what I wanted to be. As we passed through the archway there were workmen, ladders, buckets of paint and people laying new flooring. The rooms had twelve-foot ceilings, and wallpaper was being stripped in large sheets off the walls. Gramma boasted, "This is going to be the most beautiful house on the block!" Just then she disappeared through the floor into the basement.

That memory is still vivid because, after we found that only my grandmother's pride was hurt, we couldn't stop laughing. Apparently the flooring had been laid over a gigantic cold air duct. The flooring had not been cut to accommodate the hole so when Gramma stepped on it, down she went with the flooring and all, right into the basement.

When the tour continued, I learned that the house had a dining room *and* a kitchen. In our old house, everything happened at the kitchen table and to have a room fit only for eating seemed too good to be true. To me, I would now have two tables to make messes on and at least one I wouldn't have to cleanup before each meal.

Gramma and Grampa would have the two bedrooms downstairs and my Mom, my sister, my beloved Granny (my Grampa's mother), and I would share the upstairs rooms, along with the only bath. This new house had two very scary rooms: the attic, which was a walk-in off of my bedroom, and the basement, which was cold, dark, and unfinished. There was a big old barn out back, but it would take a few years to uncover the secrets of these places.

Gramma, Grampa, Granny and Me 1947 to 1948

These were my earliest memories. In 2011 a four generational family moving into the neighborhood would probably seem out of the ordinary. If we stood out in 1947, it's only because my mother had divorced my father and moved back home to her parents bringing her two little girls with her. Back then divorce was frowned on and even more so if you were Catholic, and we were Catholic, born and bred. If being raised without a father affected me adversely, I didn't realize it, and still can't see how it may have had a negative impact on how I turned out. The attitude of divorce being "wrong" affected me only when a divorce became an option for me later in my life.

At 609 Troy Street, I was one happy little girl. I had my best friend Granny; my grandfather's mother, and she and I would play for hours on end. We would sit in her room by the large picture window and cut out paper dolls, have tea parties and play dress up. I would comb and fix her a new hair-do or play being a nurse; one of my signature roles. I would pretend she was my patient and bandage her from head to toe. Then one day she fell on the first landing steps and broke her hip. I knew if I had been able to bandage her she would be well again soon and able to do play with me. I didn't get to bandage her. An ambulance came and took Granny away. Back then a broken hip was an almost for sure death sentence and death stole my Granny from me.

Mom, My Sister Nancy and Me 1944 to 1950

That was my first encounter with tragedy. I was inconsolable but my mother let me know she was there for me and that the sadness would go away in time. Soon I would go to school and make new friends. My mother was right, but until school started my new best friend became my Grampa. "Hey Kid, you want to walk to the corner with me?" I knew that question meant we were going to go get donuts. Just one block from our house was Schottsnider's Bakery. Several times a day, especially in summer, we would smell the heavenly aroma of baked goods drifting on the breeze. Not only was my Grampa my new very best friend, he was also my enabler. I think it may be his fault I fight the battle of the bulge to this day, as my choice of donuts were hot out of the oven crullers, and I could eat two before we ever got home.

Gramma wasn't innocent either as she was a master pie baker, making her crust with lard. "Flaky" does not even come close to describing the texture of her crust. She taught me to feel dough with my fingers, as it crumbled with the blending of the flour and the lard. "Never overwork your dough. Form your dough ball and get on with it," she explained. Any leftover dough was rolled out sprinkled with cinnamon and sugar and baked just for me.

Sundays were the best; we would all be in the house together at the same time. Gramma got up very early and went to Mass; she claimed that was when she felt the closest to the Lord. She would then come home, fix a big breakfast and send out her usual call for us to come and eat. Her call consisted of getting everyone's name wrong, but we all came to the table anyway. After which my mom, sister and I would clean up the kitchen, dress for church and walk the three blocks (which seemed to take forever) that it took to get to Mass at Our Lady of the Rosary.

When I was between four to six years old, Mass held little meaning for me because it was in Latin. I just wanted to go home, as most Sundays meant that I would be the center of attention of everything that would happen in our house.

Grampa and I would drive over to the butcher shop on Sunday mornings after church and pick out our Sunday dinner. We would buy the two plumpest hens if we were having chicken and dumplings or if it were to be fried chicken two of the youngest just- plucked chickens. I learned the difference had to do with fat; fat made a better broth for dumplings. Grampa would let me sit in his lap and "drive." If he did that in today's world, he probably would have gotten a ticket.

On Sundays, I was always in the kitchen with Gramma, standing at her elbow, learning how to cook. She would make iced tea from scratch, brewing it and then straining it through cheesecloth. The dumplings were made from flour, eggs, and lard rolled out flat and cut with a knife into pieces that I could drop in the boiling stew. Cole slaw was grated by hand and drenched in homemade dressing. Biscuits were next on the kneading board and the list went on. Is it any wonder that later in life everyone wanted to come to my house for dinner? Thanks, Gramma! I learned from the best.

After Sunday dinner and if we had company like Aunt Vera and Uncle Frank, we usually played parlor games. I learned to play cards with the best of them. I was treated like one of the grown up players and not a child, so if I won at any of the games, I won fair and square. Then it was on to "watching the radio." We would sit around staring at the radio and listening to shows like "Fibber McGee and Molly" or "Burns and Allen." Occasionally, we would visit friends and family, have picnics, go swimming, and maybe even see a movie. Sometimes, Mom would take us with her to rehearsals. She and a few of her friends had a singing group and they practiced for hours. When we were there, we played with her friends' children or just listened to the singing and the music. Yes, Sundays were the best.

My sister Nancy was my hero, and being six years older than I, of course she knew everything. She would read me stories and every once in a while would play paper dolls with me. We had our "secrets;" things that we kept from the grown-ups. For example, at Christmas we would go on spying trips to see if we could find any presents, take a peek and report back to each other.

We shared a bedroom and I infringed a bit on her space and she would cry, "Mom, can't you tell her to stay out of my stuff?" But, we would eventually make peace. When we were younger, the difference didn't seem to matter, but when she was fifteen and I was nine, it was as though we lived on different planets. She became aloof, had the attitude of a Prima Donna, ate celery sticks, read books constantly (still does), and had boyfriends. Yuck, boyfriends. Eventually I changed my mind on all of those things.

If I wanted my mother's attention, I had to get her alone and away from my grandmother. It seemed that if I asked my mother a question or wanted permission to do something and Gramma was in earshot, Gramma would answer when I was looking for mother's response.

My mother was what today is called a working mom. She worked as a receptionist and PBX operator. She was beautiful inside and out with reddish brown hair accentuated by a henna rinse. She was a talented singer and musical writer, and I believe had she not married and had children, she may have found her way to Broadway. Mom was always the fun grown up in our house; she made my sister and me feel loved beyond words and always made time for us doing things that made us happy.

My Mom Alberta Wolverton and Her Music 1940

On the other hand, most of our discipline came from Gramma and almost never from Grampa. (I'm sure there are some Freudian overtones here?). I remember one time I disobeyed my mother. She had called me in for supper one summer evening and I yelled back, "I've already eaten. I'm going to stay and play with my friend." She called out again for me to come home, and again I yelled back, "I already ate and I am not coming." The next thing I knew she was standing over me with a switch, and she switched my legs all the way home. I had welts as long as snakes running up and down the backs of my legs, and I was sure they would be deformed forever. One other time when I was disappointed with an answer she had given me, I left her presence and started up the stairs not realizing she was behind me. I said a few words under my breath, comments about her answer, only to have my mouth washed out with soap.

Despite the occasional reprimand or punishment, I consider my childhood memories priceless. My summers were filled with playing out of doors from sun up to sun set. (I was always as brown as a berry and can only hope that won't come back to haunt me.) I would come inside only for meals and can still hear the screen door banging behind me, coming or going for drinks or a Popsicle.

All summer long my fingers and tongue would turn black from eating mulberries and cherries right from the trees. Tomatoes straight from the vines, warm from the sun with just a touch of salt from a shaker kept on the windowsill. Rhubarb dipped in sugar and sucked on like a lollypop was a cheap treat as well.

Catching lightning bugs and keeping them in a jar or making rings that glowed in the dark were things that kept me busy, too. Then when it was time to come in for the night, climbing the stairs I could feel the heat rise with each step. The smells of the day rose with us, and every once in a while I think I can still smell those smells, and the memories flood back to unforgettable times. We were bathed and put to bed with all the doors and windows open, and my sister and I would quarrel about who got the most air from the swivel fan.

Wintertime brought memorable holidays. There was Halloween, Thanksgiving, Christmas and New Year's celebrations to look forward to. All the holidays were well planned for in advance and carried anticipation. If they were stressful for the grown-ups, we never knew. We had homemade decorations for all occasions. For Halloween the barn became a haunted house. Corn stalks and hay lay strewn on the dirt floor. Dry ice in the homemade cauldrons made foggy apparitions, with bats and flying witches hanging from the rafters. Traditional foods were a bonus at Thanksgiving but it was the setting of that dining room table that made it special.

Christmas of course was always my favorite. We wrote out Christmas cards by the hundreds with a few on the ready to send should we receive an errant card. In the foyer, cards were hung on the woodwork for everyone to see and read. Presents were wrapped and often the wrapping was as special as the contents. With ribbons, bows, ornaments, small toys, candy canes and the like, sometimes we just didn't want to open the boxes. We were a family that opened presents on Christmas Eve so we could focus on the celebration of the birth of Christ on Christmas Day. We had to wait for Grampa to come home from work on Christmas Eve. It seemed that hundreds of buses came and went as we watched for the bus that would bring him home, before he finally emerged from the last one. Shouts of "Hurry up, Grampa, we're waiting for you," sounded with glee and giggles as he came through the door like Santa Claus himself.

In the spring there was Easter; a time to celebrate the resurrection of Jesus Christ from the dead, the renewal of the earth from a long winter's sleep, and new undergarments. It would not be a proper Easter Sunday if we did not have new outfits to wear to church. The most important items were the new undergarments. Gramma always said, "Never wear holey underwear, as you never know when you might be in an accident; when they take you to the hospital they will see your holey underwear."

So under our new dresses, white gloves and Easter bonnets were brand new panties and petticoats. When we got older, garter belts, girdles and bras. When you have good foundation garments, you can be sure you are well dressed for any occasion. You can look good in anything with the proper undergarments; and according to Gramma, maybe even conquer the world wearing only your petticoat.

So carefree were those childhood days. No doors or windows to lock, only a screen latch to keep the door from blowing open and letting the flies in at night. My sister would say, "Good night, sweet dreams and don't let the bogeyman get you." The only way the "Bogeyman" could get you was if your arms and legs fell over the sides of the bed. So I would lie right, smack in the middle of my bed so the Bogeyman under the bed couldn't grab me.

On the last day of summer, the night before I was to enter into the world of big girls, the only fears I had were of the bogeyman and holey underwear. The next day, at the tender age of six, I would go to school, become educated and lose my childish ways. Oh, how I wish that the bogeyman and holey underwear were the only things I had to be afraid of and defeat in this lifetime.

CHAPTER 2

Let the Pecking
Order Begin

T he dawning that the universe didn't revolve around me came as a bit of a shock, as I stood at the door of my first grade classroom. I saw little girls crying and begging their mothers not to leave. Not me. I entered the world of a parochial education with my usual gusto and assumed I would conquer this new adventure.

Our Lady of the Rosary Catholic Church and School would be my home away from home for the next eight years. Located in North Dayton, established in 1888 with the church built in 1918, it served over 2,000 families and included over 1000 children in grades one through eight. Father Taske, The Society of Mary Brothers, and The Sisters of Notre Dame, made it their mission to instruct all their charges in the faith and academics. Many families sent their children to parochial schools for the superior education knowing that a firm foundation of ethics and morals would also be instilled. In other words, the no-nonsense nuns and brothers would see to it that we would all turn out to be adults whom they would be proud to call their own.

At some time within the first three years of school, I learned that everyone was not created equal, except in "God's" eyes. While God's eyes were always on me, mine were looking at a group of girls who were a lot smarter than I. I knew this because they always raised their hands with the correct answer before I could even process the question. They dressed better, had secrets, and rarely mingled with girls that didn't fit in with them. Then there were the girls that barely or rarely spoke out, dressed funny and seemed to stick together like glue. As for me, I seemed to mingle with the middle of the pack. Not smart enough to be in the elite group but not quite segregated to "the dumb or dumber" group.

Peer pressure was alive and well in the 50s, and it is alive and well today. By advocating school uniforms, the parochial school system made a huge dent in relieving that pressure. We all moaned and groaned but secretly we enjoyed the fact that we no longer had to compete in what we wore. In addition it was thought that boys and girls should not be taught in the same class rooms together. This practice vanished by the time my children started school, uniforms haven't.

During second grade the Baltimore Catechism was introduced in the curriculum, and I went to the head of the class for the first time that year. I had an affinity for the religious material and it seemed to come easy for me. The Baltimore Catechism was the foundation of teaching the faithful of the church its doctrines. The Bible contains teachings from God Himself. From these two sources I have gathered my internal and deep beliefs. There are God's Laws and there are man's laws.

God's laws were passed to mankind, starting with "Adam and Eve," and then passed on to their descendents and from there to inspired men of God, the Prophets, the learned men of their time and on to the Apostles. The laws, lessons, or stories were most likely written and preserved in a time when man began to write these revelations down on cave walls, stone tablets, scrolls and parchment paper.

The Bible serves as the most common form of spreading the word of God to Christians throughout the world. It still remains on the best sellers list. The Baltimore Catechism served as the method the church used to teach its children church doctrine. This book was written in 1885 and had little revisions made by the time I received instruction from its pages. At one point in my schooling, I could recite the Catechism verbatim. I got all A's in tests. I would be a little hard pressed today to make that same claim. However, I still hold my formal religious education responsible for my salvation, not only for my relationship with God, but my life here on this planet. Without my daily classes and assignments in exploring the depth and breadth of my being, I doubt I would be here today writing this book. I doubt I would be able to stand to the trials and tribulations that were soon to befall me.

By the second grade and the age of seven, we were told we had reached the age of reasoning. I could now reason that my First Holy Communion would bring me and the body and blood of Christ together for the first time. As much as I wanted to understand that concept I have to admit it was much later in life before I truly understood the context and meaning.

Though I was only in second grade I already had three sacraments under my belt. First came Baptism, which I don't remember, but I received my name of Linda Louise. My birth certificate had my name as Linda Lou, but neither was a saint's name so Louise would be my official Christian name from that day forward. Next was my First Confession, and the third my First Communion. The remaining sacraments were Confirmation, Marriage, Holy Orders and the final sacrament of The Last Rites. Eventually I would complete two more. One much sooner than even I thought possible.

An opportunity to go to the head of the class did not happen often for me and the fact that it happened during a spelling contest is even more amusing. Why? Well, if you promise not to tell anyone, I'll admit it; I couldn't spell. I certainly wasn't on the same playing field as the group of girls who knew all of the answers. Sister Elizabeth Ann would play the game "Are You Smarter than a Second Grader" and if you knew the answer you would clean out your old desk and move to the front of the class. Everyone wanted that prime piece of real estate. The question that day was, "What do you call hundreds of bees flying together, and how do you spell it?" One by one, girls stammered, guessed wrong or just didn't know. I knew the answer right away, and though I worried that I could spell it right, I was more worried that someone else would spoil my chance to go to the head of the class.

I prayed to the saints and my guardian angels, perhaps even "God, Himself" would hear my prayer. It was my turn and I stood proudly and blurted, "Swarm spelled S-W-A-R-M" and moved to the head of the class. At that moment I knew prayer worked because I also knew I didn't win that contest by myself. I couldn't have, because I couldn't spell very well then and I can't spell without spell check now. Thus began my intimate relationship with prayer; yes, I knew I wouldn't get everything I prayed for, but I also knew it couldn't hurt.

The second grade soon came and went and advancement to the third, fourth, fifth and sixth grades followed. These years were spent not only learning reading, writing, and arithmetic, but practicing social graces as well. Mother saw fit to introduce me to music, and the accordion was the instrument of torture. As with spelling, I could not read music very well. I bluffed my way through four years, only because I had a good ear. I could play by ear and did well enough to give recitals and receive praises for my accomplishments.

On the other hand, dancing and singing were my favorite after school activities. My how I loved to be on stage. I would entertain my family on weekly basis, and Grampa was my biggest fan. I would wait in the wings (the foyer in our home) for my cue. I remember still the laughter and applause I would receive when my act was finished. Every week during the TV show "The Schlitz Playhouse of Stars," I would make my entrance dancing, singing, playing the accordion or just play acting to the music at the beginning of the show. I would plan these events in advance and anticipate the pleasure I felt in giving my all to please others.

I know the entertainment gene was in my DNA given that my grandparents were once in the industry; Gramma played the piano and Grampa sang with a quartet for silent movies and Mom sang and acted locally with some recognition of note. Perhaps with the right outlet to show biz my life story would have gone in a different direction. Assuming we are all born with free will, my will was not strong enough to pursue the entertainment industry on long-term basis. I would, however, from time to time continue to play with the little talent I had. This would show up in many different ways throughout my life, when I worked with children in school, PTA endeavors, Rosary Alter activities, and local summer productions in theater and parks and recreation venues.

For now, I was living a childhood that all little girls should have; I had a family who loved me. Life was grand. I would go on to become a Brownie Scout, a Girl Scout, and play CYO ball. I sold flower seeds, gift-wrapping paper, and greeting cards. The rewards for these endeavors were trophies and prizes from a catalog: beautiful statues, rosaries, books and such, and where I acquired the knack for selling and my entrepreneur spirit.

I had to face death again when one of the girls in my brownie troop was hit and killed by an auto on her way home from school. Her parents wanted her brownie troop to be pallbearers. Remembering this event was especially painful; I really didn't want to be chosen as one of the pallbearers. I was urged to handle this task by being reminded it was my duty as a scout and a friend. Duty and friendship were two of the most important unspoken, invisible traits that would serve me the rest of my life. Duty comes before your own desires and friendship; true friendship is a rare commodity and must be treasured. The lesson that death can come in a blink of an eye to the very old (my Granny) and my very young friend Inez was hard for me to understand. Was my love for them not enough? I wanted love to always be enough to keep the people close to me alive and well.

During the sixth grade we prepared for our Confirmation of Faith. Understanding "The Apostles' Creed" was the basis for confirmation. With these beliefs firmly implanted into my being, I willingly accepted my confirmation into the faith of the Catholic Church at the age of twelve. These beliefs would be tested many times over the years.

During my elementary years I encountered people who lived with physical disabilities. I was always grateful that I was not afflicted. One of my classmates, Kay, had a form of epilepsy. She was in the row next to me, and I was the one who was first to help when she had an episode. I would help lay her down on the floor before she fell. As she became more spastic, I would see that she didn't hurt herself by moving objects out of the way. Sister would hurry to her side and slip a stick in her mouth, and we would wait until the seizure passed. Kay was then sent home to rest but would return either later that day or the next. We were told about brain waves and electrical currents that run though our brains and how sometimes they would short circuit. The look into Kay's eyes would be the clue to this happening; I would remember that look many years later. The look said, "There was no one there, in Kay's body. No one was at home." It is a look you don't forget, and sadly a look I would become familiar with in the future.

A major turning point came as I entered the seventh grade. I became bolder and smarter and more opinionated. I was a latch-key kid and I took the freedoms I had been given and taken for granted, and I didn't use some of them wisely. I had tagged along behind my older sister for so long that it was taken for granted I could take care of myself.

No one really monitored my after school activities closely. Yes, of course I always went to my music lessons, scout meetings, and volleyball practices. But if I went to the park all I had to do is let my folks know where I was going. My closest friends had the same freedoms I had and no one ever questioned our whereabouts.

On weekends, we would throw our roller skates over our shoulders and walk the two miles to the skating rink. We would skate all afternoon. The next weekend we might go to the movies for $.25 and spend the afternoon. In the summer it was the swimming pool. To this day I don't think our parents knew that sometimes we would "hop" trains to travel to and from these places. We never wore helmets or knee and elbow pads when we rode our bikes and the worst that ever happened was a scraped appendage.

I watched the technique used by the others to grab the slow moving train by the iron hand rail and pull myself up so that my foot had balance on the edge. I'd hold on for dear life and only let go when the train slowed for the crossing. I'd ride my bike at the "speed of light" in order to clear the patch of lawn in front of my house in one fell swoop without stopping. I'd climb the chimney at the picnic shelter to sit on the roof and not be seen. Daredevil, tomboy or someone who wanted to try everything just once, or maybe I didn't want to be left behind. Looking back now, it's a wonder any of us lived to adulthood.

At about this time I wanted to know more about the boys that went to school across the street. We still were not allowed to mingle during school hours; however, after school, we began to pay more attention to them and they to us. It started out with teasing or showing off. Then we started to write their names on our book covers with plus signs. Conversations would begin with who liked who and did we think he liked us back? Hormones were kicking in and the only education we girls had was a short movie about menstruation and how to take care of ourselves during that "time of the month." We weren't supposed to take baths, only showers or go horseback riding or play sports. Yes, we could be excused for gym if we wanted, but we never did, as that was a sure sign we were on the "rag."

There were drawings about the female organs and how the sperm met with the egg to produce a baby and when that didn't happened the lining would fall away and that was what caused menstruation. Of course, we were never told how the sperm got there or what the male anatomy looked like.

Our parents were of no help either; relying on the school to teach us what we needed to know. From our homes all we were ever told was that we were too young to know these things and when the time was right we would just somehow magically know. You would have thought my sister would have clued me in; maybe she didn't know either.

As with most things, information swirled around and eventually we had a pretty good idea of what "sex" was. If you had sex, you would be a slut and if you didn't marry the boy, your reputation would be forever ruined; no other boy would want you. For a boy he was always supposed to try and get the girl to have sex; if he were successful he was hailed as the conquering hero. That was my introduction to "sex" and the term double standard. For the next couple of years it was sufficient information.

The girls I hung out with were basically carbon copies of each other, and we all pretty much counted on doing the same things together. We all wore Spalding saddle shoes, suede jackets and "Duck Tail" haircuts; after school Levi jeans and your Dad's (in my case, my Grampa's) white dress shirts. We hung out at Stewart Patterson Park, listened to "Elvis Presley," had record collections of 45s

My Childhood Girlfriends
Donna, Lana, Me, Kathy, Eileen, Judy, Angie, and Susan 1957

and slumber parties. Life was fun as a pre-teen, or as we called it, "twelve-teen" on the verge of taking on the world.

These were the experimental years of trying adult things like smoking a cigarette, drinking a beer and kissing boys, without getting caught. Not a lot, mind you, but at least once. We denied we still like to play with dolls, and most of us wanted to be teachers, nurses, secretaries or moms. Never once did I hear any of the girls say they wanted to be doctors, lawyers or scientists. Along about the fall of the eighth grade, most of the girls had found certain boys they seemed to pair off with over the summer. I was becoming the odd girl out. They kept after me to meet this boy, whose name was Joe. Joe was in high school as were these other guys, and he had just broken up with a girl named Eileen. Joe also had an after school job and a car. "Just meet him," my friends would say. "If you don't like each other, that's OK."

My first and only boy friend up to that point was a neighborhood kid, named Johnny. We rode bikes, hung out at my Cousin Kathy's house, and we shared our first kiss. The first kiss came on a dare. We were out by the barn in my back yard, and all of a sudden Johnny motioned for me to come with him into the barn. He told me that the other boys were teasing him about stealing a kiss from me. I thought he was the most handsome boy I ever saw, so the kiss wasn't stolen; it was given.

We hung out long enough for him to ask for more than a kiss, but I was not ready for anything else, and I don't think he was either. It was just something he felt he should do; maybe that was on a dare too, so we broke off our friendship. I remember even though I wanted this "break up" it still was awkward to see Johnny out in the neighborhood from time to time. It just felt to me as if we should let our friendship go, as it was time to move on. Little did I know then my next boy friend would take me into a world that would forever change my life.

CHAPTER 3

Thirteen Going on
Twenty-one

T he exact date eludes me: however, it was in the fall of the eighth grade that my girlfriends and I were making plans to meet at Stewart Patterson Park for some after school activities. I met up with them after school and as we started to walk toward the park. Susie shouted, "I think I see Joe's car coming," and Donna said, " this is the guy we want you to meet." Coming down the street was this baby blue "51" Ford; it looked like a blue torpedo as it pulled up along side of us. There were four guys in the car, two in the front and two in the back. A boy named Tom leaned out the window and said, "Can we give you girls a ride?"

At that all the boys jumped out of the car except for the driver. Everyone seemed to know each other really well. While I was always told never to get into a car with anyone I didn't know, this didn't seem to be one of those times. I was urged into the car to sit next to the driver, and since there were two more people cramming into the front seat, I was sitting really close. There were four of us in the front seat and four in the back seat and off we roared. This felt like a setup to get me to meet this "guy," but I didn't care; it really was a lot of fun and I thought about how grown up I felt. Did this mean I was now officially part of this group?

From my angle I could tell he had sandy brown hair, cut in a "duck tail style" with a large wave of hair hung low over his forehead with a curl on one side. He wore a blue and green plaid flannel shirt and Levi jeans. Tom, a boy named Ronnie, and another other guy (whose name I can't remember) were all wearing leather jackets over tee shirts and jeans. Tom seemed to fancy Donna, and Susie and Ronnie paired up, and that left Judy and this other boy sitting together in the back seat. We took the long way to the park, just driving up and down streets to kill time, listening to the radio and of course talking. I was trying to get the feel of where I fit in with this group so I really didn't have much to say.

I did a lot of listening. I gathered that these guys became friends over the summer when I was pretty much out of the loop. I had been to camp most of the summer and was trying to bring my schoolgirl friendships back on track. It sounded like Joe had entered the group just recently too. They had been hanging out at the park over the summer, and Joe was the only one who had a car. When we arrived at the park, everyone piled out except the driver. Driver Joe announced that he needed to get to work and wanted to know if we would like him to pick us up in the morning to drive us to school? Donna and Susie replied, "Sure see you in the morning," I didn't say anything but I guessed that our next meeting was planned as he drove away.

So, what did I think? Did I like him? They all wanted to know. I didn't know what to say. I told them that we barely talked, and that I really didn't get a good look at him. I didn't have anything to report except if he wanted to pick us up to drive us to school, sure I would go along. What could it hurt? I was in the loop for now. Everyone agreed that we would make a "cute couple" and we all went inside the rec center; with me being the object of teasing, about having a new boyfriend.

The next morning as I rounded the corner on my way to school, there sat the baby blue Ford. In the back seat were Donna and Tom, so I climbed into the front seat with Joe. This time I got a good look at the driver. Joe had what some might call bedroom eyes, with long brown eyelashes, the color of hazelnuts. His smile revealed a chipped tooth and it made him look really cute. His fingers were long, and he wore a gold ring that had a letter J in the center surrounded by a sunburst. Joe wore a plaid flannel shirt and no jacket even though it was a little chilly. I think he was hoping to get a better look at me too. We started to talk to each other as we finished picking up a couple more kids for this ride to school. I began to think, "This is really cool." About a half a block from school Joe pulled over to let us out and said, "I will be back after school to pick you up, okay?" Yes, that would be okay, and from that day forward Joe became part of my life then and little did I know it, he would be for the next 25 years and then some.

In the eighth grade the school day began as every school day did with Mass, except we no longer were required to meet in the classroom and walk over to the church as a group. As long as we arrived at the church before Mass began, we met the requirement of being on time. Our Lady of the Rosary Church was built like a cathedral. There were six double paneled doors that opened to a vestibule and then smaller doors that opened to a 100-foot long aisle that led us to the front pews and a few steps more to the altar rail. It had enormous high ceilings, painted much like the Sistine Chapel in Rome. Statues of the Virgin Mary, saints, angels, and The Stations of the Cross lined the walls and alcoves.

The focal point of course was the altar with a twelve-foot wooden cross with an ivory icon of the crucified Christ. The floor was made from marble and every step could be heard as we walked single file down the aisle. To aggravate the nuns we would purposely arrive after the rest of the class had been seated and begin that long journey to our pews single file. To make matters worse; we all had metal cleats attached to the soles of our "Spaulding" saddle shoes, to help save the heels from wearing out. When these eight to sixteen or so metal cleats hit that marble floor, all at one time in the quiet church, the nuns would grimace and pray that cleats would somehow be outlawed. We weren't exactly juvenile delinquents; but we liked to push buttons to test our limits. Isn't that what is expected from youths? I have to wonder if all the things that I was exposed to at such an early age, things that seemed normal at that time, contributed to my early arrival at adulthood?

We always had the freedom to go home for lunch and in eighth grade we mostly went to the local diners near the school. Neither our parents nor the school would have approved, but no one seemed to notice. At these luncheonettes (the favorite one was Shocks) we would have our choice of hot dogs, hamburgers, grilled cheese, French fries and soda pop. School lunches had all the balanced nutritional foods, and of course we wanted none of it. We liked to listen to the jukebox music, dance and socialize. I was particularly fond of socializing. If I could have been graded in socialization, I am sure I would have gotten an "A."

The lunch counter and booths were always jam-packed and often times we would have to stand to eat if we arrived too late. Lunchtime was to us just another part to the school day, another subject added to the curriculum. After school we would go to "Hartell's," a luncheonette and bar. Back then you didn't have to be eighteen to enter without an adult. Hartell's was across the street from Kiser High School. This was the "IT" spot to go, much like the Soda Shop on "Happy Days." By the time we were in the eighth grade we were meeting boys from high school and hanging out in public places, with much older kids.

At Hartell's, I continued to perform my entertainment routines. As the jutebox played the songs sung by Patty Paige, Debbie Reynolds, Connie Francis, and all those great teenager singers of that time, I performed right along with them. I would pantomime and be the life of the after school party. The group of kids that I hung out with seemed to like my entertainment; however, there were a few of the older kids who didn't like it or me. Looking back now they may have just been jealous. The one and only physical fight I ever had in my life was over my pantomiming. April Thomas, a girl a couple years older than me, threatened if I pantomimed one more song she would take me out back and beat the living song out of me. Well, no one challenges me without some sort of confrontation, then or now. The next song was "I'm Sorry" by Theresa Brewer and one of my favorites. I started to perform, and sure enough true to her threat, she was about to lay one on me. As she swung at me, I grabbed her cardigan sweater and ripped all the buttons off in one major tug. That stopped any more aggression from her, and the fight was over with only one punch to my cheek and an embarrassing torn sweater.

Joe kept his promise to take us to school and pick us up afterward. We would all pile in the blue torpedo and off we roared, loud tail pipes and all. We would talk and exchange homework notes, make plans for after school and weekend activities and just enjoy one anther's company.

About two weeks after we started this daily taxi ride to and from school, Joe dropped everyone off at the park, but I needed to be home early that day. It was just he and I, alone in his car for the first time. Tensions were high; some expectation was felt, but Joe was a perfect gentleman, and when he dropped me off a simple "See you in the morning" was all he said. I felt that he wanted to say more, or do more, but was still not sure just what to say or do.

These early morning and after school encounters became an almost daily routine. The next thing I knew we were talked about as a couple, much like Donna and Tom and Susie and Ronnie. We became Linda and Joe. Finally on one of these after school runs, Joe, leaned over as I was about to exit the car. He put his arm around me, kissed me, and I kissed him back. That first kiss was awkward, but like most first kisses magical. As I walked the final block home, I wondered what was Joe thinking about that kiss. I had thought about the first kiss he and I would share and when it would it happen. Would it be different from the kisses Johnny and I shared? Had our fates been sealed with that first kiss? If you believe in fate the answer is, yes. We were now officially a couple. From that first tentative kiss, it was not long before we began to indulge in make out sessions.

Our conversations were now more intimate, and we began to explore our individual traits. Just who was Joseph - no middle name - Hutchison and who was Linda Lou Louise Marie Wolverton. Where would these two people be in the next couple of years, the next 25 years or even the next 50 years? Perhaps it is a good thing we didn't know these answers, as we may not have gone beyond that first kiss.

CHAPTER 4

We're Going to the Chapel and

We're Gonna Get Married

The years 1955 and 1956 were pivotal years for my family. I had entered eighth grade, my last year as a student at Our Lady of the Rosary, and my sister was preparing to marry. With many milestones achieved in life, being an eighth grader was important. We were considered the ones who had achieved stature and respect for our accomplishments. We had arrived, so to speak. The younger students looked up to us for guidance, and we relished the position we would hold if only for just this year. The next year we would be relegated back to the bottom of the food chain as a lowly freshman in high school. We would have to work our way back up the ladder again. Until then the eighth grade was a sweet ride.

My sister became engaged to a young man named Paul, who was a few years older and fresh out of the Navy. At Christmas time they were engaged with plans for a June wedding. Everyone was wrapped up in the details of this wedding, including me; no one seemed to notice that I too was growing up by leaps and bounds. In the mean time I was making my own plans.

My eighth grade teacher Sister Mary Theodosius (or Ferocious as we nicknamed her), must have picked up on my budding thespian talents and chose me as a major player in the annual production of a play by the graduates. To be chosen from the group of girls that were my companions was a surprise to everyone, especially me. For the first time, I would be playing in an arena I longed to be a part of. I didn't care if it made the others unhappy. I was having a ball. I would be living what I had practiced all those years from the foyer of my home into the limelight.

I studied my lines, painted scenery, danced, sang and played around with the theatrical make-up. I was to be in every scene as the ticket master at the train station. Yes, I was to play a man. What did you expect? We were an all girls' class and the male roles were to be played by girls. I made the part come alive for the audience. Believe it or not, years later as the class of "57" we would reprise these roles at a 25-year class reunion.

While the acting and entertaining gene was trying its best to get my attention, I let it slip by, for I was too involved with a boy named Joe to keep the dream alive. Joe had become part of my everyday life. We were not "dating" in the traditional sense nor did my mother ever catch on as to how involved our relationship was. We met before and after school, at the park, at one of my girlfriend's homes or when everyone just hung out together. When no one was expected to be home at my house, Joe would drop by and spend time.

During the spring of 1957, preparing for my sister's wedding, my eighth grade graduation, and the spring play, I had one exciting adventure after another. There were dress rehearsals for the play, dress fittings for the bridesmaid dresses, final exams and…the loss of my virginity.

I wasn't prepared for the eighth grade to end; I wasn't prepared for all of the excitement of the preparations of graduation or have the wedding to end. I wasn't prepared for the let-down and wondering what was to come. Maybe that is why I made a foolish mistake of thinking I was in love.

I knew so little about Joe and his background, but after about six months, I believed I was in love. Joe must have filled a space in my life to the point that I thought I couldn't live without him. If he was not around the corner waiting for me in the morning or parked down the street after school waiting for me, I was so disappointed.

We had many excursions as a couple and as a group. There was one Saturday the boys showed up in the morning to hang out, and it was decided we would ride up to Columbus, to see where the Ohio State Penitentiary was located. Why? Apparently, it was a favorite threat parents used on the boys at that time; parents would threaten to send them there if they didn't behave. We all thought it might be fun to see just what that horrible place looked like.

Finding the prison was easy; what we saw was mind-boggling. This medieval complex was straight out of the movies. We toured the perimeter in slow motion. I don't know what was going on in the minds of others, but I know that this was not a place I wanted to visit, let alone live in. "Let's get away from "here," I heard myself say. It was a foreshadowing, a memory was and is still vivid and unforgettable and I couldn't shake it.

Joe dropped out of school to work full time. It wasn't unusual for boys to drop out and go to work in factories or the armed service. I knew that Joe had thirteen brothers and sisters and that one of his sisters died as a small child in a tragic accident. She had slipped outside for a brief moment and went unnoticed when Joe's dad backed out of the driveway. After losing a child, I can understand the almost unbearable pain an accident like that can cause. Parents are never supposed to bury their children; their children are to bury them.

Joe lived somewhere behind the Farmer's Market in a place referred to as the "bottoms." He grew up by some accounts, as "dirt poor," meaning often times there was not enough money to take care of the essentials. Joe went to work as young as eight or so, gathering bottles to sell back to the Farmer's Market or odd jobs at the market until he was old enough to actually be an employee. His dad was often out of work and his mom stayed home to care for the home and the kids. They had come to Ohio from Cynthiana, Kentucky, and were not well educated; some might refer to them as country folk. I learned that it was Joe's desire to break out of that environment and in the process help his Mom have a better life.

I had not been taught prejudice about race, creed, origin or background. I was taught tolerance of religion. We never spoke much about who was poor or who was rich and that I should avoid any certain class of people. I did hear some minor rumbles about "WASPs" and "Dagos" and a little about the Polish and the Lithuanians, but not enough to warp my view. The only prejudice I grew up with was about the "Holy Roller Church" and the people handing out the "Watch Tower Magazines." So Joe's background didn't bother me in the least. This was long before I knew anything about hereditary traits, such as genes and DNA, or coming from the "wrong side of the tracks."

In the months that Joe and I became girlfriend and boyfriend and before we became "lovers," it never occurred to me that maybe all we should ever be is friends. Our backgrounds were so different if viewed in the light of what I know today. We should never have taken the path that we did.

Joe stopped by and we were just fooling around, listening to 45s and making out. It wasn't the first time we got to playing around, and it got a little out of hand. We had always been able to stop just short of "going all the way." This time however when we got to the point of no return I thought, "Well, let just see what this is all about." If Joe had stopped, I don't think I would have pressured him to go on, but I also felt that part of me really didn't want this. It was over so fast; I really hadn't done anything. There was no magic, no stars, no fireworks.

Once again I had tempted fate and it dealt me a quick wake –up call. Not only was I not prepared for the physical part of this decision, but I most certainly hadn't thought about how the emotional part of this decision would affect me. What there was for me was fear. Fear of what had I done. This was something I couldn't undo; I could have only one first time. What I didn't understand was this decision wasn't fatal, unfortunate, but not fatal. Like so many other things I still needed to learn how to enjoy the pleasure this act should produce under the right circumstances. Eventually I would, but that didn't come until after I was married.

My Eight Grade Graduation Bridesmaid and High School Pictures 1957to 1959

For the time being, if this was what it was like to lose my virginity what was all the fuss about? Because neither of us had the experience to fully understand what intercourse meant and how it should be. We didn't quite know what to say to each other afterward. What it did mean to me was that I had sealed my fate. Joe was to be the "man" I would have to marry some day. For now in my immature thinking that was okay; someday this will all be okay, someday because I would marry him this would be forgiven. I will have vindicated this indiscretion and made it all right with everyone, and God. I will do the right thing.

The eighth grade came and went. My sister's wedding came and went. We all had a fabulous summer before we would become freshmen. While I begged my Mom to let me go to the public High School, just a few blocks down the street at the corner of Troy and Leo; it was her desire I continue my education in the parochial school system. She had graduated from Julienne; my sister had graduated from Julienne and I would as well. At least several of my classmates from grade school would attend and I accepted the fact. Joe was all for it. I think that my being at an all-girls school was appealing to him as he was protective of me.

Joe's generosity knew no bounds. He was constantly showering me with gifts and trinkets. I remember on Easter Sunday every time we looked out on the porch there was another pot of flowers. My birthdays produced many gifts from Joe including two beautiful watches, and on my fifteenth birthday a small stereo system. One Christmas a suede jacket was mysteriously left on the porch by "Santa Claus." At first it was thought to have been left by my father. Joe might have gotten away with that one had not the girls called and asked me if I had gotten the you-know-what? Mother was listening on the other end of the line.

About my father, I only saw him twice. The first time I saw him was at Christmas time when I was about 10. He arrived unannounced made a fuss over my sister and me and then was gone. I learned about him in bits and pieces. He was a very good-looking man by what I can tell from photos. He and mom married in their early 20s in a very elaborate wedding and didn't have children right away. My mom was 27 when my sister was born and 32 when I came along. I was thought to be a miracle baby as my mom had had a tubular pregnancy after my sister was born and they told her she might never conceive again.

My dad came from a very large family with many brothers and sisters. However, because of the divorce, family ties were broken. My father was not well thought of by Gramma and Grampa; (like "Voldemort" from the Harry Potter books, we never mentioned him by name).

When I was about six months old and my sister was about six, my mother left my dad in a hurry. My sister said, one day Mom yelled at her to grab the clothes and me and get into the car. We were leaving. Rumor had it that my dad drank a lot and would show an abusive nature. Over time things got worse. Additional things would come to light later and I will share them as they become relevant. But that is how we became a divorced family.

The only thing certain in life is change and changes were coming fast. Joe and I continued to see each other. Mother accepted our friendship within what she thought was limited encounters. We never had official dates, just brief get-togethers, at the park or group outings or supervised visits. Joe was becoming more and more concerned about the future and was planning to join the Army. He wanted to finish school and still take care of his mom and me.

Mom, Dad, Nancy and Me about 1944

27

He wanted to know if I would wait for him if he joined the Army, and of course I said I would. I had no idea how long four years would be and all that would and should transpire during that time.

On a cool October morning before I got on the bus that would take me to school, I kissed Joe good-by and promised I would wait for him until he came home from basic training.

The loneliness I felt the minute I boarded that school bus took over and stayed with me until he came home in December. I kept busy with schoolwork and different projects but nothing was the same. I no longer was hanging out with the other kids; they were doing the "couple" things that Joe and I used to do, and I just didn't fit in any more. A letter came in November that read: "Will you my *"mother's name"* at Christmastime?" I had to give that some thought. It finally dawned on me that his mother's name was "Mary" and that he was asking me to "marry" him. Will you *"marry me"* at Christmastime? I wrote back and answered yes, I will marry you.

Joe and I wrote back and forth but it was his belief that we should keep this a secret and that I should finish school. In the meantime we would bank all of the allotment checks that I would receive as a wife of a soldier and when he returned we would have enough money to start a married life, maybe even enough to have a down payment on a house.

There was that huge Christmas dance each year held at Wamplers Arena and this year (1958) it was called the "Snow Ball." What a perfect setting for my wedding. I asked my mother if I could ask Joe to be my date. Joe would be home from basic training and since we had never had an official date could I please let this be our first date? She agreed and everyone in the family rallied around this "date." We all went shopping for my dress: Mom, Gramma and my sister. I was insistent that the dress be white; the entire dance theme was named after a snowball so my dress should be white, shouldn't it? What I wanted was for it to be my wedding dress as well. Everyone agreed to the white dress; however, Gramma was just as insistent that tiny red velvet bows be placed in and around the ruffles. I have to admit it was a very unique touch.

Joe came home as promised, and I was waiting. He had two weeks before he would be leaving for Fort Hood TX, for additional training and then to Germany. It was just like old times: we couldn't get enough of each other. We went horseback riding, movies, hung out with the old crowd and planned our wedding.

First we were going to cross the border into Indiana, known for letting underage people marry. We found that not to be true, as they would not accept our blood test from Ohio. Then we found that we also needed our birth certificates. We went downtown to the court house and retrieved copies that were hand written in ink and notarized. We then set out to erase the original birth dates to enter dates that would make us both 21. Normally there would be a three-day waiting period but because Joe had on his uniform the registrar didn't make us wait the three days. Everything was now in motion and married we would be on December 26, 1958. Was this fate, too?

Joe came to pick me up at about 6:30 pm on the evening of our wedding and the Snow Ball dance. He had in his hand a wrist corsage of red roses; with the tiny red velvet bows that Gramma had so lovingly place in the tulle of my dress I was breathtaking. Joe was so handsome in his full dress uniform as we took pictures in front of the Christmas tree. Within a few short hours my life and Joe's and anyone else connected to us would never be the same. Our clandestine union would eventually bring us both to our knees in triumph and in tragedy. All because we

made a decision to be married in front of a justice of the peace; in the little town of Moraine City, on a cold and snowy night the day after Christmas in 1958.

Joe's brother Frank and his wife Jereldene were our witnesses. We recited vows and in a few minutes it was all over and we were off to the Snow Ball.

Several of our friends were already there and when they learned we were married they were in disbelief.

Nevertheless, we danced and partied the rest of the night away; and since I had a curfew we left early to get something to eat and Joe dutifully brought me home by 1 a.m., kissed me goodnight and said, "I will be back in the morning, Mrs. Hutchison, sleep tight." That was how I celebrated my wedding night.

What did I do, I wondered? Did I *really* want to be married? Did I make the right decision; did I understand what the ramifications were? Did I choose this path or was this path chosen for me?

Our Wedding Day Dec. 26, 1958

CHAPTER 5

When the You Know
What Hit the Fan

Joe's had a few days before his return to Fort Knox, then to Fort Hood, Texas. They went by so fast, but we found time to be alone and consummate our marriage. Feeling freer to explore each other and experiment we were not as careful as we should have been.

Joe told me he would have his allotment checks sent to his mother's house and that I would need to open a bank account and deposit them for our savings. If I needed any money, I could always use them. He would send his mother money from time to time as well. His personal plans were to continue his education. He had already completed his G.E.D. and was planning on taking on some college courses. Joe was an avid reader, and education was important to him. He encouraged me to stay in school and assured me that all of our dreams would come true.

In the end all that was left was the dreaded "good-bye." Joe's brother, Frank, picked up Joe and stopped to get me on the way to the train that would take Joe away from me again. We had our pictures taken in a booth at the train station, put a couple of quarters in and got a strip of pictures back. We were a young wide-eyed couple. Two people headed for a life of unknown possibilities; blissfully hopeful that their plans will work out and they will live happily ever after.

I began the New Year of 1959 as a high school sophomore and a wife. I had just convinced my mother that I should have a professional photograph taken to send to Joe. She agreed that one was due for the family album as well. Just before we were ready to leave for the portrait setting, the mail was delivered. There was a letter from Joe. I read it quickly; then I took it upstairs and slipped in under my pillow. Mother and I had the best time that day laughing and making silly faces into the camera just for fun. After the portrait setting we went shopping and had lunch at the "Five and Dime." When we arrived home, Gramma was sitting at the dining room table staring at us. I felt the hair on the back of my neck stand up. I knew from her look that Gramma knew what I had done and was about to tell my mother. Gramma said, "Alberta, do you know what this girl has gone and done?"

With the news that Gramma had gleaned from reading Joe's letter, she conveyed to my Mom what had transpired. I knew I was in BIG trouble. I never saw my mother in such a furious rage. She chased me around the table and up the stairs where I proceeded to barricade myself in my room. I was terrified. Joe had left me with a telephone number in case I needed to get in touch with him. I placed a call to the number he left and got someone in his barracks. I asked them to tell Joe to call me right away.

I was now on the verge of becoming hysterical. The voice in my head was screaming at me, "Oh, my God, what have you done?" I felt I had truly hurt my mother. What do I do now? In the past, I was always able to justify my actions; how could I do that now? I was talking and praying to God for some kind of sign. I worried that everyone would come out of this OK. Would my mother hate me?

Downstairs; Mom was on the phone—calling my sister, Aunt Vera and Uncle Frank, everybody and their brother, too. I could hear voices and people moving about. Every time the phone rang I thought it would be Joe. Eventually things calmed down and quiet was again restored. I suppose "they" were all trying to figure out what was going to happen with this news. It had now been a couple of hours and Joe still hadn't called. As I sat in my room looking at my wedding band, I wondered, "Was this the end of my marriage? Why hasn't Joe called? Has he abandoned me?" When the phone rang one more time, I prayed that this time it would be Joe. I answered the upstairs line to find that is was Joe, and I was sure Mom or someone would be on the downstairs line.

I tried to tell him through tears what had happened, and he tried his best to calm me. I told him I had no idea what was being said or where this was going to go as I had barricaded myself in my room and hadn't spoken to anyone yet. Joe suggested that if they would not let me stay,

I should go to his mother's and we would work something out. At that Mom spoke up and said, "She is not going anywhere. You'll be hearing from our lawyer." She then hung up. Her tone of voice was now eerily calm. What was she going to do? Send me away, maybe to a boarding school or maybe a convent. My mind raced.

Joe told me not to worry; he would take care of me. "After all, you are my wife. We'll just have to make new plans. I love you and we will be together, but I need to go now. I will call tomorrow. I need some time to think this through." One might think that I married Joe because I had had a horrible childhood and a terrible home life, but that couldn't be farther from the truth. I married Joe because it felt right. I had committed myself to this "boy" and I needed to fulfill that commitment.

It was so quiet in the house; then there was a gentle knock on my door. It was Grampa with a tray of food. He didn't say anything important that I remember. He just set the tray down and put his hand on my shoulder. He had a look in his eye that said to me, "You have really done it now, but we all love you and everything will work out." Grampa, a gentle man of few words, offered me a small bit of hope, but I knew that eventually I would sit for an inquisition of some sort.

The next morning I was asked to come to breakfast and explain myself. I am not sure just how I worded the reasons I did what I did; however, I managed to say that I was in love with Joe and that our plan was for me to finish school and in the process prepare a "nest egg" for our future. That news elicited raised eyebrows.

"Just what do you know about Joe and his family? Where do you think you're going to live? Do you know what you're giving up? How about dances, proms, parties, social events? What about health insurance, life insurance, college?" After a while it was Gramma who said, "Are you pregnant?" "Of course not," was my answer. After all, Joe and I hadn't been together for months until he came home for Christmas. "I'm sure I'm not pregnant."

Mom then told me that she had spoken to an attorney and she was planning to have the marriage annulled. She also said that according to the law we were not legally married any way. Not only were we under age, but we had forged our birth certificates and there were legal implications.

She was looking into having Joe charged with statutory rape and having him dishonorably discharged from the service. By now I was hysterical. "If you hurt Joe in that manner, you will have killed me," I sobbed. "He does not deserve to be treated like a criminal. I am as much to blame as he is, and he never, ever forced me to do anything I hadn't consented to," I cried. "Do what you have to do with me but you leave Joe alone. He only wants to love me and take care of me."

Gramma said again, "Are you sure you're not pregnant?" Turning to my mother, she added, "Alberta, before you go off the deep end you need to get to the bottom of if she is pregnant or not."

Mom said, "Why do you keep saying that? Linda, when did you have your last period?"

"I don't know, sometime in December, I suppose. I'm never regular anyway."

"Let's get her to the doctor before we go and do anything," Gramma said. I remember thinking if this was a mistake, an annulment would be at least a justification for the loss of my virginity; perhaps this was what was meant to happen to make things OK?

Our family doctor, Dr. W. C. Madden, gave me the once over and declared that it didn't appear as if I was pregnant. Gramma with her words of wisdom declared, "Well, any damn fool knows if you miss your monthly, the only good reason is that you're pregnant." As usual she was right. A test proved I was pregnant. Wow, not only did I jump into this marriage, but I was now about to be a mother too. I wasn't yet used to being a wife and now I was going to be a mom. The only thing I could think of was that God was in control. To keep Joe from being condemned for all of this mess, a baby was just the thing to take the sting out of what everyone thought was a terrible mistake or worse a criminal act. So I took this as a sign that this was where I was meant to be.

I might have pushed God in this direction with my free will, but He OK'd it. Mother did ask me if I wanted out. If so, she would accept both the baby and me. It was my decision. I did think long and hard on this. Being an unwed mother was never in my plan. Perhaps if I hadn't been pregnant, I might have considered the annulment a way of making atonement, reconsidering whether I should be married, but not now. I got my answer when the rabbit died. This was meant to be.

It was decided that an official marriage would take place. The marriage and the baby would be legitimate. In order to be married in the Catholic Church to a non-Catholic, a sort of legal process within the church takes place. I would have to swear before God and my church that I accepted this marriage of my own free will. Joe would have to swear that he would allow the children of this marriage to be raised in the Catholic faith. Church and "legal" documents flew back and forth between Ohio and Texas to make this happen.

Joe contacted the Chaplin on the post, Father Semoniski, to begin religious instructions and pave the way for me to arrive at Fort Hood, Texas, to be married with the church's blessings. On a cold day in late January of 1959 in Dayton, Ohio, I boarded a train that would take me to Joe to be married again, only this time it would be for real and for life. Gramma pinned my money to my bra and gave me my last instructions:

"Don't talk to any strangers. Don't tell anyone where you're going or what you're going to do. And please, call us when you get there. Let us know you've arrived safely."

As I boarded the train that would take me to Texas, I was very frightened by the enormity of all that had transpired. In my heart, I knew I would make this work. I would be the best wife and mother I could be. This was just another adventure to conquer.

The train ride to Texas would take three days. When I reached Fort Hood, I wondered to myself, "Can I really count on Joe to be my partner?" I answered, "Yes, he will be there for me now and always."

Joe had made arrangements for us to stay on post at the visitors' barracks. It was like a hotel. It had individual rooms and a shared bathroom facility with limited privacy. After the mini-tour of the base, we were to have dinner in the mess hall. Not exactly romantic.

Father Semoniski warned Joe that we were not to be "together" until we were married in God's eyes, but it seemed to us that the "horse was already out of the barn" and thus it made no sense to stay apart. The following morning as I made my way to the latrine in my flannel PJs, I was asked if I had come to visit my father. Eyebrows rose when I explained I was visiting my husband. I guess the flannel PJs were a dead giveaway that I was a blushing bride.

Joe finished his instructions with Father Semoniski. Our marriage was to take place after Mass on February 2, 1959. Father asked us if we had any attendants but we didn't, so he asked a couple from the front pew if they would witness our vows, and in a few minutes we were married in "God's" eyes...until death did us part. We celebrated with dinner in the Mess Hall and went back to the guest room.

We were only permitted stay at the visitors' guest barracks two more days, so after that we went into town to the "Ranch Motel." This was where Elvis Presley stayed when he was at Fort

Our Honeymoon in Fort Hood Texas 1959

Hood for basic training. We were told we were in the same room Elvis stayed in. We just wanted to believe it. If you have ever traveled through or stayed in Killeen, Texas, in 1959, these were the best accommodations they had to offer; they were the *only* accommodations they had to offer.

Joe hoped my family would let me stay with them until the baby was born, this way we could save money needed for me to join him in Germany. He also felt that I would get better care at the Air Force Base in Fairborn. There were problems acquiring birth certificates for babies born out of the country so it was better for me to have the baby in the States. Joe would fly home in December for a visit, and we would then go back to Germany together. That was the plan when I got on the train to return to Ohio.

Back home it was obvious that my education could not continue at Julienne. They could not have a married, pregnant girl amongst the student body; I became a dropout. I had contact with a few girl friends, but even then I could tell it wouldn't be long before we had nothing in common. I took parenting classes and read books on how to manage a pregnancy and what to expect when I went into labor. I wrote letters to Joe, helped around the house, and went shopping for maternity clothes.

There was a "fire" sale at Rike's department store; first come, first served. They had maternity tops for $1.00. Just what my budget could handle. I waited outside the doors on that spring morning with hundreds of eager moms-to-be, all pushing and shoving. (It's a wonder some of them didn't give birth then and there.) The doors opened, and women reached and grabbed flinging thousands of pieces of clothing into the air. I grabbed the ones that were falling over my head and took them to a fitting room. All in all I made a few good purchases.

I now was in nesting mode. My sister had had two babies, and I was getting hands-on practice changing diapers, feeding, burping. By my fourth month I was leaking "milk" from my breasts. I took on a baby-sitting job for one of my mother's friends, intent to not only get as much practice for my impending birth but to make as much extra money as possible. It was going to take a lot to move to Germany with a small tot in tow.

As the spring turned into summer my body changes warranted more rest. I had managed a routine that included long naps in front of a fan and eating oranges by the bushel. It's a wonder my baby wasn't born tinted orange. I continued to walk to the "Five and Dime" six blocks down the street to check out the newly arrived paper doll section. Walking back with my treasure was at least a mile of healthy exercise; and afterward I would sit for hours and cut out paper dolls. My collection consisted of starlets, baby dolls, period costumes, and comic book characters.

In between indulging my paper doll passion, I prepared a nursery. A neighbor gave me an old fashioned white crib with spindle bars. I gave it a coat of fresh paint and began to make a canopy to hang above it. I bought an unfinished chest and finished it with decals of bunnies and ducks. I found a used dressing table that had a baby's bath underneath the tabletop. Everything was ready to go.

I sent pictures of my growing tummy to Joe along with and letters about every new feeling and thoughts about becoming a mom. I shared with him my expectations of just what kind a mother I would be and my hopes that he would like being a father as well. He would write back with assurances of his commitment to our family.

To make things easier on everyone, I learned to drive and shortly after my sweet sixteen, and passed my driver's test with baby on board. I was now able to take mom to work and drive myself to doctor appointments and other important errands. A short vacation to Traverse City, Michigan, to visit Aunt Millie and Uncle Bud topped off the summer. While there, I got to see the Aurora Borealis for the first time. We swam in the lake and boated every day. On the surface life was as normal as one could expect under the circumstances.

Joe continued with his desire to give me everything he possibly could. He often sent wonderful surprises. One day out of the blue the postman brought six crates from Germany. Inside was an eight-piece dinnerware set; Bavarian bone white china with a platinum filigree of roses. There were serving platters, soup tureens as well as a sugar and creamer and a teapot, and, as an added attraction, toothpick holders, ashtrays and bud vases. I would be ready for our first big dinner party, but would not have guessed that it would be in Germany and therefore this set of china would take several trips across the "pond." There were also cuckoo clocks, lederhosen, baby clothes and a hand painted portrait of me. Joe had an artist do the painting from the photograph I had taken on the day everyone found out we were married.

By the Assumption of the Blessed Virgin Mary, a holy day celebrated on August 15, the

Me in Ohio Joe in Germany 1959

birth was just a little over a month away. My friend Lana called and asked if I was planning to attend the evening Mass and if so she and Judy would be by so we could all go together. After Mass that night we all walked over to Lana's house to hang out, but when I walked through the door, there were shouts of "Surprise!" There was everyone I knew gathered for a baby shower for me. There were guesses of whether it would be a boy or a girl but most everyone was pulling for a girl. What would the name be? Well, if it were a boy it would be named after his daddy and if it were a girl it was going to be Lucinda. That was my choice until a few days later when I saw a picture of a woman in the newspaper named Lucinda. She was not the most attractive woman I had ever seen, so Lucinda would never do.

On September 12th I was asked if I felt like babysitting for the Cassano family. I agreed and my Mom drove me to their house. I was there about an hour when I was overcome with immense pain. It started in my back and radiated around the right side of my body. It took my breath away. I couldn't endure it. I was panic-stricken at the thought of feeling like this during labor.

All the preparation for labor and delivery did not prepare me for this kind of pain. I called my mom. "Mom, can you come right away? Something is terribly wrong. I can't take care of these kids. I am in so much pain." Mom was there within fifteen minutes. She called the hospital and was instructed to bring me in right away. After arrangements were made to cover the care of the children, we were off.

At the hospital I was told I was not in active labor; however, they were going to keep me overnight and run some tests. The pain finally subsided and all the tests came back negative. I was sent home to wait and, although I was grateful this was nothing serious, I had nagging doubts and a very uneasy feeling.

Eleven days later, with everybody sitting on pins and needles, a few contractions about 30 minutes apart were developing. Then all of a sudden severe pain engulfed me, and I became unnerved. We were off to the hospital again. There I labored for the next 42 hours thinking I was going to die any minute. This was pain equivalent to being stabbed and ripped opened with a knife.

By the time my doctor suggested a Caesarian section, the baby had moved to the birth canal and it was too late. I would have to deliver vaginally. On September 25, 1959, with a spinal block and the calls for me to push as hard as I could, a mirror in place so that I could see the delivery, I gave birth to my first-born, a little girl, who weighed in at 7 pounds, 4 ounces, and measured 19 inches long.

Her head was cone shaped and she was slightly blue, but she was kicking and screaming bloody murder and I was no longer in pain.

According to the doctors, her head would not make that final turn in the birth canal and without help she might not have been born and we both might not have made it.

She was perfect and none the worse for the wear; her head rounded out over the next few days. She took to nursing immediately, and we were released after three days. Upon arrival home, we settled in, and Gramma insisted that the baby wear belly-bands so that she would have a perfect navel. Whether it was Gramma's belly-bands or nature, my daughter Leeann Lynn had a perfect navel (and she still does).

I named her Leeann Lynn. I spelled her name as simply as I could, thinking it would pose no problems. Wrong! Poor Leeann. She has spent the rest of her life correcting the spelling. "No, it's not Leigh Anne, Lee Ann, Lee-ann, or Leah Ann."

Leeann was a good baby; she nursed well, slept well, and was very good at pooping all over her belly-bands and down her leg. Of course she was changed the minute she spit up one drop on her sleeper or nightie and a complete new outfit was applied.

We were home less than 24 hours when I awoke in severe pain. This was the same pain I had during labor and the same pain I had two weeks prior to delivery. We called an ambulance, as it was feared that I had some post-delivery

Leeann's First Day Home 1959

complication that could be a life and death complication. I was rushed to the hospital and examined extensively, but nothing could be found. When the pain had subsided in about 4 hours, I was again sent home with no explanation.

This scenario played out about every few days. We traveled by auto to Wright Patterson Air Force Base, looking for answers that were not forthcoming. Test after test and a short hospital stay proved inconclusive. The doctors thought the gallbladder might be the culprit, but tests were negative. For the gallbladder to be the source you needed to be "fair, fat, and forty." Well, I was fair, fat due to the pregnancy, but I wasn't forty. I didn't fit the "profile." This was the first time I became aware of how much people relied on profiles. I have never fit a traditional profile and probably never would. I have always been the oddity. This pain, however, was very real, and yet no one believed me.

Meanwhile back home, mother and baby were bonding and enjoying those first couple of months of a new life. Leeann was the most beautiful baby. She seemed to respond to my voice immediately; maybe it was because I had her breakfast, lunch and dinner, with a few snacks in between available upon demand? She was growing and outgrowing her newborns at a rapid rate. I was also losing the weight. Both of us would look smashing when "daddy came marching home" at Christmas time.

CHAPTER 6

Daddy Is Coming Home and

Mom Is Leaving

In the next few weeks the "attacks" lessened some, and I learned to live with the idea that whatever it was, wasn't going to kill me. Swallowing a few "magic pills" seemed to ease the pain and take the edge off.

Leeann was thriving despite her mother's mysterious attacks. She certainly didn't lack for attention. We never lacked for company either, and soon her Daddy would be home to meet her. Joe was due to return for two weeks in mid-December.

As the day approached, it was all I could do to contain my excitement. I hadn't had an attack for weeks and was sure they were behind me. I was getting ready to go to the airport to pick up Joe, and I couldn't decide what outfit to wear. Gramma didn't think I should take Leeann out in the cold with snow threatening, but I was determined to bring his baby to him. I looked to my Mom to help with my decision. Gramma didn't like to be overruled, but this time I said I was taking her, period. Mom backed me up, agreeing that Leeann should go with me to the airport.

We waited in the terminal at the old Dayton Airport located out in Vandalia, Ohio. Planes still debarked on the runways and passengers had to walk across the tarmac to enter the building. He emerged in full dress uniform and looked so handsome. "Joe, I want you to meet your daughter. Leeann, meet your Daddy."

It took some time to get through check out, and Joe was amusing Leeann with funny faces and playful stuffed toys that he carried back from Germany. By the time we got to the car, it was obvious that I was now the object of his affection; before we got home we christened the back seat the way we had in times past while Leeann slept in the front seat. Joe wondered out loud if he was going to be welcome. I assured him if my family was at all still angry about our marriage, they didn't show it. They could see he truly cared for me and the baby by his many letters and gifts over the past months.

Indeed this visit was going as well as expected. Joe had all the information needed to get us to Germany in the New Year. We had applied for our passports and pre shipped things like the beautiful china he had sent a few months before. Vera had given me some of her unneeded pots and pans, a set of silverware, and towels. I had sent some summer clothes and a few other things. We bought our tickets and set a date to leave: May 7, 1960. We were on a whirlwind, visiting family and friends and of course getting ready for one of those down home Christmases. All was well. I had no idea that heartache and tragedy were just around the corner.

Joe couldn't believe that this little bundle of cuteness was his baby. She was very good at wrapping her little hand around his finger and no doubt around his heart. He was every bit into being this little girl's daddy, and he was kind of fond of her mommy, too. It was funny to watch her vie for attention from her daddy and her Grampa. I think she knew that both men would give her anything she wanted. All she had to do was smile and kick the back of the sofa demanding that one of them come to her aid. They always did.

A few days before Christmas, Mom was in the bathroom getting ready for work, and she asked me to come in. She said, "Linda, do my eyes look yellow to you?" I looked and thought that maybe it was the florescent lighting or maybe the kind of make-up she was using, but yes, she did look a little yellow.

I asked, "Are you feeling ill?"

"No, just a little tired," she said. Mom went see Dr. Madden, and he ordered some tests that brought concern. He thought he saw a shadow between her gallbladder and her stomach. "It may be gallstones," he said. "But I think we should do exploratory surgery to be sure. We remove the gall bladder and you're fine." They scheduled the surgery for January 2, the day Joe was flying back to Germany.

We checked Mom into the hospital the evening of New Year's Day. Joe said his goodbyes and then we spent most of the night talking, making love and planning for our arrival in Germany and our first real home. It was a bittersweet farewell, and the emptiness that always gripped me when Joe and I had to part settled in quickly after he disappeared into the belly of the plane. It would be only a few short months and Leeann and I would be on our way to our first home as a family.

Meanwhile, the news that awaited me when I arrived home was devastating. Apparently, when they opened Mom up and got a look at what really was going on, there was nothing they could do. The mass that was showing on the x-rays was not the gallbladder; it was a tumor attached to her pancreas: malignant and inoperable. The prognosis: six months to five years. The doctors said, "As of now, there isn't treatment for this kind of cancer." There was no chemotherapy, radiation, medication, nothing, as these things had not been invented yet to treat pancreatic cancer. There was nothing we could do. I wanted to scream, "Do something!" but there was nothing anyone could do. Oh how I hate being unable to do something.

Holy Mary, Mother of God, why now? Why my Mom? The doctor said it could have been growing for a long time, as this kind of cancer was not easily detected in its early stages. It also was not as common in women as it was in men. This was Gramma and Grampa's only child, and they were both numb with grief and disbelief. My sister was raw with emotion and pregnant with her third baby. I prayed to God to make this go away, yet I knew that it would take a miracle to defeat this disease. Perhaps my faith was a little shaken, for I was actually angry with God. Here was my Mom who did the best she could, believed in You, loved her family, and You let her get sick. She is finally free of obligations to her children, now You put this in her path. How could You?

At that time, I believed that God was in control of everything and could change things on a moment's notice if He wanted to. I also worried that maybe I could have caused her illness and for this I felt so guilty. I had just eloped and broken my Mom's heart. Had that caused her illness?

The next week was spent trying to come to terms with this news, visiting Mom in the hospital, and watching her gain strength back from the surgery. She looked marvelous and appeared to be taking this revelation about her health with optimism. She would say, "What do the doctors know for sure? I'm sure it's not all that dire." I was sure she was putting on a brave front for us. Mom would come home to recuperate and planned to go back to work next month. Her job was secure at Srepco.

She was especially looking forward to getting me off to Germany. I was not sure I should go. "Look," Mother said, "they are not sure how much time I have. It could be months or then again it could be years. My happiness lies in knowing that you and Joe will be together. He so loves you and wants to make a home for you and Leeann. I want that for you too." I argued that I didn't want to leave her knowing I might never see her again. "Linda, no one gets assurances of tomorrows. We plan and we plan and then one day all those plans change in a heartbeat. This is what I want; will you do this for me?"

"Yes, but I don't want to," I replied.

In the following weeks mother seemed to be bouncing back to her "old self." We celebrated her 49th birthday on Valentine's Day in the traditional manner. She was going back to work in a few days and thought a shopping trip was just what the doctor ordered. This shopping trip mimicked the one we had just a year before when we had the portrait taken. Mother was in good spirits, and we first picked out an Easter coat and bonnet for Leeann. It was in a pink taffeta fabric; not only would this work for Easter, but it would be great for our trip to Germany, too.

Mom thought that I should have a "walking suit," as they were new on the market. This was a suit with a three quarter length coat and a matching skirt. It would be comfortable if it were chilly and if I needed to remove the coat I would still look nice in the skirt and blouse. Of course, that meant that I would be wearing hose and heels. Isn't that what people wore to travel to Europe? Thank goodness we now can travel in any attire that we want. Mom picked out a lovely dress for herself and we happily brought these treasures home for Easter Sunday.

Mom went back to work, and we all were beginning to think that mother's cancer was not going to be an immediate issue. Joe had written that he had found a place for us to live. Our address would be the lower level of a house on number 6 Strauss, Uningen, Germany. The landlord and his Frau would occupy the top floor, and we would have the lower level. Joe would move in May 1st and have everything ready. Joe was not an officer; only officers could live on base; so we would have all the privileges accorded to families of servicemen just not the accommodations. Our first home was to be shared with a German national and an Italian national family as well. His letters were filled with wonderful information and some not so wonderful information. What did he mean that he would bivouac almost as soon as I arrive?

Toward the end of April, I noticed that Mom was reading the Bible more; she said she wanted to be sure she had a good understanding of what she believed. She said she had never doubted, only had some questions. As Catholics, while the gospels and epistles were very much a part of our Sunday worship, individual Bible study was not a big part of our lives. It wasn't encouraged nor was it discouraged but Mom was getting some strength from reading this book on her own.

As I look back to remember these last few weeks of my life with my mother, she was very brave in her efforts to fight this disease. She was beginning to struggle with eating. Mother so loved her popcorn and a cold bottle of beer. We noticed she was turning down some of her favorite foods and couldn't stop belching. Just before Easter Sunday, Dr. Shaffer, her, oncologist suggested that she go back to the hospital where he would fix a shunt to take the pressure off of her stomach and give her some relief. She insisted that she would attend Easter Sunday Mass first and go to the hospital that evening.

We were all dressed for Easter, Leeann in her pink taffeta, me in my walking suit and Mom in her new dress. We all wore yellow daffodil corsages and were the picture of an Easter Parade. Later in the afternoon Mom entered St. Elizabeth's Hospital and would not leave the hospital again. The following day the doctors made some adjustments in how to reroute the digestive track, and it offered Mom some relief. In the next few days, she should be able to eat solid food again. Her hospital stay would take her past my departure day of May 7th.

Mom and I spoke again about me postponing my trip, but she was adamant that the plans stay in place. This is what she wanted. "If God wants me before you get back, Linda, so be it. I know you'll be well taken care of." What could I say to that? The day before we were to leave, I got permission to bring Leeann into her hospital room to be with her Grandmother one last time. Mom looked so beautiful and serene.

We put the sides up on the bed, and Leeann played comfortably in sight of her grandmother and to the delight of her grandmother. When it was time to go as Mom was getting tired, everyone left the room so that I would have a private moment alone with her. Yes, I knew this would be the last time I would see my Mom; I just didn't want it to be. She wanted me to be happy and reminded me that we are all where we are supposed to be. She said, "Linda, we don't always get what we pray for, because we always don't know what we need. We just think we do." She held my hand and said, "You know I love you, Linda."

"And I love you, Mom," I said, tears running down my face. "I'm sorry I caused you any pain with some choices I've made. I'm so, so sorry."

She said, "See, they turned out all right, though, didn't they?"

I kissed her goodbye. "I'll pray for you always, Mom," I said and left her bedside for the last time.

As we traveled back to the house, Gramma asked, "How can you leave, knowing your mother is so sick?"

"Gramma, this is what Mom wants. I don't want to leave her, but she said my leaving for a happy life makes her happy."

"Well, it's not making me happy, or Grampa, either."

"Gramma, if I don't go, I will not have given my Mom what she wanted. That was my only choice."

The next morning amid raindrops Leeann and I boarded a plane dressed just like my mother wanted us to be dressed. We wore our Easter outfits minus the daffodils, and my money was pinned to my underwear, per Gramma's insistence. We were bound for a life in another country with a man I had agreed to spend the rest of my life with (twice). I would turn 17 in a few days, but I felt so much older. This plane would take us to LaGuardia in New York; from there, we would board a Swiss Air plane to Zurich, Switzerland, and then go from Zurich to Frankfurt, Germany, and Joe.

Here I go again breaking people's hearts, I thought. I could see Grampa from the little window of the plane. Was it the raindrops on the windowpane or were those tears running down his cheeks. I held

Leeann up to the window for one last look at her great Grandfather, my Grampa, my next best friend, and as I took her little hand to wave a goodbye, the plane rolled away, leaving behind a life I would never know again. I had to fight the fear of the unknown and tell myself, this is where you are meant to be. This is the next step to the forever after.

So much for the excitement of flying...the seats were cramped, and the thrill of take off was short-lived. It was nothing but a very noisy bus ride in the sky. It took about an hour and a half to get to New York. The landing was even more thrilling than the take off, and I found myself holding on to Leeann for dear life.

Then they told me we were to take a helicopter to the next airport. I had in mind a tiny whirlybird, but this helicopter held 20 people and was as big as a small airplane. The take-off and landing were pretty spectacular because we didn't fly very high, and I could see more of the countryside from its windows. We had a few hours delay until we boarded the plane headed to Switzerland. Leeann and I

Leaving For Germany in Our Easter Outfits 1960

spent it looking at all the shops and stores located inside the terminal. She seemed to take this adventure in stride. Much like her mother, I mused.

At 5 p.m. we took off into the sunset and out over the ocean. Within the hour it was pitch black outside, and it would stay that way for most of the next twelve hours or so. The attendants were very helpful and brought a baby bed that fit onto the overhead compartment; it would hang just above my head. I placed her in the bed and began to relax for the first time since this adventure began. My thoughts were mixed with excitement and sorrow, hopefulness and despair; sleep was fitful at best. I wondered if I should have left my mother knowing that I might never see her again.

There was so much I still didn't know about her. I did believe she would have given her life to save her children; she proved that by sending me on my way in life. I had many questions about her. What was she like as a little girl? What were her dreams and how did she meet my daddy? Was my father her first love and what went wrong? When I was young, she didn't exchange intimate details about her life or my grand-parents'. I knew hardly anything about my father or his family. So many questions…so few answers. I brought out paper and pen and began to write my mother to tell her about our trip so far. Then I tried to sleep. I would finish this letter when we arrived at our destination.

As I drifted off to sleep, I thought about the Christmas Mom wanted a flocked Christmas tree. We had always had live twelve-foot trees, and this particular year we were going to flock it ourselves. She had the tree delivered to the barn, along with two boxes of flocking materials. It was bitter cold but we were out there ready to get the job done. The first box barely covered one branch and the second didn't even cover the next and they both looked awful. Mom had the tree picked up by the nursery and they finished the job. In the end the cost of that tree was $75. In 1956, spending $75 for a Christmas tree was something only the very rich would consider. I remember Mom saying, "You know, if someone knocked on our door and asked for $75 to help the poor I would have to tell them I don't have $75 to just give away and yet here I spent $75 on a dead tree." That was so like my Mom. I was trying to remember every little detail about her that I could.

I awoke to the sun coming up over the Swiss Alps. These snow-cov-ered mountains glistened in the sunlight, and I could almost hear the "Sounds of Music" bouncing from peak to peak. Things were not perfect but a new day was dawning.

Soon we were back on land again and rushing through customs to make the flight to Frankfurt. Leeann and I made our connection in the nick of time. It would only be a few more hours, and we would be home – wherever Joe was.

Oh! Linda what have you done, you have forsaken all others. You have entrusted your future and now your child's future to a man you have only really known as a childhood boyfriend. You are in a foreign land with only a day-to-day plan. God, we are definitely in your hands.

CHAPTER 7

"Wunderbra"
We Have Arrived

Leeann and I passed through customs and stepped into the waiting arms of my husband. This was the comfort I was looking for. It completed the feeling that this was where I was meant to be. Joe guided us out into a spring German morning and to the auto he had just purchased. It was as cute as a bug. It was a bug, a VW Volkswagen bug; steel gray, used and our first family car. We loaded up the trunk and the back seat with our luggage, and headed out onto the autobahn. Joe said, "Hold on, Linda, and hold on to Leeann, as there are no speed limits, and people here drive like bat's out of hell."

Sure enough, we were going 80 mph, and cars passed us like we were standing still. Can you imagine, and the whole time Leeann, sat on my lap with no seat belt. Fifty years later, and we would have been arrested for endangering a child and a seat belt violation. Everywhere wildflowers and sprouting crops lay on either side of the roadway. For the most part we were out in the wilderness; there were no houses, no barns, only pastures and farm lands.

About two hours later we left the autobahn for the sleepy little town of Uingen, and our new home. Traffic slowed to a crawl. The streets were so narrow that barely two small cars could pass each other going in the opposite directions. No wonder German cars were so small. Cows, chickens, horses and goats shared the roadway; we often had to wait for them to cross the road, to reach the pastures on the other side. People walked alongside their animals and everyone waved. The town, with its houses were of beige stucco with orange tile roofs and flower baskets hanging from every archway, was like a picture postcard of times gone by.

On the street where we would live the row houses looked alike save for the kinds of flowers hung from the windows; which had no screens. Window curtains blew in the breezes. The colors of spring were everywhere and fragrances filled the air.

Joe pulled up along side number 6 Strussa. As we walked along the side of the house, the gardens were beginning to show that in a couple of months there would be corn, grapes, beans, eggplants, and more. Of this bounty we would never be able to feast, as we were forbidden to eat anything grown on the open market. Sadly, it was considered unsafe for American's to eat, in so far as parasites lurked in the raw uncooked veggies and fruits grown in the soil of the country people. I would have to buy my fresh foods direct from the commissary on post.

Arriving at the back of this house, where the entrances were located, there were at least 10 steps up to the front door. This was because the first floor was above a basement portion of the house; only the basement was above ground. There was also another connected structure that looked a little like a very long summer porch; however, I found out that an itinerant Italian family would soon occupy that part of the house for the summer, while they worked the fields. From the very small porch the door opened into a long hallway with three doors; one to the left, one straight ahead and one to my direct right and in front of a beautiful staircase that lead to the third floor.

Joe took the lead and opened the door in the front that opened to a living - dining room combination. There was a horsehair sofa in red velvet like fabric, a rocking chair, full size dining table, four dining table chairs and an ornate china-buffet. The windows faced the road and the curtains were blowing outward and over the flowers. The living room ended to the right with a door that opened to the bedroom. The furniture was massive, the bed looked like two oversized twin beds pushed together. There was a wardrobe and a huge chest of drawers.

Going back through the living room into the hallway, I opened door number two and there was the kitchen. The refrigerator was small and the gas stove even smaller. The sink however was gigantic with one spigot and a drain board. A small blond kitchenette table and four chairs sat in the middle of the room and a few cabinets hung on the walls. Out in the hallway was that third door. "OK, ready? Joe asked." I nodded and the door opened to reveal a perfectly normal looking toilet. But there was a reason that it was located away from the rest of the living quarters and unheated. This toilet didn't flush. At the side of the toilet was a very tall pitcher filled with water. After you relieved yourself you would need to take the pitcher and pour the water into the bowl where it would help send everything into a holding tank located underground. It worked much like a septic system and every few weeks a "honey wagon" would come around and suck all of the contents out of that container. Then the contents were used as fertilizer in the fields, thus making produce grown on the country soil unsafe for Americans to eat. I was not prepared for this. When summer arrived you didn't spend any more time in the toilet room than necessary.

All I wanted to know now was where the bathtub or shower was located. "Joe, how will we bath, I asked?"

"Linda, we'll be sharing the bathtub room with the homeowners and it's up the stairs and down the hall," Joe said.

Well good, that is just what I was looking for a nice hot bath and a change of clothes. Joe then explained a bath would not be ready for about an hour because first we would have to build a fire below the hot water tank and wait for the water to heat.

"Joe, I don't know how to build a fire; the only fires I have ever been involved with were at camp and I didn't have to build them."

"I'll teach you," Joe said. You will have it down in no time at all."

A light bulb went off in my head and I realize that the kitchen must not have hot water either. I would need to heat all water needed for cooking and cleaning too!

"How about laundry," I asked?

Joe answered, "No problem Linda, it won't be practical to take our clothes into the post all the time. Besides, I'll have most of my laundry done by the government."

Then I realized to my horror that I would need to build a fire under something if I am going to do any laundry for Leeann and me. I quickly asked," Isn't there a laundromat close by.

Joe said, "Linda, you are in Germany, in the country, not the city, and I don't think even the city has laundromat's. Mama Donwolf will show you how it's done, when you're ready."

Though I was bewildered by all of the changes I was fascinated at the same time. Of all the things I learned or found out that first day in my new home, the one thing that bothered me the most was that Joe expected me to cook for him, that night. I had hoped that he would take me out to a nice restaurant; however, he wanted a home cooked meal, and had put provisions in the kitchen. There was a sirloin steak in the fridge, potatoes for frying up in a pan (one of his favorites), salad fixings, and his appetite for food was only second to his appetite for sex. I couldn't remember if I had ever cooked a sirloin steak before; Yes, I had eaten sirloin before, I just had never cooked one myself.

Joe said: "How hard can it be? Just throw it in a skillet and turn it over when one side looked done and cook the other side."

Dinner was cooked and to my surprise it wasn't all that bad. Joe offered to do KP duty while I took that bath I had been looking forward to.

So many new experiences in one day were overwhelming but I had one more to go. How do you make a bed with sheets that don't fit? Who cares if you are tired enough? However, where was Leeann going to sleep? Joe was waiting for me to arrive to buy the crib. In the mean time how about the middle drawer of the dresser, with an oversized feather pillow as a mattress. The drawer was deep and Joe would pull the dresser up next to our bed as added protection. Voila! Baby's bed no longer an issue. As we all fell asleep my last thoughts were of home and my Mom and the letter I needed to finish and get it in the mail.

The next day we prepared to go into Goppingen where the army base was located. On post Joe showed me around so that I would know where the commissary, infirmary, church, movie theater, and other points of interest were. From there we went into town to a department store. To my very pleasant surprise in 1960 the Deutschmark equivalent to the US dollar was about a four to one value. The baby cribs that I looked at were selling for $100 to $150 Deutschmark's meaning that we would be paying about $25 to $30 dollars for a top of the line crib. These values were found in every area of goods on the open economy. I thought about all the things I couldn't afford back home, that now I could. Talk about stretching a dollar. We purchased the bed and a few other essentials and headed home.

I was trying to memorize the route as I would be driving into the post on my own in the future and I wanted to be sure not to get lost. Before I would be able to drive I would need to take a test and get an international license, so it would be a few weeks before that would happen. In the mean time I had to take an omnibus into the base or to town.

While Joe put the crib together I finished my letter to Mom and had it ready for Joe to take to the post office. There was not much time left to get us settled in as Joe had warned me he was due to bivouac for a couple of weeks, which meant I would be on my own. Thinking we had everything covered, Joe left two days later. You would think I would be bored out of my mind; I had no TV, no car, no family, no friends but actually I was quite busy. It was very time consuming to live without hot water and travel by bus to get supplies.

Just doing the laundry was an all day event. Starting with Leeann, all of my children used cloth diapers, which required special care. First I would soak them in a bleach bath until there was enough for a load of laundry. In the early morning I would go into the quasi basement, which was no more than a dig out with bricks and stones holding up the wall. A mammoth cauldron sitting over an in-ground grate would stare back at me like a cartoon character with a big grin. It tested me every time, daring me to make a fire big enough to put its contents to boil.

I would fill "laughing" bowl with water from a hose and also its partner in crime, the bucket that would hold the rinse water. The last part in this adventure was the landlord's pride and joy, an electric spinner. Yahoo. About and hour or so later the water would be ready for soap and the dirty diapers or whatever. I would take the plunger and jab at the clothes until I thought that they were clean. Then, I would take this really long stick and pull the clothes up out of the soppy water; drain for as long as my arm would hold out, then plunge them into the cold rinse water and jab them around some more.

I would then place these washed and rinsed clothes in the pride and joy; flip a switch and all the excess water was spun away. Then I would hang these bright white tidies on a clothesline.

I had decided to try and make friends as soon as possible with other military wives, so I went into the post on many days to find out if there were any woman's groups or mommy and baby clubs. I met a few of the wives at the commissary and they told me of some of the various things I could do to get involved quickly. I went into the post daily for companionship and to check on the mail as I was hoping to hear from home. Each day there was nothing.

In the middle of the night on May 17th I awoke to Joe gently taking me by the shoulders. He was supposed to be out on bivouac, what was he doing home in the middle of the night? Joe said, "Linda, your Mom died yesterday morning."

About 24-hours prior, a telegram was delivered, it said: "In the early morning of May the 16th (stop) Mom slipped away in her sleep (stop) to be ever at peace (stop), more information to follow (stop). Love Nancy."

Never was I more acutely aware that money couldn't buy happiness, but if you are going to be miserable you might as well be miserable with money than without. I couldn't fly home for the funeral and return; there was no money to do that, but had we had the money that is exactly what I would have done.

The time difference of six hours made it somewhat difficult to get timely information. Of course I called home but at $4.00 a minute, we didn't talk long. I learned that Mom did get my first letter and was so pleased I had arrived OK. She wanted to write but was too weak and soon slipped into a coma. I have to wonder if she waited to learn that I was all right and then surrendered her life back to God.

My sister said that the nurses had persuaded her to go home around midnight to get some rest and to come back in the morning. Nancy didn't want to go but she was eight months pregnant and they convinced her she needed to get some rest. She said, "Linda, I no sooner arrived home then phone rang and the hospital sadly informed us that Mom slipped away about 2 a.m."

The thought that Mom died alone was painful to hear. My sister was devastated that she had left Mom alone as well. Death usually enters stealthily, and for those of us left behind, I am certain none of us was ready for Mom to leave. I had to tell myself over and over, this is where Mom wanted me to be.

The Army allowed Joe to stay with me for three days before he had to return to bivouac and that was some comfort. Letters filled in the blanks. Mom was laid to rest in the dress she wore on Nancy's wedding day. Nancy told me that Our Lady of the Rosary was filled with flowers and the viewing the night before brought my dad by to pay his last respects. She said she barely recognized him and he really didn't recognize her.

Mom's last will and testimony was short and to the point. After her debts were paid everything was to be divided between Nancy and me and Gramma and Grampa. I hadn't expected anything; I hadn't even given it a thought. Mom's place of work, Srepco, Inc. paid all her outstanding debts, her car was sold and I received $500 plus mementos that were lovingly put into a box and sent to me. My Mom was not a wealthy woman except for how much she was loved by all her knew her.

Had Mom known that her time was nearer than we thought, would she still have wanted me to leave? She was so adamant that I keep my planned departure. Did she send me on my way so that I could be spared the anguish of her final days? I admit I felt some guilt but I reminded myself, this is where your mother wanted you to be.

May turned into June and our first guest from home was Fr. Alfred Niehause from Vincennes, Indiana. Fr. Al was my cousin on my mother's side. We had always been close and he would send me trinkets from time to time. He knew I was in Germany and wanted to check up on me. He brought along another priest as they had just come from visiting the Vatican and other interesting places on their jaunt through Europe. There were many stories to tell. The first day of the visit ended with us taking them on a tour of all the quaint little mini Catholic churches, hidden in the hilly countryside.

Towards evening after being on the go all day, and eating all kinds of different foods, I began to feel that long forgotten overwhelming pain grip me. I hadn't had an attack for four months but lo and behold there it was again. I tried to cover it up as best as I could by telling everyone that I was ready to call it a night. Fr. Al and his traveling companion went back to their hotel room and by the time I got home I thought I was going to pass out.

Joe was troubled about my illness but I assured him that all I needed at this moment was my heating pad and the electric current reducer that would allow it to work. By morning the pain had subsided. I was a little wiped but somehow managed to prepare an old fashion fried chicken dinner for our out of town guests; corn on the cob, biscuits and strawberry shortcake too. Served for the first time on the "traveling china plates". After dinner we said our good-byes and I collapsed. Were these attacks because I was stressed? Well if they were, I was more stressed than ever as they began to happen several times a week. At first Joe was concerned but after the doctors found nothing wrong he soon began to ignore my agony as well. The doctors in Germany thought all I needed was mineral baths.

Joe left for bivouac again and one evening as I was rocking Leeann to sleep in the chair in the living room I kept hearing this crackling sound. It kept getting louder and louder and as I looked around the room I looked up at the ceiling and the ceiling was smoking. I ran out of the room as fast as I could yelling, "FIRE! FIRE!"

At that Papa Donwolf came running down the stairs in his night shirt; looking like a frightened little elf, turned around and ran back up to shut off all the electricity. As it turned out the problem was with the old wiring and it was a good thing I was still awake to catch it in the early stages.

My home was overrun with workman all talking in German. They stripped off wallpaper and dug into the walls for the wires. They looked as though they had been molded into the cement. They worked very fast and were finished by the time Joe returned from bivouac. I'd like to say I learned how to speak German, however I knew only enough to get by. "FIRE" must be universal, as everyone understood me just fine.

June turned into July and we vacationed in Garmish, Paterkurskin a favorite resort for military families. A mountain range with the most pristine lake at its base made it perfect for summer and winter venues; a Bavarian lodge surrounded it with smaller individual cabins dotted in among the evergreens. We stayed in the main lodge; a beautiful rustic setting. I was just 17, the wife of a serviceman and a mom, we had to be one of the youngest families to ever vacation at this resort. Of course I had never been to any place like this before and I don't think Joe had either. After we were shown to our room we looked over all of the activities available and chose ones that we wanted to do.

The lodge offered secured babysitting service so we made plans to water-ski one day and ride horseback the next. In my attempt to water-ski for the first time I can't tell you how many times I smacked the water before I actually stood up on those wooden boards. While I considered myself a seasoned horseback rider, I was used to the western saddles and all the resort had to offer were English saddles. Thank goodness the horses were well trained, as I felt quite uneasy not having that horn to grab just in case. The third activity we did without Leeann in tow was a dinner out at a fancy restaurant.

Neither Joe nor I were drinkers but when we were brought a menu of the wine and specialty drinks, we decided that this would be a very grown up thing to do and we both decided to order martinis. Joe asked for two "very dry martinis, stirred not shaken, with two olives." You don't suppose Joe heard that somewhere do you? When the drinks were delivered we both took sips and nearly gagged. It was like drinking perfume; just God awful. We pretended to drink and then when no one was looking dumped the contents in a potted palm.

As we were ushered to our table we noticed that many of the diners were being served food that ended up in flames as it was served. Joe said he was not interested in food set afire and so we looked over the menu very carefully and chose dishes we thought were flame proof. After dinner we were given a dessert menu and thought our concerns about flaming food were behind us. I wanted to try the baked Alaska and we discussed just what it was and how it was made. I told Joe that I thought it was ice cream and cake covered with a meringue and slipped into an oven to brown. That sounded safe. A few minutes later the waiter was rolling a most delicious looking confection on a cart in our direction. He stopped in front of our table between Joe and me, poured a golden colored liquid over this creation and proceeded to set it on fire. This was the first time I ever saw my husband wanting to disappear under a table. We laughed about this many times over the years.

It truly was a vacation I will never forget and it was probably one of the more sophisticated vacations we ever shared. Before we left the resort we shopped for gifts, mainly for my Gramma and Grampa's 50th wedding anniversary.

We spent the rest of the summer watching Leeann grow and learn to walk and talk in sentences. We had plenty of time to read books and spend sunny afternoons at the public swimming pool three blocks over from our house. We were back from our vacation just a couple of weeks when Leeann was having trouble keeping down food and soon was demanding more and more milk. Then diarrhea set in. We thought she had a virus or the flu and took her into the infirmary to be checked out. Yes, the doctor agreed that some sort of a virus was afoot and put her on medication. We no sooner arrived home than a need for a diaper change was evident. In cleaning the area I found what I thought was the remains of the suppository and as I began to try and clear it from her bottom it became longer and longer and began to move. I started screaming and that brought everyone in earshot running.

As Mama Donwolf came into the room she started to shout, "DAS ISS GOOT, das iss goot." What's so good about a 12-inch long wiggly thing coming out of my daughter's behind? We put the creature into a container and took it to the post for testing. It seems that this parasite is common, and it is good when you pass them. However, when they told me she could have up to 25 of these things in her body and they could come out her ears, nose and mouth as well as her bottom, I almost fainted. They would test this one and if it were a male she probably would not have any more.

Have you ever prayed for the sex of a bug? I have and my prayer was answered. It was a male and Leeann would be just fine. Most likely she had contracted it in the nursery when we were on vacation. We had just found another reason not to eat the food grown in the country soil. It was most likely transferred to her from one of the caregivers, maybe from under the caregiver's fingernails.

August the 15th was Gramma and Grampa's anniversary. Nancy had delivered her 3rd baby, another boy, in July (that was three sons so far) and everyone was doing okay. They missed me and couldn't wait for next spring when I would be home, bringing darling Leeann with me. I missed them but was very content to be a wife and mother. I was having a wonderful time.

A month later, Joe came home early holding another telegram: Linda and Joe (stop) I am sorry to tell you (stop) Grampa passed away last night (stop) it was a heart attack (stop) more info to come (stop) Love Nancy.

The two most important people in my life beside my husband and my daughter were now dead. They both had died without my being there. Could I go home for the funeral? No. If I went home I would not be in time for the funeral. Second, there would be no return to Germany, and now my family was here.

I called my sister and she told me Gramma and Grampa had just finished supper and Grampa had stepped out onto the back porch to listen to the baseball game on the radio. Grampa was a die-hard Cincinnati Reds fan. He hadn't been on the porch long when he got sick to his stomach and fell out of the chair. Gramma couldn't help him and called for an ambulance, but he was probably gone before they got there.

Nancy said, " Linda, all of the funeral arrangements have been made, everything is taken care of and that there is nothing you can do at this point. Gramma seemed to be holding up okay for now." Grampa was a man of few words but he had a heart of gold.

Charles Van Camp left this life to join his daughter (Alberta Marie) in heaven on Sept. 16th. He left behind his wife of 50 years (Jessie), two granddaughters (Nancy and Linda), three great grandsons' (Mark, David and Matthew) and his beloved great granddaughter (Leeann). As broken hearted as I was, it never occurred to me to go home permanently. Joe had other ideas.

"Linda, I think you should take Leeann and go back to your grandmother's; she needs you. We only have another six months here in Germany and we would be going home anyway. What do you think?"

"Well, I think you're crazy. I love my grandmother but I do not want to live with her. Joe, I haven't made all of these choices just to end up back as a child in my grandmother's house. I know this sounds selfish but I don't want to go home yet. Gramma is a very strong woman and I know she will be okay. Gramma carried this family through all our tough times."

To my surprise, Joe used my argument, as his argument: "Maybe it was time for someone to carry her for a while?"

"Please, Joe not now. My Mom's gone and now Grampa. I don't want to go home; they're not going to be there."

"Well, I have made the decision and you and Leeann are going".

This may have been our first serious disagreement, one that was going to be hard for me to accept. I couldn't make Joe understand that while I loved my Gramma she could be very controlling. Time to me back then seemed forever, only six months felt like a lifetime. Gramma would want to make all the decisions about my everyday life. There would be no one to help me buffer her "suggestions."

I was steaming mad and barely spoke to Joe through the whole process of getting ready to leave. I wondered if Joe's reasons for sending me home were purely noble. Could he be tired of being a husband and a father? Of course Gramma was happy I was coming home; she didn't ask me to come home, but she didn't tell me to stay either.

On a bright clear late October morning, Leeann and I boarded a plane back to the USA and Dayton, Ohio. My little run at being a wife and mother was over. I was now going to be a little girl again, at the direction of my Gramma and how she wanted things done. Only six months Linda, you can do this for six months can't you?

CHAPTER 8

Home Again Home Again

Jig-a-de-jig

T he trip back to Ohio was overshadowed by my unhappiness of returning home without my husband. I still hadn't made peace with Joe's decision, but no matter. Leeann and I were on our way. With stops in Iceland and Greenland to break up the long flight, we arrived back in Ohio in late October. The house at 609 Troy Street looked much the same but the inside left me with a lost and lonely feeling. Gramma looked well and was truly glad to see us. Leeann and I settled in the room she and I shared before we left as if nothing had changed. Mom's room down the hall was the same minus her personal things; only a picture remained on the vanity dresser as a reminder of her. The same was true for Grampa's room, just his picture on the chest of drawers.

We had been home less than a week when early on a Sunday morning the phone rang and woke me from a sound sleep. It was St. Elizabeth's Hospital calling, telling me that my Gramma had been in an accident and could I please come to the emergency room at once. That is all that they told me, except she seemed to be in stable condition. I called my sister with this news; she and Paul would be on their way to pick me up as soon as they could get there.

At the hospital we learned that as usual, Gramma was on her way to early Sunday Mass. It was still dark outside and apparently Gramma had stepped off the curb into the path of a bus. There was some speculation that perhaps her bone broke before the bus hit her; causing her to fall in front of the bus, but no one could say for sure. She suffered a broken pelvis and an arm and wrist fracture. At the age of 72 the outlook was optimistic but she would be in the hospital at least six to eight weeks.

The only amusing thing about this situation was that Gramma had her holy underwear on. Wasn't she the one that kept telling us "Be sure you have on good clean underwear when you leave the house, as you never know who will see it?" We teased her and she laughed at her foible as well. So where did this leave me? I hadn't thought about being mistress of the manor. Was it a good thing that I had come home, so that I could keep things going during Gramma's recuperation? If I hadn't come home would this have happened? Who knows? Just deal with it, Linda, I told myself.

Gramma was asking me to visit as often as I could but the hospital was across town and to get there I would have to take two buses with a transfer. Leeann could not go, as children were not permitted to visit. I called upon my cousin and her family for help. They were more than willing to watch Leeann and so I tried to visit every other day and Nancy visited on the weekends. Soon, Leeann and I were getting visits too. It seemed my Grandmother's house was a good place to hang out; I was happy to have the company and Leeann never had so much attention.

I wrote to Joe and told him everything that was going on and he was writing back telling me how displeased he was with my behavior. Joe, didn't think it was right that I was renewing old friendships and asked me to limit my time spent with people he perceived that could lead me to lose focus. Weren't these all the same people we ran around with when we were in school? These were the people I grew up with, were my friends and his? Granted, none of these people were married with children, but at least we once were good friends.

I wrote back that he was the one that insisted that I return home and that I would spend time with whomever I wanted to. After that, I didn't tell him anything else about what I was doing or whom I was doing it with. Gramma was healing nicely and I was having a good ole time in absence of anyone telling me what to do. From time to time I had a houseful of people, and I enjoyed playing hostess.

Right before Christmas, Gramma came home and all the good times abruptly ended. It is my desire to be around people, lots of people, so I was not ready for all of the socializing to stop. Gramma returned to her mode of wanting to know everywhere I was going and with whom.

"Why do you need to go some place every day, Linda?" she asked me. "You really shouldn't be dragging your daughter all over the place." Then she'd add caution about safety, just to make me feel guilty. "Linda, it is cold outside, and Leeann shouldn't be out in this weather."

I would answer with "Gramma I just can't stay here day in and day out or I will go nuts." I wanted to be doing something besides watching TV. It never dawned on me to take some classes and I was not interested in sewing and knitting. So, Gramma and I squabbled a lot.

Christmas came and went and the New Year brought much the same except that my mysterious attacks were back with a vengeance. Not only was I unhappy every day, I was sick too! I would go out to the base at Wright Patterson Air Force to see the doctors there; again they could offer me no explanations and referred me to a psychiatrist, again. My cousin's mother said, "Why don't you see a chiropractor and see what they have to say."

I decided to do just that. I made an appointment with a Dr. Krusch. He told me that it sounded like gallstones, but if he could align my body properly the stones would eventually dissolve. No one else thought that was a good idea including Joe; however, it was my body and my pain and nothing else was working.

By February, I felt overwhelmed by Gramma's constant presence, doctors telling me I was "crazy", and not being able to help me. I just couldn't take any more people telling me what I should do, and I moved out of Gramma's house across town. Not one of my better ideas. I rented an apartment on the bus line and tried to be as independent as I could.

I kept the appointments with Dr. Krusch and with the base doctors as well. The doctors on the base ordered pain medication, Darvon, and the prescription was for 100 pills. In early March, I awoke with the mother of all attacks. I was so doubled over in pain I couldn't take care of Leeann. By the second day this attack showed no signs of easing, and I needed help. No help came, so I devised a plan that if no one were going to help me I would make someone help me. I swallowed the whole bottle of Darvacet to kill the pain and then I called Dr. Krusch and told him what I had done. Can you say ambulance and paramedics?

Leave it to me to go out in style. All I remember of the next couple of days was someone trying to stick this tube up my nose and me fighting them like the devil. My sister had to convince the hospital, doctors, and the police that I was not trying to kill myself, only the pain. My sister's pleas kept me out of the psycho ward. I floated though the next couple of days and wondered why anyone would want to take drugs, as this was a feeling I enjoyed even less than the pain. Drugs take your ability to control what is happening to you, leaving you at the mercy of others.

I returned to see the doctors at the base. This time though I saw a civilian doctor, filling in because of a personnel shortage and low and behold, he believed me. I told him if he couldn't find an answer to these attacks that I wanted to be locked up, as I must be crazy. He said he wanted to run another test and if it came back negative he would order an exploratory surgery. While I was not happy about someone cutting me open I also knew I could not continue to live like this. By then it had been almost two years from that first attack two weeks prior to Leeann's birth. I had taken this pain to Germany and back and I just needed to have an answer, preferably sooner rather than later.

I was prepped and an IV was running some kind of fluid through my veins while I was tilted up side down on an X-Ray table. Eureka! A picture at last of a minimum of 150 gallstones dancing around a very sick gallbladder. How could these not be seen before? They told me that every time one of these particles of solid material (some as small as a grain of sand, others the size of a pea) tried to pass though the duct to my stomach it would cause this excruciating pain. It would be like glass cutting at this duct or blocking the duct altogether. The pain would subside either with the stone passing through to the stomach or floating back into the gallbladder. I was relieved and angry at the same time.

Through their ineptness or incompetence, these "doctors" left me feeling that I was stupid and too young to know what I was talking about.

This is when my mistrust of doctors started to take hold; I also harbored some ill feelings toward others who didn't believe me either. No one offered me any apologies and there was one person I especially wanted an apology from, Dr. Hood the base psychiatrist. When I told him about the diagnosis all he did was shrug his shoulders and walk away.

Surgery was scheduled for the end of April. Joe was due home about a week before the scheduled date. When he arrived he was none too happy with me. I had moved out of Gramma's house and was out on my own; I don't know if leaving my Gramma's house on my own, or being successful in doing it caused him more concern. I thought my independent nature was what attracted him to me; now it looked like it worried him or was it that I could live without him that made him more nervous? Either way we had a rough patch to overcome.

I had to decide if this marriage was what I truly wanted and he was deciding if he could trust me. He was sure I had been unfaithful. I was sure I hadn't, and I wondered if he had been unfaithful and needed me to confess to lessen his guilt. We were really two young, immature people with attitudes on both our parts, but now was not the time to debate it. I was looking at major surgery and what all that would mean.

Joe would be able to stay for the surgery but he would have to leave the next day to get his temporary duty papers and his assignment for the summer. He was almost sure he did not want to stay in the Army and wanted to know what I was thinking. I really liked being connected to the armed service. The thoughts of traveling the globe appealed to me, but it was his decision. We spoke about where we were going to go from here. I wanted to have the right to make personal decisions about things that would affect me directly. While Joe thought it was a good idea that I return home, it should have been my decision. Whether we should have more children should be a joint decision. What I wanted was to have my feelings taken into account. Joe could be insistent and would remain so on many issues. I was very headstrong and would remain so on many issues. In others words we both had to learn to pick our battles to keep the peace within our family.

Joe helped me check in to the hospital for my date with the surgeon and I settled in a room with four other surgery patients. I did not have a clue what I was in for when it came to having your body assaulted with a knife. They shaved my belly, gave me a sedative, wheeled me out of my room on a gurney, and prepped me for a day from hell.

Some hours later I awoke thinking death might be preferable. There was this nurse who resembled a bouncer, telling me I had to get up out of the bed and walk. I wanted to know if she had lost her mind. " Honey, we must get you up and moving so you can heal, she said". Why, hadn't they put enough staples in my belly so I could lay flat and die in peace? I didn't think they did because my insides felt as if they would fall out if I moved.

I slid out of the bed like an eel for there was no way I could bend myself in a sitting position. They came in every few hours after that and insisted I get out of that bed every time. Surely this was cruel and unusual punishment, wasn't it? In those days if you had a gallbladder removed it was usually by a 12-inch incision that ran from your breastbone past your navel or maybe from under your rib cage around to your back.. Today making a couple of small holes does that same surgery. I never really had a bikini body and it was for sure now I never would. Besides the long incision that would end up healing triple thick; I had a drainage tube poking out of my side too, adding insult to injury. I now have two belly buttons, one just a little to the right of the one mother-nature gave me.

Was there anything positive about this experience? Well, yes. As I was healing, I knew I would not be plagued with any more "mysterious attacks" and I had the best set of roommates to help me recover. What one of us didn't think up to cause the nurses trouble the other ones did. We became friends in need and had made the most of our trials and tribulations if you will. One of these roommates would keep us all in stitches, no pun intended. We found ourselves begging her to stop because it hurt so to laugh. Ten days of this and I was definitely ready to go home. I took with me a little jar holding my 150 gallstones as my prize, and arrived just shy of my 18th birthday.

After a few more days of rest and recuperation I would be ready to join Joe in Sparta, Wisconsin. He would be stationed there for the next four months before leaving the service for civilian life. He came back to fetch Leeann and me and take us with him on this last leg of his military life. This is what I wanted, to be with my husband and my child.

What fun we had in those last few months of Army life. We were dirt-poor living in a complex with four other "dirt-poor" military families but we were having a great time. We had one of the smaller cabins on the complex and would share a latrine type bathroom. My days were filled with raising Leeann, being a homemaker and learning how to stretch a dollar on a once a month paycheck.

Toward the end of the month we all found ourselves pooling our resources to make communal suppers. One would have the beans the other would have a ham hock and one would have some veggies. We had so much fun we forgot we were poor. I can remember we would have to take a pair of pliers to bed just in case the innerspring in the mattress would poke though and stab you in the ribs. We would then pull out the pliers and cut it off.

Joe and I were still working on the issues of trust and communication of our true feelings, but for the most part we were making progress. It's a good thing too, because I was a thrower in those early days. If we had a spontaneous verbal fight, I might just pick up something and throw it. One of those times I threw a glass-measuring cup at Joe to make my point. It missed him, crashed and broke and Joe swore that I would never have another glass-measuring cup so long as I was married to him. He kept that promise too.

We really hadn't planned to have another baby just yet, what with our future so uncertain but nature does take its course. With little entertainment on most evenings we had to think of something to do to spend time with each other. Sometime in late July or early August we conceived the second addition to our family. I was somewhat concerned that it might be too soon after my major surgery but the doctors assured me it would be all right.

The due date for this baby would be April 6, 1962 and we were very happy until Joe got his mandatory assignment to go back to Germany. The Berlin Wall had just gone up and there was a freeze on releasing anyone from active duty. I was heart broken as I thought that I would be left behind again to have this baby on my own and Joe would be back in Germany without me. At that time they were not allowing wives to join their husbands and any wives still in Germany, were sent home. It was thought war was imminent. Joe applied for a hardship release and one was granted with a sigh of relief from me as well as Joe. We stopped at the post commissary on our way back to Ohio and much to my surprise, Joe bought for me an engagement ring to add to my wedding band. I took that as a sign that everything was on track, full speed ahead on our way to ever after.

Joe resumed his job at the Farmer's Market while we were getting our bearings as to where we would go from here. We stayed with Gramma to her delight until we could find us our first home as civilians. I would need to find a doctor to see me through my pregnancy and we knew we couldn't afford an OB/GYN so we settled for the GP on the corner. Dr. Priest would take me as a patient and we felt comfortable with him. He was informed about the delivery difficulties I had had with Leeann; he assured us that it rarely happened in second deliveries and if it did he would have access to experts at all times. I can't tell you how much I enjoyed being pregnant, both with Leeann and now this baby. To feel life growing inside you is a miracle; it's a shame that men never know that feeling.

Joe soon found a job at Koontz Brothers Foundry making excellent hourly wages with benefits and promises of overtime. We found an apartment between Joe's work, Gramma's house and Joe's mom and dad's. It was perfect with two bedrooms, living room, kitchen and full bath and at $59 a month plus utilities we could would be able to save some money, too. We had enough money to buy three rooms of furniture for $395 and still pay the doctor and hospital bills for the birth of our baby. We couldn't have asked for more.

We settled in as a stable family with all the hopes and dreams young families plan for. We had plenty of family to visit on weekends and they would visit us as well. Sunday dinner was either at Gramma's or Joe's mom and dad's. Friday or Saturday nights were at one of Joe's brothers or sister's houses; or with our new neighbor friends, playing cards or board games while the children played. This was typical of the family life I was familiar with and to say we were happy and content would be correct.

The only negative was that Joe worked awfully hard at a very dirty job, but he never complained. He was doing it for his family. We ate a lot of fried baloney and Mrs. Grass's chicken noodle soup, but we had plans and were saving for a house. Our biggest family night, and for many years to come was to dress up to go grocery shopping. We often took Gramma with us and afterward we would stop for our one meal out at a restaurant. Often it was just McDonald's but still it was a treat.

Come April 1, 1962 I was ready to have this baby. While I hadn't gained as much weight with this pregnancy I was a whole lot bigger. Yet every time I kept my doctors appointments I was told, "You're not quite ready yet," or, "Any day now, be patient." By the end of April everyone was asking what was going on. My sister who by now had four boys wondered, "Why hadn't Dr. Priest induced labor yet?" I would tell her, his answer was always the same, "Let nature take it's course." He asked if we could have missed calculated?" I didn't think so, but what did I know, compared to a learned doctor of medicine?

Perhaps the baby was waiting to be born on my birthday of May 11th? As I turned 19 on Friday, May 11, I still hadn't delivered. Dr. Priest had said, "If nothing is going on by Monday, I'll consider inducement." Early on Sunday morning I awoke feeling uncomfortable and began spotting. At last we were about to have a much-anticipated delivery. We had just had a shower of rain and the sun was peeking through the clouds. We left our house to drop Leeann off at Joe's Mother's and we were off.

By 10 a.m., I was settling in at St. Elizabeth's Hospital on the labor and delivery floor. The nurses declared I was about 6 centimeters dilated and it shouldn't be too much longer. This time I was going to try a drug free delivery.

Joe was totally clueless at this point. It was amusing to see him fret about the room. I had to remember that this was a first time for Joe, to be this close to the delivery of his child. He had been in Germany when Leeann was born and they didn't allow fathers in the delivery room, but he stayed until I was transferred for the final phase. Dr. Priest was there and the last thing I heard was "Linda, don't push."

I awoke about an hour and a half later to find out I had delivered a whopping 10-pound baby boy. My lips and mouth swollen and my eyes black and blue, "My God what happened," I asked. "Is my baby okay?" Baby boy Hutchison was getting cleaned up in the nursery. It seems that Dr. Priest was unable to make the delivery as the baby would not make that last turn in the birth canal; just like Leeann 's birth, just like he said would probably not happen with a second birth. He had the attendants slap a gas mask on me and held the baby in the birth canal about 30 minutes before an OB-GYN could make the delivery. No matter, so long as my baby boy was all right. Baby boy Hutchison joined seven little girls in the nursery, all born on Mother's Day, May 13, 1962. We were so proud and happy. Nothing matched the joy that we felt with the births of our children.

In the nursery, they placed his bassinet in the center of the viewing window and positioned all the little girls around him. At 10 pounds and all the little girls a dainty 5 to 7 pounds he made quite a conversation piece amongst the visitors. I might not be able to sit down for a month, but he was here and beautiful. Despite the difficult delivery his head was perfectly round and bald as a billiard. However it was our belief he was born a month old and he proved that by giving us the sweetest smiles he could muster. When I asked the pediatrician how often I should feed him and what. His reply was, "Feed him anything he wants, anytime he wants it."

Our wishes and prayers had been answered. We got our boy and he was, to our innocent, new-parent eyes', healthy. He was a blessing and we named him Joseph David Hutchison. Joseph, for his father and David because it sounded sturdy and grounded, a name he could grow into as a man. To me he was and will always be Joey, my first-born son.

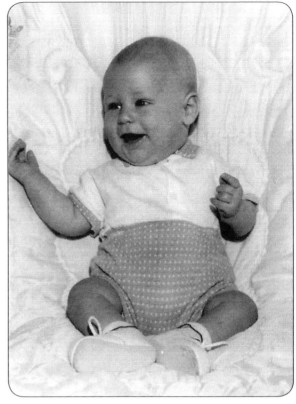

Joey's Baby Picture 1962

CHAPTER 9

A Completed Family,
A New Home Too

At 3702 Roland Circle, "Joey" met his big sister and joined the family. He was dressed in the blue outfit Leeann and I picked out; and I placed him in Leeann's lap the minute we came through the door. The books I had read said that is what should be done to over come any jealousy. We had prepared Leeann so I believed she was ready to accept her brother from the start. Joey would eventually share her bedroom, and the crib had been placed there a couple of months earlier. For now though Joey would stay in mommy and daddy's room in the bassinet until he was able to sleep through the night.

Two days later Leeann came down with the measles. While Dr. Priest said it was unlikely the baby would get the measles, Joey did. How was this going to affect him? No one knew for sure. We watched him very closely for the next couple of days as he was breaking out, at that point it looked as though everything was going to be okay. It did take a lot of food to fill him up and within three weeks he was sleeping six to seven hours at night. Another reason I believed he must have stayed too long in the womb.

Now you would think that between Dr. Priest and an OB-GYN doctor, they could have gotten the delivery done right; they didn't. This may not have been their fault but several months after Joey's birth I had to return to the hospital for a D&C procedure. This is where they dilate the cervix and scrape the uterus of the foreign matter. It appeared that all of the afterbirth was not expelled at the time of delivery and what was left behind attached itself to the uterus wall and grew. It needed to be removed to restore my body back to a non-pregnant state. This would become an issue years later when we were hoping to have another baby.

Joey was such a dear sweet baby and very smart, he was walking and talking by seven months. One morning I awoke to find Joey in our room and wondered how he got out of his crib. The next day I found him climbing over the rail. From that day forward we left the rails down just in case he might fall climbing over the rails and out of the crib. For safety we now gated the doorway to keep him in his room at night. In trying to remember every detail of Joey's life, at around a year old he came down with a strange virus. He was frighteningly sick for about ten days and would upchuck the oddest contents from his stomach with the foulest odor. It crossed our minds that maybe he had ingested something that was poisoned, but we never found anything to confirm that. Eventually he recovered except we noticed he didn't sleep as long during the night and he didn't seem to be as happy.

Joe had changed jobs and was now working at Dayton Tire and Rubber, where he had better pay, better benefits and better hours. We started to look for a house to buy. We found a three-bedroom brick ranch in the little town of Vandalia, Ohio, near the Dayton Airport. In addition to the three bedrooms, the house had a living room and kitchen; full bath, a carport and attached storage shed, patio, and a huge fenced in backyard just begging for kids to play. Could we afford it? It was $12,400 and the monthly payments would be $79.00 a month. That would be $20.00 more than we were paying to live in a two-bedroom apartment, but it would be more room and it would be ours.

As we went to sign the papers we were told I was not old enough to have my name on

421 Vista Ave., Vandalia

▶ About 1,350 sq. ft.
▶ $105,900
▶ Sales: C. Michael Royce, Realty World/Royce & Assoc. (937) 890-8732 or 718-7915
▶ Directions: National Road, south on Helke, left on Vista Ave.
▶ Open house: Jan. 25, 2-4 p.m.

Previous owners of this brick ranch added a 21-by-13-foot family room with a wood-burning fireplace and a fourth bedroom measuring 20 feet by 13 feet. They included a full bathroom between these rooms. The home was built in 1956, and its original layout includes a living room, a formal dining room, kitchen, three bedrooms and a full bath. Within the last three years, the roofing shingles, furnace, central air-conditioning unit and carpeting were replaced. The garage door was updated on the one-car garage. Extra parking is available on a concrete pad.

the mortgage and the deed, I would not be 21 for another 2 months. For the time being only Joe's name would appear on these documents. On a cold, cloudy and windy March day in 1964, we moved into the house where we would live in for the next 20 years.

The kitchen in the new house was a galley style and at the end of the counter was the perfect place for Joey's high chair. I placed Joey in his high chair with some finger foods to keep him busy while I helped to bring in things from the moving truck.

The next thing I heard were screams of terror from my new kitchen as I found Joey hanging by one foot from the high chair and his head cut open on the side bleeding profusely. My little escape artist apparently was not satisfied to sit and snack and decided to break free and join the moving team.

With only a partial move accomplished, we spent the next several hours in the ER getting stitches. I was to watch him closely for any signs of a concussion. I could hear him screaming the whole time they put in his stitches.

When we got home our family and friends had us moved in and we collapsed in fatigue. Joey protested going to bed in this new house and new bed, so we let him sleep with us. If I had to put

Our Home on Vista Ave. With the Famous Tree House and Giant Sandbox Early 1964

my finger on just when I began to notice my son's strange and destructive behavior it would have to be from that day forward. Joey was never able to focus on any one activity for more than a few minutes. He would break or throw toys across the room for no apparent reason, and meltdowns were a daily occurrence.

Our plan was for Leeann and Joey to share one bedroom as we thought we would use the third bedroom as a playroom. That would work well for the next couple of years. It was a 10x10 space that held all the most important "stuff" that my children owned. Toy boxes of building blocks and baby dolls; coloring books and paper dolls, puzzles and picture books, a perfect place to keep Leeann and Joey busy learning and playing.

Joe's job at Dayton Tire and Rubber kept him busy bouncing from first, second, and third shifts and back. I, on the other hand, was eager to become part of this new community. We registered at St. Christopher's Parish and became involved with raising our family in the parish life; Mass on Sundays, tithing, Rosary Altar Society, parish festival committees, and community work as well.

St. Chris' is where we would send our children when they were ready for school. First though, we enrolled Leeann in Vandalia pre-school classes held at the Lutheran church. It was not affiliated with the church other than using the classrooms. This was the place that a great many of the children in Vandalia began their education or so I was told. A woman known as Miss Eby had operated this school for years; she was a lady of some advanced age, perhaps in her seventies, and well respected for her knowledge of the training of children aged two through six. She would ready them for kindergarten and they would be better prepared to achieve than those who did not have pre-school experience. Joey and I would drop Leeann off at the school weekdays and then Joey and I would have some alone time before we would pick her up at noon for lunch.

Joey and I used this time to get acquainted in the neighborhood. There was a family by the name of Anderson a couple of houses down on the left. In the Andersons' household was a "granny" and it felt really comfortable to spend an hour or so visiting with her. She loved Joey and seemed not to mind that he was into everything.

As the years went by people moved away and new people moved in. When Carlene and Randal moved, Marilyn and Kenneth Livingston moved in with their little girl, Kimberly, and Marilyn became my closest and dearest friend to this day.

My early days on Vista Avenue were a whirlwind of family life. Some time was spent on housekeeping, but mostly, it was about being surrounded by children and good neighbors. Joe's days were spent as the provider for our home. We had plans to make the backyard a perfect playground for our children. There was a swing set already there; and we added a jungle gym, and soon a mammoth sand box and a tree house would be built. Add to that a picnic table for adults and a smaller one for the kids, providing everything we needed to keep our kids and their friends happy to be there. I longed to give my children the out door experience I had as a child. There would be tricycles and bicycles, hot wheels and blow–up swimming pools. We would play outside until dark in the summer and in the recreation centers in the winter.

I insisted that my kids learn to swim as soon as possible; and on hot summer days after work, Joe would take us to Miller's Grove to swim and play. Later we would join the Willow Swim Club. If the kids had been really good, on the summer weekend nights, we would take them to the drive-in movies.

Of course there were television programs like Uncle Al, Mr. Rogers' Neighborhood, Captain Kangaroo and cartoons. While I noticed that watching television did seem to keep Joey's attention more than any other activity, we had become concerned about Joey's lack of sleep, his dangerous antics, like banging his head against the walls or playing with fire. As Joey grew his behavior seemed to worsen. I would talk to my sister about the things Joey would do, and she would tell me that Joey was a boy, and I was just used to Leeann's good behavior and cooperation. Boys were supposed to be little demons on hot wheels.

Surely children were not supposed to climb out windows and sit on rooftops in the middle of the night, were they? Remove all the doorknobs from all the doors, escape and have the Vandalia police department bring them home? Have their behavior corrected and yet continue to repeat the same behavior over and over again? He could not sit quietly for five minuets let alone finish a storybook. His frustration level was at ground zero. Tantrums came and went in minutes as well. I would want to have Joey sit on my lap to read stories or just rock and rest a bit, but he would not have any of it.

After an especially exhausting day, Joey would fall asleep sometimes in a sitting position. Even today, despite all the misbehavior, I can still visualize what a beautiful baby boy he was. His hair curled in ringlets from the dampness left over from his evening bath. His chubby little hand and fingers that were once clamped in fists fighting who knows what were relaxed; and that perfect little rose bud mouth that many would envy, was perfect for a kiss. Did he know just how much he was loved, and at the same time how much we were worried about him?

As much fun as it was to dress a little girl, I was having a great time picking out little boy outfits too. There were the cowboy boots, leather bomber jackets and corduroys. One Easter there was a navy suit for Joey and the matching navy outfit for Leeann. I once tried to make a mother and daughter dress for Leeann and me for Easter. Just how hard could that be? Well, just because you can read a pattern, and cut out the fabric, doesn't make you a seamstress—no matter how hard you try. We did wear them that Easter but

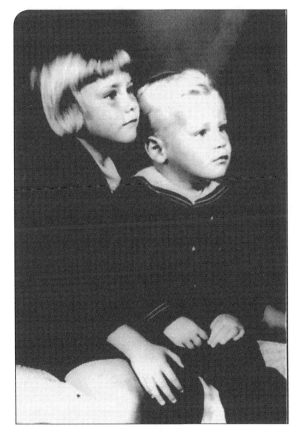

Leeann and Joey's Easter Portrait 1964

73

you would not have wanted to look too close as they were missing a lot of the pieces. Thank goodness I never tried to make a man's or little boy's dress shirt. Hats off to anyone who can.

Another thing I was not very good at was cutting hair. Again, I thought, "Just how difficult can this be?" Leeann's hair was as straight as a stick so I figured it would be easy. We ended up crying and then were off to the beauty shop with the hope that someone could rescue Leeann and save me from my arrogant undertaking. I was always eager to at least try new things; if I was interested I thought I should be able to accomplish it, right? Apparently not!

We struggled to take Joey with us to Sunday Mass for a long time; it was our belief that "God" wouldn't give you children if HE didn't want you to bring them to church as a family. But eventually we could no longer take Joey to church on Sundays; even in the quiet room he couldn't restrain himself for long. In the church itself, he would be under the pews, over the pews and running into the middle of the aisle. We hadn't been to Mass on Sunday as a family for a few months, so when Gramma came for a Sunday visit and asked, "Would you like me to stay with Joey so that you can go to Mass as a family?" we jumped at the chance.

However, when we returned home we found Gramma and Joey both in tears, and Joey with his hand in a bowl of ice water. It seems that Gramma was doing some preparations for our Sunday dinner and had warned Joey not to touch the stove. He was so quick and he must have placed his hand directly on the electric burner. The burn was painful but not serious. Gramma very upset, said, "I guess I'm not as good as a babysitter anymore." I assured her that it was not her fault; Joey was very quick and hard to keep up with.

In grocery stores I spent a lot of my time chasing him down. The looks and often times the verbal affirmations from well meaning people were easy to read: "If that were my child he wouldn't behave like that!"

We took Joey to our new family doctor, Dr. Smith, but Joey was never overly active in Dr. Smith's presence. All the doctor saw was this beautiful blond curly haired little boy, smart as a tack, but it was noted that he did seem to have a lazy eye and we were to keep a watch on that. If it didn't correct itself in the next few months he would need to see an eye doctor that specialized in this condition in children.

All The Young Great Grandchildren From 1962 to 1964

Gramma had moved into a garden apartment and seemed to be content with a group of friends to keep her company. Her routine of traveling by bus to church, card clubs, doctor appointments, and hairdressers remained the same. In the summer when we would visit, often times Gramma would leave the apartment door open to circulate air. Joey thought this was an invitation to bolt out into the hallway. We would retrieve him and explain that he must stay inside Gramma's house. Short of closing the door this wasn't working. We thought he was now playing a game of "come get me" and we decided not to chase after him. Within nano-seconds we heard a piercing scream. We ran to the door and opened it to find Joey standing there with a part of his finger dangling by a thread of flesh.

I can only assume he must have pulled on the door and it somehow caught his finger. We grabbed towels to wrap his hand and rushed him to the hospital. We now were in the ER again in less than 2 months. The doctors said they thought they could save the fingertip but it would require surgery. We gave our permission for the surgery but didn't know that it would require Joey going under anesthesia multiple times and we worried about so much anesthesia and how that might affect him, but we were told not to worry.

After this, we needed to find out just how important it was to correct Joey's eye problem. If he wasn't seeing properly, perhaps that contributed to his behavior issues. The eye specialist confirmed that indeed Joey had a lazy eye and that at his age the correct treatment would be to cover the good eye and force the lazy eye to perform. That was easier said than done. We used every trick and treatment known to mankind to get Joey to keep that patch on. The next step was surgery to tack the eye muscles in place to hold the eye straight. The doctors said that because he was so young it might not work. However since he wouldn't keep the patch on they had no choice. Unfortunately, the surgery was not as successful as they had hoped. We would now try glasses with an eye patch and see if we could get the results needed. This worked a little better but not much.

A year later with little to no improvement, and a "Mexican Stand Off" between Joey and everyone committed to helping him keep that eye patch on, another surgery was performed. This would be the last time a surgery of this nature could be done; it would either work or it wouldn't. It didn't. So it would be the glasses and patches if there were to be any hope in saving the sight in that eye. It wouldn't be that Joey would be totally blind; he would just not be using that eye to see as someone would without this problem. No one knew if this was the root of all of Joey's behavior problems, but it seemed to me it didn't help.

As hard as we tried to protect Joey from injuries, hardly a week went by that something horrific didn't occur. He was barely three when we were out in the back hanging laundry to dry and he had climbed onto the picnic table. Leeann called to tell me Joey couldn't get down and as I turned to see what Leeann was talking about Joey was falling backwards off the table, and he landed flat on the back of his head. I ran to him and as I picked him up I noticed swelling. It was like his skull was exploding into my hands. I raced him to the doctor's office feeling that I was going to lose him any second.

Dr. Smith declared, "It's possible Joey has a concussion that looks much worse than it is. Just watch him closely for the next 24 hours; don't let him go to sleep right away, and wake him every two hours through the night. The hematoma should reabsorb in the next couple of months and Joey won't be in any additional peril."

Peril! Peril was Joey's middle name. Please, Dr. Smith, tell me how do I keep Joey safe? Many a day I stayed up late to finish every day chores after Joey was asleep because they were not possible to do while keeping an eye on him.

In the next couple of years, Leeann advanced to kindergarten at Vandalia Elementary, and I joined the PTA. At 22, I was probably one of the youngest active mothers. I had always planned to be involved with my children's education for I truly missed completing my own. Joe had his GED and was now taking courses in college and getting involved with the AFL-CIO union as a leader. We traded off the time each of us needed to attend these functions and still not need to rely on babysitters to be with our children.

I found that working with the PTA was an education in itself. I was elected to an officer's position (secretary) when Leeann was in the first grade. This was a major challenge for me as I have explained how my lack of spelling has plagued me forever. Although I know what I want to say and can say it with conviction, often times I can't spell it.

However, I did undertake this job and was successful, with a lot of help from a dictionary and my sister, who is a walking-talking dictionary on call. This job allowed me to participate in the National Convention of PTA held in Washington DC and was probably the catalyst to my desires to be involved in future events of this type.

While Leeann was progressing at average to above average in kindergarten and first grade, Joey was struggling to fit in at playschool. Miss Eby had many wonderful suggestions to help me help Joey with his behavior, however they were not working. We made charts that would follow up on good behavior with stars and rewards when each level was completed. If there were special activities that Joey really liked to do, he would be permitted to do them if he were able to sit quietly for five minutes. Again and again we would try these and other techniques. Some times they would work, more often than not, they wouldn't.

Often when Joey would act out I would intervene only to find he was not totally aware of how he was behaving. I would not see conscious awareness in his eyes and wondered if Joey were having some kind of seizures. It was almost like the blank look I saw in my childhood friend Kay when she would have a seizure. I told this to the doctors and they dismissed it.

People marveled at how much patience it took to keep Joey out of trouble and most of the time I was able to do just that. He did though on occasions push my last button and I would either smack him on the bottom or yell at him to just stop, please stop. I would find myself asking him, "What is the matter with you?" –knowing I wouldn't get an answer but desperately wanting one.

Joey could flip on the TV, reach for the play dough on the table, throw it on the floor, open the fridge, break a dozen eggs and run out the back door all in a matter of a minute. I would then find him swinging from the swing upside down, having a great time, oblivious to the mess left behind.

We were asked to be godparents for Joe's sister Ella and her new baby, a boy named Christopher. When Leeann and I were part of Ella's wedding party Joe was able to keep Joey under his watch, but this time both Joe and I would be busy attending to the baptism. Joey was left to the other family members attending the ceremony and after the actual baptism they were eager to return Joey to us for supervision.

We went to the reception at Ella and Jerry's and were trying to join in the festivities. Joey was trying everyone's patience. What sealed our early departure was when he ran as fast as he could down the hallway and slid into the baby's bassinet, overturning the bassinet, with the baby in it. The baby rolled out onto the floor gently; but nonetheless this act caused a great deal of alarm. At that, we gathered up Joey and Leeann and said our goodbyes.

My head was pounding and all I wanted to do was get home and go to sleep. I had never had a migraine headache before, but I was sure this was one. As we pulled into the driveway of our home, I became aware that Joey was now barefoot, so I asked, "Where are your new shoes?" I was hoping he would say he had left them at Aunt Ella's. Leeann piped up and said that Joey had thrown them out the car window sometime ago.

To this day I truly regret my behavior, I grabbed Joey and began to smack him over and over, screaming God only knows what. My hands were flat not in a fist, but still I was so angry, and I vowed from that day forward I would never touch another child in that manner again. Forty years later I would break that vow.

As I lay in my darkened bedroom distraught over my actions and Joey's, I asked myself over and over what was wrong with my child or what was wrong with me? How could this beautiful, smart, funny nearly four year old, be so out of control? How could I not train him to have acceptable behavior? It wasn't that we were permissive parents. Was Joey not capable of learning the basics of acceptable social behavior or was I not able to teach him? An answer was very much needed.

I decided to take Joey out of pre-school as Miss Eby continued to give me grief over Joey's behavior. I found that she was ostracizing him, using him as an example of the type of behavior one shouldn't do. The last straw came the day I went to pick him up, and she had him close by her side making sure his pockets were empty of any little toys that belonged to the school. She was again making an example of his poor behavior for all of the other children to see. While I was not happy about my son's behavior I knew that this was not the way to correct it. I decided we would both be happier if I looked elsewhere for schooling. After all wasn't this entire struggle with his behavior going to be over by the time Joey would be in kindergarten? That was what everyone was telling me. "Joey will be okay by the time he goes to "real" school."

Joey was starting to make friends in the neighborhood; there were little Donnie and Kevin two houses down, and little Davy at the far end of the street. All of these little boys loved to come and play in the biggest sand box on the block. They would peddle their "Big Wheels' in mock races up and down the sidewalks; yes, I would sometimes have to send them home when Joey couldn't play nice, but at least there would be a tomorrow to play again. Tonka trucks and GI Joe's along with buckets of cowboy and Indians ruled the sand box, and kindergarten would start in the fall. Nobody goes to kindergarten without having learned basics of acceptable behavior, right?

CHAPTER 10

Everybody Goes to
School Or To Work

The first day of Kindergarten was approaching; Joey walked to school with Davy. It was three long blocks to his school and we walked it many times over the summer so it would feel familiar. Of course for the first couple of weeks I would walk along, or if the weather was really bad I would drive the boys. There were some changes in Joey's behavior; I thought for the better, at least the school was not reporting any crises the first couple of months. Yes, there was still some destructive behavior in the home but it was my hope that Joey could keep that behavior at home.

Maybe it was time to have another baby. I had wanted another child for a long time. I wanted to test my parenting skills and I wanted to know if another child would keep me from worrying about Joey so much.

Others had mentioned that I spent too much time trying to help Joey. Were I distracted by another little one, I wouldn't have time to be there every time Joey needed to be "saved." We had not been practicing any form of birth control, so it was possible I could have become pregnant again in the last five years. It was now time to see just what our options were. I took these concerns to an OB – GYN doctor, Dr Kritzer. With a thorough work up, it was thought that my major problem was ovulation. This was probably a repercussion from the afterbirth issue from Joey's delivery. We would try some new treatments (drugs) to see if we could encourage ovulation. After a few trials, Dr. Kritzer felt there was nothing else available and it would be up to Mother Nature from this point on. Well maybe that was my answer; we were not meant to have any more children. I was reluctant to accept that prognosis but I would have to for now.

I thought perhaps I could go back to school. I sent for books on how to take the GED exam and studied those for a few weeks. When I felt prepared enough to take the exam I made an appointment and took the tests. I can remember waiting for the results to arrive by mail; I was almost as anxiety ridden as if I were still in school, waiting for the teachers to place that grade on my reports. When the results arrived, they came with the knowledge that I was no longer under educated. At least I was equivalent of a high school graduate.

Next I applied for my social security card. I did not have one, nor had I ever been employed. Maybe it was time I got a J-O-B. Joe wasn't so sure about that. He was not anxious for his wife to work. Perhaps it was because he wanted to be the provider and thought that I should be a homemaker, period. That was all well and good; however, Joe was now working seven days a week plus overtime, and I was hoping if I went to work we could get some quality time as a family. However, the answer for now was, no.

For the next year, I would keep busy with the PTA and the Rosary Alter Society programs. Leeann would be a second grader at St. Christopher's and Joey had made it to kindergarten. We were settling into a family of four, with two children in school. During the second half of Joey's kindergarten, a meeting with his teacher revealed that Joey was having discipline problems. Miss Piper felt that some of it was her fault and therefore hadn't mentioned it sooner. In addition, the principal, Joe Gatton was now involved. It seemed that Joey was highly intelligent and was far beyond grade level except in his maturity and socializing skills. It was decided that Joey would work with a psychologist for the last semester and perhaps we would see improvement. The aim was to keep him moving in the right direction to advance to first grade.

On Joey's sixth birthday we were planning a celebration with his afternoon kindergarten class. Joey and I spent the morning baking cupcakes and as we put them in the oven to bake Davy came knocking at the door. Joey had gotten a tetherball as one of his birthday presents the previous evening, and Davy was eager to play with Joey before going to school. I told Joey, "Go ahead, run along and play, I'll call you when the cupcakes are ready to ice." I could hear them playing and laughing and the sound of the ball being swatted about. It was a beautiful sunny day, and Joey seemed to be doing better in school.

The cupcakes were done and I set about making the icing when I noticed the silence. I called out, "Joey, the cupcakes are ready to ice, you can come in now," but I didn't get an answer nor did I hear anything. When I went to investigate I didn't see anyone at the tetherball pit. I did see the box that the new tetherball game came packaged in lying on the cement driveway. I kept calling Joey's name over and over with no response. I walked over to the box just lying there thinking that maybe Joey went down to Davy's house. As I bent over to pick up the box I could see two little feet, inside. I said, "Joey, come on quit playing, it's time to ice the cupcakes." Still no answer, nor did those little feet move. I bent over and pulled on those feet and Joey emerged dazed and unable to speak or stand.

"Oh my God! Baby, what happened?" I screamed. I brought him inside and checked him over beginning with his head. I didn't see any lump or bump but while he knew who I was; he didn't remember it was his birthday, or that he had gotten a tetherball, or that he was playing with Davy. He also couldn't bear weight on his right leg and his right arm would not work either. Again, we were racing to Dr. Smith's office two blocks away.

This time, it was a concussion for sure, but again there was no immediate cause for alarm, according to the doctor. We could only speculate, but Joey probably got inside the box while standing up and putting it over his head or having Davy put it over his head. He then must have lost his balance and fallen with no way to break the fall and, knocked himself out when he hit the cement. Davy probably got scared and ran home instead of coming to tell me what happened. I didn't speak to Davy about the incident because I didn't want to put Davy in a position where he would have to lie and deny that he pushed Joey. I didn't want Davy to feel badly either; this was just kid's play. Needless to say, Joey's party was rescheduled for the next day.

In spite of that dramatic ending to the school year, the summer seemed to go well.

Leeann was going into the third grade at St. Christopher's and Joey was to be a big first grader at Vandalia elementary. I was more adamant about bringing in some money to help with our ever-growing household needs. Sears' department store was looking for seasonal help and I could work part time during school hours.

Joe finely relented and I tested positive for employment status. I was to be trained to work in the men's department at the Salem Mall store. I would be responsible for customer purchases, restocking of the merchandise, and inventory as well. I was thrilled to learn these different positions including the accountability of all of these areas of retail and marketing. I was made for customer service, as I have never met a stranger and I am always ready to help someone make a decision. I was given positive recognition and was one of the few seasonal personnel that were being considered for full time employment. However, things at home were not as I would have liked them to be.

Joe was still pouting over letting me work outside the home, Leeann was not thrilled that I was not always home before she got home and even less pleased if Joey got there before I did. Leeann complained Joey was hard to deal with and absolutely would not listen to her. I decided that with so much opposition to my working I would chalk it up as another adventure that I undertook, and conquered. I returned to work as a full time mom and homemaker, as that is where I needed to be.

This time though, if I were to be a stay at home mom I wanted more children. We knew we would not qualify for a newborn to adopt; we had two of our own biological children, so we decided because there was such a need for foster parents that maybe that was what we should do. Test the water and see if expanding our family was the right thing to do. We talked it over with Leeann and Joey to get their feelings about sharing our home with a new baby; a baby that really needed a place to stay until their new mommy and daddy would pick them up. Leeann was thrilled as she had asked for a little brother or sister before. Joey's reply was, "Sure. I guess it will be okay."

So in January of 1969, we applied to be foster parents through Catholic Charity's of Dayton, Ohio. We went through background checks, parenting classes, and family counseling, and received our qualifying status sooner than we thought. We had preplanned a Florida vacation for early June, and although the agency knew we were not ready to take on a child until we returned from the vacation, they asked us to start immediately.

We had signed on for newborns with possible delays for immediate adoption. Race would not be an issue; but I felt that babies with severe physical or health problems, would be something I could not handle. Most likely, I would be too sympathetic and not strong enough emotionally to be of help. We also would consider an older child, preferably a boy, thinking that this might be good for Joey to have a brother to pal around with. One was a great idea; one was not.

Our first baby arrived sometime in mid April of 1969. His name was James Todd and he was two months old. He had spent from his birthday of February 13, 1969 in a temporary foster home until a permanent foster home would open up, and we were it. When we got the call we had three days to say yes or no to the placement. James Todd's parents were college students, unmarried, and had decided they were not ready to be parents. They were pretty sure this was the right decision. James Todd would need a foster home until suitable parents were found, parents who would love him as there own. The only other thing the agency told us was that James Todd was bi-racial.

For the next three days I spent thinking, "Could I be the mother that this child needed?" I had had virtually no contact with any African Americans, and was unsure if I would be able to give him the love and support that he would need. Joe said it was up to me, but he was fine with the idea. Gramma, wanted to know if we had thought this through, "Linda, with so many white babies needing homes why do you want to take on a deviation from a normal family?"

I said, "Gramma the deciding factor was that this baby needed me and I needed this baby. There were plenty of white families for white babies but not enough black families for the black babies." I was sure this was something that God wanted me to do or otherwise I would not have been asked to do this. "Normal" had never been one of my first choices when it came to a challenge, so why should I change my commitment to challenges now?

On a spring morning this beautiful brown baby boy was carried through our front door. He was dressed in a turquoise onesie, with a matching tam hat, sitting over a mop of the curliest soft brown hair I had ever seen. His tongue seemed to be too big for his mouth as he grinned from ear to ear. How in the world could I not fall in love with this little guy? Any fears or doubts disappeared the minute I laid eyes on him. James Todd was definitely the kid who came to dinner and stayed. Jimmy, as we would call him, filled the need to care for an infant again. I suppose there are deep-seated reasons I needed to feel needed by an infant again, but I am sure they were all good.

Jimmy was meeting all of his milestones and by the end of the summer in 1969, we brought into our home a boy about Joey's age, named Phillip. Phillip had a twin sister and they both had been removed from an abusive home. Phillip was to stay with us about a year and then be reunited with his sister in a permanent family situation. Our thoughts were that this would be good for Joey to have a buddy to hang out with and both boys would gain something from the experience. Both of these boys needed counseling but not for the same reasons and this proved not to be a good placement for either of them.

However, we did our best to keep them busy. The boys were into T-Ball, Indian Guides and second grade. Joey was in counseling at the elementary school and Phillip at the social service agency.

Joey's teachers were sure that Joey's problems were from hyperactive syndrome and urged us to place him on medication. Placing Joey on drugs was the last thing we wanted to do; however, the school and his counselor thought it was the perfect answer. Dr. Smith agreed to give drugs a trial and Ritalin and Dexedrine were the drugs of choice. As I remember one had him bouncing off the walls and the other had him sleeping all day and up at night. These drugs were discontinued after about six months, as Dr. Smith thought that they didn't show any real improvement.

In January of 1970, we would have to face losing Jimmy to a prospective adoptive family. The agency said they had a family that wanted to visit with Jimmy and see if he would be a good match. The anxiety I felt was almost overwhelming as I called Joe to tell him the news. I guess I had always felt Jimmy would be part of our family forever; even though the agency had made the terms quite clear, that at no time were we ever to expect that a foster child would be a permanent placement in our home.

We had been with Jimmy when he had his umbilical hernia fixed, and he learned to walk and talk and now he would leave us. We had even been asked to and appeared on the Phil Donahue Show in Dayton, Ohio on a segment about families who took in bi-racial children—we had been through a lot of milestones with Jimmy, and when they came to take him it was devastating. I cried until I could cry no more, but took comfort in the fact that I was now pregnant with our third child, and believed that perhaps Jimmy and Phillip were somehow responsible for that. I thought because we opened our home to children in need that God had blessed us with another of our own.

The morning that they came to pick up Jimmy I had bathed him and dressed him in a new romper suit and fluffed his hair into a perfect mini Afro and he looked adorable. As he left, I thought I would never see him again. Later that afternoon, with a knock on the door there was Jimmy grinning that over the top smile and the social worker asking if they could come in. It seems that the family that looked at Jimmy thought he was not black enough to blend into their family and so they wanted to look at another baby. I could hardly believe what I heard. Nevertheless I was thrilled to have Jimmy home.

We decided we either needed to move to a larger house or to build on to our existing home. I wanted to move to the country. My thinking was that Joey would have fewer distractions and less avenues to get into trouble with the neighbors. Joe wanted to try and advance his skills by building on to our existing home. He

Joey's School Pictures Throughout The Years From 1967 to 1978

had already improved our home by adding a double driveway and patios; he also filled in the carport to make a garage and enlarged the dining room. Why not add a family room and a second full bath? He won the debate.

The summer was all about construction, swimming, and the excitement of having a new baby. Joe was handling the building of the new family room and bath and both Joey and Phillip were his helpmates. Leeann and Jimmy were helping me get ready for the new baby. The second grade was coming to a close for Joey and Phillip and before the new school year Phillip would leave us to join his sister in their new home. With the new baby due in October we decided to hold off on taking any additional foster children.

This pregnancy was so different from Leeann and Joey's. I felt so blessed. For one it was the only pregnancy we actually were hoping and planning for, and it took nine years. Neither, Leeann or Joey's had been planned, they just happened. Two, we would have the expertise of a very good OB-GYN so that any complications would be handled well. I was healthy and watching my weight and I felt so special. I truly felt like I was the only woman in the world going to give birth. Secretly, I would know if there was any thing I did or was doing to cause the problems we were having with Joey. I knew I was a good mother or I felt I was a good mother, so why couldn't I help Joey?

In spite of all the challenges we faced, Joey always seemed to be less of a problem during the summer. With my love of swimming I was pleased that it was flowing over onto my children as well, they all took to the water like ducks in a pond. Leeann was especially good. I remember one afternoon after we had joined Willow Swim Club we were at the pool when I saw Leeann on the three-meter diving board. As I watched her approach she lifted into the air and completed a one and a half somersault tuck and landed the dive perfectly. I was so astounded and proud by her performance, that I knew that if this was something she wanted to pursue I would do everything I could to support her. She did and she not only continued to grow in the sport but she went on to place seventh and tenth in the state of Ohio when she was in college.

Leeann was very much into sports, as was I, throughout school. Her second love or maybe it was her first was softball. While the emphasis was clearly on sports for boys, with the new Title One, girls were now demanding access to those privileges as well. Catholic Youth Organization ("CYO") sports and public school sports were now getting the backing they had been denied for so long. Leeann played softball and volleyball throughout her elementary, middle, and high school years and even into adulthood. She still referees volleyball and umpires softball as she enters into her 50s.

I was also proud of all my boys as they all played T-Ball, baseball, basketball, and football. Joey and Jimmy would also try wrestling. Sports allowed Joey to shine in an otherwise dismal learning environment. At least he was accepted as a team player most of the time.

James, Running Back/Safety Joey, O&D Lineman and Eric as a Nose Guard

Joey started the third grade in 1970 at Helke Elementary. My hope was that Joey would adapt to this new way of education (the open classroom) and settle into a successful year. I too was hoping I would not need to spend as much time in the classroom as I had in his first years. Leeann was now in the sixth grade and doing very well in all areas. Jimmy was almost two and didn't show any signs of the "terrible two's," and life was good in 1970.

Leeann and Joey were in school all day. Joe was home because he was still recuperating from his broken arm. He had broken it at work in September and at the time we thought it was a tragedy, however it turned out to be the best thing that could have happened. We were enjoying one another's company like never before. I can't remember when we were so happy. I was pregnant which made me happy; Joe was building a dream room that made him happy, Jimmy was a doll baby, Leeann was ever the model child and Joey was in a better frame of mind then he had been in a longtime.

There were some last minute fixes needed on the family room to have it completed by the time the baby came. It was amazing the work Joe could do even with his broken arm. However, I got to be in charge of being the "dead man" handler. You have not lived until you see an eight-month pregnant women holding up a dead man, while her husband nails in the drywall on a ceiling.

After working on the room addition during the day, the after school activities would kick in. There would of course be homework, followed by football practice and volleyball practice. We would attend the practices as well as the games. Practices were often more fun to watch as the stress of winning was not as intense for the grownups as well as for the kids. Both Leeann and Joey excelled in sports and we thought that in many ways it was a God send for Joey, so long as he didn't have to spend more time on the sidelines, than on the field.

By the first of October, Leeann and I went shopping for the outfit we would bring the new baby home in. This time, Leeann chose yellow and she also picked out a fall color plaid print long robe for me. Joey was caught up in the excitement of the new baby as well and would help his Dad get the baby furniture ready. One thing Joey learned well was how to fix things that were broken. He would work along side his Dad until something was fixed. I say he worked along side of his Dad, but I didn't say he always liked to. Yet he was always good with his hands. It must have been more satisfying to work with his hands than to read and follow written instructions.

The family room was completed by mid October and now it was just a matter of relaxing in this new beautiful room and waiting for the completion of our new family member to make his or her entrance. The new room was a step off the original house. We cut out over the kitchen sink and cupboards and added a pass through to a bar that had four high chairs so that while you were eating or playing at the bar, you also had access to the kitchen. The huge living area also had a fireplace at the end of the room, something that added a homier touch.

All activities could be monitored from the kitchen giving me an excellent advantage, since I spent most of my time there. The room was carpeted except for the bar area and the bathroom. With this family of almost six people that second bathroom was most welcomed.

Now, baby you can come any time.

CHAPTER 11

And Baby Makes Six
and Counting

A s much as I loved being pregnant I was now ready for this new little person to come into this world and leave my body. Again, all things happen for a reason, and Joe's broken arm was a blessing in disguise. We had the best family time anyone could have asked for. As usual we spent most fall Sundays taking long walks in the parks and woods or picking apples. On this fall Sunday I was twelve days beyond my due date and quite uncomfortable.

As we were walking out by the Englewood dam playing, "You Tarzan me Jane," Joe raised his hand for us to stop. Very quietly he said, "Linda, take Jimmy's hand and run as fast as you can up that hill." I thought he had lost his mind. Run? I could barely walk. He then pointed over to a clearing in the brush and there lay a huge wild hog with piglets. Knowing she would defend her offspring and that we would be no match should she decide to do so, we ran.

At the top of the hill was the time to explain to the kids just what had happened. We then could look down at the mama and her babies in relative safety. I was extremely tired on the ride home and Joe stopped for some take home dinner. I retired to the bath and Joe saw to supper and nighttime chores. After my bath it was obvious we were going to bring this baby into the world in the next few hours. I had begun spotting and was pretty sure leaking some water. I settled into the recliner and began the timing of contractions.

Joe did what Joe was good at, sleeping on the couch and waking every so often to check on the progress. "No, not yet I will keep you posted, I would tell him." At about seven AM the contractions had gone from every fifteen minutes or so to every five minutes and now it was time to go. Joe called on Marilyn our next-door neighbor, who had become my closest friend, to come and stay with the kids. Leeann had begged to stay home from school to hear about the birth and we agreed. We thought it would be better for Joey to go on to school so that it would be easier on Marilyn with just Leeann and Jimmy to look after, as Joey could be a hand full.

Eric Charles was born at 9:55 AM on October 26, 1970 and weighed in at 8 pounds 4 ounces. He was my only birth baby with hair. I was thrilled. This baby and his birth was text case perfect from gestation to the onset of labor to the delivery. Eric did present the difficult entrance but having a skilled OB made all the difference. Leeann was a little disappointed as she had wanted a sister, but I was happy he was healthy and looked perfect. I was thinking with this boy I would know for sure if the difficulty raising Joey had been mine. Joe stopped by Joey's classroom to tell him he had a new baby brother and he became the classmate of the day. Everybody wanted to congratulate him. Having him go to school was the best decision we made to help him accept this new baby; as he was the center of attention at least for a day, and his peers accepted him as someone special.

We brought Eric home all dressed in the yellow outfit Leeann picked out and we settled in as a family of six. The holidays came and went and it wasn't long before the school wanted to talk about Joey. It seemed that the open classroom concept was not for kids that presented behavioral issues like his. Joey would wander from room to room causing much distraction to all the classrooms. We were going to have to consider alternative schooling for Joey.

As we investigated our options they all came down to money. The Gas Light house would have been perfect except they wanted thousands of dollars a year in tuition. There were scholarships but we didn't qualify for them. Joe made too much money and we were not poverty stricken. So now what?

Well, there was a neurological handicap class in the public school system that would take Joey. Because of his eye problems he would qualify as neurologically handicapped. He would have to ride a "little yellow school bus" down to Merlin Heights Elementary School, a small little school located just south of Vandalia and north of Dayton, Ohio.

The classes would help educate Joey through to the sixth grade and hopefully prepare him for junior high.

When I visited the classroom, I was shocked to find boys and girls with behaviors much worse than Joey's. These kids thought nothing of picking up their desks or chairs and throwing them across the room. While Joey's behaviors were sometimes off the wall, I had never felt threatened by any physical harm. Joey was beside himself at having to go to school on the "little yellow bus." He hated the thought of being different; I think he knew just enough about feeling that he was different, and he was unwilling to accept himself as such. Perhaps in some ways we were also unwilling to accept that Joey was different and we may have conveyed this sentiment to Joey as well.

In the next several years as we entered into therapy with Joey and as a family, some of the most idiotic scenarios were to be explored. To this day there is so much psycho-babble going on it is hard to know who to trust. One psychologist says one thing and one says another. Is it any wonder we don't have a handle on how to help people with mental and emotional issues? One thing I know for sure, there are no two cases alike, period. You can't rely on profiles, alone. I am a living example of failed profiles.

What the hell is a "dysfunctional family"? How could we possibly be a dysfunctional family? We may have started out as a non-traditional family by virtue of our young ages when we married, but we stepped up to the plate and made our goals clear. Our home and family were our primary responsibilities. Maybe Joe worked too much, maybe I wanted to accomplish many different activities, but our family always came first.

There were no drugs or alcohol in our family, no illegal activities, we didn't lie, cheat or steal. There were no hidden closet behaviors we were hiding from the public. We were always there for our children and their needs. The only thing we could not get a handle on was why our son behaved in an unacceptable manner, and why we couldn't seem to do anything to help him?

By the time Joey was twelve, his behavior was no longer looked at as something he would outgrow. Joey began to lie, cheat and steal. We now suspected drugs, but how and where was he getting them? He sometimes didn't come home from school; we may or may not know where he was at any one given time. Joey began to show up on the juvenile delinquent list at the local police station. Some things were minor and probably would have been ignored if they only happened once. But from the first embarrassing trip to the Vandalia police station to the tragic last trip to the Vandalia police station our lives would never be the same.

You know it is odd now that no one at this point ever thought to consider that a mental illness or a brain dysfunction could be Joey's problem, or maybe they did, but were reluctant to suggest it to us. It did occur to us that our child could be mentally ill; but we were told children can't be mentally ill. They can have behavior issues, be hyper active, have discipline problems, suffer from birth defects, but not be mentally ill. If your child was having problems it must be because he had a dysfunctional family, had been abused, or somehow it was the parents' fault. Mental illness was thought to be something you could control unless you were totally out of your mind and then you were to be institutionalized in a straight jacket. We knew nothing about mental illness other than it happened to other people. No one was willing to explore the answer to the possibility of a mental illness.

For the time being, we tried to convince ourselves that our life was "normal". Joey had his schedule, Leeann had hers, Jimmy would become a Hutchison by an official adoption at the age of four, and Eric was growing into a perfectly normal toddler. When they came for Jimmy in the spring after he had turned four we were shocked. I guess we just thought that Jimmy would stay with us forever. With no one coming for him, we thought he was now too old to place. We were confident all we had to do is love him and raise him as our own. Wrong. It seemed that there was a white couple in Yellow Springs, Ohio that wanted to adopt a black or bi-racial child and Jimmy was being considered. Well that was what pushed us into making that assumption that Jimmy would stay forever, legal. We concluded that if Jimmy was meant to have Caucasian parents he already had them. The agency agreed and so Jimmy became a Hutchison legally, however he was a Hutchison before any legal paper said so.

Jimmy had been accepted as part of our family and had been accepted as such in the community as well. The thought that Jimmy would have any identity issues was never considered a big issue. It had been a long time since strangers would look at us with disapproving looks. In the neighborhood, at school, at church, and community functions Jimmy was more than accepted, he was "spoiled rotten" in the best sense of the term. On occasion, we would hear unflattering remarks aimed at the black race, followed quickly by "we didn't mean Jimmy." This led me to believe that hatred or prejudice is an acquired outlook by people who were taught these things by family or society. Jimmy was accepted because they knew us and because he was not a threat to them.

There was only one time when Jimmy was small that he questioned the color of his skin. It was after he had had his bath and I was dressing him for bed when he asked, "Mommy, in the morning when I wake up will I be white like the palm of my hands?"

My answer was: "No Jimmy, God made you this color and it is a beautiful color and we love you just as you are; we don't want or need you to change into any other color. We love you just as you are." That seemed to satisfy him then and it seems to satisfy him today. We are Mom and Dad and he has the same brothers and a sister he has always had.

Later in life (mid twenties) he asked me if I would mind if he looked for his biological mom. I said that I didn't mind, that it would be his choice. I did say that he should be prepared to accept the good with the bad. He might find that his biological parents might be something more or less than he was hoping for and that there would be no turning back if he were disappointed. I would always be his Mom no matter what and I could share him too, as I will always be grateful that his parents loved him enough to give him to me.

Family Picture For St. Christopher's Church Directory 1971

We kept our family, or so we thought, moving in the right directions. Joe moved up in stature with Dayton Tire and Rubber, not only in seniority but responsibilities with in the company and with the Union. He took advantage of further educational opportunities, as did I. I found a little extra time here and there to qualify as a Red Cross water safety instructor, a swimming and diving instructor, and I took courses at Sinclair Community College in business management for two years.

Leeann continued to be a joy and the "perfect child" in every way a child can be. I thought of her as my mini me and couldn't be more proud of the choices she would make in friends, activities and behaviors. She was eager to please and extremely helpful at home, in the classroom and with after school activities. She wasn't exactly in the most popular clique but she held her own. Joey, on the other hand continued to move ahead one or two spaces and then slip backward four or five. Just as soon as we thought the worst was behind him, we would find very disturbing periods would arise and knock us for a loop.

Late fall and winter were the worst of times for Joey. Seasonal affective disorder was not a well-known disorder yet, but it was at these times that Joey would be the most destructive. I always believed that Joey knew right from wrong, but for some reason he just couldn't stop himself from doing the wrong thing. I remember asking Joey why he did the things he did and his answer was always, "I don't know." And I believed him. No one else did, especially anyone in authority. When we questioned the authorities their answer was always, "Joey can behave or control his behaviors, if Joey wants too."

As an adult when we talked about some of his behaviors as a child, Joey was able to give me a better answer. He said, "Mom, when I pushed the dumpster over the ravine, broke windows, yelled fire, terrorized the neighborhood and generally caused havoc, it wasn't that I wanted to hurt anyone or damage property, it was because I just wanted to see how many times the dumpster would bounce, what the glass would sound like when it broke, and I never thought that I was doing any thing wrong until after I did it. As a child I had virtually no impulse control. I thought it and I reacted to the thought, plain and simple. I would have so many thoughts at one time that I just had to pick one thought and go with it, does that make sense?"

It didn't make sense to me and he said it didn't make sense to him either, but that was how his mind worked.

We, along with experts, struggled to understand why Joey who definitely knew right from wrong could not make decisions that would keep him out of trouble. Trouble had a name and it was now Joey. If anything was amiss with the neighbors it must have been Joey's fault. Nine times out of ten it was, but the tenth time it wasn't, and Joey, who knew he would get blamed, quit fighting the accusations. At home it was pretty much the same, if it was broken it was Joey. If it was missing it was Joey. Once you have a bad reputation it is near impossible to overcome.

Sometimes, months at a time, it would seem like Joey had turned a corner and the bad behavior was behind him, only to have it return with a vengeance. If money was missing, it was Joey who took it. Staying out all night and taking the car for joy rides was another problem, and he was only 13. His room was a disaster and very little that he owned was in working condition. It is extremely hard to live with a person like this. Yet at times he could be a gentle soul not sure of where he was going but wanting to get there to please us and himself. Love has no boundaries, but loving Joey was a challenge.

It must be easy to love a child who has a devastating, even a fatal illness, even one who will have lifelong physical disabilities such as blindness or deafness. But how do you love a child that has behavioral disabilities? One day at a time. One day you want to wrap your arms around him and thank God he is over the rough patch. The next day, you want to lock him up and throw away the key. You want to keep him safe and keep him from being hurt. To do that, you have to run your home like a prison. On guard at all times, preemptive if you will and all the while knowing you can't be this child's jailer.

CHAPTER 12

Beware of a Wolf in
Sheep's Clothing

Having a special needs child was definitely taking a toll on the dynamics of our family, but we were so involved we didn't see it. The first thing we didn't recognize was that Joey was a special needs child. That was not a well-known term before the 1980s. I remember thinking that if Joey was mentally retarded or born with Down's syndrome or muscular dystrophy or any number of physical impairments, there was help.

Children with these challenges take a toll on the family, but in my opinion it's nothing like having a child whose behavior is out of control. When you have a child with behavioral issues the world looks at you (the parents) as the reason this child is incorrigible. We were so determined to somehow save our child from self-destruction that we may have lost how to save ourselves in the process.

Each time Joey presented a challenge, we listened to the so-called experts and tried to work with their approaches to discipline, kinds of foods that should help, kinds of therapy, and of course education. Failure was all we ever got in return. Successes were fleeting, much like a change in the weather when one was not expected. I would cry myself to sleep and Joe would not accept that something was wrong with his son that he wouldn't outgrow.

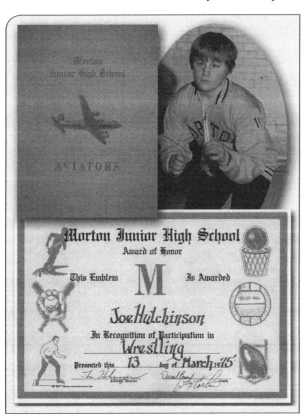

Joey Wrestling in Seventh Grade at Morton Junior High 1975

Joey entered junior high with high hopes, and we had those same feelings as well. We had hoped that after his mainstreaming from Merlin Heights and the neurological program, he would be ready. He had to be, as there was nowhere else for him to go. He was signed up to play CYO football at St. Christopher's and wrestling at Morton Junior High.

Between the times of 1968 through 1973 we had fostered a total of nine children. There was Frannie, David, Davey, Phillip, Martha, Annie, Theresa, Angela, We finished with Mary Ann whose parents were injured in the 1973 Xenia, Ohio tornado. Mary Ann was our ninth foster baby and we felt we now needed to concentrate on the children we would see to adulthood. We continued to try to find programs and counseling, as much for us, as for Joey.

One psychologist, Dr. Larry Levine from Good Samaritan Hospitals Mental Health Center, seemed to work best. It began with sessions in the home and eventually moved to Joey attending their in-house program at the hospital. Joey would spend his freshman year at the hospital on an outpatient basis and have family counseling in the home.

What we found as strange was that, after everything we had been through with Joey, no one ever alluded to the possibility that Joey could have a mental illness. It was always behavioral issues and hyperactive disorder with vision problems. Joey's IQ remained at a range of 150+ and most of his learning was achieved by hearing and oral instruction.

As Joey struggled to fit into our family life, we continued to try to appear as normal a family as we could to the outside world. It was just something we had to work with every day, and yet go about business as usual. Oh, how my heart ached to know that I could be such an influence with other children and not be able to help my own son.

Everyone else in the family was progressing with their talents and interests. I continued to work with children at every opportunity. I began to teach swimming, diving, and synchronized swimming at Willow Swim Club. I did some teaching in the CCD program at St. Christopher as well. We still had our backyard set up as a neighborhood playground, and to the outside world few people knew of our painful journey with Joey.

Joe and I covered for each other to keep Joey moving in the right directions. Sometimes we did an excellent job and at other times we failed. It seemed to me that the only thing that Joe and I seemed to do now as a couple was to keep our eye on Joey. We no longer had enough time in a day or a week to just be us, to do something for ourselves as a couple. We were working, going to school, teaching or being involved with the kids. We were losing just being a couple and didn't know it.

Apparently, the devil knows when there is a crack and begins to lay plans to move in. On an ordinary day with the only issue to address a problem with the TV in our family room, I was confronted with a life-changing moment. With this seemingly minor breakdown of a household appliance, my family's core values would hurtle toward total destruction.

I had called for a TV repairman, Jerry Micher, from Micher's TV repair shop. Jerry had serviced our TVs for as long as I could remember. He advertised on the back of St. Christopher's Church bulletin, and we always tried to do business with fellow parishioners. On this particular day Jerry asked me if I had ever studied the Bible, and I had to admit that I hadn't to any significant degree. He went on to say that he and his wife Betty, were now doing Bible studies and wondered if Joe and I might be interested in having them come by for an informal evening. It was not so much that I wanted to study the Bible; it was his offer to do something as a couple that caught my attention. I said that I would talk to Joe and let him know if we would be interested.

When I brought up the subject of the Bible studies at dinner that evening, Joe wrinkled his nose and said, "Ah, Linda, I don't think I want to do that just now." I went on to say that we did so little together that didn't include kids, that I thought that if nothing else it might be fun to interact with another couple. I don't remember how long now it was since we had done anything outside of the home as a couple and yet here was a couple willing to come to our home and visit. If it worked out and we liked the studies we would at least be doing something for ourselves, and I really wanted to do this. Joe agreed to at least host them once.

We were set to have them visit the following week, and I had prepared a fine dessert and coffee to enjoy after the study. I had seen Betty at church, but I hadn't met her until that night. She and Jerry were a little older than Joe and I, but we seemed to hit it off rather well. Jerry took charge and began a crash course of how the Bible came into being fascinating Joe and me with the narrative.

We had a basic understanding that the original writings were in Aramaic, Greek, Hebrew and other dead languages. Jerry, however, knew just exactly how they were translated. While his information was fascinating, I really didn't think it had any bearing on how I viewed the English version. I certainly didn't want to learn any other language, as English was hard enough for me, and I trusted that much smarter academic minds had translated it just fine.

Jerry, though, was saying that it did make a lot of difference because if the Bible were not translated correctly we truly didn't have the right understanding of the Word of God. Okay, point taken, but again I thought to myself that I had the utmost trust that the Bible translations I had been exposed to were correct enough for me. As the evening continued, it was pleasant enough to want to invite Jerry and Betty to return the following week. We shared the dessert I had prepared and enjoyed pleasant friendly conversation to end the evening.

The following week we learned that according to the "real" translation of the "Word" there is no Hell. Well now, isn't that interesting. Boy, I sure would like to believe that Hell didn't exist, but I was not convinced. Again we had a lovely evening of conversation that ended with dessert and coffee. On Jerry and Betty's third visit we were told that our soul was not immortal and indeed when we died, were we not saved, we would just cease to exist. "You mean," I asked Jerry, "it would be as if I had never been born?"

"Yes," Jerry said. Well, that did it for me. I spoke up and said, "Just when did the Catholic Church change their opinion on the immortality of the soul?" Jerry said, "They haven't but their teachings are faulty."

"Well, just whose teachings are you alluding to?" I asked.

"Linda, Betty and I left the Catholic Church when we discovered their teachings were not of the true translation of the Bible. We had questions, and Father Aufderhide (pastor of St. Christopher's) could not answer them to our satisfaction. We found that through the Jehovah Witnesses we could find the true meanings of the Bible."

Oh My God. What have I done? I had invited these people into my home. Were these not the people I was taught not to let get near me? Were these not the people who stood on corners and handed out the "Watch Tower" or as we called it as kids, "The Witch Tower"? I tried to remain cordial through the end of this session, but it was mind numbing to me.

After they left I said to Joe, "We can't do this; this is something that is totally against everything we have been taught. We can't continue to have these people in our home."

Joe's reply was, "Well, you're the one who invited them, and I am interested enough to see just where this is going."

"Please, Joe, this isn't right!"

Joe said, "Let's give it another couple of weeks."

I said, "I can't do this. I won't."

Again, Joe said he wanted to and would I please just give it another week.

The following week Jerry explained that the Trinity did not exist. There was, however, only one God, but the Son, and the Holy Spirit were totally separate. Apparently they fell into the category of many gods. The idea of a triune God was totally false. They seemed to put this whole idea on the "correct" translation of John 1:1. Their translation read, "In the beginning was the Word and the Word was with God and the Word was "a god." Therefore, the Trinity was a false assumption by many religions and should not be believed. "After all, how could there be three individual persons in one being?" Jerry said. My answer was, "Why not?" My next answer was, "By faith I believed in the Trinity, and I have to have faith to believe that there is a God at all."

My belief was as strong as their disbelief; I had no intention of abandoning my understanding of the Blessed Trinity because of their translations, and the evening ended for me right then and there. Why at this point I didn't run to our pastor and tell him what was happening I don't know. Perhaps I was too embarrassed to acknowledge that I had let these people into my home. Eventually I would have to ask for help. I would have to admit I couldn't overcome this intrusion into lives. It was my belief the devil was now in my home. I let him in, and I couldn't get him out. I couldn't fix this, as I was no match against him.

Jerry and Betty Micher continued to come to our home on a weekly basis, and I no longer participated in these "bible" studies nor did I offer refreshments to these people. Joe and I continued to have heated discussions about his participation, and I could not get him to see what this was doing to our family. His answer was always, "Linda, you are too worldly and blinded by your being raised in the Catholic Church to see the Truth. I can't make you participate in these studies, but if you would just open your eyes, you would see what I see and find that knowing the truth will set you free."

"Free from what?" I said. "I am perfectly happy being a Catholic. I am not looking to be bamboozled into turning my back on my heritage. Your problem is that you failed to embrace the religion you promised to raise your children in. If you are looking to find the true meaning and why you should honor your promise, go and see Fr. Aufterhide and tell him what you are doing. For God's sake, Joe, can't you see you are embracing a religious concept barely 200 years old compared to 2000 years of documented history?"

On one of these evenings, I greeted Jerry Micher at the door and told him that he was not welcome in my home. His reply was, "Linda, Joe is the head of this household and until he tells me I am no longer welcome, I will be coming."

I said, "Do you realize what you are doing to our marriage?"

He said, "Linda, whatever is happening with your marriage, you are the one at fault."

At that point I truly believe I saw the devil in this man's eyes, and it frightened and chilled me to my bones. His eyes were dancing with fire and his dirty little laugh was pure evil. This impression lasted only a few seconds but still is vivid in my memory.

As these weekly "bible" studies continued, I would keep the children in the family room with me, watching TV, or we would leave and do other things outside the home. On one of these evenings when the Michers made their weekly visit, Leeann asked me why her father was doing this. I couldn't give her a reason. She seemed to be confused by his desire to continue these studies and wondered why I was not joining them. Not wanting to put her father down, I said nothing. Perhaps I should have. Shortly after that Joe started to go to the Kingdom Hall for the studies, and Jerry Micher no longer came to the house.

One evening Leeann and I were watching a movie on TV about Queen Elizabeth during one of those times England was about to be overtaken by an enemy. Betty Davis was playing Queen Elizabeth and she was ranting and raving in her bed chambers about the imminent invasion. One of her lines was, "If I were thrown out into the streets in my petticoat, I would conquer all of Christendom." Leeann turned to me and said, "Mom, that sounds like you." I made a mental note that if I were to ever write a book that would be a good title.

Leeann was my rock. She kept me grounded and helped me to believe that I was a good mother, that I could raise children despite the problems I had with Joey. Leeann was about to graduate from high school with honors; I was about to become the manager of Castle Hills swimming pool for the City of Vandalia, Ohio, and although Joe was still studying with the JWs, I no longer fussed with him. We just sort of went through the motions of our marriage, pretending we were all right.

A week or two before Leeann's graduation, during a very competitive softball game, she slid into second base and caught her foot under the second base bag. She not only broke her ankle, she "really broke it." The official diagnosis was an open reduction and internal fixation of the fractured mellius and distal fibula and a tubular/fibular separation of the left leg. Now say that ten times fast. Can you say painful? She had a pin and a screw put in her ankle and a wire wrapped around her tubular and fibula to help bring them together. The following year she had all the hardware removed.

What a shame for her to have to go though the graduation week of festivities on crutches. We were proud parents, and we were prouder that Leeann handled this adversity well. Leeann and I had what I thought to be a solid mother and daughter relationship. We seemed to think alike and enjoy each other's company. I counted our relationship as one of my most cherished and satisfying accomplishments. I was especially thankful we had good communication. I looked back over her childhood and couldn't think of one thing I would have done differently. Well, maybe I wouldn't have tried to cut her hair. We could talk about anything: boys, sex, grades, sports and dreams. I was hopeful she would be a happy young woman with a bright promise of good things to come. She was going to stay at home and go to school at Wright State University for the first year of college.

We took great pride that we were able to raise our daughter through high school to become a college-bound young woman. She was poised and confident and seemed to be well grounded in who she was as a person. I couldn't have been more pleased. I wasn't worried that we or I had failed her in any way. On the other hand, Joey was not able to be at the graduation of his sister as he was in detention. His absence was felt deeply as you can see from the look on my face in a family picture taken on graduation day, minus Joey.

As soon as Leeann's ankle healed, she went to Castle Hills Swimming Pool as one of my lifeguards and we had a wonderful summer. I had the whole City of Vandalia as my employers, and they were a demanding bunch.

I did a fantastic job, implementing many successful programs and proving that Mr. Rusty Tomlinson, Park and Recreational Director, had made the right choice in hiring me. This was a seasonal job, and I could take my kids to work with me; a perfect job for a mom. It had benefits for a husband as well. Joe could spend evenings at the pool with his wife and kids while his wife was making a little extra money.

As that first season ended, I was assured I would be coming back as the manager the next year. Only one thing spoiled the offer. The City had adopted a new policy on nepotism, and I would not be allowed to hire my daughter as a lifeguard the following year. We had hoped that since this was a temp job, classified as seasonal, that policy would not apply, but of course it did.

Leeann had a fantastic first year at Wright State and she placed seventh on the 3-meter diving board and tenth on the one-meter for the state competition. Her grades were good as well. Now she would have to look for summer employment again. She was still upset over not coming back to Castle Hills but found she could be employed with the City of Dayton at one of their pools, though she would have to live in Dayton to work there. The solution was to move in with Gramma, and with that decision she had her summer job. But, she found that living with Gramma was not as easy as it sounded. Gramma did her "Gramma thing," wanting to know exactly where and when and whom she would be going out with, and when she would be home. It took its toll. If she came in late she would have to explain. Sound familiar? I had found living with Gramma tedious as well.

Leeann thought she had another solution; she and a couple of girlfriends would rent their own apartment. Would we object? Well, I thought I knew my daughter pretty well, and she had shown herself to be extremely responsible; besides the apartment would be a small stop-off from her father's route home from work, and he would be able to keep an eye on things, so we agreed. My baby girl was all but emancipated and not quite 20 years old. She would be a sophomore at Wright State and working at Lerner's, a department store in the evenings.

The success I felt with managing Castle Hills and Leeann's progress was tempered with knowing we still hadn't been able to bring forth much success for Joey. We had taken all the so-called positive suggestions from the experts and tried to implement them. We had to let the courts place him in residential detention centers as a wake-up call, so to speak. We thought if he were sent to Juvenile Detention it might get his attention, and he would be willing to conform to what was expected of him as a child on the verge of adulthood.

While we were trying to figure out how to have a gentle wake-up call, Joey was sent to Buckeye Boys Ranch for inducing panic. What had happened was on a stormy evening Joey had taken the bull horn that I used when I was coaching swim team, aimed it out his bedroom window, and announced to the neighborhood that a tornado was coming. Joey thought this was funny and didn't see it at all as something wrong, let alone illegal. He thought it, he did it: there was that impulse factor again. I was convinced that if he were able to think things through he would not act on these impulses. I was equally convinced there had to be some kind of mental disconnect that stopped that process from happening for Joey.

Others believed I wanted to make excuses for his behavior. The police were called, and they arrested him on a charge of inducing panic. While Joe and I thought this was a little extreme, we were convinced the sentence would act as a deterrent for future behaviors. I wonder now if that was a good decision. I learned later that while at the Ranch things were not run as efficiently as the public was led to believe.

After the short stay at the Buckeye Ranch, Joey, came home interested only in self-medicating. This was when Joey had made his first suicide attempt. He was 13 years old when we found him unconscious and rushed him to the hospital. He had had a close call with an overdose of some sort of intoxicant, but had convinced the doctors in the ER that he was not trying to take his life. We weren't so sure.

On December 15, 1977 Joey wrote this letter from one of his detentions. This was written at the top of the letter and the rest followed.

Time Don't Matter
Just as long as
I get Help
Love Joe
I mean it

Dear Mom -n- Dad
Im(sic) not going to bore you I just want to say I love you and don't forget about me I want you to be proud of me I am going to be all rite (sic)I am a man so I got to start acting like one Im (sic)not a man man I mean a young man and would you buy a chritmas(sic) present for Jim, Eric, Lee, grandma, and ect,(sic) and say its from me and tell them I love them and get my shop project from school you know I would have like to finised (sic)it so bad well Im gota(sic) go know Hay yove(sic) got a son to live with and love as soon as I git out.

Love you Joe
hope to see you soon I love you

* * *

Heart breaking as this letter was, we believed every word he wrote, and I think he believed every word that he wrote as well.

On another occasion Joey was arrested for burglary. He had dashed into an office building where he took a replica of a gun off the wall and ran out of the building. Joey had said he was being teased at school again, and on a dare he did the deed. He threw the framed gun in a dumpster and ran home. The police came and arrested him again. This time he was 15 years old and was sent to the forensic center in Columbus. While in custody he attempted to slit his wrists. The authorities thought it was an attempt to get attention. Well yes, I guess it was. This child was miserable and couldn't get anyone's attention. He was viewed as a teenager bent on doing outlandish behavior for his own amusement. His wrists were taped up but no counseling was given to him at that time. By then we had seen and been seen by so many child psychologists and social workers that I began to wonder about my own sanity. Just how did we allow this child to behave in an unlawful manner? Certainly, we did not want this for our child; however, not wanting it did not make it better. I knew something much more serious was wrong with Joey, but I didn't know what it was. The experts all said that Joey was capable of behaving in an acceptable manner, but he just didn't want to.

It was suggested that perhaps Joey's behavior might improve if he were removed from the home for a period of time, perhaps into foster care. Foster care. My God, here we were a certified, qualified foster home and parents, and I couldn't be a parent to my own child. What a huge blow to my self esteem, but we agreed. We were willing to try anything if it would help our son. Joey's first placement lasted two weeks, mainly because he wouldn't stay. He kept running away.

The second home lasted a little longer. These people were eager to become parents and in the meantime agreed to take in older children until a baby could be found for an adoption or that she would eventually conceive. Joey told me many years later that this couple wanted children so badly that the wife seduced him. Joey believed that the baby she gave birth to might have been his.

This placement didn't last more than a couple of months. One night I was awakened by a loud scuffle, taking place in our bedroom. Joey and his father were wrestling. Joe was trying to subdue Joey, and Joey was trying to break free. Joe had long been sleeping with his wallet under the mattress to keep Joey from slipping money out. Even though Joey was no longer in the house, Joe still kept his wallet there. I did not know that until that night. Joey had run away from the foster home and was now trying to get some money from his father's wallet.

As Joey lay quietly on the floor next to his father's side of the bed, slipping his hand under the mattress reaching for the wallet, Joe awoke in a protective stance. I am not sure if Joe knew it was Joey but the chase was on. The yelling and the screaming were terrifying, and I was calling the police before I knew what was going on. Joe had Joey pinned by the front door and I thought he was going to kill him. Joey did not fight back.

The police arrived, and Joey was arrested again. I wondered just how much worse this could get. Surely this had to be the worst, wasn't it? Would this be the end?

After another stint in Juvenile Detention in Columbus, the juvenile probation department wanted to release Joey back to us. We said, "No." We believed that Joey was out of control and we wanted him in a psychiatric hospital. Something was terribly wrong with him mentally and no one was seeing what we were seeing. You see Joey was not the typical incorrigible teenager. Joey was never disrespectful to us; we were not afraid of him, but always afraid *for* him. His struggle had been a life-long struggle, not just when he turned into a teenager. With as much attention as he had been given coupled with all the trials and mistrials, a normal person would have had better results. To put it simply, there has to be something seriously wrong for a person to continue to put his hand in the same fire over and over and not learn how to stop doing that.

I can't believe that a child is born to lose, as was suggested on several occasions in whispers behind our backs. We also hadn't realized just how much Joey was into self-medicating. We knew on occasion that Joey had experimented with drugs and alcohol, but we never realized how much. He hid it very well and we were so stupid not to see it.

I didn't even know what marijuana smelled liked, let alone know anything about huffing and other illegal drugs. We were told by the juvenile authorities that Joey appeared to have quite an attraction to altering his state of mind and that he had admitted to engaging in substance abuse from about the age of twelve. He was now 17.

We thought that if we stood our ground the state would have to keep him. We no longer knew how to help him, nor did we have the means to send Joey to a rehabilitation center. Some might say that we gave up on him or abandoned him. We just didn't know what to do for him that we had not already done. We were not prepared to deal with Joey's issues; we hadn't been for a long time. Where in the "training manual" of how to be a parent does it tell you, "If you have a kid who is all screwed up, here is what you do?"

The state's answer, or at least Joey's probation officer's answer, was to place him at the YMCA in downtown Dayton, Ohio; get him a job at a car wash; and let the chips fall where they may. He would be 18 in a few months, and the whole ballgame would change.

CHAPTER 13

Law and Order, CSI, and Miami

Vice Come Calling

W hile we were dealing with major concerns about Joey, Leeann was creating her own challenges. Early in February 1980, we got an unexpected call from the hospital, only this time it was about our daughter. Leeann was in the emergency room. Could we come right away? She was stable but refusing a blood transfusion. Joe and I raced to the hospital and found that Leeann was experiencing a miscarriage, and even though a transfusion could be lifesaving, she was refusing one. The shock that she had been pregnant was one thing, but the refusal of a transfusion was even more troubling to me. Where was this coming from? I looked to her father for help, but it didn't come. He agreed: no transfusion.

If you are a Jehovah Witness, you are forbidden to have blood transfusions. A passage in the Old Testament says that it is an abomination to God to drink blood under any circumstances. OK, so what did that have to do with Leeann? The father of this baby was a Jehovah Witness, and Leeann had crossed over to please him, and I guessed now she was trying to please her father as well. I lost it. I screamed at Joe that if my daughter died over this occult religion, I would never forgive him. I assumed that her father had introduced her to this man, and I was livid.

Leeann managed to pull through without the transfusion, but for the first time in our lives we were unable to talk. I was in so much pain from this revelation I just withdrew. No one corrected my assumption of how she met this man, but I did learn that he was a married man and was on the verge of being dis-fellowshiped because of his relationship with Leeann. After this episode, he did return to his wife, but Leeann remained with her father as a Jehovah Witness, and I felt betrayed and disillusioned by them both. My family was coming apart at the core, and there was nothing I could do. I suppose I could have joined them by turning my back on my beliefs, but I just couldn't, not yet, not then. A month later Joe lost his job at Dayton Tire and Rubber due to the plant closing.

The State of Ohio said there was nothing else they had to offer Joey, and they wanted to parole him back to our custody. I think they thought that he would be 18 in a few more months, and he would soon be off their radar and into the adult system. Our objections fell on deaf ears. We pleaded with them to place him in a psychiatric environment for evaluation again. Since he had attempted suicide twice I was afraid if he came home, he would die or worse.

They placed him at the YMCA in downtown Dayton, Ohio. They helped him get a job at a car wash and were to monitor his behavior with a parole officer. We thought if we held to our guns and lobbied for treatment, they would have to listen. We also knew if left on his own for long, it was just a matter of time before he would make poor choices that would lead to self destruction, either by overdosing or doing something incredibly stupid. I wonder now if we had allowed Joey to come home, could we have altered history.

Leeann was trying to recover from her misfortune or mistake, whichever way you choose to see this episode in her life. Her girlfriends wanted her to go on spring break to Florida. I thought that this just might be a good way for these girls to help her heal her broken heart and get this Jehovah Witness business out of her head. Joe would be needed for at least a few months to help with the plant closure. Joey would call every few days to just touch base, and I was hoping he would ask to come home, promising that things would be better.

I was planning the third season of managing Castle Hills Pool and looking forward to implementing the biggest and best of the end of the season Water Shows. I had implemented swimming, diving, and synchronized swimming into a water show production that would take place at the end of the season. I would take a musical, be it a movie or stage play, and turn the theme and characters into a production in and on the water.

We did the *Wizard of OZ, Damn Yankees, The Sound of Music* and a tribute to Walt Disney. Each year our productions got bigger and better, and they were so much fun. My staff was great and everyone worked hard to make these shows the highlights of the Park and Recreation of Vandalia summer venues.

The children were always so hyped to take part, and it was fulfilling adventure for me too. Jimmy and Eric were willing participants in these shows. In the *Wizard of OZ,* Jimmy was the scarecrow and Eric was a munchkin. "Dr. Creep" from the local TV station played the wizard that year. I was so proud.

It was about 11 pm on an April evening in 1980 and everyone was in bed but me. I was mapping out strategies for this coming season at Castle Hills when the phone rang. It was Joey, and I could barely hear him as his voice was but a husky whisper. He said, "Mom, can you come and get me? I am locked out of my room in the rain, and I am sick and soaking wet. I'm in front of the YMCA."

"OK," I answered, "I'll be right there." I went in and woke Joe to tell him what was going on. "Do you want to go with me? I'm not comfortable driving in the rain to downtown Dayton."

He said, "No, you can go. I'm already in bed. You'll be all right."

I threw a blanket in the back seat of the car and started out.

I was thinking could it rain any harder as I honed in on the bright lights of the big red YMCA neon sign and saw Joey huddled up against the building. I honked the horn, and he slowly came to the car. I reached for the blanket and told him to take off his wet clothes and wrap up. I leaned over, felt his forehead, and found that he was burning up. He just said he got back after curfew and was locked out. I didn't ask where he had been; I didn't want to know.

We traveled mostly in silence, and when we arrived home, I said, "Why don't you take a hot bath? I'll fix you something to eat." I brought

Me as Peter Pan in Synchronize Swimming Practice 1979
Coaching Swim Team 1984

him some dry, clean clothes and a couple of aspirin to help with the fever. In the morning I planned to call Dr. Smith's office as I felt sure he had Strep throat. When Joey was settled into his room, I went into the family room to finish some paperwork. I couldn't get my mind focused back into what I had been working on, so I set the work aside. I rarely went to bed when Joey was home and tonight was no exception; I would sleep on the sofa just "in case."

My mind traveled back and forth from the "good old days" to the troubled days. Joey was in his bed, safe for the time being, but with a 101 temperature. How is it with so many well-meaning people wanting to help my son that he ends up like a homeless person out on a corner in a rain storm?

I thought about Miss Eby, his playschool teacher; the doctors, school psychologist, Larry Levine at Good Samaritan Hospital, the folks at the juvenile courts, and me, his mother. What did we all do wrong? Why couldn't we help him? What were we missing? There were no answers. Was Joey beyond help? No, I couldn't believe that. I wouldn't believe that. Maybe tonight will be the night Joey will finally see the light?

Joe woke me the next morning and wanted to know what happened. I told him that Joey was in bed with a fever. "I'll take him to see Dr. Smith today. I bet he needs an antibiotic."

Joe said, "I'll call you later to find out what the doctor has to say. Do you think Joey will be coming home for good now?"

"I don't know," I said. "I'm not planning to call anyone about Joey just yet."

I got Jimmy and Eric ready for school, then phoned the doctor for an appointment at 11 a.m. Joey came out to the kitchen, I gave him two more aspirins and some juice. He said he wasn't hungry and I asked him when he last ate. He didn't remember; I didn't push. We would wait to see what the doctor said.

At the appointment, Dr. Smith was pretty sure it was strep but did a throat swab to be sure, and then he prescribed antibiotics, liquids and bed rest. Joey still wasn't in the mood to talk, so I made some lunch and said I would be back in a little while. I assumed he would go back to bed or watch TV and I left to run some errands. He did ask me, "Are you going to call anyone about where I am?"

"I don't plan to just yet, Joey," I said. I want to give you some time to get better, and I want some time for us to talk about what to do next."

Evening came and Joey was still not hungry and didn't come to the supper table. I am not even sure Jimmy and Eric knew he was home. For the last five years Joey was rarely home more than a few months at a time, and there had not been much interaction with his brothers, mostly because of the age difference. Jimmy had just turned eleven and Eric was nine. Leeann was on her way home from her Florida vacation and would be home late the next evening. She would no doubt go straight to her apartment.

As usual Joe turned in about the same time the kids did, about nine o'clock, and I was left to finish up the day's loose ends. I would be spending another night "guarding" the home and hearth. I guess I believed that nothing "bad" could happen if I stayed on watch, so to speak. I settled onto the sofa and drifted off to sleep.

I awoke to the shouts of intruders coming through the doors and windows. Doors were slamming and things breaking and my bewildered mind cried, "What the hell is happening? Am I dreaming? Is it Joey?" There were all these men dressed in black with white letters sprayed-painted on their backs, and they looked like giant ants swarming through my home. Joe was now at my side saying, "Linda, they are here to arrest Joey." Those white letters spelled "SWAT."

They had dragged Joey out of his bedroom and had him pressed up against the living room wall. I ran around the house to get to the hallway in time to see my son look at me with a look I had become so familiar with. The look said to me, "I don't believe this and I am so scared."

I heard the police officer say something like, "You are being arrested for aggravated murder and felonious assault. You have the right to remain silent as anything you say could be held against you in a court of law. You have a right to an attorney, if you cannot afford an attorney one will be appointed for you. Do you understand your rights as I have told them to you?"

I remember thinking, "What should I be doing now? Why am I still standing here? Why can't I faint? Please, God, just stop my heart from beating. I can't move; that's a good sign, isn't it? I am frozen to this spot. This has to be a dream, isn't it? My son couldn't have killed anyone, could he? He may be a lot of things, but he is not a killer. Why would they arrest him for murder?"

One of the Vandalia police officers came over and said, "We're taking Joey to the Vandalia police station. He'll be transferred to the Montgomery County Jail in the morning. You might want to think about getting him a lawyer," he added. "You two are probably in shock. Do you want to call your doctor?"

Apparently we said no and the last policeman left. Now our home was as silent as if death had paid us a visit. Joe and I looked at each other but said nothing for what seemed like an eternity. "Joe, I have got to go to Joey. Take me to the station. Here is his medicine; he will need that, won't he?" Joe went over to Marilyn's and had her come to stay with the kids. I couldn't stop shaking, and my teeth chattered so violently I thought they would break. Marilyn wanted to know if she could call for a doctor, but I still must have refused. At the station we were told we couldn't see Joey, but they did take his medicine although I doubt they gave it to him.

The next day's headline in *The Dayton Daily News* morning edition shouted at me:

Vandalia youth charged in murder

The article under that headline read:

Three teenagers, one a 17-year old from Vandalia, have been arrested and charged with aggravated murder, aggravated burglary and felonious assault in the beating death of Evelyn Kaiser of Kettering. Police are seeking a fourth suspect, a female who is believed to have driven the three youths to the area. A 16-year-old West Carrollton male, formally from Vandalia and a 15-year-old from Miami Township, along with the Vandalian were arrested last Thursday. Police had been investigating burglaries in Miami Township and Washington Township which led them to the trio.

Mrs. Kaiser, 53, was beaten to death, and her husband, Richard, who police say came to her aid, was injured in the March 30 attack.

According to police, the youths entered the home, thinking it was unoccupied. Some money was taken.

The three are under the jurisdiction of the Juvenile Court at this time.[1]

This was the first of hundreds of newspaper articles and TV news reports written over the next year. From that point on, a familiar line, "Do you swear to tell the whole truth and nothing but the truth, so help you God?" took on a new meaning for me. The "truth" it seemed was only true if it helped to keep you out of trouble.

"Do you swear to tell the whole truth" was often followed with "Well only if it keeps me out of jail. if not I will lie and put a spin on the truth to my advantage." That was what I learned that day, and for days to come.

As this case unfolded I was aware that truth is an elusive, fragile thing. We rarely get the whole truth and nothing but the truth. Sometimes when we do tell the truth no one cares, as it is not newsworthy, it has no punch, it leaves you flat, lifeless. The truth may not be interesting.

Neither Joe nor I knew whom to call; criminal attorneys were not in our address books. How we chose the attorneys we did talk to I don't remember, but we interviewed three and all three wanted a minimum of $50,000 to start. Even if we gave them that money there would be no guarantees that they could keep the courts from seeking to try Joey as an adult. Before they were through, it could possibly take far more

---

1 Dayton Daily News & Journal Herald from April of 1980 to February of 1981 ~ Various Writers

money. We were to encourage Joey not to speak to any one until he had an attorney present.

Joe and I discussed our options, and the only one we had was to mortgage our home, which was worth about $50,000. This would put the rest of our family in financial jeopardy, as Joe was soon to be unemployed. Again it came down to money. The greatest, most serious issues in our lives always came down to money. My heart wanted to spend the money, but my common sense said it wasn't what we should do, so I had to agree with Joe. We would have to accept that public defenders could help our son navigate the system and this journey.

The following day Larry Levine from Good Samaritan Mental Health Center called. He wanted to tell us how sorry he was to hear the news and wanted to confirm that it was Joey the newspapers were referring to. I confirmed that his assumptions were correct.

He offered his apologies and said, "Linda, we knew that Joey was headed for prison but certainly not for these charges." He went on to say that he did not think Joey was capable of killing anyone and wanted to know if there was anything he could do for us. I told him, "We're not sure how we'll handle this, so no. There's nothing you can do."

He answered, "I hope you don't blame yourselves for this. I'm in your corner, Linda. You know that. I always have been."

I remember thinking, If you thought Joey was headed to prison, why didn't you say anything? I wanted to say, "What else did you know that you didn't share with us? Did you know that Joey was mentally ill?"

In the next few days we met with a juvenile defense attorney by the name of Sanford (Sandy) Edelman, who was the court-appointed attorney for Joey. He seemed to want to help. We filled him in on Joey's background, and the first thing he wanted to do was get a psychological evaluation done. "Our only hope to keep Joey in the juvenile system is if we can get the court to see that the failure was due to the system's negligence in its efforts to secure proper care for Joey. The next thing is to try to have the deals made with the other defendants negated."

"What deals?" we asked.

"The others that are involved are willing to testify against Joey if they can be guaranteed to be tried in juvenile court, or not charged at all."

"They can do that?" I asked Mr. Edelman.

He answered, "Yes, it's done all the time."

They say that life's tragedies either bring people closer or split them apart. Joe and I had pulled through a lot in our lives. Could we make it through this? I was 37 years old and Joe had just turned 42. If someone was coming to our rescue, I didn't see anyone. In fact, no one came. It was just me and Joe.

Perhaps people stayed away because no one knew how to help us? We rattled around, each in our own misery not knowing how to help one another. How can you expect anyone to know how to help in cases like this? Joe withdrew into himself and I pretended everything would be OK. I believed that the courts would see that Joey was not sane enough to stand trial and he would finally receive the medical help he needed all his life.

It wasn't that I was unconcerned that an innocent person lost her life and that my son may have had a part in that. It was just so surreal that I couldn't process it fully. I wasn't even sure I knew what had happened on the night this crime took place. I was not ready to hear all the details yet.

As had been the case for several years, I was scheduled to be a presiding judge at the May elections. So far all the newspaper and television coverage had not named these juveniles. Joe said, "Are you sure you are up to being a presiding judge?"

"Yes, I have to. I made a commitment, didn't I?" I didn't expect that by mid-afternoon on Election Day the conversation would have turned to the identity of the Vandalia boy involved in that murder in Kettering. People gave all sorts of explanations for this act: He had come from the wrong side of the tracks, or it had to be the parents' fault, or teenagers should be tried as adults in cases like this.

I thought to myself, very soon these same people will learn who they were talking about and they will realize that they spent Election Day with the kid's mother. I didn't want them to be able to say, "Can you believe we spent Election Day with his mother and she didn't say a word?" So I said, "Would you believe that I am this boy's mother?" That shut them up and took the steam out of their speculation.

Joey's attorneys said they didn't want us talking to the media, no matter what. This is a request we honored, and a request I now regret. Joey's name didn't come out until the courts made him an adult on his 18th birthday May 13, 1980.

The media had plenty to say, even though we refused to speak with reporters. A headline in the Dayton Daily News on April 26, 1980, screamed: *Youth was looking to kill, Kaiser case defendant says.*

The article made the following claim: *Evelyn Kaiser apparently was a chance victim. She was beaten to death by a 17 year-old boy who had wanted to kill two other people that same night, according to statements read in court yesterday. A 15 year-old boy – one of three youths charged in the March 30 death of Mrs. Evelyn Kaiser, 53- year old Sinclair Community College Instructor – gave the statement to police, and it was read yesterday in Montgomery County Court. The judge found probable cause to continue the case against the youths, 15 and 16.*[2]

---

2 Headlines and excerpts taken from The Dayton Daily News & The Journal Herald from April of 1980 to February of 1981 ~ Various Writers; reprinted with permission from Cox Media Group.

I never understood why all the people that were involved in this crime were not held accountable? In addition to Joey, Jerry Arnett and Kenny Flynn, there were two girls in the get-a-way van—Dana Pierce (the driver) and Renee Muse, and one young lady back in the hotel room—Kirby Flynn (over 18), the brother of the 15-year-old who acted as the fence, and the person handling the business that received the stolen property. That's a total of six youths and two adults. Yet only three were held accountable? Why were these three treated differently? Why was my son the only one to be tried as an adult? The case against my son was incredibly weak—as you will soon see. The others changed their testimony when they made deals to stay in Juvenile Court, or not to be charged at all. Can you believe everything that a co-conspirator says when they are trying to save their own skin? Perhaps that is for a juror to decide but certainly not the media.

An Example of the Media Taking Liberties In Reporting

In the statement read in court, the 15 year-old said:

"The 17-year-old was the ringleader of the three youths, who were wandering the Kaisers' Kettering neighborhood the night of the killing.

They saw an elderly women in a rocking chair inside her home and the 17-year old said, "Let's go in there and kill her." The others refused.

The three entered the Kaiser home, 4350 Delco Del Road, and the 17-year -old beat Mrs. Kaiser's husband Richard.

Mrs. Kaiser was beaten when she entered the room where her husband was being attacked.

The 17-year-old told the younger boy to kill Mrs. Kaiser, but the 15-year-old refused.

The 17-year-old killed Mrs. Kaiser.

Also in the courtroom yesterday, Richard Kaiser, 54 identified the 17 year-old as his assailant.

Is the 17 year old Joey? Most of these printed statements were speculation, not all were true. They contained partial truth and some fiction mixed with lies.

From the Newspaper: *Juvenile Court Judge Arthur O Fisher yesterday found probable cause that the 15-year-old from Miami Township and the 17-year-old from Vandalia burglarized the Kaisers home and bludgeoned the Kaisers.*

"Both boys will undergo physical and mental examinations. Another hearing, probably in about four to six weeks, will determine whether they will be tried as juveniles or adults".

From the Dayton Daily Newspaper, "Judge Fisher had just come out in the press about how his new policy was to take away the freedoms of juveniles "You'll go to jail" is his new mantra. He was all for sending these kids to adult court. He wanted to give " juveniles a strong dose of medicine'".

From the Newspaper, "A third person arrested in this case, a 16-year-old boy from West Carrollton, had his hearing continued. Little was said in court yesterday about the role of the 16-year-old".

Almost everything said in this statement was an exaggeration except for the identification from Richard Kaiser. Apparently, Mr. Kaiser believed through collusion that what he said was true. It appeared to me, though, that Mr. Kaiser was manipulated into identifying my son as his assailant. He couldn't identify him in a line-up, but after being shown photographs, he was able to pick Joey out because Joey's photo was the only photograph in the list that he saw in the line-up.

I asked Mr. Edelman, Joey's attorney, "Why wasn't Joey allowed to make a statement of what happened?"

He replied, "That is not how this is played." He did not want the prosecution to have statements from Joey with which to work.

I said, "It looks like Joey did everything and the others were just along for the ride." I knew there were actually two girlfriends involved, the older brother of the 15-year-old, and the guy who acted as a fence for the stolen property, plus those that bought the stolen goods. Why weren't they being charged? I said, "It's a game, isn't it? Truth has nothing to do with this, does it, Sandy?"

Sandy didn't answer my question; he just said, "Just let me do my job."

Headlines from the Dayton Daily News read: *"Teen to be tried as adult," "Local man indicted, pleads innocent," "Youth tried as adult in Kettering murder,"* and *"18-year-old enters plea of innocence in slaying."*

Another newspaper article printed, *"Joseph D. Hutchison, who turned 18 yesterday, will be tried as an adult in the killing of Evelyn Kaiser, a Kettering woman who died after burglars broke into her home and beat her with a croquet mallet."*[3]

Judge Fisher got his wish to send at least one of these juveniles to adult court and Joey was it. The truth didn't matter. He was going to see that at least one of these boys was going down and the most vulnerable one was his target.

Enter court appointed attorneys for Joey's defense, Thomas Schaffer and Richard Divine. These two fresh-faced 30-somethings felt Joey

---

3 Headlines and excerpts taken from The Dayton Daily News & The Journal Herald from April of 1980 to February of 1981 ~ Various Writers; reprinted with permission from Cox Media Group.

should plead not guilty by reason of insanity. We said, "What about the truth?"

"Linda, the truth is while we know that Joey didn't kill Evelyn Kaiser, it is unlikely we can prove that he wasn't there. He will be convicted by virtue of being there. The only way to keep Joey out of adult prison is if we can get a not guilty by reason of insanity. We can then get him placed into a psychiatric facility where he can get treatment."

"Can you do that?" I asked.

"Yes, we think we can," Tom said.

Dayton Daily News, Headline: *"Murder suspect pleads insanity."*

CHAPTER 14

What Choices
Do You Have Left?

I suppose there were choices of how to carry on, but for me it was to continue to do the things I would have done if this hadn't happened. I spoke to Rusty Tomlinson about my returning to manage the city swimming pool. I needed to know if he thought that the sensationalism of the upcoming trial of my son would cause any issues for him or the city. Rusty said, " Linda, I hired you, and I trust you, and I will support you. I know this will be a difficult time for you, but I have the confidence you can do the job. I will have your back against any opposition."

I returned to the hectic schedule of getting the pool ready for the season. Jimmy and Eric were doing well in school and had only a couple of unpleasant instances of name calling. It seemed to me that most people went out of their way to pretend that nothing had happened. I don't know if that was the right thing to do but it was the way it was. Maybe they didn't want to believe this was happening either. Joe still had to close down the plant at Dayton Tire and Rubber, and we became ships passing in the night.

Joe couldn't or I wouldn't let him help me with the pain. I couldn't help him as he was drowning in the studies with the Jehovah Witness propaganda, and I wasn't going there. I stopped praying. How could God allow this to happen to our family? I had built a wall around me and wouldn't let anyone in. Perhaps there were people that wanted to help me, but I couldn't let anyone see how fragile my state of mind was. There was no way to fix this and for someone who sees herself as a fixer, this was a devastating blow.

While I lost my communication line to God; He never left me, I know that now, as I write this book. I am a firm believer that no "man" can get you through a crisis and while it is helpful to have human support, in the end, it is just you and God that matter.

Joey was doing everything asked of him. What choice did he have? I had to stay sane for Jimmy and Eric, as they were my major concern, and hope for better days. They hadn't lost any friendships. Their playmates were still coming over to the house, and they were invited out as well. Holding down my job was a way of keeping as much normalcy in our lives as possible.

The summer was passing in a flash, and that only meant that the trial would be starting soon.

Dayton Daily News Headlines: *"Hutchison's murder trial to begin Sept. 2," "Kaiser murder trial to start tomorrow," "Kaiser jury selection begins."*

As we prepared for the trial we were asked to get a wardrobe ready. Joey would need to look like a normal teen. Not too flashy, some corduroy slacks and some plaid button down collar shirts. Tom and Richard were sure this was the best insanity case they had ever tried. I think it was the only one they had ever tried. By now we had dubbed them *Starsky and Hutch* in trench coats. The defense would be " Insanity Due to a Mental Condition Previously Undiagnosed." The psychiatrist for Joey, Dr. Joseph Kavtschitsch, would testify that Joey, even though he knew right from wrong, was unable to keep from doing things that were wrong.

Dr. Kavtschitsch spoke with us briefly after he evaluated Joey. He talked with us about Manic Depression. (In the future this would be known as bi-polar disorder. Until the 1980's it was not a common belief that a child could be mentally ill, let alone with a disorder as severe as manic depression. Even in the year 2010, there are those that still fight this diagnosis in children. We don't, because we lived it.) Dr. Kavtschitsch told us that if he had had Joey as a patient, he would have been able to help him with treatments and with a drug called lithium. We were under the impression that this would be Dr. Kavtschitsch's testimony when it came time for him to testify at the trial.

We had an answer, it wasn't what we longed to hear, we didn't want our son to be mentally ill, but there was validation in knowing that Joey did not always have control over his actions. It was acknowledgment to all the pain and heartache over the years, that there was an underlying reason for Joey's behaviors. It did not lessen my guilt over the mistakes I had made in trusting the so-called experts. In fact, it made me feel guilty that I hadn't fought harder to find better help for Joey. There were times we punished Joey for his behavior, because that is what the "experts" said we should do, when he really needed a different approach to understanding his behaviors. I tried to find everything I could on Manic Depression to educate myself on the signs and symptoms, but I could find nothing on children having this disorder.

What I did find out about Manic Depression is that the medical term Manic Depression Insanity was first used 1896. They actually called it insanity back then. They renamed it Bipolar Disorder sometime in the 1980's. The first medication used to treat Manic Depression in the 1940's was lithium. They said that the average onset of the disorder is thought to be in the early twenty's, and most are not correctly diagnosed until age 40. Alcohol and substance abuse are present in at least 60% of Manic Depressive sufferers, and suicide rates are at least 25% with up to 29% of those successful. Over one half of all suicides are attributed to the Manic Depressive Bipolar Disorder, the highest rate among all of the psychiatric disorders. It was thought to be biological and possibly hereditary.

I looked for answers about our family background. Information was not very forth coming, and I did not know how to explore it any deeper. What I did learn was that my father was an alcoholic, and most likely died from years of alcohol abuse. I had to wonder if he also suffered from Manic Depression. Was that why my mother left him? My father's mother died in a mental institution in her late seventies or so with some form of dementia. Apparently she suffered from bouts of depression in her early years as well. My father had four siblings, Jack, Ermine, Alice, and Mary. It is my understanding that Ermine suffered from mental health issues along with one of her daughter's. My uncle Jack had a daughter who was in and out of hospitals for mental health issues as well.

On Joe's side of the family was a history of early mental deterioration, thought mainly due to diabetic issues. While his father died from colon cancer, his last days were fraught with dementia. Some of Joe's siblings were a bit slow, so it is quite possible that the DNA passed on to Joey contributed to his predisposition for mental illness. While this was all very interesting, it didn't help with his defense. We were relying on the defense psychiatrist to adequately convey these issues to a jury.

There was more news that was not good. Joey's court appointed attorney, Sanford Edelman, was now an assistant prosecutor. Edelman would have access to files that Tom said, could be predigested. Joey's attorneys wanted anyone associated with the DA's office removed from the case immediately. A search went out for a special prosecutor. This was a big stumbling block. A special prosecutor could be a lot tougher to work with. Most likely Joey's attorneys would know very little about his or her tactics. The judge for Joey's trial would be Common Pleas Judge Carl D Kessler, known as somewhat of a rogue judge who does what he wants and gets away with it.

We found out that as we would be called to testify, Joey's attorneys did not want us in the courtroom during the trial. "Tom, how can we support our son if we can't be there?" I asked. Tom said he made arrangements to allow Joey to call home every day. Leeann would be able to attend and bring us up to date reality-wise, as we knew that the media would report on the days' proceedings with bias.

Tom said he had just heard that the morning paper would make this announcement: "Judge Kessler has ruled that television and newspaper photographers will not have access to the trial, citing Hutchison's right to a fair trial." This was a tremendous relief. We were so against having Joey and our lives played out on local and maybe even national television on the nightly news.

Dayton Daily News Headline: *"Kaiser jury selection begins."*

From the Dayton Daily Newspaper: *"Hutchison, who is being held in Montgomery County Jail, faces mandatory life in prison if convicted of aggravated murder. He was originally charged as a Juvenile because he was 17 at the time of the attack, but was ordered to stand trial as an adult. The trial is expected to last two weeks."*

The jury selection begins but stalls. Dayton Daily News Headlines: *"Kessler mulls camera rule as trial waits."*

From the Dayton Daily: *"The trial has been set aside for at least two weeks while Kessler battles the Ohio Supreme Court to keep cameras out of his court room. The Supreme Court ruled that Kessler must allow cameras in his courtroom. Kessler so far has refused. If he proceeds with the trial without allowing the cameras in, Kessler faces contempt charges in the Supreme Court. And if he allows the cameras in despite his own disdain for them there's reversible error in this trial right from the onset" Kessler maintains, because Hutchison objects to their presence."*

"Yesterday, two prospective jurors in Hutchison's trial asked to be heard in court and said "they too were opposed to having cameras in the court room." One said he felt being photographed in the courtroom invaded his right to privacy another said, "the presence of cameras would affect his decision in the case."

"Kessler has said evidence has been presented in Hutchison's case that he could not receive a fair trial if cameras were allowed in, including testimony by clinical psychologist that said being photographed would put Hutchison in a "very angry, resentful state of mind."

Dayton Daily News Headline: *"Kessler excuses Hutchison jurors"*

Kessler now seems to be on trial in the court of public opinion. We have never wanted cameras in the courtroom during the trial. It was our opinion that they are a distraction to any proceeding, be it traffic court or criminal court. It tends to sensationalize the proceedings period.

A letter to the Editor of the Dayton Daily News read: *"What's Kessler hiding?"*

> *Judge Kessler... is worried about Joseph E Hutchinson receiving a fair trial... Did Hutchinson give Mrs. (Evelyn) Kaiser a fair trial when he beat her over the head until she was dead? Don't hand me that bull about him being innocent until proven guilty. That's just another loophole for shyster lawyers to use to get criminals released. Is Carl Kessler afraid the public will see what really goes on in the courtrooms? … They [members of the bar] had better clean their house or someday the people will clean it for them."*
>
> *E.V. Rinehart SR*

I was so glad this man was not in the jury pool. This editorial shows that most people believe what is printed in the newspapers. If this man would have paid more attention to all the pretrial trial information he would have learned that "Hutchinson was actually Hutchison, and middle initial D not E, and that he did not beat Mrs. (Evelyn) Kaiser over the head until she was dead." I too believed that the cameras would only televise the parts of the trial "they deem newsworthy" which would not be fair.

The wrangling over cameras had been going on for months, and we were now entering into the holidays. The grim prospect of celebrating Thanksgiving and Christmas without Joey, and along with the pending trial, was more than I could bear but I knew I had to make these holidays as normal as possible for Jimmy and Eric's sake.

The plan would be to go to early Mass, and then pick up Gramma. Family would visit and neighbors as well. I wanted this Thanksgiving to be as close to the same as we could muster. I asked Joe if he would participate this year and he said, "No Linda, and I have decided we will not be having a Thanksgiving dinner here. If you want, you can have everybody over on Friday."

I said, "Joe, that's not the same, and you know it."

"Well that is how it is going to be," he said.

I thought about this for about two seconds and begged him to relent, but again his answer was no. I said, "Joe, I need this, I need the family to all be together. I need the normalcy of this holiday. Please let me do this."

There are moments in your life that are defining and this was one. I found myself looking at my wedding ring. Joe had placed it on my finger for the second time, February 2, 1959 in a Fort Hood Texas Chapel, and I had not taken it off since. In fact, I had been unable to take it off even if I had wanted too. It was like it had grown to my finger. I placed my right hand over my left; grabbed the ring with my fingers, and pulled as hard as I could, it flew off my finger nearly hitting Joe, but falling on the table in front of him. I said," Take this ring and shove it, I will not wear this ever again." That night I left his bed, never to return as his partner. I would have to go the next miles alone, as I was never going to beg him for another thing.

The boys and I picked up Gramma and went to my sisters for Thanksgiving. It was assumed that Joe was just not up to celebrating because of Joey and all. I didn't tell them it was because of his "new religion." What Joe did on that Thanksgiving Day, I don't know, but we never shared another holiday again.

By Dec. 24th the Dayton Daily News read: *"Media wins stand on cameras."*

Now the media has the right to go to court and fight to have their cameras in the courtroom again. Everyone has the right to a speedy trial. Because of the media intervention into Joey's trial, and Judge Kessler's error of not noting the delay properly, Joey should have been released. That's the law. Well it may be the law, but if you are a "nobody" and have no money, the law does not favor you. Your opinion means nothing.

On December 29th Joey's attorney's asked the court to dismiss the charges against their client, because, "the 90-day delay time Ohio law set for his trial to begin had expired." The main task facing the court, said, Thomas Schaffer, one of Hutchison's attorney's told Rice, is to determine if the defendant's right to a speedy trial can be tossed aside by the Ohio Supreme Court in favor of the television media."

"What the Ohio Supreme Court did was give standing to a non-party in a criminal case because the television media didn't get it's way... Never in the history of American jurisprudence has this been allowed. Schaffer urged Rice "to put a stop to the television media's bullying, if you will, of the Ohio Supreme Court, into delaying the trial."

Dayton Daily News Headline:*"Camera tiff may free defendant," "Throw out charges in slaying trial, Hutchison pleads!" "Jurisdiction ruling due from Rice."*

"Rice does not have to rule on a speedy trial issue because Hutchison can appeal his case if convicted, Crim said."

Now this statement was to be important over the next couple of weeks when Joey was offered a deal. For now though it was just one more mistake the courts made, and nothing was going to make them uphold the law. Joey would go on trial, and it looked like the media had won.

Christmas had come and gone, and the Christmas present I wanted I didn't get. I wanted this trial thrown out of court. I wanted my son in a mental hospital, getting the treatment he needed to fight his mental illness, and to have a shot at a "normal" life. My Joey was still in jail in solitary confinement since April 10, 1980. He started sinking into his depression phase which hit sometime in December and lasted until spring. Joey now had manic and seasonal depression along with attention deficit syndrome. No wonder we were unable to help this child.

Even with the psychiatrist diagnosis, Joey was not offered any medications or treatments for his disorders. His depression was even more pronounced while being on trial for these charges. There were times he was near psychotic and suicidal in his thoughts. He wrote a note to Judge Kessler, and somehow the media got a hold of this note, and it ended up on the front page of the Dayton Daily News. Not just what the note said, but an exact copy of the hand written note. Don't tell me you can trust the system.

"I don't want to be in court with any people from the TV they put me thru so much I can't stand to be in the same room with them please help me," ~ Joe Hutchison

I didn't burden Joey with what was going on at home. Why add to his discomfort? I was working part time for the Vandalia Park and Recreation Department as a volleyball referee, and Joe and I were barely talking. One evening I returned home and Jimmy and Eric greeted me with "Mommy, Daddy's burning the Christmas tree and Easter baskets!" Sure enough, he had the living room Christmas Tree, what was once the adult Christmas Tree, burning away in the fire pit along with some of the Easter baskets. The children Christmas tree that we kept in the family room; with all of their handmade decorations, was ready to be thrown on the fire, and in his hand was the crucifix that hung in our bedroom, a gift from Gramma a few years ago as a Christmas present.

"Joe! How dare you destroy these things! They belong to me and our children. We want them. You do not have the right to destroy them. Have you lost your mind?" I was able to put a stop to the defamation of these traditional

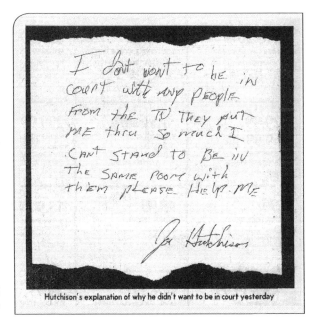

Hutchison's explanation of why he didn't want to be in court yesterday

Exact Copy of the Newspaper Print 1980

keepsakes, including the crucifix, but I didn't think I would be able to save this marriage. I pleaded to God to help me get through this trial. I couldn't handle much more. I couldn't fight God's laws and man's laws. There wasn't enough of me left to fight them both. I begged to God to help me hold on to my sanity, but I vowed to never beg another human being for comfort.

Apparently the JW's think these religious items are idols of some kind. I can assure you that I have never been taught to worship anything but God. Catholics have never been taught that these and other traditional icon's of the Catholic faith, like statues and rosary beads, were to be worshiped. I realized that Joe must have been out of his mind with grief.

Our son's troubles must have caused him to go looking for answers to take his pain away. The feeling of helplessness that we both were feeling left him vulnerable. There was no way I was going to let this happen to me. Burning Christmas trees and Easter baskets would not bring my son home, sane, happy and healthy, nor solve any of our other problems. I was not turning my life or the lives of my children over to some religious cult. Period.

I still have those childhood ornaments in a box for keepsakes. I no longer have the Christmas tree I saved from the fire, but I do have the crucifix, and it hangs in Joey's room today. Joe didn't attempt to burn these keepsakes again.

CHAPTER 15

Hear Ye, Hear Ye,

Court Is Now In Session

The Dayton Daily News Headline: "Hutchison jury selection begins for second time"

For the first couple of weeks in January of 1981 a flurry of activity took place between Judge Kessler's courtroom, the DA's office, and Joey's defense team. It looked as though Kessler would prevail in keeping the cameras out of his courtroom at least for the State of Ohio Vs. Joseph Hutchison. The new prosecutor William F. McKee was secured, and a new pool of potential jurors waited to be questioned.

The Dayton Daily News: "*The only other two that were charged in the case -a 17 year- old West Carrollton boy and a 15-year-old Miami Twp. Youth – have already been convicted of identical charges and have been sentenced to juvenile institutions until they are 21.*"

Before the jury was seated and the trial was about to begin, the prosecution put a negotiated deal on the table for my son to plead guilty. That deal consisted of a plea of guilty to a murder charge, felonious assault, and aggravated burglary. Just why did they do that? Presumably by dropping the aggravated murder charge to just murder, it would be possible to keep Joey from being sentenced to the Lucasville State

Prison, (where the worst of the worst go). He could then be diverted to the Chillicothe State Prison if found guilty. They wanted to reduce the 15-year to life sentence to a 12-year to life sentence. My personal opinion is that the State of Ohio wanted or needed to prove to the people of the State of Ohio that they could sentence at least one of these kids to do time in an adult prison for this murder.

People cry out for justice, yet most do not have a handle on what justice is. A good majority will invoke the Bible passage of "*an eye for an eye.*" Some will want the guilty to die the same kind of death inflicted on the victim, yet others will say prison is too good for any lawbreaker. Of course those are usually the one's who have no firsthand knowledge of what it is like to be a part of a criminal court proceeding from a defendant's perspective. The elected officials (judges and prosecutors) need to do all they can to please the public, as that is how they get reelected. Look at all the heat that Judge Kessler took with this case so far. The media can be brutal.

In Joey's case it was thought that Joey could possibly be found not guilty by reason of insanity, and that would not sit well with the general public. They certainly did not want to do Joey any favors, for, if they did, they would have upheld his right to a speedy trial, which they did not.

When Tom (Schaffer), Joey's attorney, asked us to come in and discuss with Joey the possibilities of accepting this deal, we were skeptical. So far we had little trust that anything would be in Joey's best interest, but because we didn't know what would be in his best interest, we had to trust somebody.

Tom began by telling us that he believed in his not guilty by reason of insanity case, but obviously couldn't guarantee the jury would return that verdict. He also said that if he failed, he believed he could win in the appeals court on the issues of speedy trial impediment and the cameras in the courtroom. He felt he could take this case all the way to the United States Supreme Court. He would call it the Hutchison Law. Pretty impressive, right…except he was playing with our son's life. The lawyerly ego trip he was on did sound good, and gave us a back up plan: win now or win in a couple of years. And if it failed, he said the only thing Joey had to lose was three years of his life, twelve versus fifteen.

We were also led to believe that with a good prison record Joey would be paroled on the twelfth or fifteenth year of the sentence, even though the law states that they could keep him for life. Oh, how naive could I have been to believe everything I heard about the justice system? But I did. Without some kind of a fight, Joey was going to go to an adult prison, period. In fairness to Tom, he did say that the deal was a sure thing and that court was a gamble; he recommended Joey take the deal. Whichever way Joey chose to go he was going to be there for him.

Well Joey, what do you want to do?
January 26, 1981- 10:15 A.M.

From **The Court Recorded Transcript**:
Let the record reflect that we are in chambers. Present are the court reporter, Thomas Schaffer, Richard Divine and Dennis Schram, for the defendant, along with the defendant, Joey Hutchison and along with Deputy Sheriff Bryan Isembletter."

Mr. Divine: Joey, at this time I would like to ask you—you have been advised that the Prosecutor has offered you a negotiated deal: is that right

Defendant: Yes.

Mr. Divine: And that negotiated deal consisted of a plea of guilty to a murder charge, felonious assault, and aggravated burglary; is that right?

Defendant: Yes.

Mr. Divine: And there has been some talk of giving you consideration in sentencing to Chillicothe—not a promise but the Court would do everything in it's power that you were sentenced to Chillicothe rather than Lucasville; is that right?

Defendant: Yes.

Mr. Divine: At this point, is it your desire to accept the plea bargain and plead guilty or go out in court?

Defendant: No. No deal.

Mr. Divine: No deal. Okay.

Mr. Schaffer: Deputy, what happened here, this is strictly confidential.

Deputy: No problem with that. I am aware of that.

Mr. Schaffer: I didn't think I had to say that, but because of repercussions and everything- -

Mr. Divine: The Press and everything.

Deputy: I'm well aware of the Press.

Mr. Schaffer: Judge, one other thing on the record I think we ought to do. We did this the last time. We had filed a motion to suppress identification, and prior to the last trial you indicated that issue had already been raised in Juvenile Court. We are just going to renew that motion because we never did get a hearing.

The Court: Which motion was it?

Mr. Schaffer: That was the motion to suppress the identification of Dr. **Kaiser.** Let's go off the record.

You have to wonder why all the "off-the-record" stuff is necessary. As I read the transcripts I found a lot of off the record talks. I wanted to know just what was being said? It seemed to me though that "the truth and nothing but the truth" did not exist.

The identification of Joey by Dr. Kaiser was not done according to proper eyewitness procedures. Dr. Kaiser did not identify Joey in a line-up that had Joey as the only one who could have possibly been in his home on the night in question until he was later shown a series of mug shots of possible suspects that included Joey and did not include Jerry Arnett and Kenny Flynn. Dr. Kaiser then indicated the picture of Joey. We believe that Dr. Kaiser was led to identify Joey. We also believe that he believed that he had correctly identified his wife's killer. This biased and improper identification of suspects happens more often than the general public is led to believe. It is a fact that eyewitnesses make just as many wrong identifications as they do right ones. Joey believed that it would have been impossible for Dr. Kaiser to identify any of them because it was so dark and there were no lights on in the house at all.

We thought Joey had a better than even chance in court as we counted on the testimony to show that Joey was not the ringleader, nor the one who actually killed the homeowner. How naive we were. We believed that Joey's dynamic duo, Thomas Schaffer and Richard Divine, knew just what they were doing and could actually do it.

We also believed in all of the others we trusted with Joey's life over the years, teachers, doctors, psychologists, psychiatrists and therapists, that they knew just what Joey needed as well. How can a child be so mishandled all these years by all these experts?

The jury was selected and sent off to view the crime scene. The court reminded the jurors that what they were about to view was not to be considered evidence unless it was brought up in court. In addition, nothing said in opening statements was to be considered evidence. It merely served to focus the issues and tell the jurors why they were there.

Mr. McKee's opening statement was long and covered the charges against Joey of burglary, aggravated assault and aggravated murder, his defense of not guilty, and not guilty by reason of insanity.

From The Transcript:
"Mr. McKee, ...*tells the jurors that the players he will focus on are: Joe Hutchison; two co-conspirators, Kenny Flynn and Jerry Arnett; the female cast: Dana Pierce, Donna Hill, Renee Muse; and another participant, Kirby Flynn, the brother of Kenny Flynn."* He (McKee) *readily admits that it was not Joey's idea to commit a burglary, that it was Arnett's. That it was Arnett who got the others to agree to the deed. It was Flynn's idea for the target as he had burglarized homes in that area before."*

However, after making this statement in his opening, the prosecution went on to say that Joey was responsible for beating Dr. Kaiser with a tire iron and striking Mrs. Kaiser with a crochet mallet until she was dead, jumping on her head after she was dead and shouting out orders to shoot and kill anyone that moved. Mr. McKee did not at this time indicate that Arnett or Flynn did anything but standby watching Joey run amok, beating and killing people.

From The Transcript:
Mr. McKee: *"And, as in any situation, you'll find that the testimony fits together in an overall picture and yet, as is normal in human existence, there are discrepancies as to the exact acts of each player or exactly what occurs".*

"There is some conflict as to who took the two mallets. In any event, there's no question but that Kenny Flynn had a mallet, Joe had a tire iron, Arnett may have had a mallet originally, or Hutchison may have had a mallet and tire iron, both, originally".

Of the 98 fingerprints lifted from the crime scene, none belonged to Joey, only Arnett and Flynn's. Joey's fingerprints were never found on any of the weapons, nor were the boots that supposedly left prints in blood, found or any bloody clothes.

From The Transcript:
The Court: Mr. Schaffer, you may make opening statements.
Mr. Schaffer: May it please the Court, we respectfully request permission to present statements at a later point in the case.
Mr. McKee: Your honor, I would object to reserving opening statements, as the trial procedure set forth in the Rules of Criminal Procedure indicates the opening statements, including defendant's are presented to the jury at this point in the trial.
The Court: We would exercise our discretion and grant your request. **Mr. Schaffer:** Thanks the Court.
[The trial continues without an opening statement on Joey's behalf. I don't know why Mr. Schaffer went this route but he did. Was it the right move? I don't know. At this point, everything was so out of my realm of understanding.]
Mr. McKee calls Dr. Kaiser as the first witness.

Dr. Kaiser was questioned about the night that this crime took place. He testified to the recollection of the events as he remembered them. He spoke about waking to find himself being assaulted by at least two people and trying to protect himself from the blows. He remembered only seeing shoes and possible heights of the perpetrators, and finally, from a split second of light, did he see the face of the defendant. He told of finding his wife in the hallway and determining that she was dead and yelling for his son, Burk, to go for help. There was no doubt that this event took place and he was a victim. There is no doubt that his wife was killed. There was doubt, however, as to who did what and in what order. To me this is understandable, as I can't imagine what I would remember with certainty if it had happened to me.

I do remember the night when Joey came into our bedroom and tried to get his father's wallet from under the mattress. I didn't know it was Joey until his father had him pinned by the front door, because it was so dark. All I saw was two shadowy figures grappling and yelling. Joey never fought back. He was just trying to flee. In the past when confronted with danger, Joey always choose to flee or dissolve into a stupor.

Mr. McKee calls Kenneth William Flynn to the stand:

Kenny Flynn is now a witness in behalf of the State. Kenny has already been tried in Juvenile Court and found guilty of the same charges that Joey has been charged with. He is now going to testify against Joey. He will testify that he only knew Joey two weeks before this happened and this was the second time they had worked together, yet he had been doing burglaries for over two years. He admitted to picking the neighborhood that night. He also admitted to drinking heavy and taking Quaalude's and smoking Marijuana usually bought by Robin Muse, because she was the eldest of the group, eighteen or nineteen.

He told of all of these kids, Arnett, the Flynn's, the Muses and Joey doing drugs the night of the break-in. He first said Joey gave him and Jerry the mallets yet another time he tells of picking up the mallets just in case anyone was home. His fingerprints were all over the crime scene. No, he didn't see Joey hit Mrs. Kaiser or jump on her head. Then yes, he did see Joey hit Mrs. Kaiser. Yes, Joey did assault Dr. Kaiser and ordered him to shoot Dr. Kaiser if he moved. No, he (Kenny) never touched the Dr. or Mrs. Kaiser. Yes, Joey dropped the tire iron and took the mallet from him when he left the room.

Mr. McKee calls Dana Pierce to the stand:

Dana confirms her presence during the crime as the driver of the get-away van and her additional involvement in this case after the home invasion. She confirms that she was offered immunity from any prosecution from the first time she was questioned. Dana said, "Joey kept saying if they got caught he would take the blame." Dana admitted to driving a get-away van on numerous occasions for Jerry Arnett and sometimes Joey was with him. She confirmed that Jerry was arrested first, then Kenny, and then they came for her. Dana had only Jerry's version of what happened inside the Kaiser's home on that night and the following day as they pawned the goods. Dana was recalled for the defense, with astounding revelations brought about by insightful questions by Joey's attorneys.

Mr. McKee calls Kirby Flynn to the stand:

Kirby Flynn, brother to Kenny Flynn tells his tale more or less about the night of the break-in at the Kaisers. He was part of the group that gathered at the Days Inn Motel before the break-in and after the break-in. Apparently he was not part of the actual crime team. He does admit however to having been given immunity for his testimony. He admitted to other B & E's (breaking and entering) and of fencing the goods from those burglaries and those from the Kaiser B and E. He had little to say about Joey's direct actions on that night except what was told to him by his brother. "He only said that Joey told him that somebody might have died that night and that Joey had said he hit a man." When asked if he could recall anything about the lady, he said, "I remember him saying she was screaming and that she ran up the hall — and I can't remember the rest." When asked about seeing any blood on Joey's clothes that night, he didn't remember seeing any blood on Joey's clothes or anybody's for that matter.

Mr. McKee calls Jerry Arnett to the stand:

Of the three major players in this case Jerry was on the witness stand the longest. Had Jerry not been tried and convicted in Juvenile Court he would not have testified at all. Why? Because his answers would have been "I choose to take the 5th amendment." Having been convicted of the same charges Joey is accused of he had nothing to lose. Jerry told of knowing Joey from Vandalia when he lived a couple of blocks over from where Joey lived. He had moved to West Carrolloton a couple of years ago and only renewed his friendship with Joey when he found Joey was working at the same car wash he was.

I remember thinking had not the Juvenile system placed Joey at the "Y" and got him the job at the car wash, that maybe this would not have happened. If they had listened to us, Joey would have been in a residential treatment program for people with mental illnesses. Maybe we would not be going through this trial and maybe Mrs. Kaiser would not have been killed. But maybes don't count. Again, was it fate that Joey found himself working with Jerry Arnett at the car wash?

Jerry told of how he hooked Joey up with the Kirby's and the Muse's and vouched for Joey's expertise in breaking into places. Remember,

133

Joey had been breaking into and out of places from age two and I guess he was quite good at it. Only now instead of climbing out his own bedroom windows, he was now climbing into strangers'. Jerry testified that it was his idea to do the B and E's that night and that Kenny picked the area.

According to his version, he never hit either the Dr. or Mrs. Kaiser. Jerry said only after Joey put a mallet into his hand did he swing it at Mrs. Kaiser three times and on the third time the mallet hit the floor, broke and flew up and hit her. Yet in an earlier written statement he was to have said he hit her once. Jerry's inconsistencies were flagrant and I am not sure if the jurors picked up on them or not.

In his testimony he revealed that he took a polygraph which opened up a whole new can of worms and caused Joey's attorney to ask for a mistrial. It seemed that the results were not turned over to the defense and that was against Rule 16 of the Ohio Rules of Criminal Procedure code. Questioning was stopped and this was debated for hours in chambers, out of hearing range. The issues must have been resolved as no mistrial was called and questioning resumed with the agreement that Jerry Arnett could be called as a witness for the defense at some later point.

Tom opened up a line of questions that we were not prepared for. He asked Arnett if he knew how Joey felt about women.

Question: He didn't like women, did he?
Answer: He beat the prostitutes and him and David Alberti of Vandalia robbed a woman at Mercury Dodge—and got three thousand dollars from them.

I doubt that what Arnett said was true or that it happened at all and wondered why this was not considered hearsay. No one came forth to bring charges of assault or theft. I believe it was just another statement made by Arnett to make Joey look bad, and take the heat off himself. There was no corroborating testimony to back up Arnett's statement. Why, did Tom allow this to stand?

Question: Tom asked Arnett if he knew how Joey felt about his mother?
Answer: Arnett's answer was, "no."
Question: "Tom asked if he thought that Joey was trying to kill his mother?"
Answer: Jerry's answer was, "no."
Question: "Tom asked if he thought Joey disliked women?"
Answer: Jerry's answer was, "no."

Now just where was Tom going with this line of questions? We wouldn't know until the defense had their turn.

Jerry threw Joey under the bus while trying his best to put a good spin on his involvement. It was at this time that Jerry also said for the first time in public that he saw Joey jump on Mrs. Kaiser's head. He also said that he had thrown Joey's clothes away but now it was Joey that threw them away in the river. It was also noted that Jerry Arnett and Kenny Flynn were allowed to travel to this trial together in the same bus from Indian River where they had been sentenced and were being housed in Juvenile Detention together as well. Was that legal? Maybe not, but it was permitted.

The forensic evidence was presented: the securing of the crime scene, finding and collecting of the evidence including: the mallets, the fingerprints, the tire iron, bloody footprints, Joey's old boots, the autopsy results, the assault evidence, a ring. Of the forensic evidence none could be traced to Joey. No fingerprints, no footprints, no bloody clothes.

The only piece of forensic evidence that could have tied Joey to the crime was an opal ring. It was said to have been found in a pocket of Joey's jacket. The ring had been identified by Dr. Kaiser on his examination as belonging to his wife. There was one problem with that ring, they couldn't without a shadow of a doubt be sure it was actually found in Joey's possessions, as the chain of evidence had been breached. Anyone could have placed that ring in Joey's possessions. Joey claimed he never had it.

There were no fingerprint matches to Joey anywhere in the house or on the weapons. His boots tested negative for the footprints found at the scene in blood and they were his old boots, nor were there any bloody clothes found or even looked for. Those that were involved in gathering evidence never went to Arnett's or Flynn's to get their boots for testing or their clothes either. Believe it or not the mallets were never tested for prints.

McKee calls the coroner Dr. Robert E. Zipf to the stand:

Dr. Zipf testifies that the autopsy showed that Mrs. Kaiser died from several blows to her head. The death occurred do to severe trauma to her head, resulting in a skull fracture. That her large vessel in her chest was ruptured by force, presumably by exerting a great force on her head and neck and that occurred after she was already dead. Also she would have been passive due to the fact she had a blood alcohol level of .29 and probably would not have been combative and most likely could not run or scream.

Dayton Daily News Headline: "Witnesses tell story of Evalyn Kaiser killing," "Boy says Kaiser died for nothing," "2nd mistrial plea rejected in slaying case."

Leeann brought home the view of the trial so far, she said, "Trials are not like Perry Mason's TV shows that's for sure, they are extremely dragged out with sidebars, motions, repeat questions, objections, often times the jurors fall asleep, no kidding, I watched a couple of them nod off," she said.

The media usually captures the "Oh My God" moments and cuts out the significance of the testimony leading to that moment, thus painting their very own picture.

Perhaps, if people want to know how the court system works they should have to attend and view the entire due process and make up their own minds. Letting the newspapers or television tell you their versions is not the way to mete out justice. The prosecution rests.

CHAPTER 16

Defending
The Indefensible

Leeann would call or bring home her views of the days proceedings from the courthouse. We of course read what the newspapers printed and TV news. Leeann confirmed our suspicions, "you just had to be there, as that is not how things were said in court today."

However we were asked not to attend any court sessions; Tom didn't think it would be a good idea for the jury to see our reactions to the testimony, as he was sure the jury would be watching us as well as Joey. At times I found it was just hard to take a breath, like I had been sucker-punched, and couldn't fight back. I got into the habit of taking long walks in the chilly winter night air. Watching my breaths come and go in puffs of steam, and asking God, "Why am I still able to breathe?" It never crossed my mind to end my life, but I wouldn't have cared if I didn't wake up tomorrow either.

Walking around our neighborhood with Eba our mixed pound hound, by my side; I felt like a visitor, like I no longer belonged, a stranger in this familiar land. If they hadn't closed their curtains yet you could see the neighbors in the day's dimming light, secured in their own little world. What was going on in their lives, were they feeling the world was a wonderful place tonight, or did they have a life and death struggle going on too? Were they struggling with something so painful they would rather not wake up tomorrow? If they looked out their window and watched me pass, would they give me a friendly wave or would they feel pity or maybe they would feel disgusted by what our family was going through?

I was told that tomorrow I would testify first for the defense. I was going to have to try and make the jury understand that there was something wrong with my son from the time he was little more than a baby. Could I possible make them see Joey's life as we saw it? Would this be the last time I would have to tell this story, trying to get someone to help Joey? Would the jury believe me?

Joe asked me if I wanted to sleep in our bed tonight, as he thought I should try and get a good night's sleep. He and I had not slept together since Thanksgiving week when I threw my wedding band at him and vowed I would never wear it again. I had forgotten what sleeping in a bed felt like; the sofa had been my resting place, as I had lost hope that our marriage could be salvaged. I accepted his gesture as it was sincere but I doubted I would sleep much.

Tossing and turning that night I thought about how Joe, such a private man, would handle this public exposure when it was his turn to take the stand. Joe never sought the spotlight nor would he call attention to himself in public. He was a good man but I felt he had left me unprotected for his new "god" at a crucial time in our lives. I was so angry that I couldn't forgive him. His abandonment of our family life and the church, and our way of life as Christians, was just another confirmation I am in a fight for survival against terrible odds.

The fight with man's law and God's law was bringing me to the edge of despair. We may have shared a bed that night but we were not sharing our grief and hurt, I might have just as well slept on the couch.

Dayton Daily News Headline: "Hutchison defense set for Monday"

The day in court didn't start in our favor. In chambers were arguments over how the jury was to be instructed. The term of aggravated burglary was being questioned as to whether it had been dropped to just burglary or was to be charged at all. No one could agree whose view was correct. Even Judge Kessler couldn't make up his mind. Of course Judge Kessler finally made a ruling leaving Joe's defense team unsure as to how the Judge would instruct the jury when it came time. Here is the court's answer.

The Court: You will know at the proper time though.
Mr. Schaffer: We are beginning our defense and we don't know what we are defending. State vs. Beech says you can't go forward this way. We are in a position where we are told that one of three is being used, and we don't know which one, and that is contrary to the law as we see it. [Either it was to be aggravated burglary, or burglary or drop the burglary charge all together.]

Judge Kessler apparently ran a sloppy court. It was only fair that Joey's defense should know how Judge Kessler was going to instruct the jury as it means what the jury can find the defendant guilty or not guilty of. However counsel was instructed to proceed.

The Court: Bring in the jury.
The Court: Want to call your first witness?
Mr. Schaffer: May it please the Court, Mr. McKee, Ladies and Gentleman. Good morning. If you will recall when this case began we requested permission of the Court and were granted permission to reserve time for our opening statement. That we would like to employ now and tell you what we feel the defense will present to you during the latter part of the case.

Thus began Joey's defense. Mr. Schaffer walked the jury though Joey's life beginning with his birth. He acknowledged Joey as part of a family and explained how by the age of two his life became a challenge, how he was accident prone and smart but had no self-control, frustrating not only his parents but others as well. Reading the opening statement I found many inaccurate statements by Mr. Schaffer. Names and dates were incorrect. Joey's first principal was Joe Gatton and was a witness for the defense, yet he called him "Mr. Kapella." It seemed his preparation of the case was not thorough. His main goal was to get the jury to reach a verdict of not guilty by reason of insanity. It was quite complicated.

To reach a verdict of not guilty by reason of insanity you must meet certain criteria; and in Joey's case the defense attempted to prove Joey was a borderline personality, meeting the criteria of insanity. I thought the psychiatrist was going to say Joey was suffering from manic-depressive disorder. I had not heard the term borderline personality before today. They needed to prove all six of the criteria of borderline personality to find him not guilty by reason of insanity. One: self-damaging acts. Two: unstable relationships. Three: frequent episodes of anger, loss of control. Four: identity disturbance. Five: affective instability. Six: physically abusive acts. Was Joey a borderline personality? A sociopath? A psychopath? Was he brain damaged? Was he manic-depressive? Was he mentally ill?

Trying to prove this began with me being called to the stand.

Dayton Daily News Headlines: "Hutchison made "home a prison," and "Former principal, parents testify to Hutchison's unruly behavior."

Of all the remarks from the testimony heard on the first day of the defense, the media chose a headline that they thought would hold an impact. They focused on a part of a statement made by me under questioning from Mr. Devine.

> **Mr. Divine**: Did you want him home?
> **Me**: No.
> **Mr. Divine**: Why, didn't you want him home?
> **Me**: You have no idea what it was like to live with him. You were never sure of anything. Nothing could be taken for granted, nothing. No security, no stability—nothing, when he was home.
> **Mr. Divine**: Did it affect the other family members?
> **Me**: Yes
> **Mr. Divine**: In what way?
> **Mr. McKee**: Objection.
> **The Court**: We would overrule the objection.
> **Mr. Divine:** How did it affect the family, Mrs. Hutchison?
> **Me**: It made our home a prison. It made us cautious. We took our—we never knew what would be missing. We never knew what would be destroyed. We never knew what things were going to happen next. The constant bickering, the constant fighting. He didn't get along with his brothers and sister. There was just no assurance of a day-to-day peaceful life.

My overall testimony consisted of telling the jury about Joey's physical problems. I wanted the jury to hear them in this way, but that didn't happen. Difficult Birth: Due April 6, born May 13, Held in birth canal approximately 30 minutes before a specialist was called in to assist the birth. Measles: At two weeks of age. First Concussion: At 18 months, from a fall out of a high chair. Severed fingertip: At age two, underwent surgery four times for this. Second Concussion: At three years old, falling from picnic table onto cement. Eye surgery: At three, for a lazy eye. Unsuccessful. Tonsillectomy: At four years. Eye surgery: At four years old, unsuccessful. Third Concussion: At six years old, loss of recent memory and use of right leg for about 24 hours. Possible Hyperactivity: from ages of two to six, treated by family doctor with diet and behavior modification techniques.

No real success. Diagnosed Hyperactive: At age seven to current. First treated with Dexadrine and Ritalin no real success, soiling of underwear and loss of patches of hair. Fourth Concussion: At eleven years old, from a fall from a 25 ft. tree; a broken wrist and clavicle. Drug Use: Starting at age twelve: glue, PCP, alcohol, mostly downers. Intelligence Test: ranging from above average to near genius. These are the things I wanted the jury to know about Joey's behavior and in this order, but that didn't happen.

After Joey's first concussion his sleeping habits changed, he withdrew from most affection and gestures of praise. We worried continually about his safety and his propensity for being destructive. It was obvious he was becoming unwelcome in the neighborhood, family groups and outings of any kind. One minute he could be playing nicely and the next punching, hitting or destroying who or whatever was near.

His eyes told a story in themselves. Often after misbehaving or being destructive his eyes would say "I don't see anything wrong with what I did" or they would look hurt because he had just destroyed a favorite toy and didn't know why or he would appear as if in a trance. As he grew older his attitude changed to, "I don't care" or "I don't believe I did that so I must not have done it."

As society pressed in on Joey and us, we struggled with constructive discipline, outright punishment, ignoring, praying, crying, and screaming. To hell with the Dr. Spock's of child psychology. We would remove Joey from the top of the fridge or the roof telling him that little boys should not do this as they might hurt themselves and divert his attention to something else. We would tell him that once you are put to bed you don't have to go to sleep but you must stay in your room. You can't run and jump on your sister's back as you might hurt her. You can't write on the walls as they are for holding the house up but here is paper and coloring books. Just how many times do you divert child's attention from things he shouldn't do to things he can do. Two? Ten? Twenty? Nothing worked. I had thoughts of taking Joey and running away to an island, chaining him to a wall until he was grown and God help me, as he neared his teens, a lobotomy so that I could alleviate the pain for us all.

As Joey started into criminal activity at about the age of twelve, I knew one of us was "crazy." I wanted Joey hospitalized at Dayton Childrens Psychiatric Hospital but they refused. As a family we went into counseling. Joey continued to be arrested for minor issues and was finally sent to the Ohio Youth Commission Diagnostic Center for observation. We went into counseling at Good Samaritan Mental Health Center. Joey eventually went to school at the hospital. Joey was arrested again, more counseling. There was a year spent at a Youth Center, two foster homes. More arrests, until the Ohio Youth Commission wanted to release him back to us. We said, "No." We felt Joey was sick and out of control and that they had done nothing to help him gain control . If Joey were to come home irreparable damage would be done to all of us. We wanted him in a hospital for his own protection and that of others. They didn't agree. They said "Joey can make it if he wants to" They told us "that very few children are mentally ill enough to require hospitalization and psychiatrists."

What the jury heard in my opinion, was a disjointed sort of rambling of these events. The attorney's would ask a question like:

> **Mr. Divine**: Was Joey sent back to the Ohio Youth commission in 1978?
> **Me**: Yes.
> **Mr. Divine**: As the result of another further criminal offense?
> **Me**: I think so
> **Mr. Divine**: How long was he committed to the Ohio Youth commission this time?
> **Me**: About six months

This went on for hours. In the end I guess the jury had a picture of Joey's behavior, but had I known that we would someday have to testify about Joey's life in minute detail I would have been better prepared. I wish I had kept a journal especially when it came to the names of all the doctors, psychologists, social workers, psychiatrists, and teachers to whom we pleaded with for help.

Mr. Schaffer was laying the groundwork for the insanity defense. I was not sure my testimony would be a deciding factor. I had hoped it would show the jury that Joey's behavior stemmed from lifelong problems. I had wanted the jury to see that we had asked for help repeatedly and while some tried to help, we were not given the right kind of help. Joey should have been identified as having a mental illness.

I now believe he wasn't because the "experts" didn't believe that a child could be mentally ill. Should Joey have been given medications to help with his behavior? Dr. Kavtschitsch said he would have treated Joey with lithium. Why were these drugs not administered? It was a matter of unacceptable practice to diagnose a child with mental illnesses as severe as manic depression, schizophrenia or paranoia. This matter of "unacceptable practice" is what needs to be changed.

CROSS EXAMINATION BY MR. MCKEE:

> **Mr. McKee**: Mrs. Hutchison, throughout all this Joey was actually a pretty bright young man, wasn't he?
> **Me**: They told me he was.

Mr. McKee: He was able to pretty well manipulate people to get what he wanted?
Me: Sometimes.
Mr. McKee: Now after the event at the Kaiser home took place, he was actually at your home when he was arrested, wasn't he?
Me: Yes.
Mr. McKee: He was sick and you brought him home?
Me: Yes.
Mr. McKee: Was that the flu or something such as that?
Me: Yes
Mr. Mc Kee: And then you found out why the police wanted him. And you've talked to him since he was arrested on this Kaiser charge; is that right:
Me: I have never asked him exactly what happened, no. There have been some things, yes.
Mr. Mc Kee: What has he told you happened?
Me: He told me he did not murder Mrs. Kaiser. I told him I did not want to know any of the details of anything.

Readers you have to understand that I was distraught over the events that had transpired. I was afraid and in denial and did not want to hear the events that I had already heard about from the other witnesses from my son's perspective. He told me that he did not kill Mrs. Kaiser. I knew the facts as others had told them, and that was enough. I couldn't bear to hear anything from his mouth.

Mr. McKee tried his best to get me to tell what Joey told me about that event. I am so glad that I had refused to let Joey tell me anything more about that night. Then I was excused.

The Court: Let's recess now. Can you come back at one, or is that going to interfere with your plans?

February 2, 1981 – 1:00 PM

The Court: Call your next witness.
Mr. Schaffer: Call Joseph Gatton to the stand.

Mr. Gatton was Joey's principal at Vandalia Elementary School, kindergarten through second grade. We knew each other through my activity with the PTA and our interaction with Joey in the classroom. His wife, Beverly, was one of the swimming instructors that I had hired to teach at Cassel Hills Pool. He was the first one to suggest a physiologist get involved with Joey when he was in kindergarten.

> **Mr. Schaffer:** Describe for the jury, if you would, please how it is you came in contact with Joey as Principal of Vandalia Elementary.
> **Mr. Gatton:** Well, you become acquainted with all of your students in the normal day's work but because of his behavior he was sent to my office a number of times. I couldn't tell you how many.
> **Mr. Schaffer:** Now, when he had these behavior problems, I presume you talked to him about them—about the problems?
> **Mr. Gatton:** Yes.
> **Mr. Schaffer:** Do you feel Joe learned anything from the discussions he had with you about his behavior?
> **Mr. Gatton:** Momentarily
> **Mr. Schaffer:** How long would it last?
> **Mr. Gatton:** Probably until the next time he had a problem. I think he realized it, but I don't think he could control it actually.

Mr. Gatton went on to say he thought Joey had a compulsion to be destructive. With his courses in abnormal psychology, Joey didn't fit in any textbook cases. He was convinced his behavior was something he did not understand and had never seen before. He likened Joey's behavior to "flipping a switch." Mr. McKee tried to get Mr. Gatton to say that Joey's behavior was done to get attention but Mr. Gatton confirmed it was not.

Joe and I were now waiting out in the hallway between courtrooms for Joe to take the stand. The bailiff came out to tell Joe he would be needed soon and for him to go on in. We looked at each other for a few seconds, and for those seconds we acknowledged each others uneasiness. Left in the hallway alone, I felt despair and hopelessness.

There were two paunchy police guards standing by the courtroom doors, presumably to guard the entry and exit of people. They were having a great deal of fun talking about the case. One of them said to the other; "Can you believe that the mother said this all happened because he fell out of a high chair when he was a baby?" They both had a hard laugh. I so wanted to wipe that smirk off their faces but I controlled my temper, and I thought this is just what Joey cannot do. He can't contain himself.

When reading the transcripts of Joe's testimony, I was really impressed with his answers from questions from both Mr. Schaffer and Mr. McKee. Joe was able to bring out things about how he thought the various placements of Joey with-in the Ohio juvenile system were so inadequate. He was able to tell about Joey's attempts at suicide and how we fought for placement in a secure environment for Joey.

Mr. Schaffer: When they put Joey in that room all by himself did you have a conversation with the Youth Commission about this?
Joe: Definitely did.
Mr. Schaffer: How long was he in that room by himself prior to this incident? (When he was at the YMCA)
Joe: Well, it was for several months.
Mr. Schaffer: Did you see him during this time period?
Joe: Yes.
Mr. Schaffer: What was he like during this time?
Joe: Well, he would call home and say that he was severely depressed, and you could tell it from his tone, the way he was talking, that he was unhappy there. He couldn't find a job. He was looking. I think he had, for a short while he had a job, at a car wash, and they went into a full time and they done away with part time. And I went to the Probation Officer, Mr. Jim Martinson, and told him Joe wasn't making it there, that he was in a severe state of depression and I wanted him to do something to get him out of there. I also felt that Joe was on drugs and I went first to Mr. Martinson and told him. I met with him once and he wanted to meet every two weeks and I said I wanted to meet every week, so he started every week but changed it to every two weeks. And I told him I wasn't satisfied with him; I wanted to talk to a supervisor.
Mr. Schaffer: Did Joey, if you know, do anything physically to himself?
Joe: Well, there was— during this period of time he had an O.D. at the Ambulatory Care Center.
Mr. Schaffer: On what?
Joe: I would assume it was on drugs.
Mr. Schaffer: Do you know that for a fact?
Joe: Yes. Because they sent us a six hundred dollar bill!
Mr. Schaffer: Did you go see him at the Ambulatory Care Center?
Joe: Wasn't aware of it. Didn't know anything about it until it was all over. Wasn't reported to me by the Youth Commission or anybody until I received the bill and then I had—even before that I had met with his senior staff--
Mr. McKee: Your Honor, I'm going to object to this
The Court: Sustain the objection.
Mr. Schaffer: Did you talk to Joey after you found out about this?
Joe: This-- when I found out about this, Joe was arrested.

Mr. Schaffer: While Joey was at the YMCA did you try to get him to come home?

Joe: No

Mr. Schaffer: Why not?

Joe: It was the assumption I got from them that they wanted him to come home and go to Good Samaritan Mental Health Center as an out-patient. I said, "Joey is not ready to come home. He's too sick to be home." And they had a staff meeting and said they agreed with me, that he was sick, but first they had to do something with his dope problem. And I said, "Put him in Synanon *[a local rehab center]* and he said," We don't have anything like that, and I said" I don't believe that, as I had read about a lot of places--

Mr. McKee: Objection.

Mr. Schaffer: So nothing was done?

Mr. McKee: Objection.

Joe: No. They wouldn't do anything. You couldn't make them do anything.

On cross examination Mr. McKee asked only four questions, arriving at nothing useful for or against the issues at hand.

The Court: Let's take an indeterminate recess. [A recess was taken, after which the trial resumed.]

CHAPTER 17

One Psychiatrists –

Two Psychiatrists – How Many More?

IN OPEN COURT

Dana Pierce, the girlfriend of Jerry Arnett was called on behalf of the defendant, having been previously sworn, testified as follows:

The Court: You were sworn the other day. You won't be sworn again, but your testimony is still under oath?
The Witness/Dana Pierce: Okay.
The Court: You understand that?
Dana Pierce: Yes.
The Court: Mr. Schaffer your witness
The Court: Did you have an occasion to talk to Jerry Arnett the night of March 30th when they came back to the motel?
Dana Pierce: Yes, I did.
The Court: During that conversation with Jerry Arnett, did he tell you that he had hit Mrs. Kaiser?
Dana Pierce: Yes, he did.

The Court: Did he describe how it happened?
Dana Pierce: He said that he had swung at her three times and on the third time it hit her.
Mr. Schaffer: Nothing further.

CROSS EXAMINATION OF DANA PIERCE BY MR. MCKEE:

Mr. McKee: Did he tell you how hard he hit her?
Dana Pierce: He said he hit her, it would not have hurt a flea.
Mr. McKee: Did he tell you what happened after that?
Dana Pierce: He said that he got—it made him sick, so he put a sweater over the face and ran to the bathroom and got sick.
Mr. McKee: No further questions.

JERRY ARNETT CALLED ON BEHALF OF DEFENDANT BY MR. SCHAFFER:

Mr. Schaffer: All Right. Mr. Arnett, when you were here before you indicated to the jury that you never intentionally struck Mrs. Kaiser; is that correct?
Jerry Arnett: Yes, sir.
Mr. Schaffer: Did you ever tell your girlfriend, Dana Pierce, that you hit Mrs. Kaiser?
Jerry Arnett: Possibly.
Mr. Schaffer: Do you deny or do you admit that you told your girlfriend that you hit Mrs. Kaiser?
Jerry Arnett: I don't know, I don't remember that far back.
Mr. Schaffer: Is it your testimony you don't remember you told Dana you hit Mrs. Kaiser with a croquet mallet?
Jerry Arnett: I just can't remember.
Mr. Schaffer: Is that the only person you have told—strike that. Do you still deny telling Detective Caudill?
Jerry Arnett: I don't—
Mr. McKee: Object.

At this point Jerry Arnett answered any additional questions with mostly "I don't remember" answers. The court then recessed until the next day. The testimony so far should have told the jury that Joey did not kill Mrs. Kaiser. Yes, Joey was there, he participated in this botched burglary, but was he the ringleader? The testimony said, "No." Was he the killer? The testimony said, "No." Was he aggressive with Dr. Kaiser and most likely one of the two that assaulted him? Yes, but why was he there in the first place? And would this matter to the jury?

Mr. Schaffer said he was pleased so far as to how the events were playing out. He told us that we did a good job on the stand as well. However he warned us that the most difficult part was just beginning. He had to convince the jury that Joey was legally insane. This was a huge leap of faith to help the jury see that Joey should not have been there that night at all. That he should have been in a secured environment for his and other's protection.

Dayton Daily News Headline: *"Hutchison called self-destructive"* *"Hutchison has conscience, but is nearly psychotic, expert testifies."*

The Court: You want to call your next witness?
Mr. Schaffer: Call Dr. Kathleen McNamara

Dr. McNamara was a doctor of Psychology steeped in degrees and child psychology. She evaluated Joey on several occasions including his past medical history. She was requested to evaluate Joey on neuro/psychological dysfunctions. Joey's impairment index showed the presence of mild neuro/psychological dysfunctions.

Mr. Schaffer: Would you characterize what you found as a mental defect?
Dr. Kathleen McNamara: Yes.
Mr. Schaffer: And your diagnosis of it was?
Dr. Kathleen McNamara: That it was an attention deficit.
Mr. Schaffer: And is that the minimal brain dysfunction that you spoke of earlier?
Dr. Kathleen McNamara: Yes, it is.

On cross examination Mr. McKee tried to downplay Dr. McNamara's testimony with questions that were meant to confuse the jury as to their significance. Next to be called to the stand was Dr. Joseph Kavtschitsch and he will be referred to as Dr. K from this point forward. Dr. K was educated in Germany from 1953 to 1955, he came to the U.S. to study medicine and decided to stay. He received his specialization in psychiatry at Ohio State University.

Mr. Schaffer: Call Dr. Joseph Kavtschitsch
Question: All Right. Doctor, have you had an occasion in the past to see and interview Joey Hutchison?

Dr. Joseph Kavtschitsch: Yes. I saw him on three occasions: First was 9/21/80, from 8:35 to 10:00 o'clock; the second time, 9/22/80 from 8:45 to 9:15; and then 9/23/80 from 9:30 to 9:45. I also saw the parents on 9/22/80 from 4:30 to 5:30.

Question: Now, doctor, can you explain to the jury what your purpose was first of all, at the three meetings you had with Joey?

Dr. Joseph Kavtschitsch: The purpose was to evaluate whether we are dealing with a sociopath personality or a deeper problem.

Question: Prior to seeing him or sometime during that time were you given an opportunity to review reports of other psychologists, psychiatrists, and medical doctors who had seen Joey in the past?

Dr. Joseph Kavtschitsch: Yes.

Question: Based upon your examination of him and your examination of the prior reports, did you reach a conclusion as to how you would classify his particular disorder?

Dr. Joseph Kavtschitsch: I think he is a borderline personality.

Question: What does that mean?

Dr. Joseph Kavtschitsch: A borderline personality has been established as a deeper entity just in the past ten years. Now there is an awful lot of disagreement how one goes about diagnosing that defect, but the DSM finally decided upon what criteria to use in order to diagnose him as borderline.

We never received this diagnosis (borderline personality) when we spoke with Dr. K. We thought he was going to diagnose manic depression with attention deficit syndrome. As he continued his testimony he laid out the perfect critique for insanity that fit this diagnosis. Was manic depression not enough to qualify for insanity? According to Dr. K, Joey has at least five if not probably six or seven criteria for borderline personality.

So how did Joey become a borderline personality? According to Dr. K it began at about age two. Dr. K noted that Joey was sick and accident-prone. He seemed to think that was significant because his basic emotional needs were not being met. When I told Dr. K that Joey was calm and reacted normal only when he had a fever and was sick, he must have surmised I only loved him at those times. Otherwise, if he were well, he was hell on wheels and I rejected him.

He said that Joey only felt approval, love and affection at those times when he was ill or injured. So, he would make himself sick to get what he needed or hurt himself. When he had his concussions did he plan them? How does an 18 month old plan a concussion, a three year old or even a six year old? Did he plan to sever his finger at two? Did he give himself a lazy eye condition? We saw all these doctors, psychologists, psychiatrists and social workers for 15 years and now we get this diagnosis?

Granted it was hard not to show disapproval and rejection when it came to Joey's behavior. We never rejected Joey, only his behavior. It is my contention then and it is still my contention now that Joey could not control his behavior. I still believe it is brain damage, still undiagnosed and a chemical imbalance.

> **Mr. Schaffer:** And what in your opinion, doctor, caused this disorder?
>
> **Dr. Joseph Kavtschitsch:** Probably a series of events which for some reason he adopted to incorporate in his self-concept, his lifestyle.
>
> **Mr. Schaffer:** What would his parents have had to do with it?
>
> **Dr. Joseph Kavtschitsch:** They probably unconsciously fed into it and aggravated it and probably reinforced it constantly.
>
> **Mr. Schaffer:** Reinforced it by doing what?
>
> **Dr. Joseph Kavtschitsch:** By punishing him, by rejecting him, by not accepting him, by criticizing him-- which is all punishment. Criticism, rejection, and unfair treatment is punishment. I think they (the parents) were very angry with Joey, and I can understand why they would be angry. I think they aggravated each others difficulties.

Now there are some who believed that we didn't discipline or punish Joey enough for his behaviors. Those were the people who said if that were my child he wouldn't act like that. The others were the one's that said, "Joey can if Joey wants too." It was hard to know how to constructively discipline Joey. We worked with Joey's teachers, doctors, psychologists and law enforcement, and tried to follow all of their advice and suggestions and just what did it get us…disappointment, confusion and despair.

> **Mr. Schaffer:** Doctor, based upon your consultation with Joey, and your observations, and the data you received, do you have an opinion based on reasonable psychiatric certainty as to whether or not Joey can refrain from doing wrong acts?
>
> **Dr. Joseph Kavtschitsch:** I would say yes, he cannot refrain from them. He has to keep doing them because this is part of his masochistic makeup. He has to keep punishing himself. He has to do wrong and he has to expiate the feeling of guilt by punishing himself or having somebody else punish him. It is automatic.

Mr. Schaffer: Is that the compulsion you are talking about?

Dr. Joseph Kavtschitsch: Yes.

CROSS EXAMINATION OF DR. K BY MR. MCKEE

Mr. McKee: In your report you mention several other classifications that I would think would be niches of diagnoses. You refer to Joey Hutchison as a manic depressive; is that correct?

Dr. Joseph Kavtschitsch: That's a possibility that he is that way, but I have not enough evidence to support that. Now remember his mother's mother or father's was an alcoholic and the father's mother who died in the state hospital, so there is a predisposition here which could account for this turmoil which goes on.

[My father was an alcoholic and his mother my biological grandmother on my father's side, died in the Dayton State Mental Hospital out on The Wayne Avenue Hill. You would think that this might be a pretty important fact; we thought so, but I guess medical science hadn't caught up with Dr. K yet, or maybe he didn't take very good notes.]

Mr. McKee: Did you feel that it was such that you need prescribe for this condition?

Dr. Joseph Kavtschitsch: Yes.

Mr. McKee: Did you prescribe Lithium for him?

Dr. Joseph Kavtschitsch: No. I am not treating him.

Now we hear about manic depression, but why did the prosecution bring this up? Would manic depression alone not be sufficient for an insanity defense? Did Dr. K stretch for the borderline personality diagnosis? (I didn't know the answer then and I don't know the answer now). We were more confused than ever. The prosecution also wanted to have Dr. K talk about what Joey might have told him about the night this crime took place. Mr. Schaffer nipped that line of questioning quickly with a confidentially of patient rights.

UNDER REDIRECT EXAMINATION FROM MR. SCHAFFER DR. K TESTIFIED:

Mr. Schaffer: Doctor, the Prosecutor has just talked with you about mental illness. You've testified previously that what Joey Hutchison has is a mental defect; is that not correct?

Mr. McKee: Objection, your Honor

The Court: We will sustain the objection.

Mr. Schaffer: Can you tell the jury what it is that you diagnose Joey as?

Dr. K: It's a personality disorder.

Mr. Schaffer: Is that a disease or defect of the mind?

Dr. K: You certainly can call it that because it is a way that the patient cannot really function well, and if he cannot function well he can break down.

Mr. Schaffer: You have not diagnosed him as a compulsive/ obsessive, have you?

Dr. K: No

They say if you put two psychiatrists in the same room and give them the same patient chart and even have them interview the patient, you will get two different diagnoses. If that is true how can a lay person possibly come to a conclusion of someone's mental state or condition? With a case such as this, it will be a miracle.

The prosecution will present a rebuttal witness. The State will call Joseph J Trevino. Under direct examination Dr. Trevino will tell the jury that he is a medical doctor, specializing in Psychiatry, with a sub-specialty in Forensic Psychiatry. His medical degree is from Mexico, Mexican D.F. The rest of his education was in the United States.

BY MR. MCKEE UNDER DIRECT EXAMINATION TO DR. TREVINO

Mr. McKee: Now, at the request of the State, did you have occasion to examine the defendant, Joseph Hutchison?

Dr. Trevino: I did

Mr. McKee: And when did you examine him, doctor?

Dr. Trevino: I believe I examined him on two occasions. If I may refer to my notes I can give you the exact dates.

Mr. MeKee: Sure

Dr. Trevino: Mr. Hutchison was examined on two occasions by myself, on October 6, 1980 and December 24, 1980.

Mr. McKee: And based upon this were you able to arrive at a diagnostic based upon a reasonable psychiatric certainty?

Dr. Trevino: I was.

Mr. McKee: And what was that diagnosis?

Dr. Trevino: Taking into consideration the past history as given by the individual, finding no mental illness, I did find he suffers from what we call an antisocial personality.

Mr. McKee: And would you tell us what that is, Doctor?

Dr. Trevino: An antisocial personality is a condition that we in psychiatry feel is an illness, but legally is not considered an illness.

Dr. Trevino goes on to testify that he believes that Joey is not now or has he ever been mentally ill. It is now in the hands of the defense to question Dr. Trevino and discredit Dr. Trevino's testimony. Mr. Schaffer starts out by pointing out that Dr. Trevino works for the State and that the State is prosecuting Joey. *I thought, isn't that a conflict of interest?* Yet another mistake moving forward with the trial. Mr. Schaffer will uncover that this is not the first time that Dr. Trevino has had contact with Joey.

> **Mr. Schaffer:** Doctor, isn't it a fact that you have seen Joey before?
> **Dr. Trevino:** That's right. About two years ago.
> **Mr. Schaffer:** For an attempted suicide?
> **Dr. Trevino:** Very superficial, very attention getting. Not very serious at all.
> **Mr. Schaffer:** But you hospitalized him for how many days?
> **Dr. Trevino:** It wasn't that we hospitalized him. He was in the Miami County Jail and he superficially cut his wrist, and the jailer suggested we evaluate him and we kept him three days.
> **Mr. Schaffer:** And you strapped him down?
> **Dr. Trevino:** Because he continued to try to cut himself. He was very upset because he was in jail.
> **Mr. Schaffer:** That's your opinion
> **Dr. Trevino:** Yes, my opinion

Mr. Schaffer was able to get affirmative answers to diagnose borderline personality as Joey's mental condition and Dr. Trevino confirmed that often a patient can have multiple disorders. Dr. Trevino also mentioned manic depression.

> **Mr. Schaffer:** Would you say he (Joey) has a negative image as opposed to a positive image?
> **Dr. Trevino:** I think we all have that at one time or another.
> **Mr. Schaffer:** Joey's got it consistently, doesn't he?
> **Dr. Trevino:** No. He has periods of euphoria. Reading from the other diagnostic categories made of him might indicate he might be manic depressive, because he had periods of highs, where he was very euphoric, and I am sure that's in the report I have.
> **Mr. Schaffer:** There's another term then that we are using—manic depressive?
> **Dr. Trevino:** UM—hmm
> **Mr. Schaffer:** People in the past have given him a lot of different labels haven't they?
> **Dr. Trevino:** Yes.

Mr. Schaffer: And that's really the reason they put the border-line classification in / It's a new classification?
Dr. Trevino: I would be speaking for them, and I don't want to do that.
Mr. Schaffer: And it's because those kind of people you can't put a label on have got to fit in some kind of category as you diagnose them?
Dr. Trevino: Correct.
Mr. Schaffer: I have gone through six of those keys to a border-line personality. Can you tell me where in there Joey doesn't fit?
Dr. Trevino: He does.

Mr. Schaffer continues to question Dr. Trevino and with every additional question he is able to get Dr. Trevino to agree with Dr. K's testimony. However, he will still maintain that Joey has no remorse and will stay with his diagnose of antisocial personality and legally sane.

I believe that throughout Joey's life, possibly from birth that he did not fit into any category and that no one knew just what to do for him, let alone we, as his parents. The mistakes we all made in our efforts to help Joey develop, in many ways confused and compounded to his problems. We also realized that not one person who treated Joey in the past was going to admit that they had a part in his maladjusted life. We had to ask ourselves, how many other "Joey's" were out there? How were they being handled? How many other families had been through what we were experiencing? These questions and answers took years to unearth. We did not get the answers in 1981.

The Defense rested their case. The state had no rebuttal so tomorrow we heard the summations. At this juncture I felt a lot of pain and a great deal of fear. Pain because my child, my first born son, had and was traveling a road we could not have foreseen, when we conceived him in that little makeshift camp in Sparta, Wisconsin. I feared for what would become of him no matter what the verdict. Was prison the answer? Is a mental hospital any better of an option?

No matter, he is my son, and a mother's love is unconditional and my love for him would always be there, despite the testimony that said we had abandoned him. Those were their words not ours. We may have wanted him out of the house, but he was never out of our minds or our hearts. We just recognized we could no longer help him and neither could the State.

CHAPTER 18

Has The Jury
Reached A Verdict?

By BENJAMIN KLINE
Daily News Staff Writer
...eph David Hutchison Thursday
...as found guilty of aggravated
... and felonious assault in the
... death in her Kettering home of
...ster and an attack on her

...th of Vandalia, who had
... court testimony
...son, was said
...here and after a

February 5, 1981, 10:20 A M

The Court: "…there are three things to be done for the determination of this lawsuit; First, the summation of counsel; the charges of the Court - - and we are having copies made for each of you – and the deliberations. Now, to work this out so it makes some sense, we're going to have the opening of the Prosecutor, and the opening summation of the defense, and then we're going to take our recess for lunch, come back, and allow the defense to close and the prosecution has the opportunity to come back and rebuttal, and then I will charge you and you will begin deliberations. Mr. McKee.

SUMMATION BY THE PROSECUTION BY MR. MCKEE

McKee: "We make no apology for the character of the Flynn's or Arnett, or Pierce. The State doesn't pick their witnesses for criminal cases. They have to take the witnesses who know something and who were there. Joe picked those witnesses by going with them. In all candor and frankness, it appears quite obvious that the role that Flynn played and the role that Arnett played was

157

greater than they still like to admit to. There's no question but that all three believed there was no one home when they went in the Kaiser home."

He points out Dr. Kaiser's identification of Joey, the marks on his back where he was hit with the croquet mallet. The autopsy report on Mrs. Kaiser, and Dr. Trevino's easy diagnoses of an antisocial personality vs. Dr. K's new and difficult diagnoses of a borderline personality.

At one point Mr. McKee does say," It became obvious that at the point those items (croquet mallet's) were picked up, they were intended for use, and they were used, because they entered with stealth, they beat on the doctor, they beat on Mrs. Kaiser and they killed Mrs. Kaiser,"

[Notice how he said "they." He never inferred that Joey was the only one that killed Mrs. Kaiser]

> **McKee:"** If his doctor is correct that Joe wants punishment, the facts and the law—the facts which you have received and the law which you will receive-- are good for Joe, because under the law and the facts that is exactly what he should receive by way of the over-whelming evidence. Use your regular experience and you can preform the duty which is mandated of finding the defendant guilty."

Use what regular experience? How often does a lay person have to make a judgment on someone's sanity? Even the expert's can't agree. The expert's now agree that Joey has a mental illness and a mental defect, but can't decide if it meet's the law's definition of insanity, and you want ordinary people to make that judgment? Regular experience would say,"Joey was there; Joey is guilty."

I grew up believing if you drove the get-a-way car you were as guilty as the one who did the deed. However, if the jury really wanted to see Joey's broken brain, all they had to do was listen to the testimony. If they really wanted to finally get him the help he has needed most of his life, they should find him not guilty by reason of insanity.

If there was to be justice in this case, they would have kept everyone as a juvenile or made everyone an adult. That would have been fair. They would have and should have charged them all. I knew long before this that life wasn't always fair and only with God were we all going to be judged as equals, so I had to accept this.

Since we couldn't control keeping Joey in the juvenile system or having the others charged or having Flynn and Arnett brought to the adult system with Joey, could this be fate? Was this some kind of test for the humanity of everyone who had a part in this event? This event took place years before March 30, 1980. It began in 1962 when Joey was born, someday others besides me will see this fact.

Could this be vengeance on my part, to want the others to suffer? No, I don't think so; it was knowing that because Joey was mentally ill, he was bearing the full force of the others' actions, as well as his own. Others who were as easily accountable for these misdeeds and for the death that took place; maybe even more so than Joey.

Am I making excuses for his behavior that night, absolutely not? I am angry that Joey was in the position to be a part of that motley crew. If "they" had listened to us, Joey would have been in an institution that night. If "they" had taken the posture that Joey could be mentally ill as a small child and surely by the time he was in elementary school we wouldn't be here, and Mrs. Kaiser might not be dead. However, "they" are not on trial. Perhaps "they" should be.

SUMMATION BY THE DEFENSE

Mr. Divine walked the jury through the facts of this case from the defense point of view, with the facts and the evidence to back up it up. He pointed out that Joey was the outsider, he was recruited by Jerry Arnett to join this group of kids. How Joey never had a mallet as he had the crowbar. How mallet marks were on Dr. Kaiser's back and a mallet was the weapon that was the cause of death of Mrs. Kaiser. How the two boys told their stories and made deals to stay in the juvenile system as did the others to keep from being charged at all.

> **Mr. Divine:** "Now, ladies and gentlemen, if you want to get down to the truth, you know who struck the killing blow on Mrs. Kaiser. It was Jerry Arnett, with the croquet mallet, hit her right here, and he pleaded guilty to it over in Juvenile Court. He pleaded guilty to aggravated murder over there, and that's why he did it, and now they're trying to keep themselves in the best possible position and they will be willing to say anything up here to avail themselves of all the courtesies they can in those juvenile camps. They lied to you. They just flat out lied to you."

COURT WAS RECESSED FOR LUNCH

I thought that Mr. Divine did a masterful job of painting the picture of what really happened that night and by who did what. Although it put Joey at the scene of the crime, it did show that the others were just as guilty. The only evidence that Joey was even there came from Arnett, Flynn and the coerced identification from one of the victims. All the solid evidence belonged to Arnett and Flynn. The fingerprints, the fencing of the goods, the get-a-way car, everything. Would that help the jury to see that Joey was not the leader or the killer and was caught up in the moment of this crime? He was there, but was he fully responsible for everything that happened?

Court resumed in chambers with all of the defense objections to the charges that the Court would be giving at the conclusion of arguments. These arguments were about the charges the jury would have to consider, such as involuntary manslaughter, manslaughter as well as aggravated murder, and all of the other aggravated issues and the court finally made it clear that aggravated burglary was to be dropped.

The Court: All right. Let's get the jury in.

SUMMATION CONTINUES BY MR. SCHAFFER:

Mr. Schaffer's summation was long and with in-depth descriptions of legal definition of insanity:

> **Mr. Schaffer:"** What have we got? Dr. K diagnoses Joey as a borderline personality. Dr. Trevino came in and told you he was an antisocial personality. And then when we went down each one of those characteristics for borderline personality, Dr. Trevino at the close of his testimony said Joey fits each and every one of them. Confusing.
>
> If both of the experts in this case agree that Joey Hutchison is a borderline personality, ladies and gentleman, I submit to you we have proved to you beyond the preponderance of the evidence that Joey Hutchison is not legally sane.
> Where is the rebuttal? If you believe what our psychiatrist said, and you believe what Trevino said, there isn't anybody in this courtroom who has told you anything different. He is not sane. The evidence before you on the issue of insanity is un-contradicted."

Now, for the life of me I will never understand why he didn't stop there. In my opinion he said enough to convince the jury that Joey met the criteria for legal insanity. However he went on to say:

> "Okay. It's your province to believe if you choose that Joey Hutchison did absolutely everything that Kenny and Jerry told you. You can do that. Now, if you choose to believe those two,

can you then truthfully and honestly say to yourselves and be satisfied with your decision for the rest of your life that the act of beating a strange woman for no reason, as Jerry Arnett put it, and then jumping on her head is the act of a sane child? Is that what sane people do for no reason? There had to be a reason, and the reason is that Joey is not sane. Thank you very much."

Did Mr. Schaffer just open the door for the prosecutor to put the nails in the coffin? I will let you decide.

PROSECUTIONS REBUTTAL BY MR. MCKEE:

Mr. McKee:" May it please the court, Defense Counsel:

I think I will take the "Joey didn't do it, but in case Joey did do it, he's insane," in the order in which they argued.

See, I told you so! I rest my case. Mr. Schaffer went to far. All that work went down the drain when he gave the prosecution that scenario to work with. It is my belief we lost the case for insanity right then and there.

Mr.McKee tells the jury that Joey's defense team was going for the sympathy card by using the name Joey instead of Joe. He attacked the fact that "Joe, was the leader." He eluded to the fact that Flynn and Arnett weren't treated toughly enough, but that was not the issue. If there was a mistake, we are not here to compound the error by forgiving somebody else because the first one's (Arnett and Flynn) weren't treated quite tough enough. He argued over the psychiatrist testimony, the physical evidence and in the end stated:

Mr. McKee: "We do know that it was brutal. We do know that a normal person wouldn't do it. But we also know the test is not just, "are they normal or abnormal," The test is, "Are they legally insane?" (*There is that "they" word*) Joe felt no remorse. Joe is anti-social. Joe is not insane. Joe is guilty. Thank you."

We got a call from Mr. Devine about 2:30 PM that the jury was now in deliberation. We knew that no matter what the jury decided this was not going to be over. The trial would always be a part of our lives and something Joey would never be free from. This was what nightmares were made of. I didn't know how we would survive.

I recalled the day that Joey fell out of the 25-foot tree in the back yard. He was about twelve. A few days before, Joey had been out in the tree house, working away on a project. I was curious about what he was doing and went to investigate. I found him assembling a catapult, reaching from the top of the tree to the ground. It consisted of a rusted pulley, coat hangers, some half -inch rope and a "hoppity hop" ball.

We had a conversation about Joey's idea and that it sounded like fun, but the materials were faulty and most likely would not hold his weight. I went on to explain that should he fall, if it didn't kill him, he could be paralyzed for life. We would be devastated if he died; and we surely would be sad if he were paralyzed for the rest of his life, but he would be the one that would have to live like that.

When I told this story to a psychiatrist during one of our sessions, he asked me why I needed to feel like I had won some kind of battle with Joey. Like I was trying to win a game or something. Why shouldn't I have been pleased to have felt I had made a difference in whether Joey would choose to do something so risky to his health, when typically I was too late to stop Joey from that kind of behavior.

What did I believe happened that night? I believed that Joey got mixed up with these kids because he wanted friends so badly. "Good" kids could not tolerate his erratic behaviors and "bad" kids often times used him. Joey went with these kids because he wanted to belong. He had a ticket to a concert, but they were going to burglarize homes. I wondered if I could have whispered in his ear," Joey, if you go with these kids tonight you will end up in jail, on trial for your life, would he have gone?

I don't think they meant for anyone to die that night. I believed that when they found the homeowners home, they all panicked. Just who did what and how and when, during the course of a few minutes that the madness took place we will never be 100% sure. However, I believe that Joey didn't strike the fatal blow. Joey would have tried to get away, become confused and disoriented and run from room to room. Which is how he responded his entire life.

How did I feel about what the Kaiser family was going through? What a tragic experience it must have been for them. To have had their home invaded and for a wife and mother to have lost her life. It should not have happened to them or to anyone. To know that my child had a part in that tragedy was still unfathomably surreal for me. Should we have tried to contact the family and offer some kind of an apology? I don't know, what would we have said? We're so sorry for your loss, didn't seem quite enough. If I would have said, "is there anything I can do for you, what would they have said?" Would they have wanted anything from us?

I did find myself praying for them and hoping that they would some-day be able to forgive these kids. I knew that they were probably looking for justice, but so was I. I had a feeling neither of us would find it in this life-time. Atonement , maybe, but not justice. So, no. We didn't contact them.

I must have fixed something for supper that night, but I can't remember what. We had the TV on, tuned into the evening news, but we didn't expect the verdict to come in so quickly. At 6:20 PM the jury rendered their verdict:

> **The Court:** *The caption of the case is the State of Ohio vs. Joseph David Hutchison:*
> *We, the Jury, upon the issues joined in this case, do find the defendant, Joseph David Hutchison, guilty of Felonious Assault, as he stands charged in one count of the indictment". Members of the Jury, is this your verdict, so say all twelve of you?*
> *(Jurors indicated affirmatively)*
> *The caption of this verdict is the same, State of Ohio vs. Joseph David Hutchison:*
> *We, the Jury upon the issues joined in this case, do find the defendant, Joseph David Hutchison, Guilty of the offense of Aggravated Murder as he stands charged in one count of the indictment". Members of the Jury, is this your Verdict, so say all twelve of you?*
> *(Jurors indicated affirmatively)*
>
> **The Court:** *We are going to refer this matter to the Probation Department for pre-sentence investigation.*
> *(Court was adjourned)*

The phone rings and it was Joey, the TV news was breaking the story, and we were in a state of shock. Joey was relatively calm and he said, "I am so sorry Mom we didn't get what we hoped for, but I got what I expected. It will be OK. We will have the appeals. I don't know what to expect now. Tom said he was going to try and get me to Chillicothe. I am tired Mom, I am so tired, I am so sorry."

I told him we loved him no matter what and that we will always be there for him. I said let's sleep on this and we will talk again tomorrow. Joe took the phone and said, "I love you son, we will be here, we want to talk to Mr. Schaffer and we'll talk tomorrow."

A little after 8 0'clock Mr. Schaffer called; he offered his apologies and said he truly felt he made the right decisions and that he made the case for insanity, but the jury couldn't or wouldn't buy it. He said he had polled the jury and that the jury said that no doubt Joey was mentally ill; however they were afraid that if they found him not guilty by reason of insanity, that he would be back on the street in a few short years, and that concerned them.

Hutchison found guilty in death of Kettering woman

By BENJAMIN KLINE
Daily News Staff Writer

Joseph David Hutchison Thursday night was found guilty of aggravated murder and felonious assault in the beating death in her Kettering home of Evalyn Kaiser and an attack on her husband.

Hutchison, 18, of Vandalia, who had been characterized in court testimony as an easily agitated person, was smiling and composed before and after a jury of 10 women and 2 men returned the guilty verdicts.

After a trial that lasted nine days and involved the testimony of 18 witnesses, the jury required only about three hours to reach its decision following a lengthy description of the law by Montgomery County Common Pleas Judge Carl D. Kessler Thursday afternoon.

JURORS WENT INTO deliberation about 3 p.m. and, aside from sending out a request for soft drinks, required no assistance from the court in reaching their decision in the complex case.

Judge Kessler said he would order a pre-sentencing report by the Probation Department before he imposes sentence on Hutchison, who was one of three teenagers charged with entering the Kaiser house, beating the occupants with croquet mallets, burglarizing it and then selling the stolen goods.

The other two, both 17, already have been found delinquent in Juvenile Court and are inmates at the Indian River State School near Massillon.

Defense attorneys, who prepared an extensive defense on the premise that Hutchison was insane at the time of the Kaiser slaying, said they would have no comment Thursday night. But they already have attempted three times to have the case thrown out because of delays since the trial first began Sept. 30, and an appeal now is considered likely.

A NOTICE OF appeal cannot be filed, however, until after Judge Kessler imposes sentence in about two weeks. Aggravated murder carries a mandatory life sentence in Ohio.

Hutchison's parents, Linda and Joseph Hutchison, 421 Vista Dr., who had testified about his troubled childhood, were not present in court except when they testified and were not on hand Thursday night. Dr. Richard Kaiser, the victim's husband who had testified for the state about the attack he survived

File Photo
Hutchison — sentencing next

Mansfield, who was assigned to the case after a defense motion alleging a possible conflict of interest when a previous defense attorney took a prosecution job, warmly shook hands with Kettering Police Detective Dennis Braun, who sat by his side throughout the trial.

"We have an old saying," McKee said before the verdict was announced, "that the worse the crime, the easier the prosecution."

JURORS SENT OUT a message they would not wish to comment on how they reached their verdict. Hutchison could have been found guilty of involuntary manslaughter in Mrs. Kaiser's death or simple assault in her husband's beating. Or, he could have been found not guilty by reason of insanity to both counts of the indictment against him.

Defense lawyers Thomas A. Schaffer and Richard W. Divine put forth the argument that Hutchison was neurologically handicapped, was a "borderline" personality who could not avoid an impulse to do wrong, and that intense dislike of his punishing mother could have led him to believe he was killing his mother instead of Evalyn Kaiser.

McKee argued the defendant was anti-social but not mentally ill.

Just before Thursday night's verdict was read, a smiling Hutchison turned to one of the lawyers who had helped to defend him and said, "Do you have your

Verdict Headline 1981

Their fears may have been valid. We heard about people being released from mental hospitals only to relapse. Would that have happened to Joey? Mr. Schaffer, said he would try and keep Joey, out of Lucasville, during the pre-sentencing phase and that he would make arrangements for us to see Joey, one on one during the next few days.

The Dayton Daily News Headline: "Hutchison found guilty, smiles"
The Dayton Daily News Headline: "Hutchison found guilty in death of Kettering woman"
The Dayton Daily News Headline: "Vandalian gets life in croquet murder"

"Joseph David Hutchison was sentenced to life in prison yesterday for the murder last year of Kettering resident Evalyn Kaiser."

"Judge Carl D Kessler, also ordered he serve 3 to 15 years for the beating of Mrs. Kaiser's husband, Richard. Kessler rules that the eighteen year old Vandalian man should serve the sentences consecutively."

"Mr. Schaffer, asked Kessler, to try and assign Hutchison to Chillicothe Correctional, as they had psychiatric and psychological counseling that would be more suited for people with Hutchison's background. At least he can get some treatment. He's a young guy, and who knows, it just may change his life. Kessler said he would consider the request."

We prepared to see our son for the last time before he would be transferred to the old Ohio State Penitentiary in Columbus. There, he would be processed into the system and transferred to the Southern Ohio State Penitentiary in Lucasville, Ohio. It seems that Mr. Schaffer couldn't win anything for Joey. Perhaps Judge Kessler was getting some kind of satisfaction for all of the bad press this case caused him.

We met with Mr. Schaffer and Mr. Divine, just after Judge Kessler, gave Joey his sentence. They talked about the appeals process and thought they had rock solid arguments for the speedy trial issue among other errors. They warned us that it could take several years to get the appeals processed and heard. We were not hopeful but we would not convey that to Joey for now.

As we left the courthouse that February afternoon, the skies were a cloudy gray and sharp winds cut through me like a knife. Mr. Schaffer and Mr. Divine, in their light beige trench coats flapping in the wind, turned and walked away from us, and never looked back. Tom had just told us he was on his way to Switzerland to ski. He said, "This case was so emotionally draining that he just had to get away for a break, before they started the appeals process." Just where were we supposed to go, I thought?

I looked at them, then I looked at Joe, and then I thought about having to go home to Vista Avenue and the life I had waiting there for me. There would be no ski trips to Switzerland, no respite of any kind. I would be going home to fight for the rest of my life the unforgettable events of the last eighteen years, especially the last six. I had to think about the future and just how I would meet it. I called this a Scarlet O'Hara moment. "As God is my witness" I would not let this take me under. It would have to be one day at a time. Surely it couldn't get any worse, can it?

When we said our goodbyes after our last visit with Joey; I left some things with the jailer that I was told Joey could take with him. He didn't want us to come up to Columbus to see him. He said, "Wait until I get to Lucasville, Mom. I remember that story you told about the time you and Dad drove up to Columbus, when you were teenagers. You said you felt an uneasiness when you drove by the Penitentiary and I don't want that for you again."

This statement from my manic-depressive, antisocial/borderline personality son, my son who cared for no one else but himself. The son that "hated his mother." The son that was not remorseful. How could those people be so blind?

For the next couple of months our only contact with Joey would be by letters. There would be no phone calls. He was in prison for aggravated murder and felonious assault. He would be there for at least 17 years unless he could get probation on his twelfth year. I couldn't protect him as a child, and I couldn't protect him now. "Please God, he is in your hands, but then he always was, wasn't he?"

Joey wrote about this transfer experience to the Ohio State Penitentiary some twenty-six years later. This is what he would remember about that day.

Joseph Hutchison
ENG.111,M&W, 3:00/5:15
Professor Beki Test
01/17/2007

Take The Long Way Home

Small baby steps are all I can take without the tendons in my ankles screaming. If I fall, the chains holding my hands tightly to my waist will render me with no way to break the fall. "The rest of your natural life in the Ohio penitentiary" are the words that stain my every thought.

Slow and heavy steel doors grind open to reveal overcast skies, but the fresh clean air only adds to the list of things that are gone. There is no resisting the efforts of this man, who could pass for Jackie Gleason's twin, to pull me any faster than my chains will permit. I wonder if he is getting paid by the minute. I feel like merchandise being moved from one shelf to another; there is no element of shared human experience. There's no wasted motion with this guy; he has me to his plain light brown car with the baby moon hubcaps in what seems the blink of an eye, despite all the painful steps it took to get there.

The back door pops open with the sound of opening something that's vacuumed sealed. I begin to make the awkward bends it will take me to enter, and with a quick firm grip, he pulls me back and turns me so we are uncomfortably close, eye to eye. In a gruff smokers voice he asks, "am I going to have any problems out of you?"

Several stupid things crossed my mind to say but a simple no is my reply.

Now, tucked in with steel mesh wire separating ole' Jackie Gleason and me, I could not feel more alone if I was on mars. A jailer comes running across the lot with a stack of books in his hand, says something to Jackie and opens my door, and sets the books on the seat next to me. " your Mom left these for you, " the jailer says, and adds sarcastically, " little late if you ask me." G.E.D preparation and other such help books.

Did he mean it's to late for me to learn or just echoing the sentiments of all those who have been telling me juveniles do not fair to good in adult prison? The engine starts up triggering adrenaline to course through my body, Jackie, more talking to himself than to me, says" the medias waiting for you out front, better take the back way."

"Transport south exit clear to O.S.P," the radio squawks. "So you think you're a Romeo playing a part in a picture show take the long way home,"are the opening words of the song now coming out of the car's back speakers. Those words, "take the long way home," rattle thru my brain like pocket change that finds its way into the dryer.

Cos you're the joke of the neighborhood
Why should you care if you're feeling good
Take the long way home
Take the long way home
Could I be any bigger joke in my hometown? This song is hitting me
from all directions.
But there are times that you feel you're part of the scenery
all the greenery is comin' down, boy
Take the long way home
Take the long way home"
Does it feel that your life's become a catastrophe?
Yes, my life could not be in any worse shape.
Oh, it has to be for you to grow, boy.
When you look through the years and see what you could
Have been oh, what might have been.
If you'd had more time.
According to the judge, there's no more time for me.
So, when the day comes to settle down,
Who's to blame if you're not around?
You took the long way home
You took the long way home.
These lyrics are telling my life story. Other songs are coming and
going on the radio, and all I can hear is this playing over and over in
my mind.
When lonely days turn to lonely nights
You take a trip to the city lights
And take the long way home
Take the long way home.

What powers in the universe had this song begun to play, as if this
were a movie. At the moment I start to head off into the abyss of fear
and darkness, this sweet melody plays in the background. Staring
out the window, I look at the trees and grass, things that have always
been there but never really seen until I became banished from them.
Yet, the words "take the long way home" seem to pamper my fear, as
if to say to myself."It will be a really unimaginable amount of time, but
I'm just taking the long way home."

How fast you can get somewhere when you don't wish to be there?
Jackie's done his job. I'm here; what a Gothic looking place this is.
Hugh stone walls that must be at least twenty feet tall flank giant,
rusty, solid steel gates. In moments, these gates swallow this car and
me in it, like Jonah and the whale. Can I make it home, even if it's only
the long way home?

"TO BE CONTINUED"

CHAPTER 19

Lord This Time

You Gave Me A Mountain

A s Joe and I traveled home from our last visit with Joey at the Montgomery County jail, the silence spoke about us emerged in our own private hell. I wanted to think about the future but I couldn't permit myself that luxury. I couldn't see a future, all I could think about was the past. How did we end up here and in these circumstances? We once thought we had the world by the tail and doing exactly what we had planned for both of our futures. I remembered our wedding, our plans to save for a house and family. We had made it work, hadn't we?

I remembered the births of our first two babies, Leeann and then Joey, how happy we were; a normal, happy family for the first five or so years. Then, for the next five years we were sure that whatever was causing Joey's problems would clear as Joey became older and matured. Even then we held on to hope. As we bounced from one program to another with Joey we still held onto hope that we wouldn't lose sight of our dreams for our family. These final years we lost sight of those dreams. We needed a safety line and there just wasn't one.

Perhaps we blamed each other for what happened? Did I think that somehow Joe could have made our problems go away and "fix" Joey? Did he think I could have taught Joey differently and it was my fault? All I knew was that we did everything we knew how to and could do, up to the point when we told the authorities we couldn't handle him anymore. Should we have let him come back home? It wouldn't have mattered. What happened with and to Joey was in the works for years. We thought that by not letting Joey come home it was tough love, not abandonment, and that it would force someone to help Joey and us. If this hadn't happened; it wouldn't have been much longer, we would have had to ask Joey to leave the house, for the sake of Jimmy and Eric's rights to have a peaceful home life, or he would have left on his own. Is that how people with mental illness are left homeless?

Was there going to be another knock on the door telling me Joey made an escape attempt or was killed? I couldn't go there. I needed to believe he was safe and warm. That he would be fed and clothed and maybe, just maybe get the help he needed. I would always be expecting that next telephone call; that next knock on the door.

For the next few weeks it was hard just to get moving at the beginning of each day, but I had to for I still had Jimmy and Eric to think about. I am amazed at how well we kept Jimmy and Eric from feeling the fallout of what we were going through. When I thought about writing this book I asked them and Jimmy said," Mom, all I remember is that Joey was hardly ever home and it never really sunk in that there was all this turmoil over the trial and all."

Eric said while he was aware that there was sadness, he didn't feel that his life was made any different by what had happened to Joey.

Our first letter from Joey arrived about a week after he was transferred to the Ohio State Penitentiary in Columbus. He wrote about feeling surreal. This was happening to someone else and he was observing. A psychiatrist put him on a medication called Haldol. He was not sure why. He was of course lonely and afraid. He signed his letter, "*Love from your lost son, Joe.*"

Finally his transfer to Lucasville came through and we made plans to visit for the first time. I wrote and told him we would be down to see him as soon as it was allowed. I wanted him to know that we were still standing by him and would be there for him. I told him about the telephone call I had received from Miss Eby; his playschool teacher, she wanted him to know that she was thinking and praying for him, and wanted to send him some money. We would forward the money, as he was not allowed to receive money from non family members. I had to wonder why Miss Eby would do that, send him money? After all, it had been over 12 years since she had Joey in her care. I thought that just maybe this was her way to say she was sorry to have not been able to recognize the seriousness of Joey's behavior's and perhaps to have been a better supporter for Joey and for us.

I kept finding excuses for not going to Mass on Sundays. Perhaps subconsciously, I was angry with God and this was my way of expressing it. However, when I was challenged about my behavior, I sprang into action. Joe told me at the breakfast table one Sunday in March that he was planning to take the boys out of school at St. Christopher's at the end of the year. He would enroll them in the public school system and take them into the Kingdom Hall. He said that since I hadn't been to Mass for a while it was time for him to take the boys with him. My short-lived passive nature came to an abrupt end. I declared, "Over my dead, cold body would this happen."

I immediately called out to the boys to get ready, that we would be going to Mass today. In the meantime Leeann came by the house; she set herself up between the boys and me and told me, "Dad, doesn't want the boys to go with you to Mass," therefore she was not going to let me take them. She tried to bar me from getting into the car where I had sent Jimmy and Eric. I remember looking at her as someone I didn't know, trying to keep me from my children. I received a first hand understanding of what temporary insanity might feel like. For when I put my hands around her neck, and I began to choke her, (as she was telling the boys to get out of the car), my intention at that moment was to kill her. If I had succeeded would a jury have found me not guilty by reason of insanity? Would they have said she snapped under all the pressure?

How dare she assert herself into my life in this manner! I saw Joe standing on the porch, just watching. *Why isn't he stopping me?* I thought of the neighbors watching and thinking, "the whole damn family was crazy." It was divine intervention that took my hands from Leeann's throat. It was clear to me that as much pain as I felt over what happened with Joey, he was the only one with an excuse, he was mentally ill. What was their excuse, to cause this much pain? This was the pain of betrayal from the people I loved the most in my life, my husband and my beloved daughter.

It was at that moment that I felt the loss of one half of my family. I was not about to lose the other half.

I regained my composure and told Leeann that if she ever came between my children and me again she would be dead to me. It became evident to me overtime that if the devil couldn't get to me through my husband, he would try and use my daughter. I loved my daughter almost more than life itself and she turned on me as if our last twenty years as mother and daughter meant nothing to her. If Joe by abandonment of our family's core values cracked my heart and Joey broke it, Leeann crushed what was left. I felt as if I was bleeding to death and there was no one left to patch me up. Why were they doing this? I wouldn't have done this to them. I left with the boys and when I returned she was gone. I would not see her again for sometime.

The next thing I had to do was to go and see Fr. Aufterheide. This was a traumatic experience for me for I had to reveal my helplessness to hold my family together. I had to confess that I had felt a murderess rage. I was beside myself with grief over all that had happened and finally I had to tell him about the intrusion of the Jehovah Witness influence in my home. I confessed my guilt for opening the door to these people. He asked if it were Jerry Meicher and I said, "Yes how did you know?"

"Linda, yours is not the first family in this parish who have been invaded by the Meichers." He briefly told me of the conversations he had had with the Michers and that they had rejected everything he had to say, even when given written acknowledgment that their information was faulty. He wanted to know if I wanted him to talk to Joe. I said you can try, but I doubt that Joe would even talk with him. He went on to say that it was my duty as Jimmy and Eric's mother to protect them. He would be there to council me whenever I needed him.

I would need some legal advice as soon as possible. I found an attorney who told me that the only way I could protect my children from going to the Kingdom Hall was to ask the courts for full custody. At this point Joe had every right to take the boys to the Kingdom Hall and withdraw them from St. Christopher's School as I did to insist that they go to Mass on Sunday's and stay in school. Without third party intervention the children will be the one's to suffer, if we can't agree to their education and religious training.

"So does that mean I would have to divorce Joe, I asked the attorney?"

"Pretty much, so are you prepared to do that, the attorney asked?"

I told him I would have to think about this a little while longer. And, think about it I did. I prayed about it, I meditated about it, and I went to Mass every morning at six. I read the Bible and Eba and I walked every evening as I explored, in my mind, the possibilities of divorce. I would ask God to give me a sign; after all I did promise to love honor and obey, in good times and bad, in sickness and in health, until death do us part.

I tried my best to see Joe's point of view. I had to ask myself, was I too worldly? Did I only want the pleasures in life that Joe accused me of? Was it wrong of me to want to celebrate Christmas, and New Year's, Forth of July and birthdays? No, I could live without those things though it seemed silly to do so. I couldn't live denying that Jesus was the Son of God, the second person of the Blessed Trinity. I couldn't deny the Holy Spirit as the third person of the Blessed Trinity. I couldn't deny that my soul was immortal. I couldn't deny that there was a hell, or believe in a devotion to the Blessed Virgin Mary. I couldn't deny I was a Catholic, I just couldn't. I wouldn't.

As I asked God for signs that I should divorce Joe, He gave me every one I asked for, six in fact, and each time I talked myself out of believing they were from Him. How could God sanction a divorce, with that part about "let no man put asunder" thing?

Many years later, this event would remind me of a story I heard about a man trapped in a storm. This storm was going to produce a flood that would take his house away. He was sent a rescue team as the water rose but told them to go on that he would pray to God to spare him. A little later when the water had risen to his porch; a boat came by to rescue him and again he turned them away saying, God would spare him. As the water rose to his roof, a helicopter came for him, but again he waived them off saying, God will protect him. The man drowned and went to face God.

He asked Him why did you let me drown, I believed in you. You said you would save me. God said, "I sent you a rescue team, a boat and a helicopter what more could I have done?"

I had just finished asking for the seventh time for a sign from God, when I looked up to the sky and saw the most beautiful rainbow I had ever seen. There was no reason to expect a rainbow at that time for it hadn't been raining. And, wasn't that the ultimate sign of God's covenant with man? I went back to see Fr. Aufterheide and told him that I would have to divorce Joe and gain custody to keep him from taking the children into the Kingdom Hall.

Fr. said, "Then that is what you must do. You know Linda, that only relieves you from man's law, you will still be married by God's law." Yes, I understood that. The last thing on my mind now was marrying anyone else. I was going to have to fight the stigma of being a divorced woman first, a single mom raising two sons and being a breadwinner too! Oh, Linda, what have you done now?

I called Tom Schaffer and asked for a referral for a good divorce attorney. Joe was going to fight me for custody and I was frightened. I didn't see the law as my friend. I saw it as something I couldn't count on being there for me, as it wasn't there for my son, however I knew it would be in my best interest to have as good an attorney as I could afford. I had no money to speak of. What little assets we had were in Joe's name. Joe let me know in no uncertain terms that he believed the law would favor him, as he was and has always been the breadwinner. He pointed out that I had had only "play jobs" and would not be able to support myself, let alone the boys.

I had to admit I had never had to support myself, let alone two children. I wouldn't allow myself to even think about being separated from my boys. What would I do? I began to take stock of the skills I had. Education-wise I had my GED and two years of business management courses at Sinclair Community College. I could run a household and take care of children. *Housekeeper? Day care worker?* I had worked retail for 4 months. Maybe I could go back to Sears? I had worked as a cashier part time in a supermarket too. I had worked as a school crossing guard and a presiding judge at the polls on Election Day. I helped organize the $300,000 parish festival as a co-chairman for five years running and raised money for different charitable projects. My pool job, while a lucrative venture for 4 months out of the year, would not be enough to support a household. I was definitely going to need a miracle or at least a helping hand.

The only person I could turn to was Gramma. Through all that had happened Gramma was always there for me, abeit sometimes with strings attached, and I was there for her. Gramma had been recently diagnosed with cervical cancer at the age of 91. Her prognosis was optimistic after radiation, yet we all knew that the best outlook would be about five years. It was thought that she would come to live with me after the divorce, which would give me a little more stability in the home, having another adult in the house.

Gramma didn't want to go into assisted living. This would be a good alternative. I would make enough money during the summer at Castle Hills as the pool manager to pay for the divorce and I would need to look for a full time job after the pool closed for the season. With Gramma's contribution toward household expenses we could get by until I found suitable employment.

We would work the details out over the summer and that would give Gramma and me sometime to adjust to the plan. I had Joe served with the divorce papers and I truly think he was surprised that I went through with it. He did offer to back off of taking the boys out of St. Chris and into the Kingdom Hall if I would drop the divorce. I asked him, "Joe will you give up this Jehovah Witness crap? Can you refrain from bringing that influence into this home?"

His reply was, "No I can't do that".

Then I said, "I can't live with this intrusion into my life and that of our children either. I refuse to allow you to beat me over the head with Bible verses any longer. Please move out as soon as possible." Joe said he was not leaving, if I wanted out of this marriage, I should leave. So for the next five months or so, we lived under the same roof. I became Ms. Linda, as Joe would refer to me from now on.

I continued to maintain the house as usual: Cooking, cleaning, laundry and such. Joe continued to pay the bills. I moved into Leeann's old room. Soon I would be getting the pool ready for the 1981 season and planning to visit Joey in Lucasville for the first time. Joe and I both agreed not to tell Joey about the divorce on that first visit. We would wait and tell him at a later date, together. Perhaps the only reason Joe agreed not to tell Joey is that he thought I would change my mind. However, I was grateful he saw it as I did. I had told Jimmy and Eric about the divorce on the day Joe was served as they were both home when the processor served the papers.

I had told them that sometimes grownups find that they can no longer live together and be happy. It is better to live apart so that each one can follow their own paths. I assured them that it was nothing they did or anyone else did, it was something we did, Mommy and Daddy, and we were to blame. We would always be Mommy and Daddy, just not living together. We were going to try not to disrupt their lives much, "I am hoping to stay in this home with you," I said.

Jimmy at twelve years old, tried not to show he was upset, but I could tell by his eyes that he was worried. He was trying to be brave. Eric at ten, didn't seem to quite understand what a divorce meant, he just knew it was not something good. They both wanted to know if they would have to move and could they stay at St. Chris. I said I would do my best to make sure they could stay here in the house and at St. Chris too. They weren't too convinced at this point. I wasn't either but I tried not to show it.

Was I doing the right thing? All they knew at this point was that they were Catholic and went to school at St. Christopher's, if they were going to reject those concepts, let them reject them as adults. I couldn't in good conscience allow them to be subjected to the beliefs of the Jehovah Witnesses.

We were able to visit Joey just a few days before his 19th birthday. The drive down to Lucasville was about two and a half hours. I hadn't been down in Southern Ohio before and while there was plenty of beautiful scenery to see, it also was a look at poverty that I had never seen before either. Perhaps it was just the route we took, but it seemed that people were living in shanties and well-worn homes with not much up keep. Dotted along the roadsides were vendors selling all sorts of trinkets. There were pots and more pots and fireworks. We passed through several small towns that looked as if they were still trying to get into the twentieth century.

We had to make a reservation to visit Joey; name everyone who was to visit and their relationship to the inmate. There were plenty of rules and regulations to follow from what we wore to what we could bring in to eat. We could bring a picnic lunch of homemade food, so I prepared sandwiches and potato salad, chips and dips and Joey's favorite dessert, banana pudding with a meringue topping. We kept everything in coolers until we arrived and then carried everything in boxes from the parking lot. The prison was set out in the open countryside and you could see the manned towers a good mile away with all the barbed wire fences as well. As we got closer you could actually see the guards in those towers with machine guns or rifles on their shoulders. Talk about visiting a nightmare, this was it.

We entered the building, took a number and waited. When our number was called we had to pass through a body scan and were searched with a pat down, the foods were stabbed with special probes to check for contraband and we were then ushered in groups through several locked doors, gates and small buildings, to arrive at a large gymnasium with utility tables and folding chairs.

We selected a table about mid way into this room and waited. There were guards sitting at desks raised about four feet off the floor who checked the inmates into the room and again when they left. They continued to watch the visitors and inmates for any suspicious activity as well. As we watched the door that other inmates were coming through, we waited for that first glimpse of Joey. We hadn't seen him in three months. You couldn't help but look at the others that were visiting their loved ones and wonder what brought them to this place. The warehousing of human beings, what a concept to wrap your head around, let alone think that this was where one of your children was now living, and may have to live the rest of his life.

Joey stopped at the guard's desk, handed him a piece of paper, turned and looked for us. My thrill was just to see him alive. We hugged and just looked at each other for several long seconds. We spent about six hours just talking and eating the picnic lunch. He told us his cellmate was quite notorious. His name was William (Billy) Murphy, and frankly he was scared.

When "they" said that Lucasville held the worst of the worst, they were right. It is still hard to believe that my son was now considered one of the worst of the worst. Joey may have been convicted of aggravated murder and felonious assault but those were pretty big charges for a seventeen year old. Did Joey really belong in the same category with these men? Some said yes, but I will never agree. Others agreed with me; but were not able to do anything about it, as the law had spoken, and Judge Kessler made that decision. He could have sent Joey to Chillicothe but didn't. I believe he did this for political reasons. Too bad because he passed away just a year or so later; so that political decision didn't help him much.

Joey's cellie, Billy Murphy, had been convicted of multiple charges including murder, and was not expected to ever get out of prison. He didn't either, years later Billy would be killed by several other inmates with homemade shivs. In fact it wasn't but a few months after that first visit that Joey found himself thrown in the "hole" because knives were found in the light fixtures of the cell he shared with Billy. Since they couldn't prove whose knives they were, Joey got to share the blame, as well as Billy.

Joey also told us about a man called "Redbone." His given name was Rodger Hall. He told us that this man was particularly responsible for teaching him the inmate rules of conduct to help keep him out of trouble with other inmates. Redbone had another nickname, it was the "godfather." It seems that the guards gave him that one. We would learn more about both of these men as time went on.

Those first visiting hours flew by as Joey finished up the last of the banana pudding. This was probably the longest time that Jimmy and Eric had ever spent with their brother in the last five years. They seemed to enjoy the visit as best as a 10 and 12 year old could. I wanted to know more about the medications and what kind of medical treatment was being offered, but Joey didn't want to talk about it.

Most likely, it was because there weren't any treatments going on as we had thought. When it was time to go, it was so hard to say goodbye. We would not be back for a visit for a couple of months. Joey had asked for a TV and we said we would send the money for him to buy one. The TV had to be bought from a certain place and could be only 13 inches with headphones. As agreed, we said nothing to Joey about the divorce and I was grateful to have not spoiled that visit with that news.

As we left the building I was keenly aware that my son was in a prison. When we began to walk on the wrong side of the courtyard the guards in the towers pointed their guns in our direction and told us, and a few others, that we were walking on the wrong side and to please reverse our path. Jimmy and Eric asked, "What's the difference between this side and that side, they both end up at the same place?"

We said, "They have the guns, that's why."

If someone were to ask me what was the most emotionally painful experience in my life up to this point, one might expect me to say the events in the life of Joey, but that would be wrong. I was a spectator to Joey's life, and now a supporting player. My decision to divorce Joe was by far the most painful. I had spent more of my life with him than any other person on this earth. It was my core beliefs that were in danger of being shattered and lost. I felt forced to make decisions that I really didn't want to make.

My hopes and dreams were never going to come true, pushing my comfort zone aside I prayed I was doing the right thing. I had to let my Mother go, Granny and Grampa, Inez, and now my husband. Only this time I had lost my husband to a god I couldn't believe in. What if it had been another woman; could I have dealt with that issue any better; would I have put up a different fight? With death there is a finality but not so with divorce.

CHAPTER 20

One Day
At A Time

With no concrete plan in place; except that I would no longer be a married woman, I began each day with a prayer and the song in my head. *"One Day at a Time Sweet Jesus, that's all I'm asking of You."* I began to rely on my neighbor and good friend Marilyn for emotional support and friendship. Marilyn's marriage was also on the rocks (had been for years) for very different reasons, and we comforted each other. Marilyn had always worked and so was a little better equipped to take on the role of head of a household. Nonetheless, it would be a great adjustment for her as well, when and if she finally decided to leave her husband. We both started out married in our early teens to "men" much older than we were.

If only we had known then, what we know now; this being an over-used phrase, but ever so true. Would we have still married that young? I think not. Youth sometimes pays a high price for naivety and lack of wisdom.

I had asked the court to allow me to stay in the marital home until the children were out of school, emancipated or with mutual agreement to vacate. At that time the house would be sold and the proceeds divided. I had asked for the auto that I drove, the insurance policies to remain the same for the children, and child support. I wanted no alimony, however my attorney suggested that I ask for at least a dollar per year. This would be in case I would ever need financial help; without something granted at the time of the divorce, I could never go back and ask for financial help in the future, should the need arise.

I asked for sole custody with visitation privileges set up for Joe; so long as Joe, did not force the children to take part in Bible studies, or take them to the Kingdom Hall. I hated to accuse Joe of the charges of gross neglect of duty, and extreme cruelty, but those were the only choices I had, to make my case for full custody. Joe, of course, fought all of these requests, including the custody of Jimmy and Eric. Our attorneys would wrangle these issues out over the summer of 1981. I would remain a basket case every time we heard from Joe's attorney; afraid I would lose my kids, my home, and any stability that I had left. I threw myself into the opening operations of Castle Hills swimming pool for the 1981 season, and the fear subsided.

I wondered how and when to tell Joey that I was planning to divorce his Dad. Joe had reneged on us telling Joe together, so in June, I wrote and told Joey of the plan to divorce his father. I was unsure how he would take it, but I tried to assure him, that is was not his fault. Joey, responded by sending a letter to me, but he mailed the letter to Marilyn, the next door neighbor.

Loving Mother,

I received your letter today and to say the least it brought tears to my eyes!! I don't really know what to say. I'm at a loss for words at the moment. It hurts me deeply that you will be getting a divorce, but if it is what must happen to make your life livable, and allow you to gain some peace, than I will learn to accept that fact somehow. I do want you to know I cannot accept the doctrine of the Jehovah Wittiness in my life either, and I am glad to hear Jim-n-Eric will not be either. This is not to say I hate or dislike Leeann or Dad, I love them and always will, and I will respect their religion as I would expect them to do in anyone else's preference, but I will never be in favor of them trying to force it on others, and making them unhappy in doing so. I can only hope they see what it is they are caught up in. I pray for them every night! I am very worried about you, and the boys, and Lee and dad, it's hard for me to conceive you all living in different spots. I can't tell you in words the fear and pain I feel at this time! In your letter I had no idea what you were going through. I mean I knew things were not good, but my God you were living a nightmare. I hope you are not at this time. I'm so sorry for telling you so many of my problems, and looking for comfort, when you were the one who needed it most. I'm truly sorry! I don't know how all of this will turn out but I hope and pray with all my heart, all involved will be happy, given a little time to adjust. I for one know how scary it is to be thrust in to a whole different life style, but as you told me, hold on and hang in there, you will make it. I do agree you must deal with things as they are, and not play mind games with yourself. I too, believe you are a much stronger person. I was saying playing mind games with yourself can be a bad thing to do, for it avoids the truth, and gives it time to get worse. I know for I still play them at times, but I to am trying to deal with reality as it is, and not like I wish it was. I never thought Leeann would ever get herself in a spot like she was! But I am glad it turned out OK! I hope she wasn't hurt to badly over it. I also don't think she hates you. I don't think she could ever do that, in the true sense of the word! It's so hard for me to believe she is really caught up in religion like that. I mean after her up bringing at St. Christopher's and all, and then to try and stop the kid's from going! At times I find myself getting a little angry at them, but I know it's not good for them, or me. But as I said, I will not take sides in this. I love my family too much to ever choose one over the other. And I want to have a good relationship with each one of you. And I'm afraid this is going to affect that in some way. I truly hope not. And that is why I sent this letter to Marilyn's, so I would be sure you are the one who gets it, for this letter is only meant for you! I don't look at it as being sneaky, but just avoiding putting my views open to those who may not agree, and by that, avoiding any problems or bad feelings towards me. And I want you to know you have never lost me as your son. I will always be with you in my thoughts and prayers. I just wish I could help you more in the ruff times that are sure to come in getting resettled! If I am not rushing things in asking, where will you be going, where will dad be going, what about the kids, will you sell the house? I hope you will not sell the house. I love that house a lot, but if you do, I guess it's OK. What I'm asking is just what is going to happen and when. How are Jim-n-Eric taking it, do they know what is going on or what are their feelings. I really worry about them a lot. My thoughts are all mixed up right now. But I do know I love you ever so much and I only hope you will be happy, however things go. I do feel closer to you in these last years or so, then I have in a long time. I am glad you are being yourself and happy with it. I hope and pray I will be out in the world one day, and we will be able to share some good times together, but at times I feel lost in the wind forever and doubt if I will ever be out again, but all I can do is pray that I will be! I'm still doing half way decent. I'm in need of nothing at this time. Well I guess I will close for now as I said, I don't want to say to much till I sort things out and accept them! But I do love you and dad and everyone and that will never change no matter what happens. I'm just hoping for the best and I hope this letter finds you in good spirits and all going as well as it can be. Just remember, I support you and love you and always will. Take care of yourself and I will write soon bye bye for now!

Your Forever Loving Son
Joe

p.s. this is only meant for your eyes
p.s.s. I had some other poems, but I'll send this one, it meets the moment. Hope you like it

CHANGE'S

As my life burned away
before me
It broke my heart to look
and see.
As cold as reality is to me it's
the way it must be.
Please O' Lord not another
catastrophe.
--------------#----------------

For as a tree will never
stay the same.
It must continue to grow
with no one to blame.
As life's mysterious way's
we can never tame.
Sometimes I feel the laws
of nature are a shame.
--------------#----------------
But I will learn to be myself
in every way.
And to full fill my heart's desires
everyday.
Can I live another way, yes
I surely may.
Only to hope the good time's
are here to stay!
By Joseph Hutchison

**

Joey seemed to grasp what had happened and what was happening. I could tell though that he was putting on a brave face. How could he not be hurting? I let him know that I would always be there, in every way I could. I believed that his father would as well. In another letter he told me that he was studying for the G.E.D. He hoped to be able to further his education too. I wrote and asked him not to worry, that I was sure that we would all be all right in time. Just as he was taking one day at a time, so would we. The only thing for sure, I said, for any of us was change. Change for the good, change for the better, change was the best that it could be. I don't know if I wrote those words to keep Joey's spirits up or mine. I needed all the pep talks I could get, even if I had to give them myself.

Summer was hectic, seemed surreal, yet normal. Joe did not offer to move out and was still trying to get me to change my mind about the divorce. I was taking nothing for granted and tried to believe and live as though I no longer were married to him. I planned the day around Joe not being there. If he were at the house I always asked if he wanted to eat with us. It was all quite civilized, but I really wanted him gone as I needed to see if I could handle being a single mom.

On the other front of legal woes, Joey's, attorneys had begun the appeals process and kept Joey, in the loop, but they didn't feel it was necessary to tell us anything. We did know that Joey, had asked for, and was sent his trial transcripts. The same transcripts I am using to tell this story, 30 years later. Joey wanted to have input with the appeals process and we could certainly understand that, so we paid for them to be sent to him. Joe and I were in no position to have any influence on these matters. Joey was now 19 and by law an adult, and indigent. Joe and I were in no position to hire attorneys to assist him; we had to settle as interested bystanders. We were told, however, not to expect to hear anything until the first of the year.

With the start of August the most hectic part of the season at Castle Hills Swimming Pool, was winding down. Swimming, and diving championships, and invitationals were behind us. The "Water Show" would be held in a couple of weeks. In a couple of weeks, if Joe would not agree to the terms of the divorce, we would have to go to court and let a judge determine the outcome. I was terrified to have the fate of my family in the hands of a stranger.

I went to see Fr. Aufdehide, to ask for prayers, and for words of comfort, to get me through this last leg of my legal journey. Most of the pain had subsided and only a great sadness remained, and a lot of fear. Fr. Aufderhide gave me reassurance and a small bottle of holy water. He told me to go home and bless every room in my home and demand that peace be restored. He also told me to sprinkle the chair that Jerry Micher had sat in, and added that he wouldn't be surprised if it smoked!

As figuratively as this was, I did do as he suggested. The chair didn't smoke, but three days later, Joe emerged from his bedroom and said," Linda, you can have anything that you want, I will not fight you any longer, I will be gone by the end of the week."

It hit me like a ton of bricks. It would be years before I would be able to mark a box "divorced" or answer any questions about my marital status without feeling the stigma. I still prefer to mark "single." and use the prefix of Ms. to address myself.

On August 21, 1981 my marriage was dissolved by man's law. I was now on my own; after 23 years 238 days of marriage, or 25 years, if you count the time Joe and I spent together before we married. I was 38 years old and for the first time in my life, totally responsible for my life, but also for my two youngest sons.

Things were now moving along pretty fast and I still didn't have a clue of how I was going to provide for my family. Rusty Tomlinson, my supervisor with the Vandalia Parks and Recreation of Vandalia, Ohio, came to my office in late August. Rusty, asked me what my plans were for next season. I told him that at this time I had no idea if I would be available to resume the position of pool manager. I would let him know in plenty of time, if he needed to replace me for the next season.

Rusty said, "I will hate to lose you, you have been one of the most successful pool managers I have ever had. I have something you may be interested in. I need a part time person to help with the every day cleaning of the city offices, and the clubhouse. It's 30 hours a week minimum, and it will pay about $9.00 an hour. Unfortunately it won't have any benefits, but the job is yours if you want it?"

"What will I have to do?" I asked.

"You would come in about 10 to 11 pm Monday through Friday and clean the city offices, mine included, empty trash, and clean the bathrooms. Then you will drive over to the clubhouse; clean the restaurant dining room, mop the kitchen floor, clean the bathrooms and the foyer. That should take you to about 5 a.m. In addition you would still be able to referee volleyball two nights per week as well. So, what do you think?"

I did a quick calculation and realized I would make about $300.00 a week with both jobs and in lieu of any other offers. "Yes, I will do it," I said.

With this decision I would be able to resume the pool manager's position for at least one more year; a job I so loved, and looked at it as fun rather than work. It would work out well with my family. I would work while they slept and sleep while they were in school. Gramma, would have the house to herself during the day as well, and if she needed me I would be close by in a flash.

With the closing of the pool for the season; the boys back in school, Gramma moved in, and my glamorous janitor job, my new life began. It was my decision to put Gramma in the master bedroom as it had the most space. I had offered Joe, his king size bed, but I kept the dresser, chest of drawers, and night stands. Gramma, gave away her old bedroom suite to Leeann, and bought a new double bed, that gave the room even more space. We added her console TV, a radio, her comfortable occasional chair and ottoman. It was perfect for her and not a great change from what she was used to. She would have the full bath off the family room as hers as well. I filled in the missing furniture from the living room and dining room that Joe took with him, with Gramma's remaining pieces and the house looked whole again.

I must say that the boys took all this change in stride. We talked about some of the house rules that would be in place. Living with an elderly person would be somewhat of a sacrifice at times, but I would try and make it as easy on them as possible. Obviously, real loud noises would have to be limited. I said, "When I am not at home you will have to let Gramma know where you are going and when you will be back. If she needs anything you will have to step up to the plate and do what she asks." They did, and I was so proud of them.

I believe it was a little harder on me. I went to my new job each night and cried. I wasn't even sure why I was crying. Perhaps it was the realization that my life had been reduced to being a janitor. Not that there was anything wrong with being a janitor, but it wasn't something that I had aspired to. Maybe it was just what I needed though. I could wail out here in the boonies, and lament over my lot in life, and no one would know. No one would be able to tell me I told you so, or give me the "be careful of what you ask for as you just might get it" lecture. I had to believe that this too would pass. Maybe I needed this to teach me humility? I did learn to have a great respect for those who are the primary breadwinners, as this was not easy. However, most breadwinners of the male persuasion may not also have to manage a home, and children.

My nightly pity parties continued but only I knew about them. A routine was beginning to take hold, so long as I could get by with broken sleep. I still tried to get to my son's football practices and games, help with homework and shuttle them about. I spent time with Gramma

Our New Family Portrait Gramma, James, Eric and Me 1982

as she needed company too. There was little to no time left for me, and frankly I didn't want any.

Believing that all the worst was behind me; on a beautiful fall afternoon, attending one of the boys football games, I noticed that a young girl was walking across the field at halftime, she looked an awful lot like Leeann. Leeann, and I hadn't spoken or seen each other in months. This girl was obviously pregnant and indeed it was Leeann. My heart almost stood still, I couldn't breath and I thought, *Oh, my God what now!* She joined her father a few feet away from me and it was all I could do to not fall apart in plain view of everyone.

What a cruel way I thought, to announce that it appeared I was to be a grandmother. She looked well and radiant and I was beside myself. I went over to her and said," It looks as though you are expecting a baby?'

She replied, "Yes, I am."

"You couldn't have told me in some other way?" I looked at her father and said, "You knew this and didn't tell me either? How could you both do this to me in this manner, shame on you both." I returned to where I had been watching the game without any of my questions answered. I prayed that I would not embarrass Jimmy and Eric by making a scene. What in God's name was she thinking? Was she married? Who was the father? It had to be that Jehovah Wittiness boy, I thought.

I told Gramma when I got home and it made her extremely sad. Leeann had been her pride and joy from the day she was born. This news did not bring Leeann and me any closer in closing the riff in our relationship, that's for sure.

As it got closer to Christmas, I was concerned as to how I would provide a decent Christmas for the boys. Money was extremely tight and I was looking for work in the want ads daily. I just couldn't see myself staying in the janitor job. I was chasing every ad that said," No experience needed" and "You can make $50,000 a year. We train," and all of these ads were bogus.

I was so distraught after coming from an interview in downtown Dayton for a sales position that turned out to be another ruse to get me to spend money for a headhunter. I had spent my last tank of gas to go to the interview and was worried I wouldn't make it to my next paycheck. With tears streaming down my cheeks, which matched the rain streaking down the windshield, I devised a plan. I would stop at the library and get a book on how to write a resume, and with the two dollars left in my pocketbook I would spend one of them on a lottery ticket and pray.

I was preparing dinner that night and the nightly news was on. Peering through the bar area into the family room I could see the TV and cook at the same time. I had put the lottery ticket out of my mind for the moment, when the newscaster announced the winning numbers for pick three. *"And tonight's winning numbers are, 7-3-7,"* and they flashed the numbers in large easy to see numerals across the screen. I had just won $500. It didn't get me a new job, but it did get us a Christmas, with all the *"pagan pageantry."* So far, God had not let me down. He had provided me a roof over my head, clothes on my back, food in my belly, and a means to continue to raise my children. Yes, it was not exactly what I wanted, but it was all that I needed. I was thankful.

On January 25, 1982, I received a call from Joe telling me that Leeann was in the hospital and about to give birth. He thought I would want to know. I got to the hospital in time to see my first grandchild being cleaned up in the nursery. She was all arms and legs with a mountain of black hair, and beautiful. If I hadn't been aware of it before, it was now clear that this baby was black.

The joy of this new life was tempered by the thoughts of Leeann having to raise a biracial child alone. My experience with raising Jimmy was different. Jimmy, was not my *illegitimate* biracial child, he was my biracial *adopted* child. At this time, children born out of wedlock were not being viewed in a good light and those of mixed races even more so.

We were trying to bridge the gap that had grown between us. I have to admit it was not easy for me. I was still hurting from the betrayal I had felt from Leeann. I also was having a hard time understanding why she would choose to become intimate with the father of this baby, not because he was black, but because he was not a very good person, in my opinion. He had several other babies born out of wedlock.

Leeann, never told me the reasons she was involved with this man. He was just not going to be in the picture now or in the future. Recently, I asked her again about this relationship and she said, "This is something I will take to my grave. Let's just say it was not consensual." I hope she changes her mind. It is my belief that someday she will have to come to terms with this. Perhaps, someday before I am in my grave she will tell me.

I asked Leeann if there was anything I could do to help her, and the baby. I offered for her and the baby to come home with me for a few days. I truly don't remember this, later she jogged my memory with pictures of her and Brittney JeNai, at home, so it must have taken place. She also tells me that after she had worked so hard to pump some breast milk one day, she had sat the pouch on the counter, and before she could fasten the tie, the milk spilled. She told me she had burst into tears, and I said, "Leeann, there's no point in crying over spilled milk." We shared our first laugh in a long time. Leeann made a fine mother; she had had plenty of experience with the foster babies, and now she had one of her own.

Somehow it turned into spring and I was looking forward to returning to Cassel Hills for the 1982 season. Looking forward to that made everyday I had to clean the city buildings and the clubhouse tolerable. Jimmy and Eric had had a good school year and they too were looking forward to the summer break. Joey was holding on, and was just coming out of a very bad few months. The appeals were not going well. I still couldn't find out if he was getting any treatment for his mental state. He would write and talk of suicide, and I would call the prison, and ask to talk to the chaplain, and ask him for help. Joey would write back and ask me not to do that, as they would want to lock him up in the psycho ward, and he didn't want that. I would write him back and ask him what he wanted me to do with the kind of information he was writing, wait until they called me to tell me he was dead?

This would happen once or twice a year for almost every year he spent in prison. There were only a couple of years that seemed to be relatively calm, with no threats of bodily harm to himself, no deep black morose thoughts.

I was on a health kick and had lost a ton of weight, when someone asked me if I was now ready to start dating again. Since I had never ever dated in the first place, I wouldn't have known where to begin, even if I had wanted to. I couldn't have imagined telling someone I had never met before about my life.

Picture this: *Hey Mom and Dad, family and friends, I just met the most wonderful woman. She's divorced, her husband freaked out with the Jehovah Witnesses, her daughter just had a illegitimate biracial baby girl, she is raising an adopted black son, she is taking care of her 93 year old terminally ill grandmother, she is a janitor, and oh, by the way did I mention, she has another son in prison for aggravated murder, but she sure is just what I have been looking for.*

The summer of 1982 was moving along pretty quick as the summers always seem to do, when you are having fun. Fr. Aufderhide, had told me he was retiring and that he had filled in the new pastor, Fr. Robert Monnin, on my situation. "Linda, you will get to meet Fr. Bob, in a few weeks and I know you will like him," Father said. "You can rely on his guidance in your spiritual matters, as well as friendship. I am pleased he will be taking over for me here at St. Christopher's."

I wanted my life back, the one I had planned. I wanted my husband that I could once relate too, to be there for me. I wanted my daughter, who would have been better educated than me, to have made good decisions, perhaps marry a good man someday and have lots of babies, if that was what she wanted. I wanted my son Joey, to be well, happy and strong, not in prison. I wanted my home on Vista Avenue, to be happy with Jimmy and Eric meeting all of their milestones. I wanted things to progress within my home on a normal path to retirement, grandparents, and old age, as I had envisioned life to be. But life wasn't going to be like that, was it?

I met Fr. Bob during the annual festival, held each year at St. Chris. We sat and talked over dinner in the cafeteria. He acknowledged he knew of my challenges and wanted to know how he could help me. I told him that my most dire need was a full time job. He said, "I am going to need a housekeeper for a few hours a day. It wouldn't pay much, but it would have benefits."

I said, "Can I think about it for a day or two?"

Fr. said, "Sure take as long as you like, I won't need anyone for a couple of weeks yet."

It did sound like something I could do. But the pay wouldn't be enough to live on. I would have to keep the city job too. OK, here is how this could work, I thought. When the pool closed for the season, I would work for Fr. Monnin from 11 am to 2 pm, Monday through Friday. I would prepare a noon meal with enough leftovers for a supper. Do the laundry and clean the rectory. I would go home, and catch a nap until about 4 o'clock, make supper for the boys and Gramma, clean up and handle homework or the kids after school activities. I would catch some sleep until about 10 pm, go to the city job, come home about 5 am, make breakfast for everyone, get the boys off to school, then sleep to about 10 am. OK, that might work.

And work it did. Oh, I forgot to mention that I still refereed volleyball two nights a week as well. My weekends were such a treat. I would manage to sleep for about 6 hours straight if I were lucky. That was my schedule for the next year. Why was I willing and able to do that, I can't answer that question, I just did it. I didn't have much of a choice.

Joe and I had stopped going to visit Joey together for the most part. One, because it was just time to sever our ties, as it was becoming uncomfortable, and two, because Joey could look forward to more visits this way. The 1983 summer season was upon us and life would become much easier for at least three solid months. I had found a replacement for me at the rectory when I left to manage the pool. Marilyn, finally divorced her husband, and returned to school to become a nurse. She would be in need of extra income for the summer months, and it worked out wonderfully for all of us.

Fr. Bob called me during the summer and asked me if I would consider managing the school cafeteria at St. Christopher's for the up coming school year. The previous manager was retiring and he needed someone he could count on. He thought I could handle the job even though I had no experience cooking for 300 children. He said, "Linda, you can cook, I know that, you are an excellent manager of time and people, how hard could it be? You could manage the cafeteria in the morning, serve lunch, and instead of working in the rectory from 11 am to 2 pm, we could switch you to working at the rectory from 1:30 in the afternoon to supper. I will have dinner at 5 pm and you can be home by 5:30. What do you say?"

"Wow! A real job, a real daytime job! I could get everyone up and fed, and leave with my children when they went to school. Gramma, would have had her breakfast with us, and would be settled in for the day. I could go home and check on her and take her lunch, then return to the rectory to take care of things there. By George, I think I've got it. I have at last found a way to make things work for everyone, including me, this time.

At St. Christopher's With Fr. Bob 1981 to 1986 Housekeeper and Cafeteria Manager

Oh my, who would have thought I would have such a wonderful time managing the school cafeteria. In trying my hand at cooking for the masses, I had found another job that was more fun than work, or was it just a relief to be out of that janitor's position? I tried cooking things from scratch; things that I had never seen served before in St. Christopher's cafeteria, and the kid's just loved it. Of course there were the good old stand by's, like pizza and chicken nuggets, but I would make tuna salad from scratch, deviled eggs, and sweet potato pie. I once held a little contest to see if the kid's could tell me what kind of pie they had had for desert that day. They had to write it down on a piece of paper, and each teacher would tally the answers from the class. Not one got the answer right; most chose pumpkin pie. When I got on the sound system and told them they had just eaten sweet potato pie, such an uproar sounded throughout the building. It was talked about for days.

The children would ask from time to time, "Mrs. Hutchison, do you have any more surprises for us today?"

I would answer, "You never know, stick around, I may surprise you again, maybe tomorrow." All the cakes, pies and cookies were made with recipes I used every day as a homemaker. I just increased the ingredients. I did use canned vegetables and a few things that were prepared, but most of the time it was from scratch. I would always try to have a surprise or two every month. I really liked to build on the holidays. Once on President's Day, I served cupcakes with little stove top hats as decorations or on St. Patrick's Day I would serve lime Jello with 4-leaf clovers as decorations. At Christmastime I served Shepherd's pie. Cooking and entertaining has always interested me.

Gramma took a turn with her illness. The cancer had broken through to the bowel and she would need a colostomy to survive. The surgery was successful and she returned home in relatively good spirits and comfort. The hospital personnel taught me how to clean and change her appliance. While it was no picnic for me, it was much worse for Gramma. She was so humbled to have me take care of her in this way. I reminded her of all the times she took care of me; especially when I had all those horrible gallbladder attacks, it was the least I could do for her. It taught me empathy and gratefulness. It must take a lot of courage to have to live with a colostomy, but at least she was still with us for a little while longer.

We got through the school year and into the 1984 pool season. Marilyn returned to take care of Fr. Bob at the rectory for the summer, and I was off to the pool. Gramma, was losing ground and beginning to fall; she would not be able to get herself back up. Sometimes she would have to lay for hours before help came. As sad as this was, it was also unsafe. She and I both realized she needed round the clock care. Again, it came down to money. If there were money to hire in-home nursing care, Gramma could have stayed with us. But it was not to be.

We found a wonderful nursing home; Mary Scott's, clean and comfortable, and moved Gramma in before school began in the fall. She was comfortable; she had her own occasional chair and ottoman, telephone, TV, and the security of knowing help was there at all times. Was she happy, probably not, but we talked daily, and I visited a couple of times a week.

The atmosphere in my home totally changed again with Gramma living at Mary Scott's. A large empty feeling was present for many weeks. It was just the three of us, Jimmy, Eric and me. A big part of my safety line was gone when Gramma left. Not only a monetary one, but her presence as well. I truly was on my own.

CHAPTER 21

Who Knew
What Lay Ahead

In the year's leading up to Gramma leaving for Mary Scott's, there had been many life-changing decisions, with more to come. The fall of 1984 found me still at St. Christopher's as a parish housekeeper; cafeteria manager, and refereeing volleyball two nights per week. But every time I turned around there seemed to be a change. Without Gramma contributing to the household expenses, money was very tight.

Jimmy was a sophomore in high school at Vandalia Butler and Eric was in the eight grade, his last year at St. Christopher's. Eric was so hoping to be able to go to Chaminade Julienne, the Catholic high school located in Dayton, Ohio, the following year as a freshman. That would mean tuition, something I knew I couldn't afford. Jimmy had chosen to stay through high school in Vandalia, so tuition was not an issue for him, but high school was still expensive. There were athletic fees, lab fees, class rings, social expenses, proms, and possible drivers permits, with huge insurance fees to come.

Eric, would need to earn scholarship money if he were to go to Chaminade Julienne. I knew his dad wouldn't be of any help, he would not be willing to help pay to send Eric to a Catholic high school. Both boys were doing exceptionally well, and I couldn't be happier with their progress. I didn't want to deny them opportunities, if I could help it. I was going to need more income, and soon.

Leeann settled into an apartment with baby daughter Brittney, and shortly afterward she was keeping company with a new young man. I assumed she met him at her job with the city of Dayton Parks and Recreation. His name was Mark, and he was an ex Marine. He had a high school education and was also an African American. Mark's, father was an assistant high school principal, his mother was some kind of a lab technician, and he had several siblings. Apparently he cared for Leeann and Brittney, and she cared for him.

Mark, had moved in with her and Brittney, and they began planning a life together. We talked very little about her living arrangements with this man or her affiliation with her father and the Jehovah Witnesses. It was her life now, she was well over 21, and I was not about to interfere. I was still harboring a lot of hurt that I couldn't let go of. Then I got word that Leeann was expecting another baby.

Breeann JeVon was born in September of 1983, and along with her half sister Brittney, these two girls were beauties. Bi-racial babies are most always beautiful babies. They seem to have that bronze glow instead of the sometimes ruddy complexions fair skin babies have. She and Mark seemed to be happy new parents of two baby girls. Still there were no marriage plans.

In 1984, the year Gramma went to live at Mary Scott's, Leeann and Mark took their two little girls and moved to Denver, Colorado. Mark had found a job there, and Leeann, had written to say that Colorado offered a bit more tolerance of mixed race couples than did Dayton, Ohio. They thought there would be better opportunities for them as a family out there, so they planned to stay permanently. I so wanted her happiness, but felt something was not quite right. With her so far away I could only hope and pray she would be all right.

Early Visits with Joey in Prison About 1982 to 1985

These years also passed for Joey too. We found that the appeals for getting Joey's conviction overturned were not going to happen. Tom Schaffer, Joey's attorney told us he had taken the appeals as far as he could with no success. It was a major disappointment for us, and almost devastating for Joey. What happened to possibly taking five to eight years to get this settled? Did Tom, give up too quickly or was it a lost cause from the beginning? We did all we knew how to do to help him, but the right kind of help was never there. The "system" surely hadn't helped Joey or us. I became a little jaded in thinking that the "system" could ever be trusted. It may have helped others, but for whatever reason, it was not helping us.

To add insult to injustice, everyone else that had been involved with the Kaiser's case, including the boy that actually struck Mrs. Kaiser, was now free. Free to move on with their lives. I think we knew we would never be free, ever.

We didn't have the answers we needed then or now. We all tried to keep Joey's spirits up. He had almost five years completed, and there was still a chance he could be paroled on shock probation in seven more years. Well, he could, couldn't he? That was the law, wasn't it? We later learned, no one really gets shock probation for aggravated murder. Thank God, we didn't know that then. We still wanted to believe in fairy tales; we still wanted to believe that there was still some hope, some justice for the mistakes that were made to Joey by the system.

In late January of 1985, we were told Gramma would have, at best a few weeks, if that to live. We began an around the clock vigil at Gramma's bedside as she slipped into a coma.

Gramma, had the last rights given to her many times during the last few years, however we thought it couldn't hurt to have Father Monnin, come and administer them again. When Father arrived, I asked him if he would tell her that it was alright for her to go on home, that he would look after me from now on, and he did. He began the ritual; and half way through the prayers, she sprang up on the bed, opened her eyes, looked as if she had seen God only knows what, frightening all of us. It was such a surreal act. She lay back down; rested comfortable for the first time in days, and as I held her in my arms, she breathed her last breath on February 4, 1985. That was it. She was gone. My last rock was gone.

We had Gramma's services at St. Christopher's. As her casket was brought to the church steps; there stood Father Bob, and Father Dave, the assistant pastor, and on either side of them were Jimmy and Eric, in their acolyte robes. They were waiting to escort Gramma on her last visit to God's house here on earth. My heart nearly exploded with pride and blessings at this sight. What little family and friends left to mourn this strong, and in many ways a wonderful woman, were all filled with peace, love and a celebration of life.

The weather had given us a break from a heavy snowfall the past couple of days, and we were able to caravan to Calvary Cemetery. However, when we arrived at the cemetery we found that we would have to leave Gramma at the chapel, as the snow blocked the roads to the burial site. As we left the chapel, I sang to her one last time. *"Goodbye old girl, my old girl, goodbye,"* and with that song from West Side Story, I closed another chapter in my life.

Over the next few months I had many long discussions with Father Bob about my future. We talked about what options were available to me. The housekeeping job had no room for growth and the cafeteria job, while I could expect some increase in pay over the coming years, would never be a breadwinner's income either. Together neither of these jobs was going to meet the increasing financial cost of raising my family or preparing me for the rest of my life. I needed to step up my employment opportunities.

As much as Father Bob would not like to see me leave St. Christopher's as an employee, he knew I would have to move on. He said he felt blessed that he got to know me as a person; I felt blessed that I was able to spend these past five years with him as my "boss," and my spiritual adviser. It was definitely what and where I needed to be in my healing process. At no time did Father Bob ever treat me as a servant in his employ, nor did I feel like one. I was family from the very day I stepped foot into the rectory. It was a privilege that I got to see into the life of a truly dedicated priest in the Catholic Church. He was a Shepard to his flock and he was and is a servant to me.

Father Bob thought there would be no problem for Eric to earn a scholarship for school the following year, and told me not to worry about that. We reminisced about all the good times and the fun we had, had. We had ridden motorcycles, gone pontoon boating, water skiing, and Father even took me for a ride in his leased Cessna 172. I had prepared and served spectacular dinners for guests. One dinner that included twenty-five priests, and the Archbishop Daniel Pilarczyk. When I left for the summer to manage the pool, I would not be coming back. I had to try and make it on my own. My children and my future depended on it.

Just how many do-overs does a person get in a lifetime? Answer: As many as you need. Midway through the pool season of 1985, I began to look seriously for that new "job." I was pretty sure it would have to be in sales. I was not cut out for factory work, that much I knew, but my formal education was limited. On a summer day in August, I answered an ad for a sales representative, at a run down little storefront on Main Street in Dayton, Ohio. The sign on the door said, "Modern Marketing" with an arrow pointing upstairs. Was fate calling again?

I interviewed with an extremely charismatic man named, Paul. He told me he was looking for people he could train to be sales reps for his distributorship. If he were lucky he would find a super sales person. He went on to say that most of the people he would be interviewing would not make the cut. If I were to be selected, I would be able to increase my income ten fold over the next year. It was a commission based income; I would know after the training, (which was free and with no investment), whether I wanted and could do the job. The training would be four hours per day, from noon to four o'clock in the afternoon, five days per week.

He went on to say that after two week's of daily training, I would be ready to solo "show and tell" about this fantastic product. My new career would be to perform an in-home demonstration of this product that had to "be seen to be believed." The closing ratio was one out of every three, so for every three demonstrations I would produce a sale.

The commission per sale would increase from $100 a sale and top out at $300 a sale. There would be cash bonuses and other incentive opportunities as well. I could work my own hours, and with just two to three shows per day, five days per week, I would earn between four to five hundred dollars per week. As my demonstration skills improved, I could expect to even out at ten shows per week, with an average income of $900 per week. This was everything I wanted to hear. I signed on and entered into the world of direct sales.

The product did not disappoint me. Paul built the "Rainbow" and its uses, on a day-by-day basis via the training. By the time it was evident this was a water-based vacuum cleaner, I was sold. I believed that I could sell this product, and I became that superstar sales person he was looking for. In the last five years I had made a living as a janitor, a cook, a housekeeper, pool manager, swimming instructor, lifeguard, volleyball referee, teacher, cashier and now I was now going to sell vacuum cleaner's door to door. Was there anything left for me to try?

With my innate networking skills, discipline, and time management talent, I was able to produce an income above anything that I had ever made to date, selling "Rainbows." I built this business around my family, worked when the boys were in school or were properly supervised, kept my home in order and had some spare time for myself. Selling was definitely something I was very good at but would I ever be great at it?

 Soon I was selling one out of every two presentations, and making $300 per sale. I won many contests, including one for $1,000. Another was a long weekend trip to French Lick Indiana. The trip was for two, however Paul, said that I could take Jimmy and Eric as my guests. This was almost too much fun, a mini vacation in the middle of the school year. I never thought this would have been possible.

The French Lick Hotel was a tad Gothic in appearance, and held many secrets from bygone times. Some of the rumored secrets were; that in it's hay day, many of the old time movie stars, like Humphrey Bogart, and notorious gangsters like Al Capone, would vacation here, undercover. Someone said, that the ghost of Al Capone still lingered in the hallways. Of course this fascinated Jimmy and Eric, and I have to admit I felt the fun of it too.

One evening we joined Paul and his wife Pam for dinner. Paul, told the boys to order anything that they wanted from the dinner menu. Jimmy, ordered a jumbo shrimp cocktail, and much to everyone's surprise, Eric ordered escargot. Not only were these items pricy, they were totally not what I expected my boys would even want to try. Paul assured me it was okay, and not only did they both seem to enjoy a taste of the good life, I did too. In the future, I too ordered shrimp cocktail and escargot. This was the beginning of many long weekend jaunts to places I would never have been able to afford, had I not won the trips.

The only thing I did not do well in this business was recruit. As with any multilevel marketing program, recruiting was a big factor in making money. That concept, while I understood it, was hard for me to put into action. I hated to fail and I hated to see others fail. I knew how much effort it took to do what I had learned to do successfully. I was unwilling to talk someone else into trying this as a means to extra income. Why? Because I saw too many others fail. This kind of selling is not for everyone, and Paul agreed.

Except Paul would also tell me it was not up to me to decide who would or who wouldn't master this concept. "Linda, you just need to keep asking," Paul would say. Someone will see the potential and accept the offer. They just may be the next "superstar," and look what that would do for them, and it would not be too shabby for you either."

Jimmy and Eric were doing well in high school as a junior and a freshman. Eric got his scholarship to attend Chaminade Julienne. Both were playing exceptional football; Jimmy was a running back and a corner back, and Eric would play nose guard and lineman. It was thrilling to see them play, and I was a proud parent.

There was one snafu in all this hoop-la; Jimmy was becoming a black man in an all white world in Vandalia, Ohio. As a baby and then a little boy, Jimmy didn't pose a threat to the closet racists, but as he grew into a man there was an underlying rumble about Jimmy hanging out with, and dating white girls. There also seemed to me some pressure on the coaches or from the coaches to curtail Jimmy's time on the football field. Jimmy began to play less and less, yet when he did take the field there was always action; action from the fans, yelling "GO JIMMY GO!" I began to take mental notes. The fans loved him; his fellow players loved him.

Why wasn't he playing more plays? He also received plenty of "press." I had to wonder if there was a problem I was not aware of.

I was holding bed and board together and spreading my wings. In the past few years I ventured into the single adult world when time permitted. Marilyn and I were becoming best of friends as well as neighbors. We would tip toe onto the single scene together, something neither of us had ever done before. We didn't live far from a stretch of adult meeting places located on what was called the "The Dixie Strip." On a Friday or Saturday night if we didn't have anything else to do, we would head out for an evening of music, dancing, and socializing with "grown-ups." This soon became a habit and for a short time it was fun. We both thought maybe we would meet someone that would fill the need for male companionship. From time to time there would be someone that would intrigue one of us, but usually not for more than a couple of drinks and a dance or two.

One night though I did meet a man named Denny, he was different from any of the others. He wanted to know if I would like to learn how to snow ski. Well, that was a thought, here was someone who wanted to do more than hone a pick up line, he actually wanted to take me skiing. Thus began our friendship; I say friendship, as it never progressed from just being skiing buddies. He took me to the local ski resort, to Cananne Valley in West Virginia, where we were snowed in for two extra days and Sugar Loaf in New York. Most of the ski club members from Dayton, Ohio were our companions and we had a blast. We remained friends for the next couple of years, but I really didn't fit into this group of people. Most of them were doctors, lawyers and out of my league, or so I thought. Denny and his friends and I just didn't have anything else in common.

Then I met a man by the name of Kenneth, who pursued my attention. At first I was annoyed. I was not interested in this man with the name of Kenneth, he was too short, too laid back, and I just knew there was something not quite right about him. His pursuit became like a schoolboy quest until he finally got my attention. He began by taking us out for breakfast after the club closed, conning my phone number out of Marilyn, sending me flowers, and just stopping by to say "hello." Marilyn thought he was cute. Maybe I did too.

We hung out most of that summer. I learned he was in town for training out in Troy, Ohio, at the Hobart training center. He was a welder and was learning new skills to be able to work on Nuclear Reactors. He was from Michigan, but would soon be going to New York, to work on the nine-mile island nuclear reactor. We began what I thought was a summer romance. Never having had one before I was taking this slow and easy. We spent many evenings just talking about life, love and the pursuit of happiness. I opened up to him about my past, as I felt that if we were going to go anywhere he would need to know where I had been.

I also pressed him for information about his life. As I had suspected—as when that little inner voice warned me from the beginning—he confirmed he was still legally married. He said he hadn't "really" lied to me about being married, because before he came to Ohio, he and his wife had agreed to divorce. Needless to say this relationship was not going to go any further. I was glad we had not been completely intimate up to this point. As he left to go back to Michigan in mid August, I was sure I would never see him again. It was bittersweet, but I did have a summer romance, something I had never had, and I had enjoyed it. I could only hope that maybe someday there would be another one, a better one.

Two days later, in the mail I got a card that read, " I was just thinking about some of the wonderful things that God created, and you came to mind.... Love Ken."

One week later he was back. I was standing in my office at the pool dripping wet, having just finished teaching a "learn to swim" class, when I turned around, and there he stood. *Why was he back?* He came back through Ohio, on his way to New York, to tell me he was going through with the divorce, and wondered if I'd give him a chance to clear up his life? I told him I had nothing standing in my path at the moment, just be sure the next time you come to see me, have your divorce papers in your hand.

He wanted to know if he could write and call? I told him I would write him and take his calls, but that was it. Then he was off to Oswego, New York. With in two months it was all over. I would never see him again. He would tell me he couldn't leave his wife, as she had threatened suicide, and he didn't want that hanging over his head. He had promised her to try and reconcile. I told him I didn't want him hanging on to me, and I said goodbye.

Marilyn and I both pretty much decided it was time to leave the bar scene. As much fun as it was at first, it was growing old. The same people sitting on the same bar stools made us wonder if that was what we looked like to others, as well. We chalked it up to an experience we both needed to try.

Things were going so well selling "Rainbows" that I thought I could also manage the pool, at least for one more season, and sell "Rainbows" part time. Paul (my distributor at Modern Marketing) thought it was not a good idea, but I was sure I could make both jobs work. Besides Jimmy and Eric, were both glad I would be managing the pool as well, as they liked the fringe benefits.

Jimmy was looking for a summer job, and Leeann thought she could help him get on with the City of Dayton in the Parks and Recreation

Department. Leeann had come back from Colorado, bringing Brittney and Breeann. She had left Mark in Denver, and was trying to get her bearings as a single mom. She was staying with me at the "homestead" and back at her old job with the City of Dayton. It seemed that Mark had some real problems, the worst I think was gambling, which made life very difficult.

On a late April day, Leeann went to pick Jimmy up at school to take him for a job interview. I had made arrangements at the office for Jimmy's early dismissal and Leeann was waiting for him in the school lobby just outside the front office where Jimmy would come to sign out. Leeann, happened to witness the assistant principal giving Jimmy a hard time for being in the hallway during class time. Jimmy was trying to tell him he had an early dismissal, but the assistant principal was not buying Jimmy's explanation.

Apparently he was extremely disrespectful with Jimmy and Leeann stepped in with, "Is there a problem here? I'm his sister and I have come to take him for a job interview."

With that the assistant principal put his arm around Jimmy and said, "Oh, Jimmy and I are 'buds;' he knows I was just playing around." To which Jimmy said, "We are not buds." He then asked him to remove his arm, which he did, and they left for the interview. I was in the principal's office the next day.

This confirmed what I had suspected over the past several months, that Jimmy was having some problems within the school and it's personnel. They tried to sugar coat this incident. It was my hope that this was a one time incident. Jimmy was trying to become a man, and this was not the way I wanted him to perceive authority. He was not a second-class citizen, and I would not have him treated as one. I made myself clear about how a person in authority, especially one that has the obligation to help young people to grow into maturity should behave.

I also made it clear to Jimmy that he was not to push the limits of questioning authority. There are proper channels, and that is the way to go first and always, before taking the issue into your own hands.

By summer, Jimmy had had his senior pictures taken, and both boys were in practice for the up coming football season. I was planning to gear up for the fall selling season of "Rainbows" full time, when Paul handed me a bombshell announcement. He said, "Linda, I spent some time in Houston, Texas this summer, and I was really impressed with the organization of "Rainbow" distributors there. It is far superior to the organization of distributors here in Ohio. I am thinking about moving my business to Texas."

Big changes coming again! Paul went on to say that he would see to it that if I wanted to become a distributor he would do everything he could to help me. I could go to work with another distributor in Ohio or he would take me to Houston as a distributor in training.

Well, I certainly was not moving to Houston, Texas. I was conflicted as to if I wanted to become a distributor; I was not comfortable working as a lone wolf, as the closest distributor was 100 miles away.

Much to my dismay Leeann reconciled with Mark and returned to Denver at the end of the summer. It was my belief that Leeann would have to carry her family on her shoulders and my heart ached for her. She was stubborn and hated failure as much as I did. I had asked her to think really long and hard if this was what she truly wanted, I offered her an out. I thought about my mother when she told me, "Linda if you don't want to be married to this man, I will accept you and the baby, just tell me." My mother had offered me an out but I didn't take it either.

Sometimes fate just has its way with you.

CHAPTER 22

Cowboys
And Indians, Oh My

A s the school year began and the pool was bedded down for the winter, I was back selling "Rainbows" full time. Lurking in the wings was the knowledge that Paul was seriously thinking of moving his business to Houston. Football season was in full swing and again both boys were totally wrapped up in the sport. So was I. There was nothing I liked better than to be at their games, rooting for them and the team.

Toward the end of September I got a call from the principal at Vandalia Butler High School. When I arrived to see him I got the news that Jimmy was about to be suspended for a drug charge. Up to this point I had never been concerned that either of my boys were remotely involved in drugs. I was vigilant about keeping an eye open for any signs, and of course they both knew it would not be tolerated. To say I was caught off guard was an understatement. The High School had a zero tolerance policy and they were going to stick to it. In his senior year in the middle of the football season my son was going to be suspended until the next semester. More than likely he would not graduate with his class in the spring as well. What the hell happened?

The previous Friday night after the away football game, the football team was filling the buses to return to school. When Jimmy got on the bus several of the team members that had not participated in the game were already on the bus and sitting well in the back; They were passing around a joint and one of these boys handed it to Jimmy to pass on and he did. He did not take a hit but he did pass it on. Those boys got in trouble and took Jimmy down with them. Jimmy had not been in any serious trouble before, but they were not giving him any choices. I was heartsick and devastated for Jimmy.

We could have fought it with a lawyer, but to what end? Lawyers were not my friends and the school would have held their ground to the bitter end. If by chance we could have won, his senior year would have been a disaster anyway. He would have missed the remaining football season and would not have graduated anyway. There was not so much as a peep out of the coaching staff as to their disappointment that this had happened to one of their star players. I am convinced that they didn't care. It was an easy way to get rid of the "black boy/man" in their midst. Their silence said it all.

Jimmy acknowledged that he did indeed pass the joint on without smoking it. He admitted he wasn't thinking. He did not smoke, but he had been in other situations where things like this had occurred, and it was not an unusual experience. He had been caught up in talking about and reliving the game they had just played and didn't even give it a thought that he was passing on marijuana. Nevertheless he couldn't take it back. The others were suspended as well, but that was of little consolation. None of those boys were first string players.

I tried to get Jimmy enrolled in another school but that was not going to happen until the next quarter either. Private schools were not an option as there was no money for tuition. I was so concerned that he would just drop out of school; he was so discouraged.

While all of this was going on, Paul decided to move his distributorship to Houston. He again offered me the opportunity to go with him. He would pay the moving expenses for me to relocate. The intention was for me to help him establish the original office, which he would name Hydro Air, and then open a second office under his distributorship. It was an opportunity for me to establish a minority business and to become a business owner. I was all ready self-employed, but now I could actually run a full business that included opening a store front and hiring others.

I would have to sell my house and leave behind everything that meant anything to me. I would have to leave Joey, too. I would leave my St. Christopher family, my sister, my best friend, everything that was so familiar. Would Joe let me take Jimmy and Eric with me? Jimmy was almost of age, but Eric had a bit to go. Since Jimmy was already in limbo it might be a good thing for him, but Eric would have to give up Chaminade his beloved school and all of his closest friends.

This was a major decision and it had to be the right one. Too many things could go wrong. Why did I have to make all of the monumental decisions on my own? Where was that magic wand?

Jimmy said he thought it would be a good change, he was all for it. Eric of course was not so sure; he was a steady even going young man. He didn't make friends easily and he liked predictability. Could I go off and leave him? No, I couldn't. One thing was for sure, I would not leave him behind. He asked if he could live with his best friend, Scott. While I weighed that idea, I was sure his dad wouldn't allow it. I asked him if he wanted to live with his dad? He said no way, as he was sure his dad wouldn't let him stay at Chaminade and I agreed.

Then Eric said, "If this will be good for you Mom, I will go with you."

"Yes, Eric I think it will be," I said. "Can I just finish the semester at Chaminade before I come to Texas," Eric asked?

"Yes, I think we can make that happen," I said.

Joe didn't give me any static over wanting to take the children and move to Texas. He thought it might be the best thing that could happen for Jimmy under the circumstances. It almost blew me away that he didn't make this a difficult decision. Joe even helped get the house on the market and it was sold in three weeks. Eric was going to stay with Scott until Christmas break and then join Jimmy and I in time for Christmas in Houston. This had to be the right choice for all of us, otherwise there would have been obstacles, and there weren't any.

In mid November with a sold sign in the yard, I put our household goods on a Mayflower moving van, along with Paul's, and all our worldly possessions headed for Houston. Eric was staying with the Paxton's, Jimmy was staying with friends, and I flew down to Houston to find a place to live. Father Bob took me to the airport and gave me his blessings. He said he would be there to pick me up the following week and wished me the best of luck in finding a new home.

Paul met me at the airport in Houston and took me to the new house he had bought in Mission Bend. He had placed my things into the garage until I could find a place to live. By this time I had become part of his family. I liked his wife, Pam, and met some of his children. Pam and Paul were empty nesters as their children were all grown. Their new house was beautiful and because of Houston's economy, what would have cost $500,000 in Ohio, this house was only about $200,000 or so. Paul was encouraging me to buy a similar house but I was too afraid to go into debt for that kind of money. I came pretty close to buying a really big house for sale by owner, dirt cheap, but chickened out at the last minute. What did I know about buying property? Nothing. Instead I settled for a rent-to-own.

It was a lovely house, twice as nice as my house in Vandalia. It had palm trees and funny tropical bushes, and trees of every kind surrounding it. It had a dog run for Eba as well. It was a three bedroom, with a living, dinning, kitchen, laundry and family room. There was a loft, two full baths, a gigantic fireplace, patio, and two-car garage. We would be living on Bassford Dr. I would be pretending to be a very successful self-employed single parent of two teenage sons, and scared out of my wits. I felt like I was operating by the seat of my pants or at least in my petticoat. In truth, I was.

Paul and I scouted around for office space in Mission Bend. We were eager to get things started. Paul introduced me to the folks at Meador Enterprises the district distributorship for "Rainbows" in Houston. Curt Meador ran the show. He was a pleasant man, and a Texan through and through. He would call me Linda Girl from that day forward.

I was trying to get the feel for this tropical environment in what I had thought was an open range country. For some reason I had envisioned Texas to be Cowboys and Indians. It was, but with a tropical flavor I was not prepared for. With everything in place; I flew back to Ohio to finalize the closing of the house on Vista Avenue and end another chapter of my life as well.

Paul had left me to close up the office in Dayton. I had bought Paul's old van for Jimmy to drive and purchased a used sedan for me. I had intended to pull the van behind my car to Texas while Jimmy and I would take turns driving the 1200 miles to our new home. That was not going to happen; I just could not get the hang of driving and pulling another car behind me, yet I was terrified to have Jimmy drive by himself. In the end I had no choice. Jimmy and Eba (the dog) would try and follow me down to Houston.

My St. Christopher family gave me a surprise going-a-way party to end all surprise parties. It turned into a roast of sorts. They not only gave me hilarious gifts; one right after another, but the highlight was a gold watch with tiny diamonds surrounding the face. I still wear that watch today. We sat around eating and drinking and telling stories.

One particular funny one was this. On a very rainy and dreary night, Father Bob was to hear

My Surprise Going -a-Way Party at St. Christopher's 1986

confessions. He had left the rectory for the church and said, "Linda if I don't get any penitents tonight, I will come back and have dinner early. You can then go home early if you want."

In about a half hour he returned and said," I left a note on the confessional door to come to the rectory if anyone wanted to go to confession, and I'll have dinner now." As Father was enjoying his supper the doorbell rang. I went to answer it. Standing at the door was Clancy Must a long time parishioner. He was following Father Bob's instructions to come to the rectory via the note Father had left at the church. He took one look at me and said, "So you are now hearing confessions too," Clancy asked with a straight face and then a laugh? Before I could answer, Clancy asked me if I knew how to make "holy" water. With out me answering again, he said," You put it on the stove and boil the hell out of it." Who said Catholic's were dull?

St. Christopher's had been my second home. I was recognized as a permanent fixture having been involved with almost every aspect of parish life, but no, I didn't hear confessions. My family spent over 25 years working, praying and serving the parish and the City of Vandalia as well. I was going to truly miss and be missed by all of these people. Did I make the right decision to voluntarily leave this community and start a new life 1200 miles from everything that rang of security? Too late now to second-guess my motives and decisions; there was no turning back.

Our last night on Vista Avenue, Jimmy and I slept on the floor wrapped in blankets with pillows we hadn't shipped with our other things. I took one last look at every empty room in this house, as it was no longer a home, just a house now and cried. What was once my dream home and family, was no more. I turned the key in the lock; placed the key under the mat for the new owners and said a silent prayer that their life would be happy, for however long they would stay. Mine hadn't ended up so well.

As I drove down Vista Avenue, with Jimmy following me in the baby blue van, I cried again.

We came into Texas on Route 10 and this highway system was magnificent, huge and scary. I had never driven in such traffic before in my life. I learned one thing for sure, no matter where you wanted to go in Houston it would take you anywhere from one to two hours to get there, even if it was just across town. We arrived at Paul and Pam's at dusk. We spent the night as the following day the movers would be taking our belongings from Paul's garage to our new home.

We took the weekend to move in and on Monday morning I hit the road running. I couldn't wait any longer to start making money. I knew it wouldn't take long to deplete my cash reserve from the sale of the house and that was my only financial security at the moment. The new office was up and running and Paul would be interviewing from the newspaper want ads he had placed in the Sunday papers.

My job at the moment was to get out and sell. This is what I did best. Curt Meadors office had sent over some leads to get us started and I quickly set a couple appointments. The very first demonstration produced a sale and with our creative referral program, I was on my way to making a living in the Texas market.

Our first Thanksgiving was spent with Paul and Pam down on Galveston Island at the beach with awesome views of the Gulf of Mexico. We ate roasted Turkey and a few other side dishes and fed the seagulls the leftovers. This sure wasn't a traditional Thanksgiving but it served the purpose. I was thankful. Most holidays would never quite be the same as they once were, but I tried to keep traditions going.

I had Jimmy and Eric enrolled in Aleif High School but Jimmy wouldn't start until Eric did in January. Jimmy was welcome to monitor some classes and get acquainted with his teachers and this would also help when Eric came in. He would be able to help Eric adjust quickly.

As usual it didn't take Jimmy long to make friends, and he was set up and ready to go as if nothing had happened. I felt that we dodged a bullet and that Jimmy would be a high school graduate after all. Jimmy would have to spend another full year as a senior, but that was fine with me. He needed a little more time to grow and mature and I wasn't ready for him to leave the nest.

Aleif High School had over 700 seniors and from every race, religion and ethnic background. It was the first time Jimmy would not be the only black guy on campus. For Jimmy that was a huge awareness and growth experience he needed to relate to his heritage. It helped to know that this was a good decision to take Jimmy to Texas. I just prayed that it would not be at Eric's expense.

1987 began our new life as a family of three transplanted Ohioans to Texas. Eric was a sophomore and Jimmy an almost senior. I was keeping in touch with Joey by letters and he had called at Christmas. He was allowed one telephone call a year and it was so good to hear his voice. We had said our farewells in November and Joey said he understood why I needed to relocate. The only difference in our relationship would be, that I would only get to visit him once a year. We had been going down to Lucasville about every 2 to 3 months, so it wasn't like a total abandonment, but it sometimes felt that way for me. Of course his father would continue to make regular visits. I kept telling myself if this worked out well, maybe Joey could be paroled to Texas and leave all the stigma behind.

People do tend to acclimate to the environment they live in. We certainly were. In Joey's case, he had no choice. His environment was out of his control and he was doing his best. He couldn't choose his cell. He couldn't choose his "cellie." He couldn't choose when and where to take a shower. Losing one's freedom reduces your humanity. You may physically live in a cage built by man, but your spirit and soul live in a cage built by your own mind. How you come through that environment depends on how healthy you can keep your body and mind. How much support you have and how much you will accept. I prayed each day that Joey would make it through to the other side. I kept the porch light on.

For the next five years I realized how very fortunate I was to keep my little family moving in the right direction. Jimmy did graduate from high school with but one minor incident. It was in the spring, right before graduation, I got a call from the Houston police department. They had arrested Jimmy for unlawful transportation in a vehicle and littering. I was told that he and a very large group of teenagers were ripping and roaring up and down Westheimer Ave. in pick up trucks. It was illegal to ride in the back of a pick up truck. When the police pulled them over Jimmy jumped out of the truck and while waiting to be addressed he spat on the cement.

My trek to the police station in the middle of the night was traumatic. I had hoped never to set foot inside a police station again for the rest of my life. I posted his bail and told him that this was his first and last get out of jail card. I think he believed me because I was never called to bail him out of jail again. In fact, he was very contrite, as he knew how painful that was for me.

Eric survived the Houston heat, which he hated, but the separation from his friends was more painful. Eric returned to Ohio for visits and Scott came to Houston once to spend some time in the summer. Eric played football, took honors classes and went on a ski trip with some of his classmates. His grades were outstanding and he was bound for college back in Ohio. He had made no bones

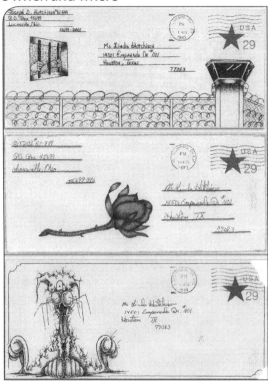

Joey Sent His Art Work in Envelopes and Cards

about going back to Ohio as soon as he graduated. He planned to stay with his dad and enroll at Wright State University.

Joe had remarried and I was happy for him. His second wife was a JW, but not as fanatical as Joe. I was not afraid that Eric could hold his own now and become the man he wanted to be, Catholic or not. I was so happy to have had him with me until he graduated. I could not have asked for more.

Jimmy had decided not to go to college. He put his efforts into learning the body building business by working at a Gold's gym. I had to help Jimmy grow up by giving him options if he were to continue to live under my roof. He did not like my options. My main complaint about the new "grown up" Jimmy was waking up and finding that Jimmy had entertained a young lady for a sleep over. I pointed out to him that I didn't bring home men to share my bed and I would not tolerate him bringing home girls to share his.

He continued to test me. I then took all of his worldly possession placed them in his car and changed the locks. He got the point. He moved into a condo with a few of his friends and shortly afterward became a very self-sufficient young man. He had a rocky few months financially until he got the hang of budgeting his money. I didn't give him money, but I did take him food from time to time. He never asked me for a penny from that day forward. I couldn't be more pleased and proud of the young man that Jimmy became.

Leeann had had two more little girls in these last five years. Brilynn Jennifer and Brooklynn JeMarka joined Brittney JeNai and Breeann JeVon and we called them the "B" sisters, sometimes the Killer Bs. Leeann also finished her education with a BA in Liberal Arts and Sciences with a double major in English (Writing Program) and Communication, and a minor in Psychology, graduating with distinction. Her Master's came in Education: Administration, Supervision and Curriculum Development with an emphasis in Instructional Technology. Eventually she was employed at the University of Colorado, Denver as the Instructional Designer for the College of Nursing, Office of Academic Programs, specializing in online education.

She was, as I suspected, pulling the weight of her family on her shoulders and would continue to do so. I was so proud of her accomplishments, earning her Master's while giving birth and raising four little girls. Yet I never understood why she put up with her husband's behavior. She was so smart and yet so unwilling to see this man was taking her self-esteem and crushing her. I was never privy to the dynamics of her marriage. I only knew enough to know I wouldn't have stayed.

On the day Eric pulled out of the driveway on Bassford Ave. bound for Ohio with all of his worldly possessions. I moved into a townhouse on Empanada Ave. in an apartment complex. I gave Jimmy all of my excess furniture and scaled my life to being a single women, responsible on a day-by-day basis for no one but myself. What a strange feeling this was after raising four children, nine foster babies and a husband mixed in there somewhere. I was truly on my own. An empty nest is exactly what I had and I liked it.

As was the plan when I moved to Texas I did take on a distributorship. I had bought out Paul's distributorship and named it Hydro Air Two. Marilyn thought she might like to try living in Texas and she came down to help me get my office started. She of course would work "Rainbow" part time while working as a nurse full time. This arrangement only lasted six months as she missed her daughter too much and returned home. We would, however, visit one another once or twice a year. Paul went on to work for Curt Meador at Meador Enterprises in an administrative capacity. I was doing all right, but after a couple of years as a distributor, I knew I didn't have what it took to be a major player. To be a major player you needed to be able to recruit and build a successful organization, and try as I might, I could never get beyond 10 to 15 sales associates. As a sales person I was used to winning all of the awards, trips, plaques, and bonus monies that were put up for monthly and quarterly goals. I didn't find it satisfying to just keep the doors open.

There were many great trips with the boys or Leeann or with my sister Nancy or with friends. There was horseback riding in Cancun, deep sea fishing trips, a ball game at the Houston Astrodome, cruises and a trip to the horse races in Louisiana.

I even sang on the stage at the Grand Ole Opera, to no one in particular, while touring Nashville. Once at an award trip for "Rainbow" someone was needed to sing the National Anthem at the opening ceremonies and I volunteered. From that day forward I was the un-official singer of the National Anthem for

Singing the Star Spangle Banner At Rainbow Functions
1987 to 1995

almost every event I attended. To say I had exceptional experiences would be an understatement, I did. I never took them for granted, nor did I ever think I hadn't deserved them. I just felt very blessed that I was able to share them with my loved ones too.

I no longer wanted the stress that came with a distributorship, the long hours and the heavy responsibilities. It was no longer a satisfying way to make a living. I had put in the long and tedious days that I needed and finished raising my family. I realized that I no longer had to do that. There had to be more to life and I wanted a change.

At the same time I didn't want to go back to just selling "Rainbows." I had out grown that job. I knew I was a good right had "man" for a job, any job. But I was not cut out to be the head honcho. It was time to rethink my goals.

As I was tinkering with the idea of laying plans to make changes in my life one more time, the phone rang. It was late on Easter Sunday, April 11, 1993. On the line was Eric and he said very calmly, "Mom, we just heard that the inmates at Lucasville are rioting and we think Joey is involved or at least his cell block is involved."

Very little was known and Eric promised to call back when he knew more.

By Monday, I found out that about 400 of the 700 prisoners in L-block were left inside the L-block buildings. About 300 were outside when the melee started. I didn't know if Joey was one of the one's that got out or if he were trapped inside with the rioters. Was he one of the rioters or one of the inmates caught inside of the building? The prison had a population of about 1,819 and was at 120 percent of capacity. One of the things Joey had written about was the over crowding and it made for a volatile atmosphere. Another was putting men together in cells made for single occupancy. Joey was due to have been transferred to a medium security prison long before the riot broke out. I couldn't help but think if he had been transferred before this riot broke out I would not be in this state of terror, and he would not have been in it.

Headline's from the Dayton Daily News: Monday, April 12, 1993: "5 Die in prison riot"

Late on Monday more information made it through. There were eight hostages accounted for and so far as was known, there were now six prisoners confirmed beaten to death. Names were being withheld.

Tuesday, April 13, 1993 Headline Read: "Siege continues"

On Tuesday April 13, 1993 after reports that there were hundreds of bodies stacked up in the prison gymnasium I was panic-stricken. There didn't seem to be any credible information coming into Texas. I called the Houston Chronicle and a reporter by the name of Stefanie Asin took my call and ran a small article about my inquiry in the News makers/ Nation section of the paper on Tuesday April 13, 1993. Included was an article titled "Talks over hostages go on at Ohio prison."

Not much press was given to the riot that day in Houston Texas.

Headline: "Houston woman yearns for news about inmate son"

A Houston woman is desperate for news about her son, who for 12 years has lived in the L-block of the Southern Ohio correctional Facility in Lucasville, Ohio. Linda Hutchison does not know if her son, Joseph, 32, is injured or even participating in the riot. Her efforts to find out have failed.

"Why can't I find out if my child is OK?" said Hutchison, who received a letter from her son on Saturday, the day before the disturbance began. Evan if he is involved, he's still my child, and I have a right to know if he's all right."

Joseph Hutchison was sentenced to life in prison in 1981 for killing a Dayton, Ohio woman with a croquet mallet during a bungled robbery.

Since his incarceration, he has complained about the conditions in the prison, she said, including unfair treatment of prisoners.

"I understand this is prison, but they are still human beings," she said

His recent letter was suicidal but did not mention any plans to riot, Hutchison said. However, she is not surprised, claiming that the prisoners were "pushed too far."

Hutchison is waiting for word on her son before deciding whether to make the trip to Ohio.

She fears that even if she goes, she won't be allowed near the prison.

Stefanie Asin

Continued Headlines from the Dayton Daily News Read:

Wednesday, April 14, 1993 "Inmate riot toll 7"
Thursday, April 15, 1993 " Food feeds hope"
Friday, April 16, 1993 "Rioters defiant"
Monday, April 19, 1993 "Hostages alive"
The riot continued….

CHAPTER 23

Inhumanity Comes From
Good Mankind and Bad Mankind

L iving in a nightmare is all I can think about when I think about the riot. What these 400 or so men were sharing at this moment in time had to be one of the most frightening experiences; akin to being in a war, and most of them cannot even protect themselves. Waiting for word of my son's safety was not nearly the nightmare of these 400 or so men, but close. Knowing whom to call to find out anything was maddening. It was for sure that traveling to Ohio would not get me any more information. Who were these men who were rioting, and what were they thinking? What was my son thinking? Was Joey a part of this uprising or a victim?

There was news that hundreds of bodies were stacked up in the gymnasium. I could not wrap my head around that vivid mental picture. Surely I would feel it if my son were dead. I didn't feel it. I just had to have more information. I got this letter on Saturday, April 10th, the day before the uprising:

Mother,
Always a special event to get a letter from you. Wish my letters were some-
thing to enjoy or look out for, but I know they're not—I can't!! I don't want
the state to tell you I'm dead and it come as a surprise and as selfish as it is
I <u>need</u> for somebody to know that I've been suffering and in pain for many,
many years. A person can endure only so long under this pressure. I want
them to look at my strength for being able to make it this long and not my
weakness for not making it out of here, does that make any sense to you?
The part of me that keeps fighting for life is tired, and I don't care, it wants to
sleep and rest and is to sick of what it sees when it looks at what's left of me.
Things have been so bad the last three months.

The letter went on to ask me to help him end his life. I can't bring myself to write exactly what he wrote, as I can't read it without crying but
he asked me to smuggle in sleeping pills and hold him until he's gone.
While these letters to me were not uncommon. I wanted to believe it
was his cry for help. This one was different though. This was the first time
he had ever asked me to help him commit suicide.

I planned to call up to the prison on Monday and try to get the
Chaplain to pay him a visit. Try to see if I could get him on sick call to see
a doctor. He needed medication. This wasn't the first time I felt I had to
do something on his behalf.

Did he know that this riot was going down when he wrote this letter
on April 4? Was he trying to tell me he didn't care if he lived through it?
Would he purposely put himself in harm's way?

There was a telephone number given to families of inmates to call.
It led to no concrete information. I finely stumbled onto a number for
the Corrections Inspection Committee. I met (by phone) a woman by
the name of Shirley Pope, who was part of the inspection committee
that organized unannounced visits to the prisons in Ohio. Shirley, the senior researcher for the state Correction Institute Inspection Committee,
was somewhat like a check and balance reporter. It seems that there
was some recourse to prisoners' complaints if filed with this committee. Shirley became my resource for information and I felt she could
be an advocate for my son in the future as well. She seemed eager to
help me.

The media of course wanted to write about the hostages families,
they were not as interested in those of us living in the same hell, of wanting to know if our sons or fathers or brothers were alive or dead. When
it was over we would learn of the horrors our loved ones faced, but no
one seemed to care? As the siege raged on and the fears mounted, it was
obvious that the righteous were at war amongst themselves. The worst
offender however was the warden, Arthur Tate.

Arthur Tate was made warden at Lucasville, after there had been a teacher murdered in a classroom there. His mantra was that he was going to whip this prison into shape. He began by making it so unbearable that the inmates began to call for him to be fired. They also began to refer to him as "King Arthur." One of his notorious activities was to encourage "snitchery." Snitches are more reviled in prison than rapists and child molesters.

In Joey's letters prior to the outbreak, all he could write about was how unlivable the prison had become under this man's leadership. This man's ideas to make things better during the summer heat, was to close all the windows, thus reducing any hope of a cross breeze in the un-air-conditioned prison. Food rationing was another irritation. Prisoners were allowed only one phone call a year, and no transfers out, even when they had earned them. Reasons to riot, maybe, maybe not… but rioting they were.

One thing I knew was that a "man" was a living, breathing human being. When you cage an animal you create a different sort of animal than the one that is free to live in its normal environment. You cage a human you contribute to an already impaired person or soon will be, and most will return to society to live next door to you. You would think you would want this human to return a better person, to be able to be law abiding.

Regardless of what these people have done to warrant a prison sentence, and I'm not saying they should run amok, but they are still human beings and should be treated as such. Prisons are no "Club Med's" despite those who claim that prison is too good for "lawbreakers." *(You know the type who say, "They got a roof over their heads, three meals a day, a shower once a week; and they don't have to pay one red cent for it either. Just how lucky can they be?").*

The riot had a very profound impact on me. Would it have had an impact on someone who did not have a loved one caught up in its drama, probably not? That's why changes are so hard to come by. Shirley Pope was able to convince me that there were not dozen's of bodies stacked on top of each other in the gymnasium; and that she thought that Joey, while still inside L-Block was alive, and did not seem to be taking an active part with the rioters. She came to that conclusion by finding out that his name was neither on the list of inmates that had made it to the yard as the riot was starting nor on a list of possible troublemakers.

Ms. Pope, would keep in touch with me, but felt that there was nothing to gain by me racing to Ohio. She did tell me though, after looking up Joey's records, that Joey should have been transferred out of Lucasville at least two years prior to this. She also said that as far as she could find out Joey was not part of any extremist group within the prison, like the Aryan Nation.

I later learned that Ms. Pope had a great deal to do with investigations of how poorly this prison had been managed over the last few years. She had written report after report of drug operations within the prison, including staff involvement in bringing the drugs in. She had warned that the prison was ripe for an uprising, yet no one listened. Even Joey would tell me it was not hard to get drugs, alcohol (prison made) and huffing substances. Joey said, "So long as you paid the guard off, and you caused no trouble they left you alone."

Joey told me that most prisons were run by the inmates anyway, and so long as order was maintained very little was done to correct any injustices. I believed him and as it turned out both he and Shirley Pope were right.

After many sloppy attempts to negotiate a truce, one was reach after 11 days.

On Thursday April 22, 1993 the Headline from the Dayton Daily News Read: "Finally, it's over"

The surrender started three o'clock in the afternoon in a cold rain. It was televised per one of the inmate's demands as part of the agreement to the surrender. The injured came out first on stretchers and then on crutches, and thank God, Joey was not one of them. Over the next several hours in groups of ten and twenty they surrendered.

It was well over a week before we heard directly from Joey. He wrote to his father first stating that he thought his letter would get to him quicker in Ohio versus me in Texas. He was not hurt but felt he had seen a glimpse of hell. He had lost all of his worldly possessions and was housed in a single cell with nothing on but a jump suit. He wasn't expecting things to change anytime soon. He expected when visits resumed that they would be by a window of glass separating the visitors from the inmates. He told

Newspaper Clippings of The Headlines For the Lucasville Riot 1993

his dad and me not to come visit. "Just please write and write often," he pleaded.

My first letter from Joey after the riot came in about a week and was written on mimeograph paper which over time has faded, so as not to be readable. It was just such a relief to hear from him. His second letter came about 10 days later, the first part of May.

Dearest Mother,

By now you know I am in one piece and that I in "NO WAY" took part in any crimes or broke anything or in anyway helped any of those who did. So no worry on that aspect of it. As of the end of the riot I've been in a cell 24 hours a day. Nothing to read or do. I've had one shower, but still feel dirty! You are right, there is no way I can describe those 11 days—but if hell is truly a place and not a figure of speech, then I received a sneak peek at the real deal in a major way. I can give you the adjectives and the best way to tell a long story short: it was murder, rape, assault, hostages, hunger, thirst, cold, darkness, flood, blood, smoke, fire, broken glass, gas masks, sticks, bats, blunt objects, knives, spears, shanks, chains, picks, shovels, queers on queers, bugs, screams, hollers, begging, bullies, Muslims, Aryan Brotherhood, Disciples, renegades, gang bangers, and for the good guys; Tanks, Humvees, FBI, state police, National Guards, SWAT teams, dogs, media, and a bad attitude. And this was only in the first week of the riot.

Joey told about holing up in the gymnasium tying to stay out of the way. He said he felt it was up to him to protect some of the younger guys from being sucked into the mess. He had been in his cell when the riot broke out and had been told that was the best place to be if there ever was a riot. So that is where he stayed. He told me about one of the inmates who was known to be a snitch, being dragged by his cell, crying out for help, but that there was nothing he could do. That inmate was killed. Later he was forced out of his cell when it was raided by men wearing hoods, and he was never able to return for the remainder of the 11 days. After, as the surrender began, he had gone back to his cell, but there was nothing left of his belongings.

Joey allowed me to share his letters about the riot with the media and some of the things he had to say were printed in the Dayton Daily News: "*11 Days In Lucasville.*" It was an insert of a 12-page story released on Sunday, June 8, 1993. One of the contributing writers was Mary McCarty and she sent both Joey and me notes of appreciation for contributing to the story.

Life went on for most folks after the riot and was forgotten, except for those who lived it. Thirteen months later the inmates were still living with the aftermath. I called the Special Prosecutor's office and demanded to talk to Mark Piepmeier, lead investigator for the DA's office. I demanded to either charge my son with a crime or release him immediately from his holding cell. I threatened a lawsuit for unfair treatment of an incarcerated person by the State of Ohio. I didn't know if I could actually do that, but it sounded pretty good to me.

It seemed as though to be released from these holding cells, you either had to be charged with taking part in the riot, or be cleared from any wrong doing. They were taking their time. If the trauma of the riot wasn't enough, being locked in a cell 24 hours out of 24 was equally as bad. Joey was now suicidal again. I told Mr. Piepmeier, "What you are doing to these men is unconscionable and possibly illegal." Much of the DA's tactics were documented in a book written by Staughton Lynd, "Lucasville: The Untold Story of a Prison Uprising" (pgs. 89 to 92 give recognition to Mr. Piepmeier and the tactic's he was using). Joey was cleared for release in the next few days after spending over 13 months in a lock down situation. I could write a good report on the riot myself from all of the letters Joey had written about the uprising from his point of view. If you want to know more about the riot you might want to read Mr. Lynd's book.

Joey also wrote to Rhine McLin, state representative from Dayton, Ohio for help. He outlined what he thought she needed to know about how the riot was an accumulation of unfair treatment and mismanagement of the prison as a whole. What he may not have known was of how much Ms. McLin was already aware of. She knew a great deal about Shirley Pope's memos and was heavily involved with the prison system and how things were being managed. Joey then made a request for help to get himself transferred out of Lucasville.

We will never know if his letters helped. I have copies, and I do know Ms. McLin received them. They have been put into files and are on record, which can only mean they were received and read. I hope they helped in getting the Lucasville prison management back on track. Arthur Tate was finally replaced as the warden for Lucasville in December of 1993. While the courts eventually granted some relief for those caught up in the up-rising, none of the inmates as far as I know, ever received any compensation or mental health counseling.

Joey was to have gotten something like $900 in restitution for his losses, but he would never see it. Betty Montgomery, Attorney General for the State of Ohio, saw to that. The public at large didn't want the inmates to be compensated for anything. Again, that mentality of treating humans as less than human prevailed.

Something good did however come out of the riot and that was Joey's transfer out of Lucasville. This happened with many thanks to Shirley Pope's help and possibly Rhine McLin. Joey spent some time in Madison, London, Chillicothe, and finally ended his time in prison at Oakwood Correctional in Lima, Ohio. Each one of these transfers was a step up in the process of getting a parole.

Unfortunately, the next ten years were not a piece of cake. Not only was Joey denied a release on a 12 year shock probation, he also was denied parole when he came up for being considered for parole in his seventeenth year. This would be the actual first time he would be eligible for a regular parole. I can't help but remember when his attorneys said that the difference between accepting the plea deal before his trial was a matter of only three additional years to the parole board. They failed to tell Joey or us; or at least help us to understand, that criminals would only be paroled if the parole board saw fit to release them. They could keep you for life if they wanted. You would have no recourse to their decision. Also the distinction between being convicted for a charge of just plain ole murder verses aggravated murder was not completely understood either.

We could discuss the different kinds of murder that one commits; but the point is, aggravated murder appears to produce a certain kind of fear, more than just an ordinary murder will, in the minds of a parole board member. I wonder if we had given more thought and had a better understanding to what that label would mean for Joey, before he went to trial, would we have encouraged Joey to take the plea?

We had wanted for our son the chance for medical treatment in a hospital so badly and we failed him again. We failed him so many times by trusting and believing others had the answers that we obviously didn't have. We failed him again, by not making sure a trial was his best choice. We didn't explore all of the consequences thoroughly enough.

Did we trust the attorney's too much or not enough? Did we buy into their enthusiasm too quickly? Still all the while knowing Joey was a participant in a crime where someone was killed, but he wasn't the killer. With all of this self-doubt the only way I could look at Joey's life at this point, was at least he was still alive. If he hadn't gone to prison would he have still been alive?

I don't have that answer either. Joey had held his death at abeyance so many times I couldn't count. He dodged death at his birth, his many falls and concussions in his youth, his flights over fences and roofs, his racing with autos at break neck speeds, his drug overdoses, alcohol consumption, dangerous companions, sliced wrists and now this riot. I had to believe he was still here for a reason. I think now I know the reason and when I am sure I will tell everyone who will listen.

CHAPTER 24

Can You Really
Go Home Again

I began to look for a way to get out of the Rainbow business. I knew I would never be a successful distributor. I had tried to the best of my ability and knew I was at the end of this adventure.

What skills did I have now to offer an employer? I was no more formally educated than I had been before I went into direct sales, but street smarts I had acquired. I had learned plenty about what it took to make a sale. I knew I was only interested in selling a product or service I could be proud of.

I spent my fiftieth birthday down on Galveston, Island. I had gone down with a friend, a woman that did my hair on a weekly basis. She was a beautician who owned her own shop, close to my business in a strip mall in Mission Bend. We became friends and I liked having someone outside of business to pal around with. Her name was Patty Alvers and she was married with a grown daughter. While staying on the sea wall in a grand hotel, Patty had some business to take care of and I decided to take a walk on the sea wall to get some air and take in the beauty of Gulf.

At the end of the sea wall was an attraction urging people come and participate in a daring feat. I had always thought I would have liked to parachute from a plane, but that was not likely going to happen. However, bungee jumping just might be away for me to see if push came to shove, would I jump. I weighed the pros and cons of if I would survive this act. "What the Hell?" I thought. Leeann was grown with a family of her own and hadn't needed my help for a long time. Joey had survived the riot, and may never come out of prison. Jimmy was out on his own living with a significant other, who I liked very much. Eric was happy, healthy and in love with a lovely girl and looked as though he would marry her and graduate from college. I laid down $60 to jump and $20 to have a video taken. I figured no one would believe me after the fact, so I'd better get it on film. I stepped on a scale so they could get my weight and match it with the strength of the rope that would be needed and waited my turn. The crowed that had gathered to watch the entertainment was beginning to swell, and they began to shout, "You go Granny! Granny!"

Well if I needed any more incentive, Granny, got my attention and my competitive spirit in high gear. Granny, huh!? I'll show them young whippersnappers! Strapped into ankle harnesses so tight I thought my feet would be amputated by the time this was over, I was ready. I got into a basket attached to a crane; with three-attraction workers we began to ascend into the air.

Upon arrival at 250 feet in the air; the safety door was unlatched, a mini platform jutted out over the huge pool of water, it was meant to keep me from killing myself, if the rope broke. Well, maybe it would, maybe it wouldn't. My "adoring fan's" below, who now looked like tiny insects, were still shouting for me to jump. I have to admit I no longer was in full bravery mode, I thought seriously that maybe I shouldn't do this. I watched others return to earth unable to make the jump. Defeat was not one of my built in traits if I could help it. I closed my eyes, said a prayer and fell forward into what may have been one of the most exhilarating things I have ever done.

I first did a swan dive, then some somersaults, and then some twists and turns as the rubber rope kept me catapulting up and down for quite some time. I was now hanging upside down perfectly still, with all my blood rushing to my head. To elevate I reached up and held onto my ankles and the crane swung me over the water and back down to the ground. My ankles were now screaming in pain, but it was worth it. Tomorrow I would be back in Houston, job hunting. *Happy Fiftieth Birthday, Linda!*

Checking out the want ads I spied one from a National company looking for someone with experience in direct sales. They were up front about having no hidden charges and would be willing to front the full cost of training, with no investment for the right person. Telemarketing skills were a plus. I called to set up an interview and worked up a very impressive resume with some help from my daughter.

The initial interview went extremely well and I was invited back for a second interview. This time they went into quite a bit of psychological testing. My third interview was with one of the owners of the company. She had flown in from Wilmington, Delaware to meet the final candidates. It was then that I finally learned the name of the company and just what services they were providing.

Laramore/Holmman Transportation was a family owned company headquartered in the East and an agent of United Van Line, one of the largest transportation companies worldwide. I was thrilled. I had heard that sales of interstate household goods moving across country were very lucrative, much like pharmaceutical sales. If I accepted the position I would train in Delaware and New York, and work in their Houston location. Again, I was very impressed. Their offer was a substantial base salary plus commission, full benefits with 401 K to boot. I would actually draw a paycheck again. I felt the pressure lifting already. I would be responsible for building their COD business and boost lagging sales in the Houston market.

I felt another, "You are where you are meant to be" moment in my life.

Could I be ready to start in two weeks? Yes. I went to work putting my rainbow distributorship to "bed." Paul didn't want to see the location in Mission Bend shut down and offered to buy it back from me for the same amount I had purchased it from him. While it was probably worth more, I was only glad to get out from under the obligation and agreed to the buy out and his terms. I thought that it was almost too easy to bow out of the business in this manner; and I am sorry to say, it did turn out to be "to good to be true."

Sadly it was not going to be as easy as I thought to put "Rainbow" out of my life. Six months later Paul and I still hadn't completely severed the financial ties that bound us. I had to take legal action to put the business behind me to protect my credit rating.

Paul had been very important to me for many years and I just couldn't believe he would take advantage of our business relationship and ruin our friendship in the process. This was a very sad event in my life. Paul was in a position with our "gentleman's agreement "to take me under financially and possible legal consequences as well." He was playing "Russian Roulette" with credit cards and the business checking account. In other words he was "Robbing Peter to pay Paul."

Paul had let the business flounder. Apparently he couldn't do both; the administration obligations for Meador Enterprises while running an individual distributorship too. Per our agreement, my name and the business bank account's would stay connected to Hydro Air Two, through to the end of the year, approximately three months. Paul would operate the business with my open accounts with the credit card companies and the business checking account. At the end of the calendar year he was to have the accounts transferred into his name and my name would be eliminated on all accounts. He had not followed through on his promise and three months into the new year I smelled trouble.

I shut the accounts down only after I had given him fair warning. He then failed to finish buying me out. Even though the courts ruled in my favor, he filed for bankruptcy and we both lost. I lost financially, because he named me as one of his creditors in his bankruptcy. He and I lost a friendship over money, a friendship that I thought would never completely end, just fade over time, ending only with sending out Christmas cards, as the last of our contacts.

Paul had given me an education in direct sales that I could not have gotten from a book or a classroom. It took time to learn both the practical hands on effort and the street smarts he taught. Unfortunately for Paul, it was some of those lessons that he taught me that did our friendship in. Fool me once shame on you; fool me twice shame on me.

In the spring of 1994, Eric shared the news that he had asked Christa Wilford to marry him. He was in his last semester of his senior year at Wright State University and Christa had graduated from the University of Dayton. There would be an August wedding. I was so excited to finally have one of my children plan a formal wedding.

I offered Eric and Christa my wedding rings to do with what ever they wanted. They chose to use the diamond from this set of rings and place it into her engagement ring. I was thrilled to be a part of this happy and exciting time. I hadn't met Christa's parents yet but, Linda and David Wilford, from what Eric had told me about them seemed like wonderful perspective in-laws. We had talked many times over the phone making the plans for the wedding. They welcomed Eric as their son-law to be and I couldn't have been happier.

As the August wedding date approached Jimmy and I planned to make the trip to Ohio together. Once there I would stay with Eric at his apartment and Jimmy would stay with a friend. Jimmy and I hosted the rehearsal dinner at La Piazza, a fine Italian restaurant. The wedding took place in a garden setting at Alliston Manor, a quaint inn. The weather was beautiful for an outdoor wedding as they said their vows under a white arbor filled with flowers; their attendants, family and friends. This was the first time I spent any length of time with Joe since I had moved to Texas. It also was the first time I met his wife, Kathleen.

Kathy, as I had been told she liked to be called, appeared to be a pleasant lady, and I took no offense to her presence. I was happy Joe had found someone to share his new life. I no longer held hatred for what I believed Joe had done to our family and me. All of that was a distant memory, which I tried hard to keep at abeyance. I no longer wanted to hold the pain in plain view anymore, I couldn't change it and it took too much effort to think and rethink it.

Eric and I shared a mother and son dance and my heart overflowed with happiness for my son and his bride, Christa. I believed this union to be a blessing and hoped this marriage would be a happy one. Jimmy and I then traveled back to Houston the following day. Little did I know, the following year I would return to Ohio permanently.

I was about to learn another very hard lesson when it came to business. Most companies can hire at will. This also means they can terminate at will, as well. I had turned the COD department at Larmore/Holman from $250,000 in gross sales to approximately $799,000 in gross sales in my very first year. I had hired two additional people to staff the department and we were growing. This is what I had been instructed to do. One of the people I had hired and trained was a former "Rainbow" associate, Diane Knowles. I had trained her for the Rainbow business and knew her to be aggressive and a closer. I went looking for her to be a part time sales person in the residential sales department and we made a fine team. I also considered her a personal friend.

Photo's From The Most Beautiful Outdoor Wedding Ever
Leeann, Joe, Kathy, Christa, Eric, Me, James, Brittney, Breann,
Brooklyn and Brilyn

However, Laramore /Holman had a change of strategy for the Houston location. It was decided by the powers that be, to downsize the COD department. The two people I hired were let go. I never really knew why they had this change of plans. At the end of my second year with sales still above average, I was dismissed as well. The industry cycle was at a low point but wouldn't they still need a COD sales person? I surmised that my overhead of benefits was one of the reasons.

I had taken some acting classes in the hope's of being "discovered" for perhaps some TV commercials. However, that endeavor was not going to pay the bills just yet. The dream of show biz was still in my blood, just not the starving part.

Much to my dismay they hired Diane back; the woman I had trained, paid her on straight commission with no benefits, worked her part time,

Preparing to do Commercial Shoots 1992 to 1994 Houston Texas

and thought that would work for them. She didn't last long, maybe six months, as she left for a job with Continental Airlines. We still remained friends and I can call her a friend today as well. I was devastated. I was not looking to go back into the rainbow business with my tail between my legs either.

I had learned enough about the moving industry, that sales positions within the industry could be as rare as hen's teeth. It was now common knowledge to me, that a moving company needed no more than one full time and one part time sales person. I was not interested in part-time, I needed a full time job. I made a few inquiries in the Houston market and there were no openings available in the major transportation companies.

Jimmy was talking about going to California. He was now involved with a young lady by the name of JoAnn. They thought California was the place they ought to be. Perhaps it was time for me to go home. At least Father Aufterhide thought so.

Marilyn, my closet friend, was working as a nurse with Mercy Scenia retirement center back in Dayton, Ohio and one of her clients was Father Aufterhide. Amazing how lives intertwine isn't it? Father Aufterhide was growing frail in his elderly years. Marilyn told the good Father, I was thinking of coming home, and his very words were "Tell her it's time she came home; she will be needed here soon."

I drove to Columbus, Ohio to stay with a friend, Susan Wilson. She had moved back to Ohio a couple of years earlier to be near family. She and I had kept in touch and she offered me a place to stay while I looked for work. I accepted her offer to stay while I checked out employment opportunities in Dayton, Cincinnati, and Columbus. I figured after living in Houston; where it took at least and hour to get anywhere, that if I found work in any one of these cities, I would be close enough to family, and all the people that I wanted to be near. Including Joey.

I interviewed with all the major moving companies in the tri-state area and the best offer came from Executive Transfer, a Mayflower agent. Tim Picciano, the sales manager for this company, and I hit it off immediately, he had shown great respect for me as a person and the skills I could bring to Executive Transfer. His offer was most generous and he was willing to cover the expenses to move me back to Ohio. Bingo! Another, you are meant to be moment, I thought. I was happy, my family was happy and I could prepare for my next chapter, not so far from my roots.

Leaving my car in Columbus, I flew back to Houston on a round trip ticket. I was back in time to prepare for the long distance move back to Ohio, as the van would be there in a week to load me up. I also prepared to say good-by to Jimmy. It was a bittersweet farewell. Jimmy and I knew that either way we would be living in different parts of the country, so it didn't matter that I was going home to Ohio and not staying in Texas. Ohio would always be home to Jimmy as well. We also knew we would only be an airplane ride away from one another.

I was sad to leave this warm tropical climate and the thrill of saying that I lived in Houston, Texas. I found Houston to be a very exciting and somewhat glamorous place to live and work.

Lord, You are still looking after me aren't You? You never let me get lost in total despair, do You? You may not have planned for me to bungee jump, but You sure do plan a whole lot of other stuff for me, don't You? I once had someone tell me that they thought that You must love me an awful lot to give me so many reasons to trust in You. I remember replying, "Will you tell Him not to love so much"

CHAPTER 25

The Long Fight For The Freedom
To Come Home

Arriving in Columbus just before Labor Day in 1996, the weather in Ohio was still beautiful. I took up residence in a brick twin single on the north side of town. I decided not to buy a house just in case Columbus wasn't going to work out. This two bedroom one floor plan with a garage was all I would need for the time being. However, it did have a spacious living room, a huge eat in kitchen, full basement and a backyard patio surrounded by lots of trees. There would even be room for Joey next year when his parole came through.

I settled into the sales department at Executive Transfer and began to make friends in Columbus, Ohio. It was harder than I thought, as most of the time my work kept me on the road. The department was headed up by Tim Picciano the VP of Sales, Scott Hughes, the national account representative, Carla Simpson, lead coordinator, and Anne Harrod, office manager. Soon Brady Linard, would join the team and from time to time a few others floated in and out. Tim would keep me in the loop with business lunches and sales meetings but for the most part I was on my own. Carla was really the only one who befriended me outside of the office. She invited me to join the "Garden Club."

The Garden Club consisted of about six to eight women that met once a month to check out unusual restaurants for dinner. There was no gardening done with these dinners, but plenty of friendly chit chat. This group of women, Carla Simpson, Janet Ayala, Vicki Martin, Irene Price, Karen Vollmuth, Madeleine Nikolaus, Karen Hirsch, and I slowly became friends and they played a part in my life for the next chapters to come and perhaps would for many more years as well.

Tim Piccianno, was the only person that I felt was trustworthy enough to share the story of my life. I don't believe I told my life story to anyone with whom I worked. Most people that I had met over the last twenty years were clueless as to the skeletons in my closet. Those that did know, those back in my former life, either had forgotten or didn't care. Life goes on, doesn't it?

The high tech information highway was making its way into the transportation industry and soon I would have to become a part of it to stay current. What scared me most was that I couldn't even play PAC-man, how on earth would I learn to do surveys on a computer? But when my training was complete, I wondered how I ever did this job without it. Along with learning the new technology, I also had to get used to snow again. I think it started to snow in October of that year and didn't stop until spring.

Marilyn was glad I was back in Ohio and living close enough to spend most weekends together. I was able to visit with Joey on a regular basis and got to see for myself how much he had matured both physically and mentally. While his formal education had not continued, he did take great pains in watching everything PBS had to offer. His understanding of social and political events never ceased to amaze me. His intelligence was never in question, His common sense only worked at 100% when it didn't concern him directly.

Joey gave a lot of credit to his survival in prison to a man named Roger Hall. Joey wrote an essay about this man some years later in an English class.

Joseph Hutchison
ENG. 111 M.W. 3:00-5:15
Professor, Becki Test
01/31/07

A Monster?
"I don't know why they call me Godfather", he says with a sheepish smile when asked. Then he says, "I'm just ole Redbone, but you can call me Bone," six feet four inches tall and a solid two hundred forty pounds out of the cage even at the age of fifty-six. "I'm somewhat heavier on lock down; dam honey buns. Can't lay off "em"

His head always shinning, reflecting any light that strikes it, makes it very easy to spot him in a crowd. Large brown eyes with heavy ruffles of skin below, he has a hound dog look, which has the ability to convey kindness and in a glance, strike fear into the most harden soul. A mixture of dark crimson and bright red facial hair, neatly kept in the goatee style, sets the tone of a light fair skinned face with a weathered cowboy look. It may be possible to read his life story from the intense graffiti covering practically every square inch of visible skin.

Each tattoo has its own tale and place in time; some even reveal his sense of humor. Kenny, one of Redbone's hommie's, recounts a summer where he saw "ME TOO" tattooed on ole Bone's left foot. Kenny recalls at the time he was too afraid to ask, "Why would you tattoo "ME TOO" on your foot?" As it turns out, Kenny tells of the following summer when he saw ole Bone's other foot. It read's, "I'M TIRED."

In the early sixties, Bone was about 18 years old. He spent seven years in the Lebanon, Ohio Reformatory for manslaughter. "A man hurt my sister pretty bad, and I done what seemed natural at the time. I was raised in the hills of Kentucky and calling the law never crossed my mind. After I was released, things were never the same. My heart was in Kentucky, but my soul had become dark and my friends even darker."

Folks back home in the hills of Harlan, County couldn't believe it, but ole Bone had become a bank robber, Tommie Gun and all. To this day, he can't really tell you why. He speculates that it might have been the anger over all those years spent locked up for doing what he still feels was the right thing to do. It could have been his drug addiction. He's just not sure. No doubts, however, as far as the world was concerned, he was armed and dangerous.

Like most bank robbers, Bone had a partner; Monk was his name. The two led their lives robbing, running, and hiding from the law. It took a couple of years for their robbery streak to come to an end. Bone got caught. Monk got killed. The Feds, Bone recounts, said it was suicide; Bone knows better, "You end up dead or in prison, and looking back on things," Bone says, "Monk received the better ending to the partnership."

So, bank robber to Godfather, how did this happen? Bone says that this "godfather reputation" had its beginnings in the Atlanta Federal penitentiary where he was serving his time for the robberies. Bone described himself as still young and wild then, about 25 years old. He had a pretty serious disagreement with this ole boy and stabbed him to death. Bone will tell you it was self-defense, him or me! Besides, in those days, he said it was rare to charge an inmate in a prison death, create a new case, go to trial or add more time to your sentence. But it did get him noticed. He was sent to the end of the line in the federal prison system, Marion Illinois. All the crime legends were in that place.

After ten years for the bank robberies, Bone was placed on furlough, a sort of halfway house situation close to home. "Unbelievable" Bone says, "but on my first day on furlough, my sister's boyfriend jumps my daddy, who was too old to be fightin'. He beat him up. So, I get home; I meet up with this boyfriend."

The words, "So you're the big bad Roger Hall that I'm hearing so much about?" come out of the boyfriend's mouth.

"Yes it's me, but I just got out and all I wanna do is have a drink and relax. You know any place we can go do that?" says Bone.

They found the boyfriend with a bullet hole in his forehead, in the ally outside his favorite bar, gun in hand and several thousand dollars in cash on him. Clearly, robbery was ruled out as a motive, and self-defense was lurking in the wings. Ole Bone's guilt was assessed at second degree murder, not first, but still came out to be a life sentence at Ohio's Lucasville Maximum Security State Prison-- the worst of the worst Ohio State Prisons.

Before Bone arrived at Lucasville, his reputation already preceded him. In actuality, it was the Lucasville prison staff, who officially dubbed him the "Godfather." Captain Blair at the Lucasville prison said that in his thirty odd years in corrections, Roger Hall is the only man he ever saw enter Lucasville prison and assume his role at the top of the food chain without ever throwing so much as one punch. Kenny, even though he is one of Bone's hommies, won't hesitate to tell you, Bone is the most dangerous human being he's ever known.

Bone doesn't like to be called Godfather, only the guards get away with that. He knows many people also call him a monster. He says that too hurts his feelings, "for people who don't even know me to think that I'm a monster. I'm just Redbone, an ole mountain man at heart."

There is no denying it, most people probably do see Rodger Lee Hall as the Godfather or a monster. Only a few will disagree. Not many see the Redbone who loves playing the guitar alongside Muddy Waters, loves playing his old eight-track tape deck, and singing the blues in a way that only someone who has lived a hard life can. Despite all his faults, he places loyalty and respect above his own well being. He despises cowards and those who pray on helpless human beings. This is a man, who throughout his years in prison, affectionately calls the new ones to prison life "Pups" and strongly suggests to them, as a father figure might do, that they stay on the porch until they are ready to play with the big dogs.

Yes, there are stories about this man, not all of which are good. But a monster? Does a monster turn his back on the innocent who need protection (whether a free man or behind bars) when there is nothing in it for him? Not all people who cross Bone's path experience the fear he can invoke. Godfather, monster, trailer trash, the list of labels that are placed on people rarely tell the whole story.

I've learned, until I know the whole story, I will always be skeptical of labels and people who prefer to use them.

Bone is currently in Tara Hut federal prison in Indiana, where the state of Ohio sent him after twenty-five years at Lucasville, so he can settle his debt for the bank robberies.

**

This is how Joey saw this man. This man befriended my son when he was new to prison life. Joey was one of the "Pups" and Roger Hall, aka, Redbone, or Godfather, taught my son how to play with the big dogs. He taught him how to keep from getting raped, robed, beaten and all the other "bad" things that can happen to 18 year-old's when subjected to the harsh realities of adult prison. I will be forever grateful that the "Godfather" took Joey under his wing. Of course he couldn't protect Joey from everything. He couldn't cure Joey's mental illnesses. Neither could I.

It was my turn to write letters. I had enlisted everyone I thought could help persuade the parole board to grant Joey his release. This meant not only family but friends as well. Friends were needed to give an unbiased assessment of his family's character. This posed some problems, as few people knew of my personal background, let alone that I had a son in prison for aggravated murder.

I felt that I could share my family's story with Tim, my sales manager, and hoped he would be able to give me a reference. Tim, not only was willing to give me a reference to my character, he was very supportive in his remarks and his follow up of how the process was going. He also, as far as I knew, kept this information he was now privy to, confidential. That's a true friend. My first letter to the parole board was sent April 16, 1997, it read:

Margaret Ghee
Ohio Adult Parole Board
1050 Freeway Dr. N
Columbus, Ohio 43229

If I thought hundreds of letters in his behalf would affect the parole board's decision regarding the release of Joseph Hutchison, 161-844, I would organize a massive letter-writing campaign in support of his freedom. I would harbor no hopes, however, for its success, for in reality, there are only a few people who care whether Joe Hutchison is ever released. I am one-- I am Joe Hutchison's mother, and as such, I will appeal to you in the only way that I know; I will speak to you from my heart. You will receive other letters in support of Joe's release, and they will be honest and genuine. They will be from people who have known Joe all of his life, and more importantly, were there when Joe's life in prison was measured in years until parole—then months until parole, then weeks, and now finally in days.

When you look at Joe's record in prison you will not find that he received the Nobel Peace Prize or developed a cure for cancer. His record will show, instead, that he entered the system at the age of seventeen. This blond haired, blue-eyed, baby faced boy went directly to Lucasville where he was lost in the cracks but somehow survived to become a man. This man with thinning hair; bad eyesight and bad teeth, and has spent half of his life behind bars.

He has earned his G.E.D. and completed many in-house programs. He has held various jobs requiring trust by the staff. He has never been involved with any gang, called a leader, or been known as a troublemaker. He is non-violent and always cooperative. He has no tattoos or body piercing. He has earned the right to be called a "convict" by his peers, the term, I am told, favored over "inmate"

I ask you to please verify the statements I will be making in this letter. My faith is strong enough to let me believe that given the enormous responsibility associated with your task, this board endeavors to carefully consider every aspect of the individual cases which come before it. I believe you hold Joe's future in your hands, and that you will make your decision based upon Joe as he is presented to you – not in consideration of someone else's failed parole, the current political environment, or on a predetermined parole limit for this month.

Joe will not deny that he took part in the crime for which he was convicted. He will agree that there were four juveniles and one adult involved in the crime. Two were never charged, two maintained their juvenile status, and Joe went to adult prison for 15 years to life.

Because of the deals that were made before Joe's arrest, Joe was left out on a limb to fend for himself. We had no money as a family then, and we have no money as a broken family now. I say this only because in this day and age, money has seemed to make a difference in the pursuit of justice. Had we been able to handle Joe's case with the skill money can buy, perhaps the outcome would have been more fair. Joe could have served time at J.D. with the others involved until he was 21, or perhaps they would have served the last 17 years with Joe in the adult prison system.

From the transcripts of the trial (see additional information) there was no physical evidence that put Joe at the crime scene. No fingerprints, no confession – just Kenny Flynn and Jerry Arnett's testimony. Kenny's fingerprints were everywhere, and Jerry Arnett failed his lie detector test including whether he did or did not strike Mrs. Kaiser with the croquet mallet (the cause of death).

The likelihood that Jerry Arnett administered the fatal blow didn't seem to matter during the trial. The prosecutor needed someone to "go down" and Joe was the easier target. Joe's father and I didn't want to see our son sent to adult prison, so we accepted the public defender's advice to plead not guilty by reason of insanity. That advice-- not Joe-- was insane, but we were too young and too scared to know better. We should have been strong enough to allow Joe to plead guilty and tell his side of the story – but we weren't.

We have accepted the fact that fairness is not always applied. It was not fair that Mrs. Kaiser lost her life, or that she was even home at all (the house was supposed to be empty-). Loss of life for anyone that night was never contemplated. The only thing "planned" was an ill-conceived burglary by a handful of misguided teenagers. "Fair" never entered the picture that night.

Joe has spent half of his life in prison for his part in this crime- at least thirteen years longer than anyone else involved. Joe has accepted his guilt and responsibility, and deeply regrets that Mrs. Kaiser lost her life. Youth and youthful stupidity played a large part in the events of that evening. At this point in his life, Joe is no longer youthful, nor ignorant of life and its consequences. His only desire now is to make something out of the rest of his life beyond what prison allows - -to make a contribution to the world from which he has been separated for so long. All of the others involved in the crime have had the opportunity to make such a new start – does my son deserve any less? I cannot believe so.

There is no grater punishment than the loss of one's freedom. Death has a finality and serves no purpose for punishment. I would surmise that in Joe's case the loss of his youth and the fact that he alone was punished more severely than the others has served to adequately punish Joe. If you continue his imprisonment it will not bring back the life that was lost; it will not take away the pain and guilt of a bad decision made during one's youth, it will not further any rehabilitation beyond that which has taken place. Most importantly, it will not serve justice any further. It will only continue non-constructive punishment which I believe is excessive and harsh and at this point, purposeless.

If paroled now, Joe has a chance to be a productive citizen. Joe's only support system is his father and I. At this time we are still healthy and able to provide that support. Joe's health, too, is okay, and physically he can do manual labor to support himself, if necessary. Right now, he has the best opportunity to adjust and not become a burden to society.

The longer Joe remains in the care of the State of Ohio, the more unlikely it becomes that he will be able to become gainfully employed. The longer Joe remains "inside," the less his father or I will be able to help him as we face the difficulties of our own aging. In our family there is a history of diabetes and heart disease (his father has both, and his sister and brother are borderline). Should Joe develop one or both of these illnesses, it will be that much harder for him to adjust to life on the "outside" and to care for himself, if he does not have the healthy head start that you can give him now.

We as his family stand ready to give Joe the support, guidance and atmosphere to ease into a life as a good citizen. All of the expectations and guidelines you will impose will be monitored carefully by us. If at anytime Joe shows signs of not being able to adjust, we will be the first to seek appropriate help and care.

His father has a large house with a barn and workshop in Tipp City, Ohio and a network of people able to give Joe employment. I live in a good neighborhood in Columbus and have an extra room for Joe. We want him home very much.

Perhaps this letter will not be the kind of letter that appeals to you and the board. If so, please disregard all of the above and accept my final comments on Joe's behalf.

Please forgive Joe. The judge said 15 years to life. I believe that this means that if Joe no longer presents a threat to society or himself, and that if his conduct and overall behavior these past 17 years have been good, Joe warrants favorable consideration for parole by this board. We understand that parole is a privilege, not a given. I humbly come before you at this time and ask in my son's behalf; please grant Joe his parole.

Further insight into my son can be given by Ms. Shirley Pope at the Ohio Correction Committee (614-466-1990) Ms. Pope has indicated to me that if you seek her input she will gladly comply with your request.,

Respectfully,

**

I was so proud of this letter and the other 10 to 12 the board should have received, and was sure we would have a positive outcome. Why did I continually believe in miracles? Why did I believe that common sense should prevail? While I knew Joey hadn't received any quality mental health treatment, I purposely didn't mention that in the letter to the parole board. The state hadn't seen fit to give my son the care he needed, I wasn't going to give them any reasons not release him. I supposed we would deal with Joey's condition when he was released.

Of course I had had conversations and written letters to Joey, concerning his emotional and mental stability. He kept assuring me that he felt if he were released that he would be able to stay on top of his issues. He said," Mom, I still have racing thoughts and weird thinking, but now I am able to slow down and think things through instead of acting out." Well, isn't that what Dr. McConnell said might happen? Isn't that what Dr. McConnell wrote and told me could happen with some men as they aged; that their hormone levels would trail off and that their reaction times would slow. Hope, without it you have nothing. So of course I wanted to believe that this time Joey could learn to live with his condition; whatever that condition was, as we were not exactly sure what he would be facing as a free man.

It had been over seventeen years since Joey's mental health had been given any labels. How sure could we be after all this time? Was Joey afflicted with an antisocial personality? Was he a psychopath? Was he Bipolar? Was he a borderline personality? Was he still ADAH? Did he have seasonal depression? Did he suffer from post-traumatic syndrome from the riot? Could he even survive in the "real world"? I didn't know, but what I did know was I wanted him to have a chance at life and I wanted to do everything I could to help him have that chance.

We were granted an interview with a parole board member, whose name was Mr. "Jim" Bedra. He could push the board for a full hearing on Joey's behalf. He came to the point quickly as he had other families to interview that day as well.

No, he would not be asking Ms. Pope for her input. He did see the original trial transcripts I held in my hand and was not impressed. What he did say is "if we insisted that the board put this to a vote now, it would probably fail, as the board is not inclined to grant parole for aggravated murder for someone until they have served at least 20 years. If we waited for the three more years he would be advocating, making it the twentieth year, Joe would have a better chance of getting his parole." I asked Mr. Bedra, if he would guarantee only three more years to the parole board again, and he agreed.

We took what the parole board member, Mr. Bedra, said back to Joey, and he was thrilled. He didn't believe he had a chance at parole, and was excited that he would be continued for only another three years. He said, "Mom, everyone else is coming back from the board with 10 to 15 year flops. I can do three years standing on my head. I can do that, thank you for all your help." He said he would get another chance in what is called half time, to ask again. So, in another year and a half he could ask the board for another look at his parole. That's the law.

The parole board faced high criticism for their hard fast line of keeping prisoners longer than necessary. They were handing out long continuances without batting an eye. Had Joe's requests for a parole been given any serious consideration; had the board even looked into Joe's record of behavior, did they read or give any thought to all the letters people had written in his behalf? Was it the nature of his crime or the terminology of his conviction that rubber-stamped their decision on his parole. I believe it wasn't about him at all. It was a line the board drew, that someone would serve at least 20 years for a crime like Joe's

no matter who they were. No matter that the judge said as little as fifteen years would be sufficient. What was upsetting was the extent of the
power of the parole board. No one had more power over an inmate's life
then they did. Once appointed to the board, the job was theirs for life.
Even the governor had no power with the board. While the governor can
ignore the parole boards recommendations he or she cannot interfere
with the parole board's decisions. Class action lawsuits were now pending against the board.

Even before Joe would reach half time, new laws would come into
effect. These new laws were called "truth in sentencing" and changed
the sentences of people convicted from this time forward. In many cases
the new laws were less severe. But in serious cases the time was much
longer before a person could be considered for parole. Also for some of-
fenses, shorter time was spent behind bars releasing the prisoner without parole at all, thus limiting the need for parole board approval. The
only way for these board members to hold on to their jobs was to deny
paroles and keep "flopping" old law prisoners.

If I had thought that the worst was behind us, I was wrong again. My
work was just beginning. I got involved with a group called the "Citizens
United for Rehabilitation of Errants" (CURE). This group worked diligently
to educate and encourage elective officials to reduce crime through criminal justice reform. From this point forward I began a written and phone
contact campaign to change laws, viewpoints, attitudes and fight for my
son's release. I even found myself lobbying the state house representatives.

If I thought the world was out to make only my son's life a living hell,
I was wrong. There were stories like my son's; some were even worse.
I thought if only the general public really knew and cared how the
Department of Rehabilitation and Corrections really operated, they'd
be outraged. Silly me, I forgot, the general public really doesn't care or
want to know, for if they did, things would change. Let me just say one
more thing here before I move on. I have learned that if we could get
the general public to care more about the treatment of mental illness,
we could then get them to care more about how the Department of
Rehabilitation and Corrections is managed for the two are so closely related. The prison population is comprised at any given time, with up to
30% to 50 % inmates with a mental illness or defect. You would think
someone would see this as a problem besides me?

As far as I knew and from everything I had read, you can't cure someone's mental illness with punishment. In fact *you can't cure mental illness
at all.* You can learn to control it, much like any chronic disease with certain medications, therapy, and rehabilitation. It takes a mountain of time
and patience and often the patient is his/her worst enemy. It may be
more difficult to treat a mental disease, than let's say diabetes, but it can

be done, *it must be done*. In Joey's case it would become clear that the state had the time to learn more about his condition and to treat his various issues, but they didn't.

Part of the department's name, "Rehabilitation" leads one to believe that anyone that spends time in one of the 30 odd prisons through out Ohio, gets to partake in rehabilitation. One would be sorely misled because significant rehabilitation may not take place for the mentally ill. Any concrete endeavors to ensure better treatment for my son, came from interventions from his family or from people we lobbied with like Shirley Pope, from the Inspection Committee. With no one on the outside to really care about someone in prison, very little is done to help inmates survive a personal crisis. Such as being lost in the cracks of what should have taken place vs. what didn't.

Who would care? How long would it take to secure Joey's release? With the new laws in place, Joey was now looking at spending at least 27 and one half years before being considered for parole. The judge said, "Fifteen years to life." Did that mean anything? Could the parole board really discard what Judge Kessler, said? Could they really make up their own rules? Apparently they could. It didn't seem as if there were any checks and balances that they must adhere to, or if there were, they were not enforced.

CHAPTER 26

Twenty-Three Years

100 Days

(Continued from the end of Chapter 18: The Long Way Home)

I ssued from the Ohio State Parole Board: Due to the disparity in the way the court handled the co-defendants, the parole board is aware of the fact that the co-defendants were much more culpable of the offense than previously indicated. "My parole is granted. Not words to a song, but in my heart, after twenty-three years and one-hundred days, it was saying: "You're done taking the long way home."

I can now see the trees and walk in the grass. Will these simple things ever become unseen to me again? Every time I hear that song I am transported back in time to ol' Jackie Gleason and me pulling out of the driveway on that overcast day.

Oh, it has to be for you to grow, boy

I'm no longer that boy, and I did use those G.E.D. books that my mother gave to me, in spite of the circumstances, and in spite of the jailer who told me it was too late for them.

**

From that first letter to the parole board in 1997 to their decision to grant Joey his parole, took six years. Six years for the board to finally understand what we had been trying to tell them. Six years out of a man's life because it wasn't important for them to follow through with the evidence that was right in front of them all of this time. Had the board come to that conclusion the first time the information was presented to them, would these past six years have made a difference in Joey's life? Make a difference in Joey having a successful reentry into society? Did those six extra years of punishment help or hurt his chances of recovery and rehabilitation? Did they give the Kaiser family any closure for their loss or the state of Ohio any more satisfaction for his crime? You have to wonder, but again that was something we would never know. There is never a going back and recouping a single minute let alone six years.

In the last six years I must have written the parole board dozens of letters. I wrote letters to the editor of the Columbus Dispatch; some of them were printed. I talked to doctors, lawyers and Indian chiefs. I pursued individual parole board members as well. I called the central parole office in Columbus, Ohio so often, that they knew my voice. I didn't have to tell them my name, they would just address me as "Oh, hello Mrs. Hutchison" and try to get me to the "right" person or persons.

In the year of 2000, three years into the campaign for Joey's release, Joey was sure he would not live to see his parole. Joey had been assigned to Oakwood Correctional in Lima, Ohio. This was another assignment attributed to the intervention of Ms. Shirley Pope from the Ohio Inspection Committee on Joey's behalf. The job at Oakwood was considered a "plumb" assignment. Oakwood housed prisoners who were deemed the most affected by mental illnesses. Joey's job at the prison would be labeled as a cadre. This assignment was considered a plumb assignment, equivalent to being selected from the best of the best inmate candidates.

Cadres were to assist the institution with the care of the hospitalized inmates. They would have no direct contact with the prisoners in the hospital units; but would do the cleaning, serving of meals, or whatever was needed to maintain the quality of the institutional care. This institution had air conditioning and cable TV. It also had a program for inmates to train and rehabilitate dogs and sometimes prepare them to be guide dogs. Every one that was spending long-term incarceration wanted to be assigned to this facility for those reasons alone. They didn't want to be housed as one of the patients though, as that would mean they were in need of intense mental health treatment. However, I was hopeful that Joey would recognize and find something helpful in this assignment.

While there, during routine testing, Joey was told he had tested positive for Hepatitis C. This virus was getting a lot of press in the late 1990's and the early years of 2000. People were told that this virus was deadly; as it led to liver failure, liver cancer and death. There were no perfect treatments for the virus and the few that were available were not being offered to inmates. Joey was convinced he would die in prison before his parole would be granted or be so sick when released, that life wouldn't be worth living.

After some research on my part I was able to help squelch his fears. The virus usually didn't present problems for about twenty years after the initial infection. I asked Joey when and how he thought he got this virus. He told me that shortly after arriving at Lucasville he got connected to people who could get drugs.

His drug of choice was always marijuana. Mental pain, due to a mental illness, goes on and on and on, finding relief is hard to come by. Joey either smoked pot or huffed, and during one of these drug induced binges, he was talked into trying something by injection. He wasn't even sure what it was he injected and claimed it was only one time. The inmate whose needle was used was not sterilized and was infected with a rare strain of Hep C. This inmate had spent time in Vietnam and southeast Asia, and was probably infected there, because the strain that was eventually detected in Joey was that same rare strain. Just as it can only take one time of unprotected sex to make a baby or contract an STD, it only takes one time to get a disease using a dirty needle.

Within the next few days Joey became extremely ill and turned yellow from head to toe. He landed in the infirmary and was diagnosed with yellow jaundice and was listed with the serious condition of liver failure. I was made aware of how serious Joey's condition was only after it happened; and Joey had recovered, which was over twenty years ago. Twenty years, isn't that the mark of time it takes for this virus to rear its ugly head. I wondered how Joey, in trouble with his physical health, and with an illness that's very expensive to treat, would do? If he were released and needed treatment for this disease or worse a liver transplant to save his life, how would he manage?

Armed with Joey's test results, I made an appointment with a prominent doctor in the treatment of Hepatitis C, here in Columbus, Ohio. I went to ask his opinion, as Joey was told he would receive no treatment for this condition. I was told without a liver biopsy to determine how progressed the disease or virus was it would not be prudent for him to give me a definite answer as to how sick Joey was or how sick he could become. [The doctor] would have ordered a liver biopsy if he had a patient with Joey's history and test results.

With this information I contacted the Department of Rehabilitation and Correction and asked to be connected to whoever handled the health of the inmates. I was assured that they would be keeping an eye on Joey through periodic testing, and if his condition deteriorated, would make the properly authorized medical treatment available.

I reminded them without a liver biopsy; (according to the independent doctor that I had spoken with) that they couldn't be sure what condition his liver was in, and because it had been twenty years since he was infected, now was the time to see how much damage had been done, if any. They in turn told me that Hepatitis C was rampant in the prison system and that they couldn't give every inmate diagnosed, a liver biopsy. "Inmate 161-844, would have to wait his turn, and that may be as short as 18 months, to as long as a 3 to 5 year wait." After several dead-end calls, I took to the editorial page again, in the Columbus Dispatch:

One of the Many Editorial I Have Written Over the Years

Prisoners Dying From Neglect

For those who are concerned that the death penalty will be abolished, don't be. The state of Ohio has thought of another way to kill its wards. In fact, it is even more inhumane than a lethal injection; it's more vicious than a lethal injection and carries more vengeance, pain and suffering than a lethal injection.

What it it? It is an epidemic of life-threatening diseases in the inmate population that is being ignored.

If an inmate is one of the hundreds, even thousands, diagnosed with a potentially life-threatening disease, he is put on a waiting list. He will wait up to 18 months before a doctor can see him to assess his condition.

If treatment is advised, he may be able to undergo it in another six months or so. But it may not be in time to help him.

If he is serving a lengthy sentence or life in prison, it won't matter because he may as well die sooner rather than later. If he has a release date, prison officials just hope he is released before they have to spend any money on his treatment. Plus, he will die anyway, in time, on a different budget than that of the Ohio Department of Rehabilitation and Correction.

If readers are as outraged as I am about this and mumble,

"Isn't that awful?" They should write or call a state representative or congressman. Write or call Gov. Bob Taft at 614-466-3555. or the head of the Rehabilitation and Correction Department, Reginald Wilkinson, at 614-752-1164.

We treat animals with more dignity and humanity than our fellow humans. Just because these inmates ran afoul of the law does not mean we should allow this. Readers can start petitions in their neighborhoods or churches. We are our brother's keepers, and it is up to us to see that this suffering is addressed today.

Send your petitions directly to ATTN: Reginald Wilkinson, Ohio Department of Rehabilitation and Corrections, 1050 Freeway Dr. N. Columbus 43229

Joey got his biopsy the following month. I think someone wanted me to keep quiet.

The biopsy showed a very rare strain of the disease and very minimal damage. No treatment at this time was needed. So long as Joey continued to take care of himself, he was expected to live a normal life span; a welcome relief as it meant one less worry for Joey to have to contend with. Without knowing the condition of his liver, there would have been the pressure of a death threat lingering over his future.

I went back to bombarding the parole board for his release. I contacted the ACLU, Catholic Social Concerns, and the Prison Reform Advocacy Center, to name a few. I struck up a dialog with a Richard Spense at the Ohio Parole Board, and for a while I felt he was in tune with the fairness for which we were asking. I called him once a month to check on any progress. He would tell me things like: in the next couple of months or in the next couple of weeks, until he no longer would take my calls. My last effort to contact Mr. Spence was by a fax I sent in April of 2003:

I don't know how to be politically correct in my efforts to help secure my son's release from prison. While there are many things I should be grateful for I am dealing with a great deal of frustration. It seems that the life of my son, from the time I can remember has always been in the hands of authorities. First with teachers, then with doctors, then with lawyers, then with Indian chiefs, and now with the parole board. As both then and now we have always tried to work within the system, we have had no choice. Six years ago, "you," meaning "the parole board," said, "Joe if you will give us three more years you will surely be released." Then "you" changed the rules, and said, "Ask us again in Nov. of 2001," we did, and you said, maybe Dec. or Jan. 2002. Then you said, Feb. or March 2003, then you said by the end of the week. Have you any idea what these last five to six years have been like for us? I am sure that this is as close to cruel and unusual punishment as you can get. I never dreamed that it would take 6 more years. Somehow in my naiveté I thought Joe would be home for Christmas in the year of 2001. Each month felt like a year. It is now March of 2003. I am losing faith that I will ever get to see my son released from prison.

I went on and on venting and begging to anyone who I thought could help. Occasionally I'd get politically correct letters in return; thanking me for my concerns, yet saying nothing. All I ever asked for was what was fair under the circumstances. Their polite and politically correct responses sickened me. Their rules and regulations or their interpretation of "their" rules and regulations, only met their reality. There was no reason Joe should not have been considered for parole in 1997, period. None. He had met the criteria for this release in1997. It was now 2003.

I found it so hard to be grateful or thankful to finally get what I'd been begging for so long. The parole board gave its two-page form letter approving Joey's release. When you get something you so desperately wanted; so fervently believed was deserved, there's a different kind of a feeling, a sort of a detached joy. The only thing I was grateful for was the hand written explanation saying they (the parole board) agreed that the culpability for the crime was not meted out justly.

I do begging well; some might liken me to a pit bull, or a mama grisly but it puts me in a place I prefer not to be, it makes me feel vulnerable, it makes me needy. I did however show my gratitude to the people in the offices of the Ohio Parole Authority, just not to the parole board members. I sent them flowers with a thank you note for putting up with me over these last six years. They were the troopers, they were the ones that took my calls and treated me with respect, kindness and empathy.

While waiting for July 19, 2003; the date set for Joey's release, Joey would have optimistic days and pessimistic ones. There were days he was sure something would happen to keep him from being released. He had seen it happen to others. We talked about the future and a little about the past. I of course was interested in what Joey planned to do about his mental health.

We knew if he got the proper amount of sleep, the right kinds of foods, and stayed away from drugs and alcohol his outlook for physical health was good. He had long ago quit smoking and that was an excellent start. We talked about him seeing a professional as soon as he was released, and he told me that was a requirement for parole as well. That certainly helped me to feel better about his taking control of his mental health.

I did know he had a great adversity to psychotropic drugs. He made mention on more than one occasion that he witnessed the seemingly over medicated men in the hospital wards. He would say, "Mom I knew these men when they were functioning out in population. They are now walking zombies. They just gave up I think." I asked, "What do you mean they just gave up?"

"They were just tired of the fight of the everyday grind of prison life, no hope," he said. "That's not gonna happen to me. Mom; they're just shuffling up and down the hallways, drooling, and swallowing pills. Not a pretty picture and Mom, once those drugs are embedded in the fat cells of your brain, you never go back to who you are. Those drugs take over your mind permanently." Now I don't know how he knew that, or if it was true, but he believed it.

He knew more about mental illnesses than he let on, but I thought Joey knew just enough about being different, yet rejected the idea that he was. Back in the third grade when we allowed Joey to attend the neurological program at Merlin Heights, it was more advantageous for the school district than it was for Joey. However, that program was all we could afford or thought we could manage. Joey was never taught about how to work with being different. We still don't have a handle on how to teach children about being different. Those that march to a different drummer are most often in great peril.

As thrilled as I was to finally have Joey come home, I had to admit I was frightened too. What would Joey's life be like after all these years? Everything I read said, "After ten years of institutional living, many can't adjust to living outside the walls of a prison. Often they have become institutionalized and can't function in society when left on their own."

If you needed proof that it may not be possible to readjust, all you had to do was look to the animal kingdom. It is a known fact that after captivity, many animals will die if returned to the wild. They no longer understand how to fend for themselves because they have relied on man to protect and feed them. Much effort is given to the animal to wean them from captivity and yet there are no guarantees. Surely the system will prepare Joey for reentry?

I am convinced that Joey is alive today because he was sent to prison. Joey couldn't handle freedom and making decisions as a child, what made anyone think he could now? They didn't believe us, or our assessment of our son's condition. It just wasn't their answer that Joey was not mentally competent; they were the experts, they knew everything about Joey's behavior, and we as Joey's parents knew nothing. Despite it, I had to believe that Joey would be ready to accept the help, should it look as though he would need it. He is older. He has matured. This time he will know the consequences of impulsive behavior and ask for help. You would think that, wouldn't you? But you'd be wrong.

Joey seemed so sure that he could transition. If our love for Joey were any indicator as to whether he could make it work, then I was sure he would thrive. After all he had two individual places he could call home. He had two parents who loved him; stood by him, who lived for this day and his successful reentry. Everything he will need to survive for the short term he will have. He won't need to sleep under a bridge and won-der about his next meal. If he could learn how to support himself, make friends, maybe fall in love, he might be able to start an independent life.

I had to interact with his father to help make the transition work. In the past twenty-three years, we had very little contact. The only time I spent with Joe in recent years was at Eric's wedding. It was pleasant, but of course it would have been, considering the occasion. We now had to submit a plan to the parole authorities of the role we would play in Joey's release.

Joe and I spoke about where the best placement would be. In my mind as much as I wanted Joey with me, I thought he would be better off with his father. Joe had several acres in Tipp City with a large four-bedroom ranch house, swimming pool, barns, horses, dogs, tools, and cars. Plus it was away from the big city. Both he and his wife were retired and would be able to shuttle Joey around during his first few months of freedom. I on the other hand, had a three bedroom condo, was working 40 to 60 hours a week, had only one car and lived in the city.

Joe agreed that his home would be the better place. Also it was good to know that his wife, Kathleen, was all for it as well. She had gotten to know Joey from prison visits with Joe. Joey would stay with his Dad dur-ing the week, work on finding a job, help his Dad take care of the ranch, and come up to Columbus on the weekends to visit me. He would report to the Miami County Parole Board as scheduled.

That was settled with no hassles at all. Joe is still a Jehovah Witness but I'd long gotten over my fears. Back in 1980 when all of this was going down; I may not have had a realistic understanding of how to handle my husbands rejection of Catholicism, and ultimately of me, and what I thought our family values were. He and the Jehovah Witnesses no lon-ger have any hold over me. I still believe he chose the wrong path, but I will judge him no more.

As for Joey, he was old enough and worldly enough to make his own religious choices as well.

What I did care about was Joey finding his own way in life. With the plan in place, the inspection of Joe's home by the parole authority in the next few days, we waited for July 19, and our son's long journey home.

CHAPTER 27

X-Con,

Another "Label"

I wondered, how reality would connect for Joey once he was out of prison? For the past twenty-three years we had built a communication level that seemed to work well. There was a certain amount of comfort knowing that my son would not be out on the streets hungry and freezing. He knew we would do what we could for him.

To me he was in many ways still 17. In reality he was a 40 year-old man soon to be an x-con. Some might wonder why I fought so hard for his release. I'm his mother. I want for my child what any mother wants, to see her child happy, healthy and free. If I could have given my life to spare him the life he had had to endure, I would have. But I couldn't. The only thing I could do is to fight for his release from man's bondage and pray that God would be with him.

He was sent to adult prison, when he should have been kept in the juvenile system and sent to a rehab facility or a hospital. I wanted to know that he could have another chance at a life cut short because of circumstances he had little to no control over. I just didn't know if it was too late. There are some I'm sure that didn't want him to ever see the light of day as a free man. I had to believe he would beat the odds. I wanted him to beat the odds. I needed him to beat the odds.

In my heart though, I was frightened. I was concerned, that even though 23 years had passed, I was no closer to understanding what went wrong in the life of my first-born son. Was he mentally ill? If so, what would he have to do to get his life on track? Did prison make his condition better or worse? Would he be able to cope? Would we? What did he think of himself? Just how would he survive? Joey, wrote:

Joseph Hutchison
ENG: 111 M.W.3-5:15
Professor: Beki Test
2007

Convict

At the early age of 12 and by all accounts a classic example of juvenile delinquency I began to experience labels used by society to separate and distinguish good children from the bad seeds. Prior to this and as far back as Pre-School the labels all had a forgiving nature, as in special needs, or neurologically handicapped. As well as a positive adjectives by all the experts; "With his I.Q. as high as it is, the sky's the limit, if we can fix the behavior."

Society begins to protect itself by the use of labels, as well as segregate when the assumption is made that the gray line of knowing right from wrong has been passed. The once positive adjectives concerning I.Q. are now reasons for negativity. Labels placed on antisocial behavior that have passed the gray line have very few if any positive connotations for the individual. The only positives favor the non-such labeled masses in their need to be safe. Even those with negative labels themselves, use labels on others as a means to judge good people from bad.

My awareness of the term convict goes as far back as cartoons; the classic black and white stripped uniform with a number printed on it, and a ball and chain on the ankle. My understanding of convict continued to mature primarily through media sources. The cartoon images were being replaced with Steve McQueen as Papillion (sic) and Paul Newman as Cool Hand Luke. The most powerful definitions came from the news media. Much like saying shark at the beach creates fear and invokes a danger response, convict triggers danger responses that go back to cartoons.

Having spent almost all my teens in one form of incarceration or another, I did not see myself as a convict, nor had I been referred to as a convict. At 17 years of age, I and three other juveniles engaged in an ill conceived adventure. One that ended up when one of my cohorts hit the victim in the head, in the temple region, that caused a cerebral hemorrhage and instant death. Bound over as an adult and found guilty, I was labeled convict. I not only had to deal with the world's view of me, but all the negative programming and reaction to this title that was within me.

My definition of convict and that of myself were not the same. But my feelings about those I would be living with did not change. Dangerous ruthless people are what they are, the fact I was now one did not change my definition of convicts at all. Having dealt with negative labels all my life in no way made this new one consumable for me. All the previous labels had the possibility to be overcome and removed from my resume in society. The convict label has no escape clauses.

Now I'm in Lucasville the states maximum-security prison where the worst of the worst convicts call home. With a well-developed definition of convict instilled in me since cartoons, the level of fear is on par with what it must feel like to be tossed into a pool full of sharks. Now the discovery that there is more than one type of convict. The trick is figuring the good cons from the bad cons. The bad cons definitely deserve every nasty word that my definition of convict was made up of, and some I had never thought of. Solid convict would be in any description of the man they call Redbone. He believed it was his responsibility as a convict to impart on the young incoming prisoners what it means to be a good convict and the standards it takes to be solid. Most all would like to live up to these standards, very few can make the personal sacrifice it takes and fall short. The simple and more important standards are to not be a snitch and not to be a coward. With my definition of what it means to be a solid convict complete within myself, much time passes.

The Regan era war on class, given the name, the war on drugs, created a massive influx. Influx, not only of low income, but due to tougher laws, middle income youths were also getting caught in the net. Prison growth at this time was massive across the nation. A clear distinction was made inside the prisons between inmates and old convicts. The inmate influx produced some good convicts but most were despicable in terms of convict standards. The forced integration of inmate and convict population boiled over on Easter Sunday, April 11, 1993; to date the nations longest prison riot, 11 days, nine dead.

It was during those eleven days it became clear there was a great deal of value in being seen as a solid convict by black and white, good convicts come in all colors. Convict standards now had a proven under fire worth to me and responsible for surviving the gory mess that was the riot.

After this period I was sent to Madison, Ohio, prison where this theme would play out again. Cell-block full of bound over juveniles was taken over by older convicts, to brutally murder one of the juveniles. Redbone was not able to school these youth. Failing to learn the lessons of Lucasville, places the blame on the system. Finally, I was sent to Oakwood, in Lima, Ohio, a forensic prison hospital. Working as a hospital aid and helper I saw where some once proud convicts, who said they could not take it any longer go. They have drugs that once entrenched on the mind are permanent.

A parallel can be made between how blacks have been given the word nigger a positive usage in the culture and a positive sense of the word convict. *Oxford English Dictionary* quotes the usage of convict and makes a connection with blacks ("The importation of negro slaves soon lowered the value of convict labor") as far back as 1530. *Blacks Law Dictionary*, current use has not changed over time ("person convicted of a crime/prison inmate"). This word is deeply engraved in our culture, just like screaming fire has universal results.

As a culture we place words to a job description to warn of danger. Convict is one of these words. In a purely random survey of twelve people; all used warning language when asked what the word meant to them. None had any positive impressions. Society has no legitimate need to try and change something so fundamental in the culture.

I cannot expect society to see me in the convict light I see myself in. However there are mainstream artistes that use convict in a very empowering positive way, ("Akron Convict, music album"). Being able to relate to these modern lyrics; gain positive thoughts and support your self-image, is one way to overcome the inherent negatives that go along with being labeled convict. In fact the convict population in this country is at all time highs and it is creating its own sub culture in our society.

Politicians are no longer screaming tough on convicts like they did in the eighty's. I believe because the legal system has reached out during its explosion and it has touched a lot of God fearing voting families. Convict has its basic meaning to the majority and only until it becomes personal do you find a definition you can live with and that will be unique to the individual.

I don't expect to see any campaigns like, black is beautiful, grass root efforts to give positive association for the word convict. However with the convicted felons list growing ever longer in the country, I don't rule out its potential sub culture growth with good associations in the future.

**

With that essay, Joey told it like he saw it. I admit I see the label convict as meaning danger, except when it is connected to my son. I couldn't help but think back to the time when, Joe and I overheard a group of people saying negative things about the black race. When they realized that Joe and I were present someone quickly added, "Oh, but we don't mean Jimmy!" Did Jimmy somehow not belong to the black culture because he was now our son, a black son who now had white parents? Would Joey somehow not be an ex-con?

Sadly Joey's label would follow him into eternity. *Please God, help me handle this and be a positive, helpful parent to my adult child, my Joey. Let him be one of the ones that "make it."* After having the experience of living as close to hell as one can, without actually going to hell, that sounded like a fair plea to fall on God's ears.

I needed to believe that after all that we had gone through, we would emerge on the other side victorious.

I then prepared to retrieve my son. I went shopping for some clothes to bring Joey home in. It felt like a rebirth to some extent. Hadn't his sister, Leeann, and I prepared an outfit to bring him home from the hospital 40 years ago, after he was born on Mother's Day? I looked for something other than dark blue and light brown. I had only seen Joey in faded dark blue work pants and baby blue button down shirts or khakis these past five years. The only thing Joey asked for was a pair of "real" Levi's but I picked out a pair of black dress slacks too. I also grabbed a couple of pullover summer shirts. There would be time for more shopping later. This whole time I kept thinking, "This is really going to happen!"

Eric wanted to drive me up to the Oakwood prison to pick up Joey. I was too excited to go by myself and was glad for the offer. We planned to meet Joe and Kathy at the prison about 9 AM on July 19, 2003.

During the two and a half hour drive to the prison in Lima, Ohio, Eric and I traveled mostly in silence. I imagined Eric was thinking about how Joey's release would impact his family. If Eric, always the thoughtful, practical son was feeling any negative concerns, he didn't have to voice them. I knew. Mothers just know these things.

In 1999, when I was sure I would be making Columbus, Ohio my home, I bought a three-bedroom condominium. I wanted a permanent place to call home, and I wanted to be prepared should I be the parent to which Joey would be paroled. I was working in my chosen field of consultation in transportation. Thinking that my success at Executive Transfer would continue gave me that permanent feeling of confidence. Even though Tim Picciano had left for a new position and even though Tim had been my biggest supporter, I was not too concerned when he left. I should have been.

When Tim left his position of vice-president of sales, the position was left unfilled, that should have been a red flag. There was a rumor that perhaps I might be tapped for a sales manager's position. I hoped not; as I didn't want the position and most likely would have turned it down, had I been asked. For the next year and a half the sales department spiraled out of control. I witnessed its faltering, but any attempts on my part to help, fell on deaf ears. Those in charge didn't quite grasp how to manage the situation. I didn't feel threatened, as I knew what my job was and how to do it. I let the others stab each other in the back. I was above that kind of folly or so I deluded myself. I should have paid attention. Backstabbing is what happens when things don't run smoothly.

When a company that relies on a sales force begins to struggle, they assume that their sales force is the root of the problem. I believe that to be wrong in most cases. If the sales people have been productive in the past and proven themselves as such, you have to look at management and the sales environment of the product. In this case, management had gone out on a limb by investing in a new facility during a market downturn of their product. Their answer was to add more sales people. Wrong answer.

I was asked to train a "potential" new COD sales person. My desire to be a teacher is part of who I am, so I eagerly took on this request. Jeff Perrin came to Executive Transfer from the restaurant industry. He had no previous sales experience in transportation. He was from Australia and I fell in love with his accent. He was also half my age and I thought of him as a kid. During his training period we got along very well. He was like a sponge and absorbed everything I taught him. Looking back now that was what happened when I brought Diana on board at Laramore in Texas? Could it be I was training my replacement?

Two weeks after I cut him loose to fly on his own, the company announced he was to be the new sales manager, not a VP of sales, only the manager. I was not concerned, as I didn't want that position anyway. Mr. Perrin took his new position seriously and began to make sales decisions that further ruined the department. Plans were laid to ultimately get me to resign. In addition to Mr. Perrin in the COD sales department was a new supervisor VP David Walton, who was known by an unspoken nick-name of "Little Hitler" in the commercial sales arena. I never had to deal directly with Mr. Walton, before this reorganization and was glad. He now became a formidable presence in the household goods sales department.

I was fired after refusing to resign. I relayed the experience of this four-month episode to the unemployment bureau and received approval for unemployment. That was a validation of a sort; because one, the company fought to pay me unemployment relief, and two, in about six months hence, almost the entire staff in the household good department at Executive Transfer was gone. I think the only one left in the department was Scott Hughes, the national account sales representative. Gone was VP Walton, Sales Manager Perrin, and some of the others who had left of their own accord.

I took a little breather and tried to lick my wounds. This was twice now in my life I had been fired from a job I knew that I had done well. I was now unemployed, bordering on becoming a senior citizen, and still working paycheck to paycheck for the most part.

I decided to try direct sales again. At least there I would have no bosses who could fire me on a whim. Exposed to a company that handled employee benefits I looked into representing Pre-Paid Legal services. I had taken out that voluntary coverage when I was employed at Executive Transfer and found it of great benefit. It was an affordable product and in my opinion extremely useful, if used properly. The only draw back was the recruiting part. I chose to do group sales and determined that recruiting was not as significant in that arena. The MLM of the Pre-Paid sales approach would not keep me from prospering, I deduced. It would be much like selling "Rainbows," except I wouldn't have to carry around the machine in the trunk of my car and clean it after every demonstration.

Until that took off I would need to have some extra income. I took a job as a reset person for a company who sold labor for restocking store shelves. In both of these jobs I could see that I would be able to offer my son Joey, a way to earn extra money until he would be able to find employment on his own. He could work under me without a background check. I would pay him direct for the work he did to help me at group signings and keep paperwork filed in my home office. The restocking company would pay him directly.

I also tried to help a man establish a local moving company and expand it into a interstate moving company. That was not a good choice on my part, as the man had no idea what it would take to make a jump, from a mom-n-pop operation to the big time. I learned he later sold the the business and moved to the Carolina's.

Working at all of these minor and multiple jobs was not new to me. However, I found that as I was just a tad older, it was a bit more challenging to my mind and body. In other words I tired more easily. I no longer wanted to work multiple jobs. But I knew I had to hang in there until I got Joey settled into the outside world. This afforded me the opportunity to work my own hours and with that, gave me the freedom to schedule personal time off if needed. That was one of the few perks to being self employed I particularly liked.

The morning of July 19, 2003 the dawn broke in typical gray Ohio fashion. The sun was up there somewhere, I knew that, but it was just not shinning through the mist yet. I felt the excitement of something almost too good to be true about to happen. This was the day I had waited for, for over 23 years. It felt like I was about to win the lottery; get something I had been praying for, but was never sure I would ever get.

I reminded myself to be careful. *Linda you are about to enter into unknown territory. I can do this, can't I? I can be a rock upon which Joey can find his way, right? Between his dad and I we can be Joey's support system. His brothers and sister will do what they can as well. This is just going to have to work. We all have come too far to fail.*

I thought that even though Joey would leave prison without the benefit of a mental health treatment plan, we would at least have access to quality mental health care if needed. I thought that the after care and support of someone who had spent 23 years in prison would be a given. There would be a certain amount of help in readjustment, like helping Joey to find a job and apply for health care. It's not that I thought Joey was cured in any sense of what the word cured meant, it was just that we knew so much more now about mental health, or so we thought. Joey knew so much more about mental health. He would be better prepared to deal with his condition; accept his condition(s), work with his condition(s) in an adult manner, there would be programs to help him.

As Eric and I drove onto the prison grounds I couldn't help but feel the joy of never having to enter onto prison grounds again to visit my son. The Oakwood prison was the least restrictive and formidable of the institutional facilities that Joey had been in, but it was still a prison, an institution; a place where you are locked away from the "real world." A place where you are a number (161844) not thought to be good enough to even have a name.

Greeted by the officer on duty, I proudly exclaimed, "We are here to pick up my son, Joseph Hutchison 161844 and take him home. I have brought him these clothes to wear." I handed him the bag that held the new clothes. The guard told us to take a seat as Joseph was in the process of being cleared for release. "He will be coming through that door," he said as he pointed at the door with the automatic locking system. His first time in over 23 years, to come through a door that would lead to freedom, without handcuffs or restraints. I wondered how Joey was feeling.

Joe and Kathy hadn't arrived yet and I also wondered what was keeping them. They missed the moment. Joey bounced through the door as nervous and high strung as I had seen him in quite some time. He later told me he was so afraid that at any moment he expected them to change their mind and tell him they were just kidding. Several of the prison personnel came out to say good-bye and wish him well. One particular woman, and I can't remember her name, came over to me and said, "I know Joe is one who will make it. He is a good man. I will miss him." What a wonderful thing to say to his mother, it caused me to smile and give her a hug.

There was some last minute paperwork for Joey to sign before he collected the $60 in cash from the state, and a 1.5 cubic foot box that held all his personal possessions from the last 23 years. He left behind his TV, radio and fan, to the custody of others, who would need them more than he would. Asked if he wanted to wait for his father and Kathy to arrive before we went through the doors to freedom, his reply was a quick firm, "No." The three of us, Eric, Joey and I, walked though the double doors to Joey's freedom and a little bit of sunshine. *Oh, Linda what are you going to do now, now that you've got what you prayed for? Answer: Love him. Just love him.*

CHAPTER 28

Promises

Of Fulfillment

Joey headed straight for the parking lot and didn't look back. "What kind of car you driving now?" he asked Eric. Eric replied, "It's that black Subaru WRX/STI." Cool, Joey, said, "That had to set you back a pretty penny." Joey walked around the car looking at all the features. Eric popped the trunk and Joey set his small box of possessions down inside and headed for the back seat. He didn't even offer to take the front seat. Habit I thought. A few minuets later Joe and Kathy pulled up next to us. We made some casual remarks like "Want to race out of the parking lot" and "Let's see who can get off this property the fastest without getting arrested." Finally we decided to meet and have lunch at an Outback Steak House on the way back to Tipp City, and the long homecoming for Joey.

As we drove we made telephone calls to Leeann in Denver and Jimmy in San Diego, and Joey got to share his good news with them. It was a way to keep them in the loop and a part of this great day. It was also Joey's first time using a cell phone. Lunch at the Outback was every-thing Joey had hoped it would be. He ordered a T-bone with fries and a salad. Topped it off with a glass of ice tea with lemon. At first he didn't seem to know that silverware was wrapped in a cloth napkin or where to put the napkin once he released its contents. I watched him watch us, and he soon followed suit. This was to be one of the many things Joey would have to relearn. Prison doesn't have steak knives or cloth napkins.

Joey Was Remodeling This House and Taking Care of His Favorite Horse Brandy 2007

It wasn't far now to Joe and Kathy's, but first Joey wanted to see his old house in Vandalia. The house looked pretty much the same, although the tree house was now gone and the front porch was a little different. We then drove by St. Christopher's and Morton Junior High, past the defunct Willow Swim Club, whose pool was filled in and no longer in use. Joey drank in all the memories of these places. Was he remembering only the good one's? I hoped so, but I didn't ask. We then headed to the ranch.

At Joe's house, Kathy had set aside a bedroom for Joey, the first one on the left down the hall. It had it's own bathroom so Joey would have some privacy. Joey sat his meager belongings on the bed and continued to tour the house. I had never been inside Joe's house before; I had been on the property a couple of times when Leeann had come to visit, but never inside, so I took the tour as well. Outside was a barn with two horses, a dog named Snickers, a swimming pool, a second barn and a garage full of tools. I saw every kind of tool known to modern man; as I remembered, if one hammer was good, five or six were even better, that was Joey's dad's motto.

We spent the rest of the afternoon in the family room telling and remembering wonderful stories and playing pool. Eventually it was time for Eric and I to leave. Lord, I can't tell you how hard it was for me to leave him there. It wasn't that I was concerned he wouldn't be OK it was that *I wouldn't be*. Joey promised to call me the next day and let me know how his first night at home went. I kissed and hugged him good-bye and told him how happy I was that he was home. I would be back Friday evening to pick him up for his first visit to my home yet it seemed that Friday would be so far away, and I didn't want to miss a day of the rest of his life.

As Eric and I drove back to Columbus, we both agreed that Joey's homecoming went well. Joey, phoned the next morning and said he hadn't slept well, I asked him why and he said, "Mom do you know how dark is it out here? Do you know how quiet it is too?"

"I hadn't ever given it much thought, but it is the country," I said.

Joey went on to say, "In prison there were always lights on some-where; and noise of some kind, someone was always hollering about something all night long. "I'm not used to the darkness and silence. I guess that is something I will have to get used to," he said.

"You will," I promised. "Do you think you will need some help with that?" I asked?

"I don't think so," Joey replied.

"What are you going to do today?" I asked?"

"I need to go and check in with the Miami County Parole Authority," Joey said. "I will have to see what kind of restrictions I will have. Then dad is going to take me to see an eye doctor for a check up and new glasses. These state-issue, Coke bottle glasses meet my needs, but dad wants me to have new ones. Also we want to see if there is anything that can be done to strengthen my eye. That should be enough for today."

"Good, you should take it slow and ease into things," I advised. "Call me later."

By Friday, Joey had his temporary driver's permit and a civilian I.D. and new modern glasses. The optometrist confirmed that Joey's eye condition was permanent, as his brain was now wired to how his vision would be the rest of his life. In other words there were no treatments or surgery that could correct it.

He was getting used to taking care of the horses and with each new day, sleeping a little bit better each night. He had met his parole offi-cer, Mr. Brian Algeo, and was set up for reentry counseling at the Miami County Mental Health Center in Troy, Ohio. He was required to report once a week and take a urine test if requested. He had a 10 PM curfew and of course was not permitted any alcohol or drugs. He was told they would be helping him to find a job as well.

I picked him up on Friday evening and he was full of stories about the horses and what he had been doing to help his dad. He told me he was concerned about his dad's health. "I think he's a lot sicker then he lets on," Joey said. "I want to be able to make his life a little easier now. I have already organized the tool barn. And Mom, you know what's funny? Remember when I was a child and dad was always on me to put tools back where I got 'um?" "Yes," I said. "Well, now it's me telling him to put 'um back where he got 'um. Kinda like a roll reversal, don't you think," he said?" I got a little chuckle out of that story.

We stopped for fast food and spent that first night at home. I had fixed up the guest room for Joey but hoped he wouldn't feel like a guest. I think he knew the room was his anytime he needed it.

It would be his choice if he wanted to attend Mass on Sunday's when he was here. Most of the time if I went to Mass, which wasn't every

Sunday, he would go with me. We talked some about religion, but not much. Joey told me he had a little understanding about many religions. He said, "Mom because of all the exposure in prison from almost all forms of religions, from Baptist to Muslim, I don't get all misty eyed about religions. They would always ask me on forms that I had to fill out if I had a preference and I've always thought of myself as a Catholic, and would mark that box. To be honest with you I don't really think much about religion." "That's okay," I said, "It is after all only a label. It's what you believe in your heart that counts. Some day it may be important to you and if you ever want to talk about religion or God, I will listen."

I took Joey back to his father's Sunday night and from there the next few months seemed to go well aside from Joey not being able to find a full time job. Joey's uncle Frank (his dad's brother) gave him a car, a van really, and Joey was tickled to death. He worked on that van constantly. He literally tore it apart at the seams and brought it back to life. He called it his "Hoopty." This van was his pride and joy; it also gave him the feeling of independence. He could now go anyplace he wanted at anytime he wanted. I no longer had to go down to Tipp City on weekends to pick him up for visits. He drove himself up to Columbus.

Joey would also come up to work on jobs with me. He would help me on Saturdays with safety meetings for interstate truck drivers. He would handle setting up the tables and laying out the paperwork. Then as the truckers would fill out the membership forms after my explanation of the benefits, Joey would hand out the membership packets. We made a fine team and I paid Joey for his help.

Joey had thought he might like to drive a truck, he aced the written exam with only two days of studying the manual however he failed the eye exam. His eye problem hurt his peripheral vision and therefore his sight was not good enough for a commercial driver's license.

He also went with me into restocking and resetting retail and grocery shelves. We would enter a store about 10 or 11 pm at night and by 7 am in the morning we had completely restocked or reset a department. We actually had fun doing this, and the company we worked for paid him by direct deposit. That meant that Joey could have his own checking account and handle his own personal needs such as auto insurance. With his ever-growing stability he was issued a credit card as well.

One major project that Joey took on was a total makeover of my good friend Marilyn's bathroom. I marveled at his ability to do these renovations. How did he know how to tear out a bathtub, toilet and sink? Remove all the drywall and tile and replace it? Even the plumbing and electricity was no problem for him. I knew he'd learned from his father, but how after all these years could he remember just what to do? Marilyn paid him well for his labor and was completely satisfied. I still admire his work every time I visit her.

Joey went on job interviews but hadn't been able to find a permanent job. The interviews Joey was sent on were often heartbreaking. Joey said, "Mom, do you know what it's like to sit across a desk from a young lady in the employment office, and answer questions about where you have been for the last twenty five years and why? I have to tell her I have been in prison for aggravated murder and felonious assault and that I have never held a full time job, ever? They look at me with fright in their eyes and move their chairs a little further back, and say, "We don't have anything in your category just now, but we will keep you application on file and call you if any thing comes up." I get so discouraged," he said.

I told him things would work out. Maybe he knew I was trying to be upbeat for him, as I too was becoming concerned. Why, wasn't there more help from the parole authority for someone like Joey? He has proven to be a good worker and a hard worker. He needs a break. Just about this time Joey's parole officer, Mr. Algeo, was replaced by a man named Andrew Barnes. There was definitely a different attitude on Joey's part about checking in with Barnes.

The New Year brought some distinct changes in Joey's behavior, not all were good. We had what I thought was a great Christmas. Joey wanted to decorate. He knew his dad wouldn't be celebrating the holiday and asked me if he could decorate my house. I got a little excited. I said, "Everything is up in the attic, go to it." We had decorations everywhere. We had the tree of course but we also had the doorknobs and lamp shades decorated. Joey found the box that had all the Christmas stockings from his childhood and hung them all on the fireplace mantel. We went to mid-night Mass and had Christmas Day dinner with Eric and Christa. We attended several Christmas gatherings with Marilyn, and her family and also with my sister, and her family. Every celebration went well and it looked as if Joey never missed a beat in all the glad tidings, yet there was still something I couldn't put my finger on. He was extremely agitated, restless and hyper.

One cold Sunday night in early January of 2004; after Joey had helped put the Christmas decorations away and was about to go back to his dad's, with tears in his eyes, he confessed, "Mom I'm not going to make it." I asked, "Joey why would you say such a thing?" He said, "Can't you see I'm damaged goods?" I said, "Joey we are all damaged goods in one way or another. Your dad has heart trouble and sugar diabetes. Marilyn has diabetes. I fight obesity. Can't you see that none of us are perfect? Come on now, we just had a great Christmas, it's a New Year, things will get better, and they're not so bad now. I love you and I think you're doing great. It's just going to take a little more time to get where you want to be. We got the time, Joey," I said.

I called Joe after Joey left and we talked about Joey's depression. Joe told me that he thought that Joey was having some problems with huffing. I said, "Why haven't you said anything before now." He said he thought it was just a phase, and didn't want to worry me. Joey also asked him not to tell me as well and he promised not to do it again. He also told me that since Joey had a change in parole officers, he thought that might have had something to do with it. He was almost sure there was a personality conflict between Joey and Barnes. This was not something I wanted to hear. Should I intervene? Should I be calling somebody?

Joey kept all of his visits with counselors and according to him they had given him a clean bill of health. Was I being paranoid? Should I worry? I decided I would wait until Joey gave up a few more flags, before I played the "paranoid mommy" card. His dad and I walked a fine line in trying not to be overly protective.

I decided that next weekend I would try and start a little dialog with Joey about seeing a professional counselor again. Maybe it would help him put some things in perspective. Hopefully he would open up about what was going on, if not he will know he can talk to me, if he wants. What else could I do, I thought?

The following week I answered the phone and the voice on the other end was Joey's. "Mom," he said, "I got something to tell you." The tone and the words were all I had to hear to know this was not going to be good. "What's happened Joey," I asked. "I tested positive for a dirty urine today," he replied. Joey went on to tell me that in the past he had been able to get past urine tests by drinking a lot of water several days before a test. This had worked well in prison; because the prison didn't use the most sophisticated testing tools, because of the expense. "So what does this mean," I asked? Joey thought he was just going to have to submit to weekly reporting and urine tests again. He had been reduced to checking in every three weeks; and that was how he got caught. He counted on cleaning out his system with abstinence and plenty of water at least 10 days before his next check in. So for now Drew Barnes, was having him return to weekly visits. "I should be glad," he said, "because he could have jailed me on the spot."

"It seems that you dodged a bullet Joey, but the bottom line is what are you going to do about using substances period, not only are they illegal, but they can hurt you physically? You know your liver has to process the chemicals, right? And Joey I know you know that while you are on parole you can't afford to have a slip. Have you given any thought to seeing a drug counselor again, I asked?" *Damn, I sounded just like I did when he was a teenager, why did I do that. I knew that everything that I said he already knew. Please God let him see the light on his own, and if he can't, please tell me what I should do. I just can't let him ruin this second chance. Why does one need these kinds of drugs to get through a day?*

I tried to cover myself from being a bitchy, preaching mother, and said, "Joey, I love you so much, but son, its up to you. I will help you if I can, I think you know that, but I can't stop you now any more than I could when you were a boy. I can't take the pain away either, or I would do that too. You are the only one who can, please want to, please try and find the answer. You are so worth it. Are you coming up this weekend, I asked? "Yes, Mom I will see you Friday night," he said. But I didn't see him Friday night. Instead, he went to jail.

At his next check in, Drew Barnes had him arrested for the dirty urine and jailed. What a sneaky thing to do. He let Joey think that his only punishment was to return to weekly drugs tests. Without warning he was sent to jail for something he thought had been resolved. Whether it was Drew Barnes doing; or whether it was Drew Barnes supervisor, Jenny Christner, who insisted that Joey be jailed, we never knew.

I was prepared to accept it was Joey who got himself in this mess, and it was Joey who would have to get himself out of this mess. Joey accepted what had happened. He didn't ask for help or intervention. He said that while he knew they could return him to prison for a parole violation he was pretty sure that wasn't going to happen this time. He was prepared to change his ways and avoid this happening again. However, a saint he wasn't.

Joey liked to vent and his twenty-three years of prison talk surfaced. He made no bones about how he felt about being blindsided by Drew Barnes. I recalled he called him several unflattering names, one being an ugly, maggot/faggot, his favorite phrase for those he disliked. It was obvious he would not be holding this man and his position in high esteem. I just let him vent. At no time did I take anything he said as being anything to be taken literally. There were a lot of "I'd like to," and "maybes." Perhaps some awful curses, like warts, should befall this man. However, nothing that was said could be remotely construed as anything Joey would follow through on, just talk.

I don't remember how long he was in jail, a week or ten days maybe, but eventually he was released. The next thing Joey did was to seek out help at Dettimer Hospital and the UVMC, Miami County Mental Health Center. There he connected with a man by the name of Gordon Buckner, MRC, LSW. Gordon was an Outpatient Therapist. Joey also spent a couple of days at Twin Valley Behavioral Healthcare, Dayton Campus and was discharged on Zoloft and Ambien.

I took this as a positive sign. Was this episode that proverbial wake -up call that Joey always seemed to need, and would Joey pay attention this time? He was after all an adult male. I made a call to Joey's parole officer to let him know we were behind our son 100% and would do everything we could to help him with any problems he might encounter. I wanted to confirm with Mr. Barnes, that Joey was seeking treatment on his own. I then gave the phone to Joey. I had the phone on speaker and heard Mr. Barnes tell Joey, to never have his mother call him again. He didn't like my attitude and he had no time to deal with mothers. He was the rudest and most unhelpful man. I could see why Joey would have issues with him.

It is my belief that most lay people can't understand why people with mental illnesses can't seem to stop destructive behaviors. It is my belief the mentally ill want to, they know they need to, they try and they fail. They berate themselves then try again. They think that they cure their behavior on their own. They can't. What a mentally ill person must come to terms with is that they can't cure themselves on their own. Until they accept that, they need our help to keep them from themselves, their own worst enemy.

Yes, Joey needed help and again I (we) couldn't help him. All we could do is encourage him to seek help from the experts. Joey was doing that and the good people at the Adult Parole Authority thought it would be a good idea to arrest Joey for aggravated menacing.

Joey and his dad were doing some maintenance on the roof of their home, when several officers arrived and arrested Joey for aggravated menacing. It seemed that a couple of jail house snitches told their parole officer, Drew Barnes, that Joey was talking about harming Mr. Barnes. They apparently had overheard his conversations with me on the phone about how much he disliked Mr. Barnes. Mr. Barnes then embellished on these statements to file charges against Joey. The snitches were looking for favors and probably got them.

This was of course a serious threat to Joey's parole. With these charges pending in a court of law the parole board could and would hold a revocation hearing. If found guilty at the hearing he would return to prison and the charges before the court would be dropped. If found innocent, the charges would be dropped as well, do to lack of evidence and Joey would be released to resume his parole. For a chance of a favorable outcome, we were going to need an attorney.

In fighting these charges we hired an attorney familiar with Miami County and its court system, as every county has its own way of doing business. Mr. Jose Lopez was a laid back sort of person and at times I wondered if he took this case seriously. His fee, a $2,500 retainer, could be more by the time the verdict was rendered.

We learned that this was a favorite tactic of the APA in Miami County. If they wanted to return a parolee back to the system, they could charge the parolee with a misdemeanor; hold a revocation hearing, find the parolee guilty, the civil charges would then be dropped and the parolee would return to prison. If the parolee didn't have adequate representation, most certainly he would go back to prison.

Mr. Lopez told us that the original charges of aggravated menacing were bogus. The evidence the APA had against Joey did not fit the laws for aggravated menacing charges. He told us that you could say anything you want against, or about a person at any time, in other words trash another person—that in itself was not unlawful. You must however be able to follow through with any harmful action for it to be considered a crime. Joey was not able to follow through with any statements he may or may not have made as he was in jail; a pure example of a misuse of power by the APA. However, a hearing would still be held.

On the day of the hearing, thank goodness Mr. Lopez was able to handle these tactics in a professional manner. It didn't take him long to prove the incompetence of the persons who brought these charges and the witnesses that were lined up to testify. It was a total joke, and it was obvious that the hearing officer, sent from headquarters in Cincinnati, Ohio was not pleased. She as much said that this case was obviously mishandled by the local APA and Joey should be released.

Another two months out of Joey's life spent in jail; several thousands of dollars and the only thing accomplished was punishment, and more hatred for the system. It was up to Joey to find positive solutions for his survival in the real world. There were no easy answers. There were none forty years ago and there are none now. What's a family to do?

The next few months in Tipp City with his dad would be pure hell. Joey was seeing Gordon Buckner at UVMC and had spent a few days in Twin Valley Mental Hospital in Troy, Ohio. There he was put on Zanax and Zoloft. We would later find out that these anti anxiety drugs and others can sometimes exacerbate mental illnesses like bipolar disorder and schizophrenia. Since no one yet had seen fit to give Joey an official diagnoses of his mental health he was prescribed these drugs. Joey was getting worse. Perhaps Joey should come to live with me in Columbus. The APA in Columbus may be a better fit for Joey than Miami County.

In the meantime we made plans to visit Leeann in Denver and attend the High School graduation of her daughter, Brooklyn. This would mean traveling by plane to Colorado. Joey had never flown before and was so excited over the possibility. Another first I thought, it was like watching someone catching up to life. For Joey to experience things that he could only partake in from watching on a television news story or a movie was thrilling and gratifying for me. We had a great family reunion.

CHAPTER 29

Completing One Journey
and Starting the Next

Joey and I returned from Colorado eager to continue making the changes needed to move forward. I decided to return to the transportation industry. Carla Simpson, who coordinated sales orders from Executive Transfer, was now working with Trowbridge, a United Agent in the Columbus market. Tim Meeks who had been a dispatcher at Executive was also there, and I was asked to join them. This is not unusual in this industry. It seems that if you can wait long enough between jobs, you will eventually be picked up by another company in the local market. In most cases, you will find yourself working with the same people you once worked with in a prior company. A little like musical chairs, and possibly a touch of insanity to boot.

There would still be part time work for Joey with restocking retail stores and helping me with my in home business. However, he very much needed full time work if he were to progress into independent living. Joey made the rounds again at Miami County Department of Job and Family Services. He talked with CBS Companies (partners in human resource solutions) and Goodwill Industries. He sat on the doorsteps of construction companies and delivery service venders. We all read the newspaper want ads, looking to help him find an opportunity and yet nothing broke.

It was approaching winter again and the rehab properties Joey was working on with his dad slowed as well. Christmas was around the corner and we were planning a huge Christmas party at the clubhouse where I lived. This time everyone would be here, including Jimmy and his family from San Diego.

To have all of my children "home" for Christmas was something I had looked forward to for 25 years. While Leeann was still harboring the beliefs of the JW's she would not interfere with the celebration.

Oh, what fun it was to ride, in a one horse open sleigh. They all came, some bunked at Eric and Christa's, some in sleeping bags on my floor. The party included all but one of my grandchildren, Britney, as she had just given birth to twins. My sister and brother-in-law and all her kids and grandkids, friends and neighbors all arrived in a festive mood. Joey invited a couple of his buddies that he knew from prison and their families. One came from Chillcothe and one from Dayton. We had music and games and great food. Leeann and I made about six gallons of homemade chili; Buffalo wings in all flavors, baked beans and mac-n-cheese, Christmas cookies and cakes in shapes of candy canes and Christmas trees. Yum!

Our First Christmas In 25 Years That All My Children Were Home 2006

Later in the week we all went to The Rapids, an indoor water park. What a sight it was to see this 60 something great grandmother, slip sliding down water shoots, to the laughter of her grandchildren. We spent time together; that was what counted. It was the happiest Christmas ever. A family Christmas…so long overdue.

Joey was showing signs of seasonal depression and I was urging him to get back to Tipp City and stop in to see Gordon Buckner. He said he would when he left. I felt he wasn't taking the right meds and was concerned he was not participating in any programs. He was still not working well with Drew Barnes either. He had asked to be reassigned to another officer numerous times but a transfer hadn't come.

Joe called me January 2, 2005 to tell me that Joey was out in the barn hallucinating and he was afraid he had overdosed. I told him to call an ambulance and I would be right there. I called Eric and he and I drove to Tipp. When we arrived at the hospital Joey was coming around, he had been huffing again according to his dad. "How long had this been going on," I asked? "On and off for a while." Joe said. We asked the emergency personnel at Dettmer hospital to admit Joey to the Psych unit but they couldn't if Joey would not agree, for now he was no longer a danger to himself. Joey told them that he was not trying to kill himself.

I asked them to call Gordon Buckner, without Joey's permission; they said they couldn't do that either. Of course Joey was apologetic and said he would take control of the situation himself, tomorrow. He insisted he was not trying to kill himself. I countered with, "Joey you need professional help. Your dad and I are not equipped to help you. This behavior has to stop. Please do this for me, even if you won't do it for yourself." But Joey still refused, saying "I will be OK and I will call Gordon tomorrow."

I was helpless to stop it. I could hear the knocks? Those damn knocks. They're here. I asked for help, I begged for help and help was not banging down the door. Joey was not going to be able to do this for himself. He couldn't when he was a child. He didn't do it in prison and he wasn't doing it well now. Why? Where were the answers?

I tried my best to get Joey to see what he was doing to himself. I reminded him how hard this was on his dad. "Joey, you have helped your dad get through his open heart surgery. He couldn't have done it without you. You were there every step of the way. He wants to be there for you now. You're sliding into dangerous waters. We don't want to lose you. If you won't check yourself into a hospital, please ask Gordon if he can get you in to see a psychiatrist. Your thinking is off line."

I asked him to come up to Columbus. "Maybe the opportunities for employment will be better in a larger city," I said. Joey said he would think about it.

Joey came up midweek and we began to take steps to get his parole moved to Franklin county. Joey was drinking coffee by the gallons and pacing the floors and picking at his body. He had been chewing his fingernails till they bled. It was obvious something was not right.

On a cold dreary January evening I was on my way home from work when my cell phone rang. It was Joey! He was almost incoherent and shouting, "Mom, I'm lost I don't know where I am or where my car is." It was pouring down rain and I was a mile or two from home. "Where do you think you are and I will come get you," I said. "Mom, I think I hit somebody or a car on Georgesville," he said. *Oh God, no I thought.* I said, "Just calm down, think. Do you recognize any kind of landmark, a store, a gas station, anything?" Joey, then said to me, "Mom, can you hear sirens? I think the police are after me? I hit something! I know I did! Oh, God, I don't know where I left the car either!" "Joey, can you get home on foot," I asked? "Try to get home, and in the meantime I will be looking for you. I am going to hang up now and call your brother to come and help. Don't lose your phone, I will call you back," I said.

I thought about calling the police, but instead I called Eric. Eric told me to go home and wait for him, as he didn't want me running around in this weather, panic stricken as well. When I got home, Joey was there and agitated. " How did you get here?" I asked? He didn't remember, maybe in a cab, he thought. He went from not being able to shut-up to totally unresponsive at all. He was covered in mud and his jacket was ripped. What could have happened, all the worst case scenarios kept playing over in my mind. Had he been in a fight, had he been robbed, had he hit someone or something? What?

By the time Eric arrived, Joey had calmed down somewhat. What was left was to try and piece together what happened and find the car. Should we have called the police, well maybe under normal circumstances; but we really didn't know how serious this was going to be, and if it turned out to be something we could handle ourselves, we wanted to wait. Joey still couldn't remember where he had been, but he did remember that he hit something and that people were yelling at him to pull over.

He remembered he left the major roadway and turned onto a side street; he then left the car and ran, climbing over fences and through backyards.

We got into Eric's car and drove up and down Georgesville Rd., first looking for a possible crime scene with police and ambulances. We found none. We then went street by street, parking lot by parking lot looking for Joey's car. We were just about to give up, when we spotted an apartment complex off to one side with a fairly large parking lot. There at the back of the lot sat "Hoop-tee" with a smashed left front fender and headlight and looking as forlorn as Joey. Wounded but still ticking, I thought. It also looked as if someone had riffled through the glove compartment and some paperwork was missing. Joey concluded it had to be the police, and that it was only a matter of time before they would come for him. "Someone was sure to have turned him in," Joey said.

Should we cut to the chase and call the police ourselves? I thought if the police were involved, that the car would have been towed as evidence, and I tried to convince Joey of that fact. Let's go home and plan our next step. Joey wanted to drive the car home, and Eric stepped in and said, "You go with Mom. I will drive it back to the condo." Joey still didn't remember what had happened. I asked him if he thought he had been drinking and he said he couldn't remember, but if he had been, he had surely blacked out.

Eric, more or less told Joey that this behavior had to stop and that he needed to make some decisions about his life. He would check in on him in the morning to find out what he planned to do. "In the meantime I suggest you stay put for the night," Eric said.

Joey paced all night long. His fingers and parts of his arms and legs were covered in blood from constant picking. I convinced him to let me take him to "Net Care." "Joey, that is the quickest way to get help," I said. I had been doing some research into mental health care and thought this might be just what Joey needed. Net Care serviced people in crisis for mental illness, drugs and alcohol. I told Joey if the police were to get involved, it might look better if he had voluntarily gone for help.

My heart was breaking knowing that for the most part Joey was trying his best to get on with life and when the times were good they were really good. We had had so much fun being together, he had been a great housemate. He just needed more care than I could give him and more care than he was getting. I can't tell you how hard it was to not be able to help your child. Joey had not been treated for a serious mental illness for the last 25 years—from the time that the psychiatrists had testified during his trial that he definitely was mentally ill, maybe not insane, but definitely mentally ill. And let's face it, people just don't spontaneously recover from severe mental illnesses.

If you are a borderline personality, bipolar, schizophrenic, paranoid or whatever, you need treatment. As far as I know punishment will not cure you or even help you over come these demons. It is my understanding you can't wish away or mandate acts of self-control to over come other diseases such as diabetes, cancer, allergies or other life long ills. You sure as hell can't do it with mental illnesses either. Yet there are some that think you can.

We need answers and we need them now. I knew that Joey was more than an alcoholic or a drug addict; mental illness was at the root. I knew he was basically a good man. He was also in a great deal of pain and was suffering. If he did not accept his condition, it was our responsibility to help him because his disease got in the way of him helping himself.

I have come to believe that a mentally ill person or an alcoholic/ drug addict can be treated; but, until they can come to terms with their condition, treatment won't work. The damnedest thing is while the medical community knows this too they are helpless without the patient consent, but the patient won't give consent, because they do not recognize they need help. A Catch-22.

Finally, Joey agreed.

As we pulled into the parking lot at Net Care, Joey balked, "Mom, I think I can do this on my own.""Joey we have come this far, please, let's at least go inside and see what they have to offer," I said. Joey sat there for a few minutes then got out of the car. We walked hand and hand into the building. At the front desk I told them that my son was having a breakdown and needed to see someone right away. A loud buzzer sounded, and two burly men stepped out into the waiting room to escort Joey inside.

I was told that someone would be out to see me in a few minuets to get some background information. An intake person took my assessment of why I brought my son in. I explained that I believed that my son was suicidal, having blackouts, self medicating and had never been properly diagnosed. I further went on to explain his history in detail.

I could hear a scuffle in the background, in the area where they had taken Joey. I could hear Joey begging to be able to go home, before long he was totally out of control, wild. What a scene this was, I was so frightened for him, even though I knew this was for his own good, I had to let them do their job. Oh, God this was so painful for him; yes, and for me too, but it had to be the right thing. Broken minds are painful, as painful as broken bodies. *Please God, give us both the strength to persevere.*

They told me to go home and that they would call me if I were needed. I went home empty, drained and in despair, yet convinced I had done the right thing. There were still no clues as to what might have happened the night before. I listened to the news and read the newspaper cover to cover; but there were no unexplained accidents reported, that might have included something Joey could have been involved in. I surmised that Joey must have hit some inanimate object and freaked out; another blessing in disguise. I called Joe's dad and asked him to come up and take Joey's car back to his house. It would need repair and it couldn't sit on my property or it would be towed. I also told him that more than likely Joey would not need a car and why. He agreed that I did the right thing.

Later that afternoon, Net Care, called and informed me that they were going to transfer Joey to Twin Valley Behavioral Healthcare. Twin Valley is the State of Ohio's Main Psychiatric Hospital located in Columbus. Joey had spent two days at the Twin Valley complex in Dayton, in March of 2004, but only stayed two days and checked himself out. They told me that Joey had been heavily sedated and was resting comfortably. They went on to say I should call the hospital tomorrow and check on his status as to when he could have visitors.

Our first visit took place a couple of days later. Joey was so drugged I was shocked. I had never seen him so medicated on legal drugs before. Over time with these anti psychotic drugs, Joey became what he had described to me as some of the patients at Oakwood looked like. He became a shuffling, drooling, handshaking "zombie," just what he feared. The doctors all told me that once Joey began to tolerate the medications that these symptoms would or should disappear. Joey asked to come home every day. However with his diagnoses of Bipolar, Mixed, Poly-substance abuse, paranoia and with moderate to severe stressors, he just couldn't check himself out of the hospital this time. Dr. Gary Davis was his doctor of record, and while he wouldn't win any personality contests, he did seem to know what he was talking about.

Joey spent six weeks at Twin Valley and left medicated on four drugs: Depakote, Lithium, Thorazine and Prolixin. His follow up care would be at CSN (Community Support Network), an outpatient program for Twin Valley patients. The discharge plan was to live with me. They strongly recommended that he be continued on combination therapy for his bipolar disorder with Depakote and lithium being the foundation of that treatment. The tapering of his Prolixin may be able to be completed as an outpatient. It was not clear whether he would require continued treatment with Thorazine. However, any decrease in any of his medications were to be done very slowly and with great caution.

We now had an official medical report on file. Joey had and in all likelihood had always been bipolar. The severity of his bipolar condition had been substantiated. I learned that there are varying degrees of bipolar conditions and Joey's were severe. Just how many years did it take to get this documentation and treatment? I now felt we could get the help and the treatment my son needed for the last 40 years. We could look forward to recovery. All's well that ends well, right? Well, the more you know about mental health issues, the more you realize you know nothing. This was not going to be easy. I learned that Joey might fight the diagnoses, consciously and sub-consciously.

Coming home Joey was still experiencing some side effects. He was still drooling a bit and his hands still shook some and his gate was slow. I kept his spirits up by reminding him that soon these symptoms would go away. They would keep tweaking the doses of the meds to get the right combination. He just needed to give it a little more time. I couldn't help but think had we had an earlier assessment and treatment plan how much heartache and pain could have been eliminated. Eliminated for Joey, for his family, and yes, for the Kaisers. For that night in March of 1980 may not have happened, and if it had happened, maybe Joey would not have had a part in it. I had to go forward. I could not look back.

Forward here we come. "Joey, do you know you are now eligible for disability and programs that were denied to you before?" I said. "Like what kind of programs," Joey asked? "Well for starters, you should be eligible for social security. You can apply for that tomorrow. I know your transfer of parole has been granted and your permanent address will now be here with me. No more Drew Barns, Yea!!"

"Jane Klosterman at the Ohio Rehabilitation Services Commission called, she wants you to come in. She wants to talk to you about a job or going back to school. What do you think about that?" I said. "I think I might like to do that," Joey said. He was slowly making progress with his medications and improving every day.

Over the next few months Joey stabilized under the care of CSN and a Dr. Asim Ashraf Farooqi. I met with Dr. Farooqi and his nurse Joy L McFadden many times. Dr. Farooqi had been a Psychiatrist with the State of Ohio and worked in the prison system. He told me he was not comfortable with how the prison system handled their mental health programs and was happy to leave. He thought Joey could be weaned off Thorazine. According to him, that drug should not be used, as it was too strong and hadn't been used much in the last few years. Joy McFadden RN seemed to show an almost motherly interest in Joey and I took a certain amount of comfort in that.

Ohio Rehab Services helped Joey apply for grants that he was eligible for, and Joey enrolled at Columbus State Community College as a freshman. He tested out for basic classes of 101 in English, Math and Science and would major in automotive. Joe Rammelsburg was Joey's new parole officer. I had never met the man; nor had he come to the house to check out where Joey was living, but we spoke by phone. I thought that quite odd as Joey's parole officer in Miami County couldn't stay away from home visits. Mr. Rammelsburg put Joey on a two week check in and eventually every three weeks.

With a mental disorder it is imperative that you maintain a strict routine. Sleep well, eat well and take your meds on time. Reduce stress and limit caffeinated beverages. Moderation is key. Full time anything, be it work or school, were to be avoided until Joey could adjust to a routine and his meds. In the six additional weeks that it took for Joey to stabilize on medications, fix poor "Hoop-tee's" fender and get ready to start the spring quarter, he couldn't be doing any better. In fact he was no longer chewing his fingernails and all his tiny bleeding sores that he picked at on his arms and legs disappeared. Even Joey was amazed at his recovery, he said, "Look Mom! Look how good my skin looks." He was finally happy again.

For the next twenty or so months, life was "normal." I worked days and Joey went to school nights. It was his choice as he was not a morning person. The schedule was perfect. His first classes began around one in the afternoon and ended around ten at night. He could go into CSN to see his doctor and get his meds mid morning, or on the days he didn't have an early one o'clock class, have lunch then go on to school. He could attend programs aimed at education on how to handle stress, alcohol, and on overall information on how he could recover and control his illness. I also attended some of these programs on how to be a support person in his recovery. Isn't it odd how when things go well you tend to think that nothing can stop your progress?

Nothing was standing in Joey's way. He was making the Dean's List every quarter. He was staying on schedule with meds, eating properly, resting and beginning to think life was pretty good.

CHAPTER 30

It Is Never
Really Over, Is It

In late February or early March of 2007, I began to notice a change in Joey's behavior. He was sleeping more and I suspected he might be changing out decaf in the coffee jar for regular coffee. I also knew that caffeine has the reverse affect on Joey. Instead of pumping him up, it took him down. I'm not a coffee drinker so I couldn't tell for sure. Often his answers to my questions were evasive or with doubletalk. I had never insisted that he take his meds in front of me but now I felt a need to check his pill case to see if he was taking them at all. An invasion of his privacy, maybe; but something was just not quite right. It did look as if he was taking his meds. Nevertheless, there were those red flags.

By April Joey was definitely showing signs of overall agitation, loss of focus and some paranoia. I thought it might be due to his pending graduation and the pressure of entering the final stretch that he worked so hard for. There were days he was unable or unwilling to get out of bed if he didn't have school. I became concerned he was seriously depressed. When I pressed him he told me he had had a disagreement with Dr. Farooqui. He refused to go back for his appointments and attend the recovery programs to which he had been assigned. Then came the "Big" one, he thought he had been exposed to HIV.

"Oh, Sh--! Joey, you just can't stop taking your medications," I said. "Well they weren't helping me and I'm doing just fine without them," Joey said. "Oh, right and that's why you're doing so well now," I said. "I have been seeing Doctor LaBronz Davis. He's up on the hilltop, and he's put me on Seroquel and told me that is all I need to take." "Joey, I want to talk to this doctor. Make an appointment and we will go in to see him to-gether, OK?" I wondered why the staff at CSN hadn't contacted me when Joey failed to keep his appointments or have his medicines refilled. They had all the proper paperwork on file and knew I had power of attorney for Joey?

I went to see what this Dr. Davis, had to say, sometime in April of 2007. I pulled no punches in telling Dr. Davis what I thought was going on with Joey. First, I wanted tests done to check out Joey's liver enzymes, and since Joey thought he had been exposed to HIV, we needed to have that checked out. I had the "talk" with Joey when he first came home about relationships, and that keeping a condom handy might be a good idea. He's smart, but naive and things happen, but still.

Dr. LaBronz Davis, was an internist; not a psychiatrist, but he told me he had first hand experience with bipolar disorder, as his brother has the illness. He said that his brother had spent time in prison because of it as well. According to Dr. Davis, his brother was doing fine on Seroquel, and felt that Joey would too. Well that made me feel a little better, surely as a doctor he would not want to treat Joey, if he thought he wasn't capable of helping him. Dr. Davis, tweaked the dosage on the Seroquel, and or-dered blood drawn for the requested tests. Although I was concerned that Dr. Davis was not the right doctor for Joey, I was prepared to give him the benefit of doubt. At least Joey had reached out to a doctor on his own.

Happily, when the tests came back they were negative for HIV and Joey's liver enzymes were within a stable range. With this pressure re-duced, Joey opened up and told me what happened to freak him out. It seems that his "good" buddy in Chillicothe had set him up with this girl and then casually mentioned afterward that she had been exposed to the HIV virus. Not only did it put him into a tailspin, it put this friendship in jeopardy. As far as I knew, Joey, never went down to Chillicothe again.

Things were a little strained now between Joey and I. For almost two years Joey and I had never had heated words. Joey was in school making the Dean's List, letting me know most of the time where he would be 'just in case I needed him.' He seemed happy and focused and working to-wards goals that were amazing. My trust in his behavior at that time was secure. Now Joey, had broken my trust in believing everything was un-der control, and it seemed we were always cross with one another. I tried to talk to him about going back to CSN. I said, "You seemed to do much better there." Joey, countered with, "You don't need to worry, as soon as I graduate, I will be gone." I asked him where he thought he would go and he replied snippily, "I'll graduate to please you and dad and then I plan to run out into traffic. I'm only going to graduate to please you."

"Just what do you want me to say to that statement," I said? I was angry now, and said, "If that is the only reason you are going through to graduation you can just stop now, as it will do nothing for me. I don't care if you graduate or not, it's you that will benefit not me. It's your choice, but don't make it mine, as it's not a diploma for me. I didn't earn it, you did." Just what did this exchange of nastiness mean? Just banter I thought, he didn't mean what he was saying. Why can't I keep my mouth shut?

During the next few days things quieted down but before long, Joey sailed into my bedroom one night, so excited he could hardly contain himself. "Mom, I just met the girl I'm gonna marry," he said. "She's beautiful, funny and smart and I think she likes me too." What was I supposed to say as to not take the edge off of his enthusiasm, but help him to come back down to earth? All I could think to say was, "Well how did you meet her and what's her name?"

"Her name is Vicki, and I met her tonight over at where Redbone's staying with some friends," he said. "Redbone? Isn't that the guy from prison you have talked so much about," I asked. "Yes, he just got out and he's here in Columbus. He called me and asked me to come by and see him. He's staying across the street from where Vicki lives and we all were sitting around a bonfire and I had the best time," he beamed. For the next couple of months I knew where Joey was if he wasn't home, in school or down at his dad's.

I was so happy for Joey, it seemed he found a reason to stay on track, now that he had Vicki in his life. He began to tell me little things about the love of his life. She was divorced, a few years older than him and had grown children. She owned her own business and had a couple of employee's and owned her own home. He was so enamored I didn't have the heart to throw any cold water on his dreams. I just prayed that God would look after him, on this one. What did I know about romance? I didn't have much of a track record.

As for Redbone, he had been Joey's "godfather" from the Lucasville days. On the day I met him, he was nothing like I had imagined. Joey brought him by the house for dinner. I had thought from everything Joey had told me about this man that he would have been a lot older looking. He was a good 10 to 15 years older than Joey but he didn't look it. I envisioned he would have somewhat of a "rode hard and put away wet" look about him, but he didn't fit anything close to it. He was rather good looking.

Redbone was polite and enjoyed the spaghetti dinner I had pre-pared. They didn't stay long, as Joey was going to take Redbone down to his father's place in Tipp. Redbone was in need of a car and Joey was go-ing to sell him the van he had been working on. My best friend Marilyn, had given Joey an older van as payment for some extensive yard work he had completed. He had just finished restoring it to working order and planned to use it as a back up work van.

I pulled Joey aside and cautioned him to be sure to get his name off the title before he let Redbone have it. I also asked how Redbone was planning to buy a van? "He will make payments as soon as he gets a job," Joey said.

I asked, "What will you do if Redbone doesn't pay you?"

Joey said, "Mom if he doesn't pay me, all I can do is chalk it up to all that man done for me in prison, I owe him that, and my debt to him is paid. Mom, he doesn't have anyone out here like I do, and I want to help him if I can. Uncle Frank gave me my first car. I want to do this for o'l Bone."

Just what could I say to that? I gave Joey a hug, told him he had a big heart, and I loved him.

A couple of weeks later Redbone, wrapped the van around a tree. He wasn't hurt and of course he never paid Joey for the van. He then left the Columbus area. As far as I knew Joey never saw or heard from him again. Joey was sad, I could tell, but felt he did the right thing by Redbone and held no regrets. In fact, if it were not for Redbone he would not have met Vicki. Vicki was worth the loss of the van, he thought.

Joey had been partial to driving vans. Joey's Hoop-tee bit the dust just before school started in 2006. Eric, sold his brother his Honda Civic, instead of trading it in when he bought his new car. Joey made pay-ments to his brother every month for two years and never missed a pay-ment. Joey was very frugal with money; which was not supposed to be a trait of someone with bipolar disorder. It was the only profile of being bipolar that Joey didn't have; excessive spending. The Civic was in great shape and was serving Joey's needs, so the loss of the back up van was not a crisis. I had to think that losing Redbone was, but Joey was keeping that to himself.

On June 8, 2007 the day broke with sunshine. Joey had his cap and gown pressed and ready to go. Invitations had been sent out, gradua-tion pictures taken and we were headed to the Veterans Memorial for commencement. In my wildest dreams this was a day that only someone who loved Joey could have imagined. It's a day books are written about. It's a day that practically no one could have thought possible, except maybe for me. Yet it was here.

Leeann and Jimmy were not available to come in because they lived so far away. They sent their best wishes. However, Eric and Christa attended, Joe's dad and his wife Kathleen, my sister Nancy and my brother-in- law Paul, Shirley Pope from the State of Ohio Inspection Committee and Miss Vicki and her mother. All of these people loved Joey and were so proud of him.

After the commencement we all went over to the Spaghetti Warehouse for lunch, except for Ms. Pope, as she said she would not be allowed to accept the meal, due to her job restrictions of accepting favors. Ms. Pope was and is one of the people in state government that can be said to truly be a friend of the underdog. Thank God for the Ms. Pope's of the world. I'm sure there are many, but in our experience, she may be the only one who ever gave 110% for Joey's welfare.

During lunch, Joey was indeed the honored guest. Among his gifts was a ticket to San Diego for a vacation at his brother's and his chance to see the Pacific ocean. The trip would take place in August. It was decided that Joey would take the summer off, look around and see if there was anything open in the automotive field for full time employment. He would then decide whether or not to return to school for a second degree. Somewhere in Joey's mind he was thinking that if he were off parole, that maybe more doors would open up for him. I didn't agree or disagree; I did know Joey was not afraid to work. He just couldn't get past his past in the outside world.

Summer was passing; August brought the first vacation Joey ever took by himself since being released from prison. He would be flying 2400 miles to San Diego. He landed in San Diego, drunk. Jimmy picked him up and took him immediately to the ocean and dumped his ass into the sea. Joey couldn't seem to remember that he couldn't have just "one drink." With only one drink, his mind went berserk and he couldn't stop drinking until he was almost comatose.

I believed him when he said he didn't like the taste of alcohol. It was just one of the substances his body craved. He said he wanted to be like the other adult passengers on the plane, ordering drinks. He wanted to fit in. He would order one drink and that would be it, he thought. After his dump in the surf, Joey said he had a

Joey's Graduation Pictures Accepting His Diploma From Dr. Moeller 2007

283

sort of an epiphany, he said he felt the hand of God touch him. He felt at peace, as he had never felt before. He told me he got the feeling that everything would be alright soon.

Joey spent most of the time at the beach. He made a new friend, by the name of Maty Baca. Maty had worked with Jimmy as a youth counselor, and Jimmy worked as a Recreation Therapist for Social Services of San Diego County. Maty and Joey became inseparable during Joey's visit. Jimmy maintained the beach property where he would take the youths he worked with for surfing and fishing trips. Joey fit right in with the kids, and along with Maty, and Jimmy, Joey spent two weeks being a beach bum and having a ball.

Jimmy was always good with children. Back in Houston he would organize street hockey and baseball games for the kids that lived in our neighborhood. It was natural that he would gravitate to working with kids. He told me that he owed his calling for working with children to me. "Mom, I saw how good you were with kids and all that you did for me, that I just naturally wanted to do that too," he said. He just wanted to give back for everything he received, and give back he did. The kids he worked with had been abused in some way or they were dealing with mental issues. Many were bipolar or had behavioral issues and some were suicidal. Jimmy was always on call for crises at the group homes he worked in.

Each of my children played a part in helping Joey recover his life. Jimmy, with his insights to mental health; Leeann, with her skills in academics and the ability to help Joey with his class assignments; Eric, available in crises and picking up the pieces when needed. Joey tried to do his very best to overcome his trials and tribulations in outstanding ways as well. Just as he was able to graduate from college with honors, with his background alone, is amazing. With all of this support how could Joey lose?

Joey arrived home after two weeks in sunny California tan, wearing shorts, sporting a great attitude, and sober. I couldn't help wonder if he should have stayed in California. He looked great, seemed very happy, but he missed Vicki.

He had decided to go for another degree in heating and cooling, and prepared to register for the fall semester at CSCC. His argument again was, "I'll do better finding a job, when I'm not on parole." I didn't disagree with him, but he at least had to stay in school to make this work. We fell back into the routine of me working days and Joey going to school nights.

Just having Joey in the house made me happy. I loved his sense of humor, our discussions on current topics, and his ability to change a light bulb when needed. *Kidding!* I didn't have to worry though, because if any thing needing fixing, Joey got it done. Joey also loved to do laundry and was a bit of a neat freak. The kitchen was always clean and he loved to vacuum with the "Rainbow." Yes, my 15 year-old Rainbow was still cleaning away. We were definitely in the groove again. Things were on track and Joey's was taking his meds, I thought.

So when the phone rang at an odd time and Joey wasn't at home or there was some unexpected person at my front door, my brain automatically went into disaster mode. On October 8, 2007 I got a call. "Linda, Joey's been arrested. He's in the county jail. I'm going up to bail him out," Joe said. "What for this time?" I asked. "I'm not sure, but I think for disorderly conduct and assaulting a police officer. He say's he is hurt. I will call you when I know more," Joe said. The story went like this, in Joey's own type written words for an essay he was working on. I found it on his computer many months later:

Beware of Free Drinks from Friendly Strangers
Dad has gone to bed this Saturday and my Ohio State Buckeyes are playing Purdue. I am lonely and bored as well as hungry from helping dad all day. Dad does not have Cable TV in his home and the game is on. I will have to listen on the radio and root for them alone. Oh how I wish I had a friend to watch the game with and talk football with. Brainstorm, I will go to the little Mom and Pop restaurant just a couple of miles up the road, get me a order of their locally famous chicken wings and watch the game on there numerous TV screens. Dressed in shorts, T-shirt and flip-flops I come inside Hinders restaurant and man is this place packed elbow to elbow. Everybody is going crazy over the game we are playing. Purdue, lights out and I was worried how good we would be after loosing so many players from last year. I get my order of wings and I join in on the Go Buckeye cheers taking place, man this is great, I'm having so much fun, when minutes before I could just cry over being lonely and having no friends. OH-IO and the crowd next to me all raise and drink their drinks and slam there empty drinks to the table and scream GO BUCKS. I join the cheers with great enthusiasm, the group turns to me as if on cue and look at me as if I offended them. [It stopped here.]

Joey was back at his dad's and injured. Joe said, "He looks as if he has been beaten. They charged him, and he wants to come back up there tonight.

"All right send him on. Do you think he needs a doctor?" I asked, then added. "I guess we will need an attorney, right?"

"Looks like it," Joe said. "Joey doesn't remember too much of what happened yet, he said he went up town to get something to eat and from there all he can remember is being hog tied in a police car."

Joey arrived home about five o'clock. His wrist and ankles were black and blue and he said his back hurt something awful. He told me he lay on the jail floor hog tied for hours. Apparently he remembered ordering a glass of beer with his wings and the next thing he remembered he was in the back of a police cruiser. He remembered being in the emergency room of a hospital too. He didn't remember assaulting anybody. We can only hope that attorney Jose Lopez, could get these charges dropped. "Let's get you to the hospital and checked out for the physical injuries and get them documented," I said.

"Joey," I said, "If you are going to beat your illnesses you are going to have to get into a treatment program and stay there. There are no ifs, ands, buts, or options left. If you can't take your meds and take them on time, and without alcohol, you will die. You can't do this on your own. You need to be admitted to a treatment center. Do you understand, Joey, Do You Understand?"

He said he did, but I knew he didn't. "Joey you are not alone, others face the same illnesses and succeed. Maybe subconsciously you want to go back to prison, is that it?"

Joey looked as if I had struck him. He said, "Are you nuts?"

I said to him, "No are you?"

The pressure of another court hearing and school starting nearly put Joey over the edge. I found him unconscious in the garage with the car running. He had been huffing. He swore to me that he was not trying to kill himself.

I called CSN and talked to Joy McFadden. I told her that Joey was out of control and I feared he would be dead if we didn't intervene. She told me they couldn't take Joey back in to the program unless he came back through Twin Valley. She then asked, "Why don't you see if you can get Joey to agree to go into Net Care and from there transfer over to Twin Valley. That will be he quickest way back into the program." I said I would try.

Joey agreed, and the next morning I drove him to Net Care. I saw him safely inside, left him in their care and went in to work. I called once during the day and they told me was resting comfortably. I arrived at Net Care around 5 PM that afternoon. They had Joey in a stripped down single bed cubical. He said they had not given him anything for pain and his back was killing him. He also said they had not given him anything to eat as well. At about three that afternoon a psychiatrist came in and spoke with him. She asked him what the problem was and he told her he just didn't want to live. He said she got angry and told him not to waste her time, as it was too valuable. He said he told her then to leave, that he didn't need her.

I didn't react well to this information. I went out to check with the desk on why Joey had not been fed and they said he had not asked for any food. I asked them if he was offered any food or even asked if he were hungry, and they said no. I then said "Do you know what it took for me to get him to agree to come in here? Do you realize how close he has come to taking his own life? I'm taking him out of here, I will find some other place that he can get help." They immediately told me that I couldn't take him with me as he had been "pink slipped" and if I took him out I would be arrested.

I left and tried to reach Dr. Davis to see if I could get him to help with this situation, but I was unable to reach him. I returned to Net Care with some hot food and found that they had brought Joey some vending machine packets, cheese crackers, cookies and a drink. They had also given him some "Tylenol" for pain. They didn't know when he would be transferred to Twin Valley, however they thought it would be before morning.

Indeed Joey was transferred and by morning he was settled in at Twin Valley. I felt a certain amount of relief. I just knew that they would be able to get him back on track, just like they did in 2005. I hoped that Dr. Gary Davis was still there and that Joey would be assigned to his care. Dr. Davis was still there, however Joey was assigned to a doctor by the name of M. Meredith Dobyns. I received a call on the second day of this commitment to come in for a consultation on Joey's case.

Arriving in the afternoon I was asked to join a team of caregivers in the conference room. There were social workers, physical therapists, out patient caseworkers and of course Dr. Dobyns. I found that Dr. Dobyns had spoken with Joey a total of maybe five minutes. She relied on the information given to her by all the people gathered around the table and from all of their notes. I thought to myself, why do you need a psychiatrist when they let all these other people do their work?

Dr. Dobyns came to the conclusion that Joey was not bipolar or at least he was not bipolar today, and perhaps he never was. She was going to discharge him to CSN for follow up care. I said to her do you realize that he is but a few steps from "accidentally killing himself."

She replied, "I just don't see it."

I said, "Dr. Davis, diagnosed him in 2005. He's spent 23 years in prison mentally ill, social security is paying him for the disability of being mentally ill, and you are saying he's not?" She didn't respond.

"I can't believe this, what does he have to do, stand in front of you people with a gun to his head, I shouted." I left the floor and ran right into Dr. Davis, standing in the hall. I said many things to him and one was, "Do you know they are saying that Joey is not bipolar?" He didn't say one word to me. He just shrugged his shoulders and walked away. He went through the door and it closed behind him. Joey then came out the same door that Dr. Davis had disappeared through, and said to me, "See I told you they don't care." This was in October of 2007.

Joey however did return to CSN with the determination to succeed. He was assigned to a Dr. Mark E. Blair as his psychiatrist. I attended this first visit. Dr. Blair was a slight man dressed in a very expensive suit and seemed to me to be a little out of place in this environment. He had the file from the last Twin Valley two-day stay. Since there was no diagnosis of any bipolar symptoms, Joey was not put on medications that I felt he needed. Instead he was prescribed Lamictal, Hydroxyzine and Atenolol. Where was the Seroquel or Lithium or Resperdol? Where was the in house treatment Joey would need to regain his control? I knew Joey didn't want in-house treatments. Could you blame him after 23 years in prison? I knew he didn't want to be confined, but I knew he would die without confinement. I believe they knew this too. I had been able to talk him into voluntary confinement last week, but I wouldn't be able to this week. It looked as if it did not matter what I thought or knew.

CHAPTER 31

The Long
Hard Way Home

We were enjoying being all together as a family these past few years, so it was decided we would go out to San Diego for Thanksgiving. Leeann would come in from Denver and Eric and Christa and Joey and I would fly in from Columbus. The only snafu in this plan was Joey's court date for his last episode. Joey was so sure that his parole was going to be revoked that he had to be reminded daily that Jose Lopez was doing everything he could to see that that wouldn't happen. The worst of it was all the court date continuances. Joey was all set to appear on a certain date, mentally and emotionally and the courts would postpone or his attorney would need to postpone. The tension was high and the pressure never ending for Joey.

On a mid October morning in 2007, about 4 am I awoke to a humming sound. I could see a dim light coming from the hallway. I immediately got a knot in my stomach, something wasn't right. I jumped out of bed in a panic. I went flying out into the hallway; arriving in the dining area. There sat Joey, on the floor, rocking back and forth, holding a fathom rag up to his nose and mouth. He was totally out of it. Relieved he was still alive, and at the same time so angry. I began to slap him, flat handed, over and over again. He swatted at me as if he were trying to get away from a cobweb. Wasn't this something I promised I would never do again four decades ago? Joey why are you doing this, I shouted and cried hysterically. I was desperate to help him but I didn't know how, I just didn't know how. "Please let me help you," I cried, as I cradled him in my arms.

That huffing shit will kill you or give you brain damage so severe that you might as well be dead, I was saying to him through tears, though I'm sure he didn't hear me. *Joy McFadden, Joey's nurse at CSN told me there are no treatment programs for those who play around with huffing, surely there had to be something. There are private sanatoriums that would take him, but we couldn't afford them. How could anyone think that a 48 to 72 hour stay in a confined environment could help someone? It might save their life for the next 48 to 72 hours, but then you're right back to square one.*

Joey was always so apologetic after one of these episodes. His life must seem so unbearable to him, yet I couldn't comprehend what it must be like to want to consistently leave this world behind? This is when you know that "Love is Not Enough." This is where I knew that professional help was the only way my son was going to be able to live. Yet the professional help we'd gotten so far was less than stellar. I lamented to myself. They couldn't help me with Joey when he was a child; it looks as though they can't help him now. I could almost forgive them for not knowing what to do when Joey was a baby, a toddler and a youngster, but what was their excuse now that we knew he had severe mental issues?

Most folks from what I had read, that were living in recovery, were at death's door multiple times. They didn't recover doing it alone and they had help in the nick of time, sometimes just barely. Two people came to mind. One is Terri Cheney who wrote *"Manic."* The other one is Marya Hornbacher, and her memoir is *"Madness."* These two women wrote about their terrifying struggle to live with a debilitating mental illness. I do not have a severe mental illness so I can't speak about what it is like to be mentally ill but they can. What I do know something about is the feeling of helplessness as a bystander, having been faced with the fact that one of my children had to suffer most of his life.

I had the opportunity to meet Terri Cheney at an Evening with Authors presentation at Thurber House. Ms. Cheney's descriptions of her chaotic life were so vivid and so much like what Joey's life must feel like to him: Her repeated trips and commitments into clinics and hospitals; her disbelief in her condition and treatments; her close encounters with death, were so like what I saw happening with Joey. My son's life is a life lived in the extremes as well.

I wondered if Joey didn't have the support system he had, would it have made a difference? I wondered that same thing when he was little boy as well. I wondered if Joey weren't as intelligent as he was, would he have received different treatment? I wondered if he were homeless and unkempt in appearance, would he get different care. Did they give him more credit than he could deal with because of his support system? Did they think because he was in the above level of intelligence he could handle his mental illness any better? Did they think because of all the stable things in his life he could do this without intervention?

I remembered the psychiatrist at Joey's trial 25 years ago who said, "Oh, he has a very good understanding of right and wrong, more than most, he just can't refrain from doing wrong." That's because he is mentally ill and needs stabilizing medications to help him control his mind from choosing wrong decisions on the spur of the moment. What was different today, that they refused to understand that? The drugs on the market to treat bipolar disorders are by no means perfect, but they are better than no treatments at all. They can help produce remissions from symptoms, but they must be carefully administered and monitored. I believed Joey needed in-house treatment to get him stabilized again.

Joey had a winning personality when he is in control of his illness or his illness was in remission. If you met my son and didn't know his background you would like him. He's funny, articulate, interesting, and intelligent. His concentration on a project, whether it's remodeling a house or putting a car back together or putting together numbers on football tickets, (his great passion) or his writings and essays were amazing.

I could tell when he was forcing himself to control his thinking. In down time, you might find him hunched over, holding his head in his hands, willing his brain to just stop. He talks about racing thoughts and images that just won't quit. This is when he would drink coffee by the gallons to calm his "nerves" just to get his brain to slow down.

From everything I read it often takes multiple in house treatments (at hospitals, rehab treatment centers, etc.) before the person can come to terms with their disorder. I asked myself one question, just one. Linda, when do you give up and just let him go? I didn't want to lose him. The last time I gave up and said I couldn't help him, he was seventeen and he landed in prison for 23 years. There must be a way to get through to him and "them." I had to keep trying; I just had to.

I also read that most of the time the mentally ill don't see themselves as sick. They often refuse treatment because they don't think they need it or that it will help. Or perhaps they do begin to see that treatment may help them but they don't stay with the drugs or programs long enough for the treatments to make a permanent change in their illness. Whose fault was that, or was it part of the disease?

The theme that is the most common thread that I saw in all the articles was: " *I feel OK now, so I must not need these drugs/medicines and treatments any longer. I'm good to go now, plus these drugs keep me from doing the things I want to do. They make me sleep to much, I bounce into walls, I'm nauseous most of the time, my vision blurs, my head and hands shake, I shuffle when I walk, I can't seem to work full time. My mind is not as sharp and creative. I gain weight on these drugs. I lose weight on these drugs. I'm not crazy anymore, they are."* This is when they stop taking the drugs or the drugs have stopped working, and in time their symptoms return.

Now the really frustrating part: When do "they" stop trying to help these people? Today, tomorrow, or do "they" give them an ultimatum such as, this is the last time and let them die or do "they" just put them in prison? Are prison or death the only answers? According to Joey's history, he had only one successful treatment plan initiated and followed through on and that was in 2005. That diagnoses and treatment came after an amazing 23 years of confinement in various prisons without any significant rehabilitation or medical treatments to speak of. Joey's first successful commitment to Twin Valley Psychiatric Facility allowed him to function so well that he graduated from college and he fell in love for the first time.

He was first diagnosed with a mental illness in 1980 at the age of 17, (of course we know he was ill much sooner than that) yet never treated. How did we allow that to happen? Now that he was out of prison, "they" gave him only one chance to overcome his mental illness. In addition, he had to learn to live in a society he left behind. I could help him with that but I couldn't treat the mental illness. His history alone should have warranted a need for extensive and aggressive care. Why was I the only one that saw this? "They" parole the mentally ill every day and expect them to recover on their own. Now, that to me is insanity.

Do we ever stop trying to treat someone who has a physical disease? Yes, we do, when it is determined through the best that medical science has to offer, that the body can not survive, as it is in a terminal condition, we stop treatments? Then at least, these people are made as comfortable as possible until the death of the body is complete. If we stop treating or we fail to treat properly the illnesses of the mind; do we in essence say, "Sorry about your lot in life," and let them slowly or in some cases fast and furiously kill themselves? Is that all they can do? Is that all I was left to do for my son, to stand by and watch him kill himself? No, I won't quit.

Today I would try again. As Joey began to come back to the real world, I ushered him back to his room, and put him to bed. I decided to call Joy McFadden later today and ask her again to help me get Joey placed in some kind of a treatment center, at the very least get him in to see Dr. Blair, today.

Joey went into CSN again and began to participate in the programs laid out for him. He saw Dr. Blair every other week for about 20 minutes. Joey said, "You know Mom, seeing a psychiatrist is not like it is portrayed in the movies. Maybe it's because I am on the State's health plan. I can tell you I am not lying comfortable on a couch and having the undivided attention of the doctor for an hour. I'm lucky to get 20 minutes. Mom, I just don't fit in with these people. I have tried; really I have."

All I could say was "Joey, try a little harder."

From the end of October, uncertainty filled the house. Joey seemed to be taking his meds that had been prescribed. I was monitoring his drugs closely. He was attending school and I thought he was sober most of the time. I talked to Joy at CSN weekly maybe more, for support; but I came home one evening and found the garage door was up. I could see Joey's car in the stall. It was dark and I thought, *shouldn't Joey have left for school by now?* My headlights lit up the garage and as I pulled to a stop, Joey, stood up and grabbed the hood. I damn near had a coronary. I had just come within inches of running him over. He was sobering up, most likely from huffing. He had lost his glasses and had been looking for them, he said. I found them out in the street. He wanted to drive to school as he had a very important test. I tried to reason with him to let me take him for safety's sake and he finally agreed.

Later that night when I picked him up from school and asked, "How did the test go?"

"It went fine," he replied.

I tried to engage him in conversation about what happened earlier. I asked him if he thought the pressure of the impending test was too much. His reply was a no; he knew the material. He went on to say he was not seeing life as clearly as he thought he should. He said Vicki was just becoming aware that his issues were a little more than she had bargained for, and she was giving him some time to get things under control.

I asked him if they had broken up and he said no, not exactly, it was just that they were not going to move their friendship to the next level just yet. I took that to mean they were not going to be married anywhere near soon. I wanted to say, *"If you want things under control this isn't the way to do it."* Then I bit my tongue. He knew that as well as I did. I said," Joey you are the only one that can make the changes and if you can't, you are going to have to let others help you. That doesn't mean you are weak. It means that you are smart. Please be smart."

"Mom, I will try," he said.

He was trying on a daily basis. That blasted court date was still hanging over his head. Jose Lopez was trying to convince him that more than likely he would just be looking at a fine. Nothing guaranteed mind you, but we all tried to help him relax. Joey knew as well as I, that there were no guarantees when it came to dealing with "Joey" issues and the courts.

Trying to convince him wasn't working; his paranoia couldn't be calmed. I believed he was medicating himself with every chance he got, even though I couldn't prove it.

I kept asking Joy for an involuntary commitment; I was convinced that we were going to lose him, and "they" kept telling me that if Joey wouldn't agree, there was nothing they could do. They also never missed telling me that Joey had to want to get better. Of course Joey wanted to get better; but his reasoning was all screwed up. He's mentally ill; he doesn't know how to make those decisions without help. He does not want to be locked up, why couldn't they understand that? If you spent over half of your life locked up, would you want to be locked up again? I'll bet if he committed a crime they would have no trouble locking him up in a secure environment and take the credit for getting him off the street.

Reasoning, that was all I was asking for. After a successful commitment of about six weeks; he was able to go to college for almost two years, graduate with honors, and then fall apart. He needed another "tune up." You would have thought that these people didn't know how a mentally ill person reacts. Either everything I read about the kind of illnesses my son had was a lie, or these people should have been charged with practicing medicine while under the influence of ignorance. He was not going to be able to bring himself back from the edge of this cliff, no matter how much he thought he could. They should know that too. *Why didn't they know this?*

Our family Thanksgiving vacation in San Diego was festive. We rented a beach house and we all stayed under the same roof for a marvelous five days. Thanksgiving was spectacular. The turkey was deep fried in one of those outdoor fryers and every other side dish was so yummy. We sat down to dinner on the outdoor porch just as the sun set out over the ocean. "Uncle Eric" was the hero of all the grand kids, as he brought along to share a new game called a "Wii." I don't think it was shut down the entire time we were there. We played. We ate; we played some more.

We took one day to go into "The City of Angels" Los Angeles, to sight see. We got wrapped up in a parade of "striking writers" union people. We all picked up signs that were offered to us and marched right along side the writers. What a neat bunch of eccentric people we met that day. We fit right in. Alicia Keys was performing with her entourage, singing and riding along with the marchers as well. Of course we visited the Grauman's Chinese Theater and the Hollywood Walk of Fame. We ate at a Blues Brothers Restaurant and visited the Wax Museum and Ripley's Believe It or Not. We enjoyed the attractions, but more importantly we enjoyed each other.

Something I remembered later when I thought about that last trip we took together, was that Joey had his palm read by a street vendor. He said he asked her about his lifeline and what lay ahead. He said she mentioned all the wonderful things that would happen in his life and that he would have a very long life. He was laughing when he said he told her the "truth" after she had given him his reading. He said when he told her about what his life had been so far, she freaked out. Was death on his mind then, did he have a pre-monition about how much time was left?

Joey Joins in With the Writers Strike in Los Angeles, CA. November 2007

Back in Ohio and the reality of everyday liv-ing kicked in. Was the diversion of a holiday to recharge your batteries so to speak, not a good idea? Joey went back to school and I went back to work. On the horizon would be Christmas and Joey's court date. I was in contact with CSN asking how to be supportive and what I should be doing to help Joey handle his paranoia regarding this court date issue. Joey was keeping all of his appointments with CSN and trying to par-ticipate in-group sessions. I told Joy, I didn't think group was what Joey needed now. I didn't feel group adequately met his needs. He wasn't ready for group. He needed more one on one sessions but Joy disagreed.

Joey's rescheduled court date for the third time was to be Friday, December 14, 2007. He stopped in at CSN December 13 to try and get a legal prescription for an anti anxiety pill. They refused to give him a pre-scription, as they said they could not reach Dr. Blair. Joey then went on down to his Dad's to spend the night, so that he could be in court early the next day. I got a call from Jose Lopez's office telling me that the court date had been postponed again. *How cruel was this?* Joey would not see this as a positive sign. I then called Joey, who had reached his dad's and told him the news.

"Are you going to stay down at your Dad's or will you be coming home tonight," I asked him?

Joey said, "I've got a lot of homework. I think I will come back up to Columbus."

"Call me if you change your mind," I said.

As the clock neared 9 pm, Joey still hadn't come in. I called down to his dad's and found that Joey had left about 6 pm and should have been here around 7:30 pm. Well, maybe he went over to Vicki's, I thought. I couldn't reach Vicki and calls to Joey's cell phone came back unan-swered. By midnight when I still couldn't reach him and he hadn't called, I knew something was wrong. Where could he be? I told him to call me if ever he felt he couldn't or shouldn't drive and I would come and get him, no questions asked. He never took me up on that offer.

By morning, still no Joey. I had a 7:30 a.m. meeting and decided to go on and keep it. My gut told me I was not going to like the news, when and if it found its way to me. I needed to keep busy as there was nothing I could do to stem the inevitable. I was just finishing up the meeting at around 8:30 am when my cell phone rang. It was the hospital in Madison County. Madison County is located between Tipp City and Columbus, along state highway 70. The girl on the line told me Joey was in the emergency room. A Sheriff's officer found him lying down alongside a country road, totally incoherent. No, he was not hurt nor under arrest as far as she knew. However, he had recovered enough to be discharged and did I want to come and get him.

It was a good bet Joey had decided he couldn't take the pressure of another postponement. If he couldn't beat his problems, he was going out on his terms. He either took some kind of pills, drank some kind of alcohol, or inhaled some kind of an inhalant, or maybe a combination of them all. I called Joy at CSN from the car on my way to the hospital. I told her it looks like Joey just dodged another chance to kill himself. Could she please try and help me get him into an in house treatment program? I told her I didn't care which program, so long as it would get him off the street, where he had access to chemicals. He was not strong enough to stop the cravings on his own.

At the hospital Joey looked as he always had under these circumstances, remorseful and somewhat belligerent at the same time. Was he mad he was still here? He was sure that the officer that was placed outside the door was going to arrest him the minute he stepped outside, but the doctor released him. His car however had been impounded. Should I have left it impounded? Maybe. However, when I thought of all the impound charges building up I didn't want that to add to Joey's worries. I certainly wasn't about to pay the charges.

We retrieved his car and he followed me home. I advised him to call Joy and tell her what was going on. "I have clients to see," I said. "Joey, I will do everything in my power to help you, but I no longer know what to do for you. Please work out a solution with Joy today, as this behavior cannot continue. If you can't find a solution today, I will have no choice but to call your parole officer and give him a full report. I expect you to do this by the time I return. I will not let you die on my watch, do you understand?"

He said nothing; he just hung his head.

"Joey, I love you so. You just have to want to get better, please. I don't understand your pain, I want to and those who want to help you do too. You have to let them," I said and I left.

On Saturday morning, December 15, I had one client to see at 9 am. Joey was up and we talked a bit. I asked him if he had talked to Joy at CSN and he assured me he had and that he was going in on Monday. I thought to myself, this was bullshit; this can't wait till Monday. I said, "Joey, how would you feel about going into OSU (Ohio State University) emergency room and see if we can get you checked into the psychiatric unit? I just don't think you are getting the right attention with these people at CSN. I don't know if it will be possible, but we have to try something today, agreed?"

He agreed.

"I will be home around noon and we'll go in then, OK?"

"Alright," he said.

The day was a bit overcast as I left to keep my scheduled appointment. By the time I reached home about eleven a.m., it had started to snow. It was snowing giant snowflakes, and it was coming down fast and furious. I found Joey in the garage, under the influence of an inhalant; not completely unconscious, but subdued and resigned to allow me to drive him over to OSU. We got into the car and drove very slowly as the streets were extremely slick. As we reached the overpass of Interstate 270, we were about to take the ramp. Joey decided he needed an overnight bag. I told him I would bring him everything he needed later.

At that, Joey jumped from my car and ran down the embankment. I began to panic as I had no way to turn the car around for at least a couple of miles. *Oh, God what do I do?* My mind raced in all directions. You've got to get home, I thought. Traffic was a nightmare and so slow. Surely Joey was headed home. Where else would he go? My fears were confirmed; when I finely made it home, the garage door was up and his car was gone, he obviously was in no shape to drive, especially in this weather. I picked up the phone and called the police.

"911. What's your emergency?"

"My son is mentally ill and under the influence of drugs, and he's behind the wheel of his car," I said.

I gave them all the information that they asked for, and was told an officer would be by to get the rest. My next call was to the emergency number Joy gave me to call if I needed help. Joy didn't answer, and the woman who did didn't seem happy I had access to this particular line. From the notes written by this particular crisis manager, this was her interpretation of this call: "*Due to clients need for outpatient psychiatric services, client's mother contacted the on-call Manager due to crisis. Mother discussed current events and was very upset. Client's mother frantic to locate client and to have something done to help client. Discussed options for treatment and AOD treatment. Discussed crisis options and possible options for care. Discussed protocols and procedures for crisis intervention.*

Talked with mother about family responsibility and when it's time to let go. Advised client was an adult and making bad decisions but they were his decisions. Advised when he reappears, support is fine but enabling is not. Advised would pass on information to MD, RN and CSP for follow up."

CHAPTER 32

Fulfillment of a

Contract

Well let's hope he turns up alive, so that I can learn how not to enable him, I thought. As the day wore on, there was no news, good or bad. About 8 o'clock that night, I got a call from Joey's step-brother, John Rickert. "Linda, Mt. Camel East Hospital contacted me and said Joey has bolted from the ER. Joey was brought in by the security personnel after they found him in the parking lot rambling around incoherently. They had just begun testing him for head trauma injuries when he disappeared. Camera's caught him walking out the doors wrapped only in a sheet and barefooted. He also had an IV inserted to ward off dehydration, and he left a trail of blood. He was left alone for a few minutes and when the nurse came back in the cubicle he was gone.

"My God John, where could he have gone in this snow storm, naked and barefoot," I said, panic-stricken.

John said, "I am going over to the hospital and see what more I can find out. I will pick up his clothes too. I think I'll look around and see if I can find his car. I'll call as soon as I find out anything new." "Oh, God, John you have to find him," I cried, "He'll freeze to death out there tonight. Have they called the police, should I call them again?" John thought the police knew and were looking for his car as well. God, how much more

299

could we take? I was near exhaustion. I had convinced myself we would find him dead. I started calling everyone I thought Joey might contact, all agreed to contact me if they heard from him. The wait and watch began. John hadn't come up with any more news. In the morning, I started to call around to other hospitals, the police stations and the impound lot, where I found Joey's car.

Eric drove me over to the impound lot to claim the car. The car was not damaged. I had hoped I would find the trunk empty. It was not. Joey's winter survival clothes and boots were still in there, which meant he must still be naked and barefooted.

"Oh God, Eric where can he be," I said?

"Mom, he'll show up; I'm sure," Eric said.

We came back home and waited by the phone.

The following day Joey did call. He was somewhat incoherent and wouldn't say where he was. He was going to get himself under control before he came home.

At that I said, "Joey do what you have to do, but if you can't see that you need in depth intervention, you just may need to stay where you are. I can't live like this any longer. There is help out there, you have to reach for it."

He promised that when and if he came home he would have a plan, and then he was gone…again.

For the next few days we heard nothing. On Monday, I talked with his parole officer, Joe Rummelsburg. I told him that I feared that Joey could very well be dead. I asked him if and when Joey surfaced, would he please find an in-house treatment program. Anything! I was so angry that CSN and the staff was not meeting Joey's needs. Joey needed an involuntary commitment, period. I did plead with him not to send Joey back to prison, as there hadn't been any medical help there either. He promised he would do what he could and should I hear from Joey he asked me to call him.

On Wednesday December 19, I left for work, still not knowing where Joey was. Something unusual happened though as I lifted the garage door. There on the ground lay a single glove; I thought that was odd. I looked around to see if there was anything else unusual and then dismissed this clue. Later that afternoon my cell phone rang and it was Joey telling me he was in the Franklin County jail. He had been arrested in our complex a couple of blocks away from home. The charge: a parole violation of changing his address without notifying his parole officer. At least he was alive and in a secure place, I thought.

"Mom, I rented a car to get home; it's parked across the street from the house. Can you see if you can get it returned to the airport rental before midnight."

"Yes, I can do that," I said. "Are you alright?"

"Yes, I'm OK for now," he said.

"I'll call Joe Rummesburg in the morning," I said. "I'll see if he can get you placed into a hospital. Joey, it's either that or back to prison, and at this point you may not have a choice."

"Whatever, I just want this over with," he said.

He also told me that "Ronnie" had his credit card and that I should call him and get it back.

"What's Ronnie doing with your credit card? Never mind, I don't want to know right now," I said.

Joey spent the next 6 days in jail; he would be there through Christmas. My present that year was that he was still alive. Joe Rummelsburg said he couldn't keep Joey in jail any longer and wanted CSN to make the decisions on how to go forward with Joey's care. I argued that we were going to lose him if we couldn't get him off the streets. I had had his car taken down to his dad's so his transportation would be limited, but that was still the mother in me making that decision, not Joey.

I picked Joey up on a windswept seedy looking downtown corner in Columbus, on a gray December night. He looked thin and lost. On our way home, he told me some things about what had happened to bring him to this point. He said he remembered coming around in the emergency room and thinking he was still alive, but back in prison. He then realized it was actually a hospital and he panicked. He ran not thinking of the consequences, found his car and slid it into a ditch. He ran again, through the woods and came eye to eye with a deer. He said they both were spooked. At that point he knew he was in trouble and looked for help.

"I knew I would freeze to death and I didn't want to go that way," he said.

He found his way into an apartment complex and the first door he knocked on, let him in. He thought it was a Hispanic couple. They put shoes on his feet, clothes on his body and gave him a cup of hot chocolate to warm him. He thanked them and asked if he could call for a cab and they did that for him too. As he left they gave him an orange. He took the cab over to "Ronnie's." There he said he talked Ronnie into driving him down to Tipp City, where he planned to stay in one of the rehab houses he and his dad had been working on. Ronnie needed gas money, so Joey gave him his credit card to buy gas, and he forgot to get the credit card back. He stopped at a Wal-Mart and bought some things he thought he would need. His plan was to get himself together and make sure that his plans would work. He felt this was what he needed to do.

It turned out later that this friend whom Joey trusted tried to max out his credit card. There were purchases of additional gas fill-ups and other items charged as well. The credit card company picked up on the fraudulent purchases and shut the card down. When Joey learned of it, it almost broke his heart. Of course his friend denied doing it, but nonetheless it was another emotional blow for Joey.

He apologized for all the stress he had caused everyone, especially the worry he caused me. "I truly didn't mean to cause you pain; I love you Mom, but I am so lost and I can't see a clear picture of where my life is going. One thing for sure, I'm not wanting to go back to prison, been there done that, ain't doing it again. I'll go in to CSN and work with them and their programs," he said.

I said, "Joey I don't think you can do this without getting yourself dried out. Your body is craving these chemicals now and it's gonna take a helluva lot of willpower to do this out there, on your own, don't you think?"

"I can do it Mom. I can!" he said.

Dear God, I prayed, he's in your hands. If you can't help him, help me understand why. The following week Aunt Nancy and Uncle Paul stopped by and we had a little post Christmas lunch and exchanged gifts. Joey seemed laid back and relaxed. He went into CSN and came home with a plan to leave school and try to start his own company. BVR was to help him apply and get grants and loans for a work van and the tools he would need to get started. I knew this was what the counselors at CSN wanted, but was this what Joey wanted?

Joey's court date in Miami County was rescheduled and this time Dr. Blair prescribed two anti-anxiety pills to help Joey face the day in court. Joey said that he was feeling pretty good about the outcome. Of course, he had just taken a pill. For the past four months of untold anxiety, it was over in about 30 minuets. In fact, he didn't even need to see the judge. Jose Lopez, Joey's attorney, took care of everything in chambers and all Joey had to do was pay a fine. Jose Lopez, last words to Joey were, "Stay on your meds."

At least for that day, with these anti-anxiety pills in Joey's system and a great outcome in court, Joey was OK.

I heard Joey come in from school and go to his room. I then heard him crying. I stepped in and asked if there was something I could do for him. He said no, he had told his teachers he was withdrawing and they were not happy to hear of his decision. According to him they were disappointed in him and had called him a quitter. Maybe they did or maybe that is how he saw himself in their eyes. I assured him that if this was not what he wanted to do, he didn't have to withdraw in the middle of the quarter.

"You could finish this quarter and then decide," I said.

"No," he replied, "I've done it and now I will live with it."

What I didn't know was that on January 9, he had told these health care workers through a written exercise, that he was severely troubled. He told them that he was "scared" and saw his life as a "hit or miss." He only pretended things were "OK." He would "cry out of the blue" and feared that he was "out of control." He wanted a "normal life" and couldn't believe that he was " mentally ill." There were a number of very distressing thoughts that were running through his mind. I called them red flags. Why didn't they see them as red flags?

If they read about those feelings and the thoughts that Joey was having on that day, what did they say to him? What did they do for him? I never knew, but it was quite clear he needed help and he was not getting it.

On the morning of January 16, 2008, the day dawned bright with a beautiful blue sky. The air had a crispness that gave you a little boost that made you want to get the day going. My first appointment was east of the city and about an hour and a half drive. Joey was up and sitting in the recliner reading the morning paper. I asked him about his day, and he said he was going into CSN to meet with the vocational counselor for her help with the paper work he needed for the BVR. I told him I had an early meeting to stop at and then would be out east for the remainder of the day. I'd give him a call later to let him know what time I'd be home. With that, I kissed him on the top of his shinny bald head and told him I loved him. He jumped out of the chair and gave me a hug, and I was gone.

At that early morning meeting I picked up an address of a property that was for sale, one that Joey could live in and rehab at the same time. I would drop by and look at it first, before I said anything to Joey. I called Eric on my way out of town and told him about the house and asked him if it looked to be a good deal, would he help me buy it. My contact said he would sell it to me with little to no down payment, just to get it off his rental properties. We could then hold the mortgage on it till Joey was ready to take over the payments. He said, "Sure Mom, sounds like a plan. Let me know what you decide." My perspective client was a grieving widow and needed to sell her house to move closer to her children. She liked my quote and said as soon as her house sold, she would use my company to move her things. Well, two good deals today, I thought.

By one o'clock, I had driven by the property and decided it was worth looking at and called Joey. Joey was still home. He said that the counseling for today had been postponed, something about a problem with the counselor's car. I told him about the property I thought we should go look at when I got home, and he agreed it sounded like something he would be interested in and that he could do. He then went on talking about everything and anything; all these grand plans he had in mind.

"I'm going to paint my bedroom after I make these lists I need for the BVR and I need to get a new watchband," he said. He also told me he was writing another essay, I didn't think to ask, why? "I'll be home about 5:30, will you be there," I asked? He said he would be.

"Great, I'll see you then."

"Mom, I love you, don't worry everything will be alright soon, I promise," he said.

I said, "Yes, I know it will be too. See ya."

I was running behind since my last client took a little longer than expected. I stopped at the grocery store to pick up some things for dinner. When I arrived home, it was a little after 6 PM. Joey's car was not in the garage. All the lights in the house were on, the TV's and music was blaring. His computer was on and his room looked as if he were about to start painting. I concluded that he would be back in a few minuets; he must have needed something at the store and decided to just pop out to get it and would be right back.

I started dinner but after thirty minutes, I decided to call his cell. No answer. Not to worry, maybe he left it in the car while he went in to shop. Dinner was ready and still no Joey. Where could he be and why would he leave the house all lit up like this? OK, it's now eight and still no answer on his cell, I began to make calls to friends. I called his dad to see if he knew anything, he didn't. I called Eric about eight fifteen, looking for comfort. I said, "I just can't figure out where he could be under the circumstances of how I found the house when I got home."

Eric tried to be reassuring and said, "Mom he'll show up, he always does."

Sometime around nine o'clock the phone rang. The man on the other end of the line introduced himself as Matt Marx from the Columbus Dispatch. He wanted to know if I knew where my son was? I told him I was waiting for him to come home. Mr. Marx went on to say that there had been an accident and there had been a fatality. He wanted to know if I had been contacted by the police. No, I hadn't heard anything and I pressed him for more information. He said that that the police would be able to fill in the blanks. He then gave me a telephone number to call, and hung up.

I called Eric, bordering close to a state of hysteria. "Eric, I need you, something terrible has happened and I don't know where to go from here. There's been an accident and either Joey has killed somebody or he's dead. I don't know which will be the worse." Oh God! Oh God! Oh God! I couldn't deal with this alone.

"I'll be there Mom, I'm coming," he said.

I tried to call the police and got nowhere; no one seemed to know anything about an accident. Eric arrived just as the late news was coming on; there on the TV screen I saw an active picture of an accident scene and a body wrapped in a white sheet lying on the pavement. The newscaster said that three auto's had been involved and that one of the occupants had run down over the embankment and straight into interstate traffic. This accident happened at the 270 overpass at Georgesville Road. The same place that Joey had bailed from my car just about a month ago.

Just then, I heard the knock on my door and I knew my baby boy, was never coming home again.

"I'm Free
Don't grieve for me, for now I'm free,
I'm following the path God has laid you
see.
I took His hand when I heard Him call,
I turned my back and left it all.
I could not stay another day,
To laugh, to love, to work, to play.
Tasks left undone must stay that way,
I found that peace at the close of day.

If my parting has left a void,
Then fill it with remembered joys.
Friendship shared, a laugh, a kiss,
Oh, yes, these things I too will miss.
Be not burdened with times of sorrow,
I wish you the sunshine of tomorrow.

My life's been full, I've savored much,
Good friends, good times, a loved one's
touch.
Perhaps my time seemed all too brief,
Don't lengthen it now with undue grief.
Lift up your heart and peace to thee,
God wanted me now---He Set Me Free.
--Author Unknown-

Columbus police investigate the death of man who ran onto the northbound lanes of I-270 at Georgesville Road on the West Side last night. The man had just caused two hit-and-run crashes, witnesses told police.

Driver runs from crashes, is struck, killed on I-270

Northbound lanes on West Side shut down for 5 hours

By Matthew Marx
THE COLUMBUS DISPATCH
and Andy Hirsch
WBNS-10TV

A man was killed while running across the Outerbelt after he fled from two accidents he caused along Georgesville Road last night.

Three cars struck the man as he tried to cross the northbound lanes of I-270 at 8:17 p.m., Columbus police said. Moments earlier, he had caused two hit-and-run crashes along Georgesville Road on the West Side, witnesses told police.

The man, whose identity was being withheld late last night pending notification of his family, died at the scene. No one else suffered a serious injury.

All northbound lanes of I-270 just north of Georgesville were closed for nearly five hours as crash investigators interviewed motorists and pieced together what happened.

The man was driving a Dodge sedan when he struck a car in the parking lot of the Meijer store, 775 Georgesville Rd., accident investigator David Cornute told WBNS-TV (Channel 10).

The man took off in the Dodge, and the first car that he struck tried to follow but lost him after he started going the wrong way on Georgesville

Road. The Dodge then collided head-on with another car at I-270.

After the second collision, the driver abandoned the Dodge and ran down the embankment, where he tried to run across the highway. That's when three northbound cars hit him, investigators said.

One of those drivers left, not realizing at first that a person had been struck, but that driver later came forward.

Why the man fled in the first place was unclear to officers last night, although investigators suggested that he had been in trouble with the law previously.

mmarx@dispatch.com
andy.hirsch@10tv.com

Newspaper Report on The Accident 2008

CHAPTER 33

After the Last Knock
on the Door

What do you do after the knock on the door that has been expected for over forty years happens? Silence, I remember the silence, total silence; deathly silence. The tears wouldn't stop; they flowed like a river in spring, yet there was no noise. Eric was there to hold me and absorb some of the pain. I saw in his eyes the suffering over the loss of a brother, his disbelief that this day had come as well. In the fog of this overwhelming pain, we made the necessary calls. We called Joey's dad, Leeann, and Jimmy. I called my sister Nancy, my best friend Marilyn, and then Father Bob. These calls were all brief and I don't remember anything that was said, either to them or what they said to me. I just felt them, along with Eric, their spirit in the moments of this excruciating mind numbing grief.

During the next few days while planning Joey's funereal, I called out to the Lord many, many times. Please, help me understand. At first, I couldn't hear His voice. I couldn't hear anything. Why, oh why, have you forsaken my son? Why have You left me in such despair? The Lord, He is patient, and finally He got though all of my wailing and reached my heart once again.

HUTCHISON

Joseph David Hutchison, went home to meet his Lord on January 16, 2008. He leaves behind to mourn his mother, Linda Hutchison of Columbus; father, Joseph (Kathy) Hutchison of Tipp City; sister, Leeann (Mark) Fields of Colorado; and brothers, James (Jessica) of California and Eric (Christa) of Westerville. There will be a memorial celebration of his life on Saturday, January 26, 2008, at 3 p.m. at St. Christopher Parish, 450 National Rd., Vandalia, Ohio. Officiating Rev. Robert Monnin. Family and friends will be received 30 minutes prior to service. Joseph was a recent graduate of Columbus State Community College and in lieu of flowers, contributions can be made to the college's scholarship fund in Joseph's name.

"Linda, be still and listen. I share in your pain. I lost My only begotten Son with the death of His human body, so I understand what you are feeling. I comforted His mother, much like I will comfort you, if you will let Me. Linda. Do you know where Joey is, He asked?"

"Yes, Lord, I have his cremains; he is sitting on his dresser, he is safe and warm and the world can't hurt him anymore."

" Right!" said the Lord, "And Linda, I have his soul. Do you have any idea what a brave soldier Joey was?

"Lord, what do You mean," I said?

"Linda, listen carefully, I want you to do the eulogy and here is what I want you to say about your son." He whispered in my ear, I listened.

Eric, stayed by my side, he rarely left me for a minute. Leeann flew in from Denver, and Jimmy from San Diego. Marilyn spent as much time as she could. Father Bob and Linda Comstock helped me plan the memorial service at St. Christopher's.

Even though Linda was facing a health crisis of her own, she arranged for the service programs and the liturgical readings and the music the choir would perform. My sister arranged for the flowers and the memorial afghan. The bereavement committee prepared refreshments for after the service. My good friends from the "Garden Club" saw to the foods we would need at the house for all the out of town guests. I can only hope I thanked all of them properly.

On the day of the service there were over 100 people in the church. Most had traveled to Vandalia, Ohio from out of town. I had to wonder if Joey knew how many came to pay their last respects, what would he think? Many were concerned that I wouldn't be able to do the eulogy, including me. However, I had been instructed by You Know Who and said, "I have to do this."

After Father Bob gave his homily and his remembrances of the weekend that he and Joey and Linda and I spent together in a little log cabin, down in beautiful Hocking Hills. He told of Joey's wit, and the reactions Joey had of participating in the Mass held on the kitchen table in that little log cabin that Sunday morning. Joey had been overwhelmed with the significance of this reenactment of the last supper, in this setting. Father Bob then turned to me. I began by saying,

I want to thank each and everyone of you for coming. Some of you have never even met my son, some of you only knew him as a small boy, and some of you have only known him for these past five years. As you probably have guessed, I have had many talks with God over these past few days, and you can bet I did most of the talking. However I was quiet long enough for me to hear what He wants me to tell you. First He wants me to tell you about His Son then I can tell you about mine.

You know, He lost his Son to a cruel physical death too. He had to comfort His Son's mother as well. He wants you to know that through His son's death we are all saved. However, we still have a purpose to fulfill while we are visitors here on earth. Jesus Christ, fulfilled His purpose, and so did Joey.

He said you should read in Matthew, Chapter 25 verse 34 to 40 and you will find the answers to why Joey was here. The basic message is: Lord, when were you hungry or thirsty? When were you a stranger or naked? When were you sick or in prison? It ends with 'Amen I say to you, as long as you did it for one of these, the least of my brethren, you did it for me.'

Joey was one of His special soldiers. He was a tester. He was sent to separate the sheep from the goats. If you had come in contact with Joey, he would have tested you in some way. He certainly tested me.

Just last month when Joey bolted from the ER naked into a snowstorm, a stranger opened the door to him and gave him shelter, clothing, and food. Within the next few hours a "friend" took his credit card and ripped him off. While he was in prison many were called to minister to him, some did, most did not. Are you getting the picture?

Joey also was a caretaker, he offered shelter in that prison gymnasium and friendship to those caught up in the prison riot of "93." He was there when his dad had open-heart surgery and helped nurse him back to health. He was there when his stepbrother was dying from breast cancer and kept him company in his final

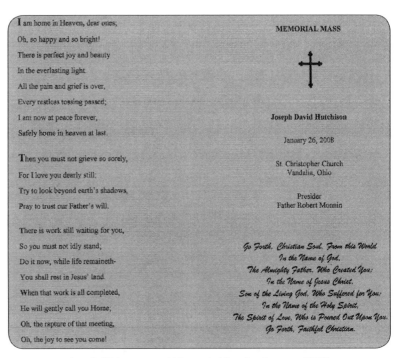

Joey's Obituary and Memorial Service January 2008

days. He was loyal to those who deserve loyalty. Yes, if Joey crossed your path you felt the need for some kind of reaction to his presence. His greatest test was for his caregivers. Only you know if you passed or failed that test. His being will be felt for many years to come.

I would like to read you something Joey wrote, so that you may get to know him a little better. I read Joey's essay "Take the Long Way Home." I finished the eulogy with a song of pure love for my son, a song just from me. *"Where are you going my little one, little one--- Where are you going my little bay—be, turn around and your two, turn around and your four, turn around your a young man gone home to his Lord. Turn around, Turn around and your a young man, that took a long, long way home."*

I had carried Joey in my arms into church as a baby to be christened, and I now carried him in my arms out of church, after his remains had been consecrated back to his Father in heaven. Joe didn't attend this service for his son; however, I carried his son back to him as well. After the service out of respect, we all went over to Joe and Kathy's. Kathy had prepared a reception for the immediate family. It was much appreciated.

The days that followed the memorial service were filled with many unanswered questions. Joey was killed at the same overpass as the day he bolted from my car in that snowstorm a month ago. Was that significant? He was always in flight to get back home, when things went wrong. Was it because he looked at his home as his safety net? What caused him to leave the safety of that home that afternoon? What caused him to medicate himself to the point of total destruction? Could anyone have stopped him from getting behind the wheel of his car that day? Answers to these questions we will never know. Surely, this was not to be the end of what I thought Joey's life had been about. There just had to be more, but what?

I thought that maybe somehow I was to avenge his untimely death. I decided that if the world knew how poor the mental health system was that failed him that would be the ultimate reason for his being. I set out to bring to justice the people I felt were responsible for his death. I knew from research and reading about mental illnesses that many suffer the untold stigma and pain of these diseases. Were others looking for relief too? I was going to get it for them.

I was going to find an attorney to sue the State of Ohio and the people whom I felt had let my son die. I started by using my Prepaid Legal Services membership. It was Prepaid Legal's belief that I had a reasonable case of wrongful death, negligence and medical malpractice. They referred me to an attorney that considered my claim of wrongful death and neglect. I was heartened by this referral.

Ms. Valentine, a respected medical malpractice attorney, was sympathetic but declined to take the case, citing how difficult it would be to get a judgment against the State of Ohio. It would be very time consuming and the rewards few, if any. However, she did recommend three other attorneys to contact. This turned out to be the standard practice of most attorneys that I spoke with. When you call their referrals they most always tell you, if attorney so-in-so didn't want to take the case they wouldn't want to either. All in all I probably talked to 25 to 30 attorneys statewide.

Almost all of them thought I had a case of neglect and wrongful death, until they found that the defendant would be the State of Ohio. Second, because it was not a win/win situation they were unwilling to take on the beast. Most thought it would take at least a minimum of $50,000 to prosecute and an awful lot of work. With the odds not being very good, they were unwilling to go forward on their dime and of course I didn't have $50,000 up front.

I did find a very prominent and very kind older attorney by the name of Hans Scherner. Mr. Scherner was on the fence about how successful he could be with this case. He asked me to give him a couple of days to think about it. He then called to say he would be willing to look into the case further if I were willing to cover the initial expenses of the investigation. He wanted just the costs of getting the investigation started. He would take no fees. If he were convinced after his investigation and reviewing all of Joey's medical records, and an opinion from a prominent psychiatrist, he would then take the case, and cover the expense from that point on.

It was during that investigation I learned that Joey's last doctor of record was as impaired as Joey. It seemed that Dr. Mark E Blair had had his license suspended again. He had been medically discharged from the armed services with a diagnosis of bipolar disorder, with poly-substance abuse and social paranoia. His license was reinstated and the State of Ohio hired him. His license was suspended again in June of 08, and at that time, he was currently being treated in a five star rehabilitation treatment center in southern Ohio. Why did the State of Ohio hire him and why was he allowed to treat my son? I thought this was a nail in the coffin for a case against neglect. I was wrong. The only thing it proved is, the State of Ohio will hire just about anybody.

I'm sorry Dr. Blair has a mental illness but I don't think he should be treating patients. Mental illnesses do not always allow you to use sound judgment. Wouldn't it be better if physicians with mental illnesses use their knowledge in research where their findings could be tested by others? Mr. Scherner decided against taking the case when his friend, a psychiatrist and classmate from Harvard, didn't think the case was strong enough and that we could win against the State. I tried to engage a few more attorneys, but time was running out on the statute of limitations, and I had to accept the writing on the wall. This was not going to happen in a court of law, man's law.

I took my story to a reporter from the Columbus Dispatch, Alan Johnson. Alan, was preparing to report on the state of the mental health system in the State of Ohio, and with the story about my son's untimely death, he had his expo. On March 8, 2009, Alan's story was on the front page of the Sunday paper, including a full inside page. Tom Dodge did the audio and video presentations that became a part of major stories that the Dispatch printed. Please feel free to go to the Columbus Dispatch archives and read the full story (March 8, 2009 front page). Within a year, the story won a first place in journalism for the Columbus Dispatch and Alan Johnson. Yet the mental health budget was still cut.

Front Page Story With a Full Inside Page With an Audio and Visual Display March 2009

If I couldn't sue the State of Ohio for neglect and it's employees for medical malpractice in a real court of law, I would sue them in effigy. The following is the letter I sent to the people I believed directly or indirectly responsible for my son's death. I included the last pictures of my son's broken and mangled body, taken at the scene of the accident, as well. Perhaps you may see this as a vigilante attempt on my part. I see it as telling it like it is, and I pulled no punches.

I FIND THE FOLLOWING PERSONS OR ENTITIES DIRECTLY OR INDIRECTLY RESPONSIBLE FOR THE UNTIMELY DEATH OF JOSEPH DAVID HUTCHISON

BORN MAY 13, 1962   DIED JAN. 16, 2008

I believe you need to bear witness to the last pictures of this man taken on this earth. May these pictures haunt your dreams and trouble your soul to the day you leave this world. You held his life in your hands and you not only fatally failed him you failed humanity as well. You need to see and feel the reality of the decisions you made on this man's behalf.

Gov. Ted Strickland / Community Support Systems

Mark E Blair, MD
Senator Ray Miller / Ohio Adult Parole Authority
Joe Rammelsburg.
State Representative Dan Stewart
Gary M. Davis, MD / Staff of CSN,
The Attorney General of Ohio
Asim Ashraf Farooqui, MD /   MHM Solutions
Ohio Department of Mental Health
LaBronz Davis, MD
Twin Valley Psychiatric Systems / M.Meredith Dobyns, MD
All State Representatives / Joy L McFadden, RN

For the past eighteen months and with a deadline to file a medical malpractice wrongful death lawsuit, I have been in contact with individual attorneys and law firms. The individual attorneys and firms all told me my case had merit until they found that the State of Ohio was involved. At that point they suggested I contact another attorney that would want to take on the State of Ohio, as they were not willing to take this case.

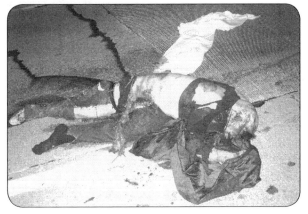

This Is A Real Face and The Truth Of Untreated Mental Illness and The Lack Of Quality Mental Healthcare For the Diagnosed Mentally Ill 2009

One, because they had connections with the State and there would be a conflict of interest and two, because this case would have to be tried in the Court of Common Pleas (or as many referred to it as "The court of NO PLEAS"), and therefore, they were unwilling to do what it would take to bring this case to resolution. Third, because this case would be near impossible to win in the Court of Common Pleas because the Governor appoints the judges. They told me the judge's work at the pleasure of the Governor and must be reappointed to the bench to keep their jobs. Assuming they would want to keep their jobs they would not want to rule in my favor, and hence against the State. Fourth, in the unlikely event I would have a favorable verdict from one of the judges, one not interested in returning to the bench, the monies awarded would be somewhere in the breakeven zone.

In other words, the cost of litigation would certainly not be enough to warrant all the time and effort a case like this would take. So much for "JUSTICE!" I DIDN'T WANT ANY MONEY. I WANTED JUSTICE FOR JOEY AND HIS FAMILY. The attorneys didn't care; they wanted to win and they wanted the money.

With a complete set of medical records, sworn testimony, and hand written testimony from the victim himself as to his state of mind prior to his death, I believe a jury would find you guilty of neglect, medical malpractice, and dereliction of duty; therefore:

FOR THE STATE OF OHIO ELECTED OFFICIALS AS INDIRECT DEFENDANTS

Gov. Strickland you of all people because of your education and background should know how critical the funding is for mental illness. You know that at anyone time 30% to 50% of the State of Ohio's prisoners are mentally ill. Yet, you continue to short change the mental health system for the State. You as a psychologist have a first hand understanding of mental illness. You were serving as a psychologist at Lucasville during the riot of 1993. Joseph D. Hutchison was caught up in that mêlée and spent over a year in solitary confinement before being found totally innocent of any wrongdoing. Not only was he mentally ill then, that incident and confinement added post traumatic stress to his list of illnesses. When I tried to meet with you regarding my issues with the mental health system and budget cuts, you pawned me off to one of your flunkies.

You are responsible for how the Department of Mental Health is run. Do you really know what is going on over there? Do you know that the top 10 salaries paid out to state employees are paid to Psychiatrist's? The Mental Health Department admits to cracks in the system and that my son fell through a crack. Well I say "they threw him through a cavern."

In 1890, the medical profession found that manic depression insanity was a viable illness. It took almost 100 years for the profession to admit that children can be afflicted with mental illnesses. Yet, the State of Ohio would rather put the mentally ill in our jails and prisons than to properly treat them. The State of Ohio would rather prosecute the mentally ill and pay attorneys and psychiatrists to mislead the general public that these people are fully accountable for their actions and punish them. You then lock them up and fail to treat them for their illnesses.

Senator Ray Miller, you never returned any of my calls or emails. You have failed to respond to one of your constituents.

You have failed to vote in a responsible pattern for Mental Health issues. States Representative Dan Stewart, when I came to you with my story, all you wanted to do is tell me how much you had done in the past for mental illness. You had no intention of helping me write a bill to help people like me obtain the proper medical help for their loved one. In fact, you told a reporter for the Columbus Dispatch you had no intention of helping me. You are indeed a "lame-duck" with the emphasis on 'LAME," and I promise you if you ever run for another elected office, I will campaign against you. You need to remember you are only as good as your last failure. To all the rest of the legislature, (State Representatives, State Senators, etc., had you passed HB 299 I would have had the power to save my son's life without the approval of the medical professionals.

You are the indirect persons responsible for my son's death. It took the State of Ohio and thousand of so called public servants over 40 years to kill my son. For every year the State of Ohio fails to improve the mental health system is another year that more lives will be lost in this tragic fashion. It is my opinion you have no excuses. Just remember the last picture taken of my son when issues of mental health arise for your support and your vote.

Only with your full support on mental health issues can you even possible hope to make amends for the death of my son and all of the others lost while on your watch. Only with your full support can you reduce the number of mentally ill from the prison system to treatment centers. Only with your full support will we find the answers to how to alleviate the suffering of millions of citizens that suffer from mental illness.

FOR THE DIRECT DEFENDANTS
FIRST DO NO HARM

It took 40 years with 23 years and 100 days of those years in prison to finely get the diagnoses of a mental illness that Joseph David Hutchison spent his entire life fighting. The long awaited diagnoses came from Gary Davis, MD after 6 weeks at Twin Valley Behavioral Hospital. The outside world can be a cruel place when you are well. When you are mentally ill and have spent the last 23 years of your life in prison, it can be deadly.

As we suspected, his diagnosis was "Bipolar 1 with substance abuse and paranoia." His condition was never documented or treated beyond the first three months of incarceration. He endured the horrors of that environment including the 1993 Lucasville riot. This man fell through the cracks of the State of

Ohio as a child resulting in his incarceration in 1980 as well as a man released on parole in 2003

I have read extensively the signs, symptoms, and treatments of Bipolar disorder, and Joey had all of the classic signs and symptoms. There is no doubt that Joey was Bipolar, nonewhatsoever. Joey did well with his FIRST and only in house treatment program for his bipolar condition. He graduated with honors while following this program. You failed to give him continued proper treatment as warranted in his case. How could you not possibly see this man was dying on your watch with all of the warnings, yet you made me watch it happen first hand 24/7.

The CSN staff and Dr. Farooqui failed to notify me that Joey was no longer coming in for treatment in 2007. Instead I had to learn he had left treatment when his symptoms returned in the spring of 2007. I had power of attorney and my son's written permission for you to keep me informed of his mental health care. You chose not to inform me. Was he not worthy of your vigilance of his care? Did you just not have the time? Were you to over worked to pay attention? Did you just not care? You really have no excuses.

Dr. LaBronz Davis as an internal doctor of medicine you should have recognized that a psychiatrist should have been treating Joey. Dr. Davis you should not have been treating someone with as severe of a mental illness as my son had. You prescribed pills but no follow up. Did you not know that pills alone would not bring about recovery? Dr. Dobyns you failed to see how serious his condition was and discharged him from Twin Valley after only 2 days of observation. Dr. Dobyns you met with Joey for 5 min. and relied on notes and other personnel to make your decision. Do you always dispense care so rapidly and carelessly? Despite my telling you he was not under control you turned him over to a totally incompetent doctor, Mark E Blair. Dr. Blair was as ill as my son, suffering from Bipolar 1, poly substance abuse and social paranoia. Dr. Blair has had his license to practice medicine suspended numerous times.

Dr. Blair you were too involved in holding on to your own sanity to be effective in helping my son hold on to his. You also didn't want to challenge Dr. Dobyns either, did you? Was it because you didn't trust your own judgment? Was it because you couldn't look me in the eye and answer my questions? Were you too afraid they held answers you didn't want to hear as well? I see you entered a 5 star treatment center, wasn't the State of Ohio treatment centers good enough for you?

Dr. Gary Davis you shrugged your shoulders and walked away from me when I confronted you about Dr. Dobyns diagnoses. Were you afraid to challenge a colleague's opinion too? You would not even discuss it. In fact you spoke not one word to me, just shrugged your shoulders and walked away. Everyone kept passing the buck until it resulted in this man's death. Except for Dr. LaBronz Davis all of you mental health care givers are employees of the State of Ohio.

All of you doctors, Nurses and psychologists, and counselors were kept informed of Joey's critical condition on numerous occasions from Oct. of 2007 to Jan of 2008. I told you that we were going to lose him, the records told you that we were going to lose him. I begged you for help and you blew me off.

Joe Rummelsberg, as Joey's parole officer, I asked you to place Joey in a secure environment other than jail or back to prison. What did you do? You put him in jail for 6 days then turned him over to the mental health people to deal with. You were happy when Joey was your shining example of a model parolee, when he was in college making the deans list, not causing you any trouble. When he was really sick, you let him flounder. You had him arrested to cover your butt with your supervisors, pretending to do your job. Your job was to recognize Joey was in critical need of medical intervention and to see that he got it. Or was your job only to put him back in prison? He was your responsibility to help rehabilitate. However, we all know that rehabilitation's are a figment of everyone's imagination. How do I know this? Well, if it existed, Joey would have returned to society treated for his mental illness (you only had 23 years to find and treat his condition) and ready to get on with his life.

What did he have to do, stand-in front of you people with a gun to his head, a rope around his neck, a hand full of lethal pills? You killed him by your righteous indignation, your depraved indifference, your ignorance, your arrogance, your lack of capabilities, and your self-serving save your own butt mentality. First, do no harm. You all failed that test. All you had to do was place him in a secure environment for his own protection and to help him come to terms with his condition.

After all, it is a documented fact it takes many trips to a treatment environment before a bipolar patient can come to terms with their disorder. You gave this man only one long-term treatment for a condition he didn't ask for, didn't fully understand. He deserved more; he deserved better treatment than he got from people who should have known better. In my book, you are responsible for his death. I find all of you guilty. Many of you, if not all, will believe you are not responsible. Your misguided sense of importance will have you take the attitude that you can't save them all? Well this one you could have and didn't.

Perhaps you are all so hardened to the suffering of those with mental illness you no longer have the ability to feel the shame of losing someone through the cracks. It is easier to blame the victim than to take responsibility for your lack of actions. May the last image of this man remind you of what it means to be a public servant or a caregiver? May God forgive you, as HE is the only one who can?

Joey gave many of you over 4 months to see a critical need to save his life. To others (the state of Ohio law maker's, and the medical profession as a whole) you had over forty years to make things better for Joey and all of the other Joe's in your care. My Joey was your test for your humanity and you failed. Will you continue to fail or will Joey's life have made a difference? Will you now see that critical changes must be made?

This is what I had hoped to convey with a public hearing. I not only wanted to confront you publicly, I wanted the public to know what is going on daily in the State of Ohio and the Mental Health System. This is the justice I am looking for. This is the other reason the attorney's said they couldn't or wouldn't help me. They couldn't get for me what I really wanted, JUSTICE. They could only get me a monetary award, and it was not going to be big enough for them to go after.

Just what is a man's life worth? You failed to see that this man was loved and was important to his family. What if this was your son? The blank lifeless face of the icon of justice with blinders on is so true. Justice only exists for those who can afford it. Justice exist for very few. Where is King Solomon, as justice should not be this complicated? Will you now make those critical changes?

You all may have dodged your responsibility and accountability by man's law. Apparently the State of Ohio protects itself and you. I have no power beyond letting everyone know, in whatever legal manner at my disposal, just what I think of you and the State of Ohio. I have faith in a higher power you will all live to regret your part in my son's death. There is no reasonable doubt you are responsible.

Linda L Hutchison (Plaintiff)

I sent this letter to not only the people I felt were directly respon-sible, but to the top legislators as well. I received only one response. It came from Richard Cordray's office (The Attorney General for the State of Ohio). It was a politically correct response. It addressed their sympa-thy for my loss, but said that there was nothing that they could do to help me, as they would be the one's to defend the State of Ohio against a lawsuit. They did tell me I had a right to seek an independent attorney for counsel.

You don't always think clearly when dealing with grief. I don't regret anything I wrote, as I believe it all to be true. However, I realize that this letter didn't change what happened to my son. Nothing can do that. Perhaps I had to get this out of the way, so that I could begin to do what God wanted me to do. Apparently He is not as interested in man's laws, as much as I am. I went back to the original conversation I had had with Him and found that perhaps, He just wants me to tell my story, and let it do the work that needs to be done. You just can't mess with God's will.

After Thoughts

As you follow my journey from my outstanding childhood, with a loving family by my side, you will see that I couldn't have possibly envisioned the twists and turns I would later face. As for my son, I hope you will see the courage it must have taken for him to live his life for as long as he did. With all the misunderstandings of just who he really was; a brilliant and talented man with an unbelievable agenda, that will no doubt affect you, long after you finish this book.

My closest and dearest friend Marilyn Livingston's, favorite response when I am whining and crying over split milk and lost opportunities is, "Linda, you ain't dead yet."

No I am not, and I plan to go out kicking and screaming. I figure I have about 20 more years left to fight the good fight, providing that is what God has planned for me. The problem I see is that I am only one person in this sea of humanity, one of over seven billion plus, currently on this planet. I am only one of 300 million in the US, and one of only 11 million in the State of Ohio. When you think about where you fit in these terms; I am but a speck in this vast universe; a nobody. God, however, must think I am somebody, as he has laid out yet another opportunity for me. He tells me that I have much to do before I rest. Sometimes I think He doesn't realize just how old I am?

Does He realize I am not a person of great intellect? I don't have a myriad of letters behind my name. I am not a great scientist, scholar, statesman, politician, celebrity, or movie star. All I am is a Mom; a Mom who lost a son too soon; a mom who only wanted all of her children to succeed in this life better than she was able. A mom who knows what it is like to have a child afflicted with a mental illness. A mom who knows that there are other moms out there who have faced those same challenges and are facing them today. I am only one mom, I can't do much to make any changes, believe me I have tried. If there are to be great changes, it will take you to make them happen.

As I searched for and collected all of Joey's medical records for the attorney's, I found that his trip to the ER in December of 07, included a MRI. In this scan of his brain, some abnormality in his gray matter was observed that warranted further evaluation. As far as I know, no one was advised of that finding beyond that note in the records. Which makes me wonder if an MRI had been done earlier in Joey's life, could there have been a better understanding of any brain damage that Joey might have suffered from. Would that have made a difference?

In hindsight, what I could have done was given my permission to have Joey's brain donated to science for additional studies. They did an autopsy, and I am sure no one thought to preserve his brain for research. It would have served the good of all mankind. As gruesome as that might sound, it is necessary in learning how to treat and control various conditions that can befall the brain.

As with anything as serious as experiments with human body tissue, I am sure that safeguards were in place, just as I am sure that there would be a lot of controversy over a campaign for brain donations. It is my belief however, "Remember, man that thou art dust and to dust thou shall return" can only mean we will not need our brain matter once we have left the body. You might want to add that donation to your "gift of life" requests, and let your family know that you would like to donate your brain to science, as well as any other body part you may be considering.

If my story touched you in any way, consider doing one of these requests as well:

You can make a donation to the foundation for "The Love of Joey."

This foundation will make available grants for research into childhood mental illnesses. It is my belief that serious mental illnesses start in childhood, either as a result of heredity, trauma, or perhaps a physical illness such as a virus that may attack the developing brain. As with any disease, the earlier it is detected the better the outcome may be. We need new and better drug therapies.

We need new and more advanced psychiatric counseling for the seriously mentally ill. We need new and innovative educational tools and trained teachers to help these children learn in a classroom. We need to de-stigmatize mental illness.

FOR THE LOVE OF JOEY FOUNDATION

A DONOR ADVISED FUND AT THE COLUMBUS FOUNDATION
IN MEMORY OF
JOSEPH DAVID HUTCHISON

GRANTS WILL BE MADE TO STUDY AND RESEARCH CHILDHOOD
MENTAL ILLNESSES. PREVENTION, CAUSES, AND TREATMENTS,
PRIMARILY OF BIPOLAR DISORDER, SCHIZOPHRENIA, PARANORA AND
RELATED ILLNESSES.

IN ORDER TO MAKE A GIFT BY CREDIT CARD, YOU MAY DO SO VIA THE
COLUMBUS FOUNDATION'S WEBSITE AT
https://app.etapestry.com/hosted/TheColumbusFoundation/
OnlineGiving.html

IN ORDER TO MAKE A GIFT BY CHECK, PLEASE SEND THE CHECK TO:

THE COLUMBUS FOUNDATION
1234 EAST BROAD STREET
COLUMBUS, OHIO 43205-1453
614-251-4000 Fax 614-251-4010
ATTENTION:
J.BRADLEY BRITTON, J.D. LL.M

IN EITHER CASE, PLEASE INDICATE THAT YOUR DONATION SHOULD GO
TO "FOR THE LOVE OF JOEY FOUNDATION"

Join NAMI today (National Alliance for Mental Illness)

Perhaps you will consider joining your local, state, or national NAMI organization and support the programs that help the mentally ill and their families. One way to do that is through NAMIWALKS. A yearly National Campaign to raise money for clients and families of the mentally ill. NAMI and NAMIWALKS are organized in almost every state

You can donate to Columbus State Community College (CSCC) in memory of Joseph David Hutchison.

This already established scholarship fund will help a disabled and challenged person reach their potential. CSCC was the only place Joey felt valued by others, in his attempts to put his life back together.

Last but not least, please contact your Representatives in the State House, along with your Senator and Congressperson, too. It is there duty to protect the most vulnerable of our citizens. Ask them to see that mental health programs and health care issues in your State, are given top priority. We need to pursue an **"Involuntary Outpatient Commitment Program"** for all states and every community.

Call for a List Of Your State Representatives

If we treat and cure the mentally ill, we can be assured that we are going to reduce the cost of keeping the mentally ill in prisons. It is far less costly to hospitalize the mentally ill for a few months for treatments when needed than it is to jail or imprison them indefinitely. Your tax dollars will be better spent in supporting the care and treatment of the mentally ill. They will be far more able to support themselves and be productive citizens with the proper care. With the right kind of care, living with a mental illness can be no different than living with a chronic physical illness.

In providing proper assistance to the mentally ill, you may be protecting your life and that of your loved one's as well. In time, we might even be able to cure mental illnesses. If every person gave just one dollar to each of these programs; there would be in the state of Ohio alone, 11 million dollars for research, 11 million dollars for mental health programs, and 11 million dollars in scholarships, to help educate those who are mentally and physically challenged. Take that and in vision the 300 plus million in the United States, boggles the mind of what could happen, doesn't it. While that may be a tad unrealistic, with corporate sponsors some well know spokesperson, it could happen. It has to start somewhere, why not here, now, today, with you.

Yes, I want to help! Enclosed is my tax deductible gift.

Any amount you can give is appreciated

☐ _____

Donations of &250 are recognized on the Wall of Honor in the NAMI Ohio office

In Memory of _____

In Honor of _____

Full Name _____

Address _____

City _____ State _____ Zip _____

Phone _____

Email _____

Please add your email address so we can send you updates.

Make checks payable to NAMI Ohio or donate by

☐ VISA   ☐ MasterCard

Credit Card No. _____

Expiration Date _____

Print name on card _____

Signature _____

To make your contribution online, please visit our website at www.namiohio.org

---

The Columbus State Development Foundation's goal is to provide support to advance education opportunities, programs and services at Columbus State Community College. To make a gift in support of the **J.D. Hutchinson Fund at CSCC**, simply tear out this page and mail to: CSCC Development Foundation, Inc. 550 E. Spring St, Columbus, OH 43215 or go to www.csccfoundation.org to make an online gift.

Name	
Address	
City, State, & ZIP	
E-Mail	
Contact Phone	

Gift Amount:				
Gift Type:	◯ Check	◯ Visa	◯ Mastercard	◯ Discover

Credit Card Number:		Exp.	
Signature:			

My Love For Joey,

Knows No Bounds,

and I Miss Him So.

What If God Is Watching and Taking Notes?

Notes

Permission for a one-time use of the Jan.18, 2008, story and the A1 image from March 8, 2009, in the book, with credit to The Columbus Dispatch, has been granted.

Headlines and excerpts taken from the pages of the Dayton Daily News and The Journal Herald, who covered this case, have been reprinted with permission from Cox Media Group Ohio. Coverage by the Vandalia Drummer, is with their permission as well

Photo's and Inserts have been prepared for reprint by: Ted Kibble and Tom Dodge from the Columbus Dispatch, NAMI – The Columbus Foundation – Columbus State Community College – A book cover draft prepared by Paul J Reif -

12729288R00181

Made in the USA
Charleston, SC
23 May 2012